R-3742-NSF/RC

Indicators for Monitoring Mathematics and Science Education

A Sourcebook

Richard J. Shavelson, Lorraine M. McDonnell, Jeannie Oakes, editors

July 1989

Supported by the
National Science Foundation

PREFACE

This sourcebook contains a collection of papers summarizing the major research on elementary and secondary schooling conducted over the past decade, and outlining what those studies suggest for designing improved educational indicators. These papers were originally written as background material to guide RAND's recommendations to the National Science Foundation for indicators of precollege mathematics and science education.

The volume is intended as a resource for educational researchers and policy analysts who need a summary of key schooling research, organized by the major domains of the educational system, and the implications of that research for indicator development. Because the volume is designed as a sourcebook, to be read selectively depending on one's interest, Chapters 2 through 9 are each organized around a major schooling domain. Chapter 1 provides an overview of the indicator development process and a summary of each of the succeeding chapters. Chapter 10 explores the policy context in which educational indicators are defined and used.

The initial preparation of these papers was supported by the National Science Foundation; their revision and the preparation of this volume were supported by The RAND Corporation from its own research funds.

ACKNOWLEDGMENTS

The papers in this volume were written and revised over the past four years. Their content and presentation were greatly improved during that period through the conscientious reading and advice of many people. We are particularly grateful to Joyce Peterson, who helped us reorganize the volume and clarify its focus, and to Paul Hill of RAND and Lyle Jones of the University of North Carolina, who reviewed the entire draft and asked the hard questions that forced us to sharpen our analysis.

Richard Berry, our National Science Foundation project officer, was a continuing source of advice and support. This volume also benefited from the counsel of a project advisory group representing mathematicians and scientists, science and mathematics educators, psychometricians, policy analysts, and policymakers. We are indebted to the following members of the committee for their useful comments on individual chapters: Leigh Burstein, Audrey Champagne, Lee Cronbach, Pascal Forgione, Bernard Gifford, Norman Hackerman, Harry Handler, Ina Mullis, Ingram Olkin, Jerome Pine, Senta Raizen, Thomas Romberg, and Ramsay Selden.

Once again, Janet DeLand has eased the reader's burden considerably with her careful editing. Deborah Lang performed the seemingly endless task of compiling and checking the bibliography with grace and efficiency. Donna Hathaway, Rachel Mitchell, and Linda Weiss provided invaluable assistance in the production of this volume.

CONTENTS

FIGURES

TABLES

Chapter 1

THE DESIGN OF EDUCATIONAL INDICATOR SYSTEMS: AN OVERVIEW

Current interest in developing better educational indicators[1] is not without precedent: The Common School Movement provides an almost perfect parallel (e.g., Travers, 1983), and indicators served as a justification for establishing a U.S. Department of Education in 1867 (Warren, 1974). In the nineteenth century, the call for indicators was a response to perceived problems plaguing the nation's schools, and the contemporary movement stems from similar concerns. Data available to the National Science Board (NSB) Commission on Precollege Education in Mathematics, Science, and Technology signaled loud and clear that science and mathematics education faced serious difficulties. However, it was also clear that available data were inadequate to pinpoint potential problems within the education system or to enable policymakers and educators to target reforms with necessary precision. What we did know was that the United States had fallen far short of the educational excellence considered both possible and necessary. Declines in mathematics and science achievement, combined with the increasing importance of science and technology in maintaining economic and strategic preeminence, led to a call for substantial improvements in those areas and for a mechanism to monitor that reform.

Indicators have been justified throughout their history not only as a mechanism for reflecting the nature of education problems, but as an instrument of education reform itself. Indeed, the rationale for federal involvement in monitoring the nation's education systems in the mid-1800s sounds surprisingly like the NSB Commission's and other groups' justification today. Federal involvement is considered necessary to:

- Ascertain the conditions of U.S. schools and reveal defects in them by providing accurate descriptions and comparisons of schools and school systems, nationally and internationally.

---

[1]Indicators are individual or composite statistics that reflect important features of an education system (see "What Is an Indicator?" on pp. 4–5 below).

- Apply external pressure on local communities to establish and improve schools (Warren, 1974).
- Equalize educational opportunity (this was especially important after the Civil War) by voluntary response to comparisons of quantity and quality of schooling.
- Increase and diffuse knowledge of education, especially popular education, and measures for its improvement.

Historically, with each indicator movement, enthusiasm ebbed and waned as optimism about what indicators might accomplish gave way to the reality of what they have achieved, both in education and more generally in society (cf. Sheldon, 1975). The current interest in developing more valid and useful educational indicators has grown significantly over the past four years as national, state, and local agencies have moved to improve the quality of elementary and secondary education. At the national level, growing concern about overall levels of scientific literacy and the future availability of scientific manpower has necessitated more systematic information about student participation and achievement in mathematics and science courses, the content of such courses, and the capability of those teaching them. At the state and local levels, the monitoring of policies such as increased academic requirements for graduation will require much more sophisticated measures of both the processes and outcomes of schooling.

Although data are currently collected on student and teacher characteristics, the schooling process, and student achievement, no comprehensive indicator system is available to measure the status of mathematics and science education in the United States. If such a system were available, policymakers could determine the nature of current and emerging problems, evaluate the factors influencing educational trends, monitor the effects of policy, and identify steps that might be taken to improve student performance.

THE RAND INDICATOR PROJECT

In its 1983 report to the nation, the NSB Commission recommended that the federal government "finance and maintain a national mechanism to measure student achievement and participation in the manner that allows national, state, and local evaluation and comparison of education progress" (p. 12). RAND assisted the National Science Foundation (NSF) in establishing a national monitoring system by identifying and evaluating alternative systems the Foundation might employ.[2]

This volume reports RAND's ongoing efforts to identify and develop indicators that will provide systematic and objective information about the quality of precollege education in the United States. The papers included here provide background material that supports RAND's recent recommendations to the NSF.[3] Each paper focuses on a single domain of mathematics and science education (e.g., resources, teachers, curriculum, achievement) and attempts to answer the following questions: What are the central features of the domain? How do these features link to other essential school conditions and outcomes? What support for these features does research provide? What would be ideal indicators of the domain? What substantive or technical issues are likely to constrain the development of these indicators? The papers then identify comprehensive, research-based sets of indicators that could be used to measure particular components of the mathematics and science education system.

Additionally, because the domains RAND selected for indicator development stem from a comprehensive model of the educational system, these indicators should also provide information about how individual components work together to shape the system as a whole. Consequently, indicator systems based on the recommendations in this set of papers should assist policymakers and educators to monitor progress in mathematics and science participation and achievement, in course content, teaching quality, and the conditions under which mathematics and science learning occurs.

The remainder of this chapter describes the concept of indicators and indicator systems and discusses their major functions and limitations. It then outlines the tasks that must be undertaken in designing an indicator system, with special emphasis on the particular focus of

---

[2]The RAND project, completed in August 1987, outlined a range of indicator systems and assessed each one's ability to measure the major domains of schooling, address relevant policy questions, and generate information cost-effectively.

The NSF has also supported a number of other projects. A committee of the National Research Council (NRC) has recommended a set of indicators to portray the condition of mathematics and science education (Murnane and Raizen, 1988). The University of Wisconsin-Madison is monitoring mathematics instruction and performance against standards developed by the mathematics profession, to determine the extent to which mathematics education is changing as a result of various reform efforts. The State Education Assessment Program (SEAP), sponsored by the Council of Chief State School Officers, has been designed to help states collect more timely, comprehensive, and comparable data on elementary and secondary education.

[3]These recommendations are a part of RAND's final report to the NSF, *Indicator Systems for Monitoring Mathematics and Science Education* (Shavelson, McDonnell, Oakes, and Carey, 1987).

this volume: using research to identify potential indicators of schooling. The chapter concludes with an overview of each of the subsequent chapters.

INDICATORS AND INDICATOR SYSTEMS

The purposes educational indicator systems serve are strikingly similar to those of indicator systems to monitor the "health" of the economy, the criminal justice system, or other social systems. In all these areas, statistical indicators are used to monitor complex conditions that we would probably judge imprecisely or miss altogether in day-to-day observations. Governments have long recognized the value of statistics that provide current information, analyze trends, and forecast impending changes. Consequently, it is not surprising that policymakers and researchers are seeking better statistical indicators of education.

The overriding purpose of indicators is to characterize the nature of a system through its components, their interrelations, and their changes over time (e.g., de Neufville, 1975; MacRae, 1985; Sheldon, 1975). This information can then be used to judge progress—toward some goal or standard, against some past benchmark, or by comparison with data from some other institution or country.

What Is an Indicator?

The term *indicator* was defined above, by apposition, as a *statistic*. After reviewing the social indicator literature,[4] Jaeger (1978) concluded that indicators are, like this definition, "anything but clear and consistent. Review of a dozen definitions has produced much that is contradictory and little that is concise and illuminating" (p. 285). He recommended that:

> all variables that (1) represent the aggregate status or change in status of any group of persons, objects, institutions, or elements under study, and that (2) are essential to a report of status or change of status of the entities under study or to an understanding of the condition of the entities under study, should be termed indicators. I would *not require that reports of status or change in status be in quantitative form,* for narrative is often a better aid to comprehension and understanding of phenomena than is a numeric report (pp. 285–287, emphasis added).

---

[4]See, for example, Bauer, 1966a,b; Duncan, 1967; Etzioni, 1979; Etzioni and Lehman, 1967; Hauser, 1975; Jaeger, 1978; Land, 1975a,b; Land and Felson, 1976; Sheldon and Parke, 1975; Sheldon and Freeman, 1971; Shonfield and Shaw, 1972, and papers therein.

Jaeger's recommendation to leave open, as far as possible, the definition of an indicator and to determine the status of potential indicators on pragmatic rather than strict definitional grounds is a wise one.

An education system can also be conceived as having underlying properties that are not directly or perfectly measurable (cf. de Neufville, 1978–79). For example, we can talk of the quality of the teaching force but also recognize that this notion, concept, or "construct" has no direct measure. At best, several statistics can be aggregated into an *indicator* that "gets at" our notion of "teacher quality." An indicator of teacher quality might be some aggregate of years of academic training in the discipline taught; possession (or lack of) a credential in the subject matter taught; measured subject-matter knowledge; measured pedagogical knowledge; measured ability to translate subject-matter knowledge into a form that communicates to students of a given age, background, and prior knowledge; and so on.

Education indicators are statistics that reflect important aspects of the education system, but not all statistics about education are indicators. Statistics qualify as indicators only if they serve as yardsticks. That is, they must tell a great deal about the entire system by reporting the condition of a few particularly significant features of it. For example, the number of students enrolled in schools is an important fact, but it does little to inform judgments about how *well the education system is functioning*. On the other hand, data on the proportion of secondary students who have successfully completed advanced study in mathematics can provide considerable insight into the condition, or "health," of the system, and can be appropriately considered an indicator.

For our purposes, the following *working definition* serves as a heuristic guide: An indicator is an individual or composite statistic that relates to a basic construct in education and is useful in a policy context.

What Are Indicator Systems?

Another central concept in the discussion of indicators is that of the "indicator system." Whether indicators are single or composite statistics, a single indicator can rarely provide useful information about complex phenomena such as schooling. Indicator systems are usually designed to generate more, and more accurate, information about conditions. However, an indicator system is more than just a collection of indicator statistics. Ideally, a system of indicators measures *distinct* components of the system and also provides information about how the individual components work together to produce the overall effect. In other words, the whole of the information provided by a system of indicators is greater than the sum of its parts.

National indicators can and probably should be conceived as something more comprehensive than a time series of educational outcomes (e.g., achievement, participation). This was the type of indicator system developed by the NSB Commission (Hall, Jaeger, Kearney, and Wiley, 1985; MacRae, 1985), but simply monitoring outcomes does not provide explanations for observed trends. Might these trends, for example, be explained by demographic changes, educational improvements, or some combination of these? Moreover, education policy influences outcomes indirectly by actions such as increasing standards for teacher certification or for high school graduation. The direct effects of these policies will be reflected in changes in teachers' qualifications (e.g., an increase in teachers with bachelor's degrees in the disciplines taught, not in education), in better matches between teachers' subject-matter and pedagogical training and their teaching assignments, and in the number of academic courses students take in high school.

National indicators must represent, at least roughly, the important components of an educational system (see Fig. 1.1). In addition to monitoring outcomes, indicators should reflect the characteristics of students and communities served by schools, the financial and human

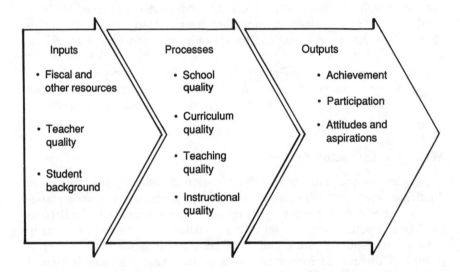

Fig. 1.1—Components of an educational system

resources (especially teachers) available to the schools, and other educational *inputs*. Moreover, they should reflect the adequacy of the curriculum and instruction received by students, the nature of the school as an organization in pursuit of educational excellence and equity, and other educational *processes*. Finally, indicators must be related to one another so that their relationships, and changes in these relationships, can be ascertained to suggest possible "explanations" for observed changes in outcomes.

Reasonable Expectations for an Indicator System

A good education indicator system is expected to provide accurate and precise information to illuminate the condition of education and contribute to its improvement. The information generated will be neither possible to grasp through casual observation nor generally available from other efforts to collect, report, and analyze data about schooling. Indicators are thus expected to assist policymakers as they formulate schooling goals and translate those goals into actions.

Whenever social indicators have been heralded as a stimulus for reform, their promise has quickly given way to realism. Promises of policy applications have been overly optimistic. Indicator systems were, for example, unable to provide detailed and accurate enough information for evaluating government programs. Moreover, indicator databases, often lacking essential theoretical prerequisites, fell short of expectations for research applications (Sheldon and Parke, 1975; see also Warren, 1974). These events led to more realistic assessments of what indicators can and cannot do (e.g., de Neufville, 1975; MacRae, 1985).

What Indicators Cannot Do. The literature on social indicators appears to have reached consensus on what indicators *cannot* do (e.g., de Neufville, 1975; Hauser, 1975; Shavelson, Oakes, and Carey, 1986; Sheldon, 1975; Sheldon and Freeman, 1971; Sheldon and Parke, 1975):

- *Set goals and priorities.* Educational goals and priorities are established by the public through its elected representatives. The information generated by an indicator system can inform those objectives, but it is just one factor among many in shaping decisions about policy preferences and priorities.
- *Evaluate programs.* Social indicators cannot substitute for well-designed, in-depth social program evaluation. They do not provide the level of rigor or detail necessary.[5]

---

[5]MacRae (1985) points out, and we agree, that program evaluation and policy analysis should be used to examine alternative policy options with well-designed studies that per-

- *Develop a balance sheet.* Social indicators lack the common referent available to economic indicators. Evoking an economic analogy and proposing a parallel development for social indicators is misleading because education cannot put each of its constructs on a common dollar metric as can be done, say, for Gross National Product (GNP). As Rivlin (1973, p. 419) pointed out, "No amount of disaggregation of inputs . . . will provide a basis for answering the how-are-we-doing question in the education sector. As long as cost is used as a proxy for value there is no way to compare inputs with outputs or to see whether a given *amount* of education is being produced with fewer resources." Rivlin also noted that because students help produce education, it is difficult to disentangle the quality of the output from student input.

What Social Indicators Can Do. The expectations for social indicators are now quite modest: to describe and state problems more clearly; to signal new problems more quickly; to obtain clues about promising educational programs; and the like. The following statements illustrate the realistic tone currently taken by the social indicator movement:

> We will be able to describe the state of the society and its dynamics and thus improve immensely our ability *to state problems in a productive fashion, obtain clues as to promising lines of endeavor, and ask good questions* (Sheldon and Parke, 1975, p. 698; see also de Neufville, 1975; Kaagan and Smith, 1985; Sheldon and Freeman, 1971; Thomas and Tyack, 1983).
>
> . . . .
>
> The fruit of these [social indicator] efforts will be more directly a contribution to the policy-maker's cognition than to his decisions. Decision emerges from a mosaic of inputs, including valuational and political, as well technical components (Sheldon and Parke, 1975, p. 698; see also de Neufville, 1975).

STEPS IN DESIGNING AN INDICATOR SYSTEM

The development of even a single indicator is an iterative process that de Neufville (1975) estimates takes about ten years to complete. The process is time-consuming because indicators are developed in a policy context; thus their interpretation goes beyond the traditional

---

mit, if possible, causal interpretations. Such studies should be linked closely to the indicator system by using similarly defined variables.

canons of science and enters the realm of politics (cf. de Neufville, 1978–79).[6] With this caveat, some steps in the identification of an *initial* set of indicators and the development of alternative indicator systems can be enumerated.[7]

Conceptualizing Potential Indicators

A reasonable first step is to determine which components (constructs) and their indicators adequately specify a "comprehensive" monitoring system. In our NSF project, we formulated a model of the education system and the potential indicators for measuring each component on the basis of an extensive review of the social indicator and educational research literature. The model contains inputs (the human and financial resources available to the education system), processes (a set of nested systems that create the educational environment that children experience in school), and outputs (the consequences of schooling for students from different backgrounds). For each of these components, we identified a large potential pool of constructs for which indicators might be developed. Each construct appeared either to be an important enabling condition (e.g., it moderated the link between an input or process indicator and an outcome indicator) or to have a direct link to the desired outcomes of mathematics and science education.

Refining the Indicator Pool

No manageable indicator system could accommodate all of the potentially important indicators identified by such a comprehensive identification process. A necessary second step, then, is to develop a valid, useful, and parsimonious set of indicators. The purposes the indicator system is to serve (e.g., description of trends, information for

---

[6]For example, preliminary indicators used to chart educational achievement from the early 1970s to the present have been criticized on the grounds that they measure aptitude, not school achievement (e.g., the SAT), or, if they measure achievement (e.g., the National Assessment of Educational Progress (NAEP)), they focus primarily on basic skills and not necessarily on a deep understanding of mathematical and scientific concepts and students' ability to apply them to solve everyday problems (see Chapter 7 of this volume). In response to policy priorities focused on students' understanding of mathematical and scientific concepts, the U.S. Department of Education (ED) is considering changes in national achievement indicators that will better reflect these priorities. Such a process is a lengthy one involving considerable discussion and debate among policymakers and researchers.

[7]For detailed discussions that include, but go beyond, initial frameworks to address the iterative process of indicator development, see de Neufville (1975, 1978–79) and MacRae (1985).

accountability purposes) constitute one criterion for reducing the initial pool of potential indicators. System designers need to consult potential users to determine what those purposes should be, since the purposes will dictate the type of information that must be collected and the level to which it should be disaggregated.

We applied eight criteria derived from our working definition of indicators.[8] We assumed that indicators should:

1. Reflect the central features of mathematics and science education.
2. Provide information pertinent to current or potential problems.
3. Measure factors that policy can influence.
4. Measure observed behavior rather than perceptions.
5. Measure reliably and validly.
6. Provide analytical links.
7. Be feasible to implement.
8. Address a broad range of audiences.

These criteria were used to select indicators that reflect the major components of schooling, are reliable and valid (to some minimal extent), and meet basic standards of usefulness to the policy community. These measures then became the core around which different indicator system options were generated.

We should warn indicator system developers that applying these criteria may produce some casualties. For example, some highly desirable indicators may have to be eliminated because they cannot be measured reliably. This exercise suggests that some potential indicators that are not sufficiently developed to be included in an indicator system at this time are critical to a better understanding of mathematics and science education and should be part of a developmental research agenda. Once these indicators meet our criteria, they can be incorporated into the indicator system.

---

[8]Some of these criteria create tradeoffs with each other. For example, describing the central features of schooling assumes that indicators will be relatively stable over time. On the other hand, providing policy-relevant information means that indicators may need to change as areas of policy emphasis change. The consequence of these competing requirements is that indicator systems are likely to expand over time. However, if the system is based on a comprehensive model of schooling, the addition of new indicators can be guided by that model, thus ensuring that they are conceptually sound. One way of meeting these dual information needs is to develop a system that measures the central features of schooling, using a stable set of indicators, but also provides "empty slots" that can be used for policy-specific indicators that change as policies shift.

Designing Alternative Indicator System Options

Once a model of the education system is defined and indicators are selected, the next step is to identify alternative data collection strategies that could be used to build the system. In the NSF project, we surveyed existing databases to determine what information was already being collected, and we identified areas where new indicator data were needed. In addition, we costed out each data point in an "ideal" indicator system to estimate costs for implementing alternative indicator systems. We were thereby able to generate alternatives, assess their likely utility, and provide cost estimates for each. We identified five generic options that ranged from simply relying on whatever data are available at the time a report is produced or policy issue considered (status quo) to developing and fielding a comprehensive data collection system that spans the major components of education (independent).[9]

Evaluating the Options

If indicator system alternatives are to be considered seriously by educators and policymakers, they need to be evaluated on a number of criteria. We evaluated each option according to its utility, feasibility, and cost. We asked whether each could (1) describe national trends (e.g., in achievement, teacher quality, and curriculum quality); (2) describe those trends state by state; (3) identify emerging problems on the horizon; (4) link teacher and curriculum quality to achievement, thus enabling policymakers to target reforms; and (5) enable the NSF to provide leadership by monitoring curricular and achievement areas that are currently ignored.

Begin Developing or Refining Individual Indicators

Once an indicator system alternative is selected, the process of developing or refining the individual indicators begins. The first step is to evaluate the technical adequacy and usefulness of existing indicators.

The advantages and disadvantages of each major construct (potential indicator) in the model must be evaluated, using currently available data and analyses. Systematically synthesizing and contrasting information from a variety of databases will allow the usefulness of current indicators to be assessed and will lay the groundwork for developing and implementing new indicators.

---

[9]These options are detailed in the final report of the NSF project (Shavelson et al., 1987).

Many data collection efforts and analyses will fall short of indicator requirements. Some of the most important constructs may not be measured at all, and well-known difficulties with existing datasets are likely to constrain the analyses that indicators require. In many cases, sample sizes or designs will not be adequate for disaggregating data by groups of interest; some will not permit relational analyses among various components of the system. It is important to identify the shortcomings in existing data and analyses, and where these gaps and inconsistencies exist, to specify what work is needed to obtain reliable, valid, and useful indicators.

In reviewing research that might help us identify the key components and indicators of mathematics and science education, we became acutely aware of how little we know about schooling and how primitive much current measurement technology is. For example, multiple-choice tests of verbal and quantitative ability and of achievement in specific subject matters are well-understood, yet there is overwhelming evidence that these tests do not adequately reflect the erroneous "mental models" many students (and adults) have of everyday phenomena such as electricity, gravity, and force. And, to date, no technology has been developed that would enable large-scale testing of this qualitative understanding. Each component of an indicator system may suffer from the same shortcoming.

It is therefore necessary to identify a research agenda directed toward improving the system. This agenda should become a research component of the indicator system itself that enables researchers to piggyback on monitoring activities and test alternatives to indicators currently in use. With increasing confidence in research findings, new indicator technologies can be incorporated into the system.

Because this volume focuses specifically on the first step in designing an indicator system, that task is discussed in some detail below.

THE FIRST STEP: IDENTIFYING RESEARCH-BASED INDICATORS

The chapters in this volume summarize our efforts to identify an initial pool of variables that capture major components of the mathematics and science education system. In some areas, e.g., the fiscal resources available to education, statistical indicators are well-developed and have been widely used for some time. Consequently, the discussion focuses on actual indicators that might be included in a mathematics and science indicator system. However, in other areas of schooling where aggregate statistics have not typically been produced and reported as indicators (e.g., instructional processes), we are limited to discussing features (or variables) that are good candidates for future indicator development. Each chapter will identify a set of variables that either have already been used as educational indicators or could be used after additional developmental work. We refer to both categories as potential indicators.

This pool of potential indicators represents our assessment of what the social indicator and educational research literature identifies as the most essential elements of the schooling process and its outcomes. Four assumptions are reflected in the chapters of this volume:

- An indicator system should be based on a conceptual model of schooling.
- That model and its major domains should be empirically, rather than normatively, derived.
- A major criterion for selecting the potential indicators within each domain should be their ability to measure core features of schooling.
- Where possible, indicators should be derived from research that identifies the factors associated with important schooling outcomes.

Past experience with social indicators has demonstrated the need for indicator systems to be firmly grounded in a working theory or model of how the social system being measured actually operates (de Neufville, 1975). The model may be very simple and intuitive or it may be quite complex, but it must represent the phenomenon of interest and identify its most important components and the relationships among them. Only with such a model can we have a context for interpreting individual indicators and for explaining trends reported by the indicator system.

Figure 1.2 presents the model of precollege science and mathematics education that guided our work. The model's *inputs* are the human and financial resources available to education; its *processes* are what is taught and how it is taught; and its *outputs* are the consequences of schooling for students from different backgrounds. This model is based on Barr and Dreeben's (1983) concept of the educational system as a multilevel, "nested" series of organizational structures and educational processes. Each level has specific resources available to it and engages in particular kinds of activities. These activities, in turn, lead to outcomes that significantly influence what is possible and likely at the schooling level(s) nested within.

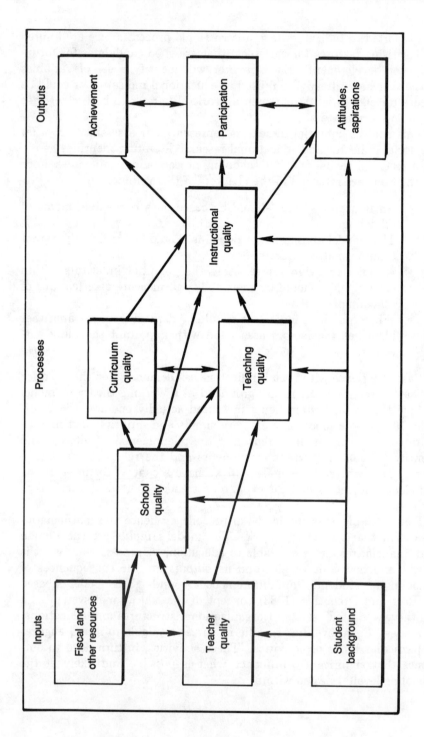

Fig. 1.2—A comprehensive model of the educational system

A multilevel, nested depiction of schooling places teacher and student classroom interaction at its center. This interaction is nested within instructional groups that are, in turn, nested within classrooms. Classroom interaction is nested within schools, schools within districts, and districts within communities. Although local communities have some degree of control over their schools, they operate within a context of federal and state policies. Barr and Dreeben indicate that only what happens at the teacher-student level is directly related to student learning. Yet what happens at this level is influenced by what happens at all levels of the system (see McPartland and Becker (1985) for a similar argument).

Understanding the educational process requires attention to all levels, as well as specification of the relationships among conditions at each level and student outcomes. This task will inevitably generate considerable methodological frustration, but neglect of multilevel elements will lead to superficial and simplistic portrayals of schooling. Far from clarifying the dynamics of the schooling process, simplification can ignore critical factors. How schools organize educational resources and learning opportunities and how schools respond to new policies and other kinds of improvement efforts are often neglected, even though few would deny their importance. However, these elements must be simplified if they are to be studied. The inevitable tension between comprehensiveness and clarity must be resolved by identifying the meaningful factors that are actually measurable in a standardized way across schools.

The model we selected identifies major domains and suggests how these elements are likely to be logically or empirically related. The relationships depicted in Fig. 1.2 do not constitute a model in either a strict predictive or causal sense, but they serve as a framework showing logical linkages among elements. Moreover, as subsequent chapters will indicate, considerable correlational research supports those links.

The second assumption—that the model and the domains comprising it should be empirically derived—was also important in shaping our work. Some have suggested models of mathematics and science education that are based on a set of desired goals and the changes needed to achieve those goals (e.g., Romberg and Stewart, 1987). This approach is more normative in that it views the primary purpose of the indicator system as aiding the reform of mathematics and science education according to a particular set of standards. Although all indicator systems and the models from which they are derived embody a set of values (e.g., high rates of participation in mathematics and science education are desirable and high-quality science and mathematics education should be available to all students), we have relied on broader and more empirically based criteria. We wanted to create a monitoring system that is broadly responsive to policymakers' information needs, regardless of the particular type of education they advocate. That is, we want the system to track those central features of schooling that are likely to be sensitive to policy changes, whatever their type or direction. The system should thus remain useful over time and place, even as policy priorities change (Shavelson et al., 1987).

This desire to develop a system that will be useful to the policy community but will still transcend specific initiatives led us to the third assumption, that potential indicators should measure core features of schooling. An indicator system that measures fundamental characteristics of mathematics and science education will enable us to generate data to monitor the condition of that system, even as particular policy interventions change. By focusing on the core features of schooling, we chose not to concentrate on specific policies (e.g., increased mathematics and science course requirements), but rather to develop indicators of basic characteristics (e.g., curriculum content, course offerings, and enrollments) that policies attempt to influence. We assumed that the importance of any one indicator to policymakers may vary considerably over time and place, but the essential construct and the indicator(s) measuring it need to remain fairly stable.

We also chose to include domains and potential indicators for which research has not yet determined relationships to particular outcomes. We believe that information is needed about some features of schooling (e.g., the amount of financial resources available, teachers' workloads, curriculum offerings) to understand how the system works and because policymakers and the public care about factors such as per-pupil expenditures and class size.

However, we also assumed that, wherever possible, indicators should be derived from research identifying the factors associated with important schooling outcomes. Therefore, we undertook an exhaustive review of the research on school finance, school context and organization, teachers and teaching, curriculum and instruction, learning, and knowledge utilization.

Within the structure provided by our four guiding assumptions, we examined relevant research in education, psychology, sociology, policy analysis, and economics. We sought the most robust and consistent findings across multiple studies to identify reliable measures of the domains of schooling. We also used the research literature as a guide in determining the most appropriate unit of analysis for different measures, identifying major problems or gaps associated with potential indicators, and suggesting how those problems might be resolved.

The subsequent chapters are briefly summarized below.

OVERVIEW OF THE VOLUME

Table 1.1 lists the major domains of the educational system model of Fig. 1.2 and indicates the chapters in which each is analyzed. The boundaries among these domains are not rigid, and all are discussed in more than one chapter. For example, teacher quality is a major resource for schools; it is also a critical component of the instructional process. However, each component is the primary focus of a separate chapter, where it is treated in depth.

Resources and Commitment

In Chapter 2, James Catterall argues that resource indicators are fundamental to indicator systems. Resource levels define what schools have available and therefore influence *how* science and mathematics education is conducted. Resource levels also indicate a level of commitment to schooling. Further, because they are salient to the public, they are frequently used as informal indicators of school quality, both in community discussions and in the popular media.

Catterall suggests that we need systematic information about budget allocations to schools and school systems, and we also need information about the whole array of human and material resources that those educational dollars buy; coupling resource levels with measures of resource use can dramatically increase their power to inform judgments

Table 1.1

MAJOR DOMAINS OF THE EDUCATIONAL
SYSTEM COVERED IN THIS VOLUME

Domain	Chapter[a]
Fiscal and other resources	2, 3, 4
Teacher quality	4, 2
Student background	8, 2, 4, 6
School quality	3, 4
Curriculum quality	5, 7
Teaching quality	4, 6
Instructional quality	6, 4
Achievement	7, 8
Participation	9, 7, 8
Attitudes and aspirations	8, 7

[a]The first chapter number listed for each domain is the primary one in which that domain is discussed.

about school quality. Catterall argues that the background characteristics of students themselves, the fiscal capacity of their communities, and the voluntarily contributed inputs of communities to schools also constitute important educational resources that must be measured.

In short, Catterall asserts that the material and human resources available and actually expended should be essential elements of an indicator system. Resource indicators are important, he argues, despite the fact that research shows that the link between student achievement and such factors as per-pupil expenditure, curricular materials, and facilities is tenuous at best. These indicators measure the parameters in which schools must operate, and they define the outer limits of what is possible. School or system performance differences across time and settings may be affected by resource levels and community commitment. Such indicators can therefore serve as important controls for context in any educational monitoring scheme and can lead to a fairer and more accurate understanding of other school processes and outcomes.

School Organization and Context

In Chapter 3, Jeannie Oakes suggests that information about schools is essential, since it is *in schools* that resources and policies are transformed into educational programs and activities for students. Decisions about school organization, activities, and procedures set conditions for science and mathematics teaching and learning in classrooms. They create the conditions that *enable* learning to take place. Oakes argues that recent research provides evidence that school characteristics are linked to educational effectiveness generally and to mathematics and science achievement specifically. She argues that these indicators are also important because a plethora of current reforms seek to foster new characteristics in schools, but there is virtually no way to track the impact of these efforts.

Based on a review of research on policy-relevant features of schools as institutions, Oakes suggests constructs for which school indicators should be developed. The first is *access to science and mathematics knowledge*—the extent to which schools provide students with opportunities to learn topics and skills in these fields. The second condition is the *expectation for science and mathematics achievement*—the extent to which schools communicate their belief that all children can succeed in these subjects. The third, *professional teaching conditions*, is a set of school circumstances that enables teachers and administrators to create an instructional program in which access is maximized and expectations are salient. Access, high expectations, and teaching conditions are viewed as "enabling" conditions; to the degree that they exist in schools, they appear to promote good teaching and good learning.

Even though these constructs are *intangibles*, Oakes suggests that they can be operationalized and assessed with measures of the ways schools use their resources to create educational programs; how schools organize their staff, time, curriculum, and materials; and what processes schools follow in conducting the work of teaching and learning. Measures of these tangible manifestations of access, expectations, and teaching conditions are likely be good indicators of the quality of science and mathematics education that a school is able to provide.

Teacher and Teaching Quality

In Chapter 4, Linda Darling-Hammond and Lisa Hudson remind us that the classroom—the place in which students and teachers interact to affect learning—lies at the heart of the educational system. They argue that it is the quality of this interaction that ultimately determines the quality of the educational system. And the quality of the teacher-student interaction is greatly affected by the qualities (e.g., qualifications, attitudes, training, beliefs) of teachers.

Darling-Hammond and Hudson analyze the literature on teacher and teaching quality and conclude that a few features of teachers and teaching are known to be consistently related to student achievement, and that some teacher characteristics and behaviors are more "effective" in some educational contexts than in others. But we do not know the distribution of these teacher qualities across the teaching force, how this distribution changes over time, or how teacher qualities relate to teachers' practices, working conditions, or career decisions. Darling-Hammond and Hudson suggest that indicators can begin to provide such information.

More specifically, the chapter suggests that three types of indicators are needed: (1) teacher characteristics that reflect their qualifications, experience, and attitudes toward mathematics and science teaching; (2) descriptors of teaching assignments and conditions; and (3) factors influencing teacher supply and demand, including retention of current teachers and trends in the supply of prospective teachers.

Teacher quality indicators should also enable educators and policymakers to explore several major issues. We need better indicators of how teachers' background features (e.g., certification status and levels of college coursework) are related to each other and to other teaching variables (e.g., teacher experience, types of students taught). Darling-Hammond and Hudson argue that it is also important to examine how—according to these various measures—teacher quality is distributed across classes and students of different types.

Curriculum

Curriculum is usually defined as content, i.e., the topics, concepts, processes, and skills that students are taught in science and mathematics classes—the "medium of exchange" in school. The content taught in school clearly makes a difference in what students learn. But curriculum includes more than just content. It includes the objectives teachers have in mind as they present content to students; the depth to which the content is explored; the way it is sequenced; the textbooks and materials used; the mode of presentation teachers employ; and decisions about what content is appropriate for various groups of students.

In Chapter 5, Jeannie Oakes and Neil Carey argue that, despite many obstacles, curriculum indicators can be identified. First, they suggest a set of indicators to monitor curriculum policies within schools, districts, and states. These indicators could provide descriptions of curriculum policies and permit comparisons. However, Oakes and Carey suggest that a set of indicators to collect information about the science and mathematics curriculum that is actually *practiced* in classrooms would be even more important. The classroom is a place where policy is often substantially modified. These indicators could provide a comprehensive description of the mathematics and science curriculum and could enable the tracking of nontrivial effects of curriculum policy on the curriculum students actually experience.

Third, Oakes and Carey suggest substantial new developmental work on curriculum materials quality indicators. The congruence of the science and mathematics curriculum with "expert" judgments of the ideal curriculum; the scientific accuracy of curriculum content; and the pedagogical appropriateness of the curriculum (e.g., how well the curriculum matches the cognitive needs of students) could be used to monitor the quality of the formal curriculum as represented in state, district, and school curriculum guides, and in commercially produced textbooks and curriculum materials.

Classroom Instruction

In Chapter 6, Neil Carey tackles the difficulties of developing valid and feasible indicators of instruction in mathematics and science classrooms. Carey argues that, for indicator purposes, instruction consists of the policies, practices, and social climate that result from the interaction of the teacher, students, and curriculum in mathematics and science classrooms. He suggests that these features of classroom life are critical for indicator development, since much of the variability in achievement may be better understood in the context of the processes through which students are engaged in mathematics and science.

Carey warns, however, that a comprehensive system for monitoring mathematics and science instruction would require detailed attention to all aspects of classroom life. Such an undertaking would overburden schools and would be economically and practically infeasible. Moreover, many crucial aspects of instructional processes cannot be measured with current technology. Carey therefore suggests a more parsimonious set: First, instructional policy indicators should focus on time allocation, the standards teachers set for students, the learning experiences in which students are engaged, and the grouping policies operating in the classroom. Second, the indicators should probably be limited to aspects that can reliably be measured with surveys (e.g., the number of pages covered in textbooks), since observational or detailed teacher record-keeping defies cost-benefit criteria for data collection and analysis. Finally, Carey suggests developing a few classroom climate indicators, such as perceived difficulty of assignments, businesslike atmosphere, and emotional warmth in classrooms. However, these should probably be developed experimentally and tested as proxies for more difficult-to-measure aspects of instruction, such as the appropriateness of teachers' expectations.

Individual-Level Outcomes

In Chapter 7, Neil Carey and Richard Shavelson review the literature on what many consider the most important domain of the mathematics and science education system: student outcomes. As Carey and Shavelson define it, this domain includes (1) students' *achievement*, viz., knowledge, understanding, and use of concepts and skills in mathematics and science; (2) student *participation* within and outside of school in mathematical and scientific activities; and (3) students' *attitudes* toward and self-confidence in these subjects.

The authors conclude that achievement outcomes—whether students have learned what they have been taught—should be given the highest priority in an indicator system. They also treat participation as an outcome for indicator development, since it is a precondition for achievement; participation provides a concrete, albeit imperfect, indicator of whether students are likely to progress toward becoming mathematicians, scientists, or engineers, or whether they are literate in those areas; and it provides a useful, indirect indicator of student attitudes. The chapter also recommends that attitudes be included in an indicator system, because they are perceived by many to be a relevant outcome of schools, they are thought to provide an early sign of mathematics and science dropouts, and data on them are easy to collect.

Carey and Shavelson recommend that outcome indicators report the extent to which students are learning problem-solving skills and developing conceptual understanding in mathematics and science. Participation indicators should reflect course-taking in required and elective mathematics and science courses, and the topics and skills covered. The indicators should also show the degree to which students participate in extracurricular activities related to mathematics and science, and students' intended college majors or career choices.

However, Carey and Shavelson warn of the difficulties of implementing these recommendations. Achievement test scores provide the most readily available indicators of achievement, yet none of the existing tests actually measures some of its most important dimensions. In the short run, an indicator system could use a specific combination of data from various achievement tests. However, new methods should be devised to assess understanding and problem solving. The importance of this recommendation goes beyond testing: Achievement tests exert a profound influence on what is taught in classrooms. The authors also warn of the conceptual and technical difficulties in measuring and interpreting correlates of participation and achievement, such as scientific attitudes, favorable attitudes toward mathematics and science, and students' self-confidence in their abilities.

Participation of Special Populations

In Chapter 8, Jeannie Oakes illustrates how indicators can be used to monitor the educational achievement and participation of women, the poor, and non-Asian minorities in mathematics and science. These groups' lower levels of achievement and participation warrant close attention because of their impact on the quality of the future workforce. Underrepresentation and underachievement also relate to the long-standing federal responsibility for ensuring equal educational opportunity for minority and disadvantaged populations.

Data describing how the precollege mathematics and science opportunities and experiences of women, minorities, and the poor typically diverge from those of more successful student groups (Asians and white males) provide considerable evidence that schooling factors may contribute to unequal outcomes. Patterns of schooling differences accompany those of lower achievement and underparticipation. Both patterns begin early in the educational process.

Oakes' review of the literature on underrepresentation in science and mathematics concludes that race-, class-, and gender-related differences appear to result, at least in part, from the insufficient and unequal access of women, minorities, and poor students to school conditions that work in favor of high achievement, continued participation, and positive attitudes. Consequently, indicators should monitor the distribution of resources and opportunities available at schools of different types, i.e., those serving different student populations. Indicators should also assess the extent to which resources and opportunities are available to different groups of students *within the same schools*. However, the ability of indicators to provide such information will be determined by technical decisions about sample sizes, analytical strategies, and reporting procedures.

School Completion and Dropouts

James Catterall's discussion of school completion and dropouts in Chapter 9 presents possible justifications for including dropout statistics in an indicator system for science and mathematics education; reviews the relevant research; and describes the current state of dropout information collection by government agencies and school systems. Catterall argues that the relevance of school dropout data to an education monitoring system depends on the purposes of the system. He suggests what those alternative purposes might be and what indicators would be appropriate for each.

Nevertheless, Catterall identifies serious challenges to the development of dropout indicators. Existing data collection efforts are unlikely to provide the type of information that is needed, and the establishment of useful data collection mechanisms is likely to be costly. Moreover, Catterall argues that there is as yet little consensus that dropout indicators will be worth their price.

The Policy Context

In Chapter 10, Lorraine McDonnell describes how the larger policy environment profoundly influences schooling in a variety of ways. Federal, state, and local policies largely determine the level and type of resources available to education. Although their effects on other components of schooling are typically less direct, these policies can also influence who is allowed to teach, what content is taught, and even how it is taught. The priorities of the policy community may also signal to educators which outcome factors are most important at a given time, thus indicating the criteria on which they will be held accountable. What is perhaps most striking about the education reform policies of the past four years is that they have moved the influence of policy well down into the educational system. In the past, policy typically focused on how schools were financed and governed; now its scope also includes what is taught and who teaches it. Consequently, McDonnell strongly recommends that the larger policy context be taken into consideration in future attempts to explain changes in the major components of schooling.

Chapter 2

RESOURCES AND COMMITMENT

James S. Catterall

INTRODUCTION

For an indicator system that can monitor the state of science and mathematics education in the nation's schools, inputs and processes of education are as important as outcomes. Before policymakers and educators can develop any strategies for improving education in those subjects, they need to know not only how well the schools are doing, but also *how* they are doing it. The resources society devotes to education strongly influence the way science and mathematics education proceeds. Thus, the resources required and expended hold considerable interest for educators and for the public officials who must juggle competing demands for public services, within and outside of education.

Educational resources are usually thought of in terms of the budget allocation to schools and school systems. However, these resources also encompass the full array of material resources and human participants involved in education, including the characteristics of the learners. How resources are conceived dictates the nature of resource indicators to be included in a science and mathematics indicator system. This chapter (1) presents justifications for including resource indicators in a mathematics and science indicator system, (2) establishes a conceptual framework for identifying and selecting resource indicators, (3) discusses the usefulness of candidate indicators, and (4) assesses the relative difficulty of obtaining data on these indicators.

WHY RESOURCE INDICATORS?

As Chapter 10 suggests, an indicator system will not be useful if it does not reflect the policy context for improving education, motivate policymakers to act, and give them the information they need for policy decisions. Resource indicators can enhance the policy relevance of an indicator system for mathematics and science in the ways discussed below.

The Correlation Between Resources and Outcomes

Resource measures may help policymakers interpret observed differences and trends in science and mathematics performance. However, it is important to recognize that resource profiles cannot provide unambiguous explanations of educational outcomes. Resources are usually conceptualized by researchers as per-pupil spending, teacher salaries, square footage of classrooms or laboratories per pupil, number of library books, and so on. But resources so conceived do not establish determined or even probabilistic outcome frontiers for our schools. Studies of the independent contributions of specific educational inputs have produced no consensus on what resources, in what particular arrangements, lead to what types of learning.

The limitations of extant input-output research in education are well known (Cohn, 1979; Blaug, 1985). The failure to identify strong relationships between the mere presence of productive resources and outcomes appears to result from multiple factors:

- The overriding importance of student characteristics, especially family educational background and support, in the functional forms identified and estimated by researchers (Coleman, et al., 1966; Jencks et al., 1972; and many others).
- Observations that resources themselves are subject to varying degrees of use and human effort over varying lengths of time (Levin, 1980; Karweit, 1983; Wiley and Harnischfeger, 1974).
- The inherent scientific limits of capturing the outcomes of education in quantitative statistics (see Chapter 7 of this volume).

However, most input-output research in education (often called *education production function research*) addresses constructs of general learning and usually employs scores on verbal or reading tests as outcome measures. Since almost none of this research examines science learning, and very little concerns quantitative skills development, we might be surprised by the relationships uncovered by a systematic and comprehensive science and mathematics indicators system that incorporates exemplary achievement, resource, and process data.

At the very least, resource profiles could trace a set of opportunities and constraints that might help educators probe the relative effectiveness of existing or proposed practices. The school whose students come from highly educated families expects impressive results when learning is measured, and if those results do not materialize, specific concerns may be flagged. The district with large class sizes and spectacular algebra achievement may warrant a closer look. In practice, useful comparisons are not likely to involve these simplistic and bivariate contrasts, but would include constellations of resource constraints and opportunities surrounding the efforts of educators to teach and students to learn.

Motivating Education Providers

Resource measures, like measures of performance and participation, may serve to motivate education providers. High-performing systems may be buoyed by their identified excellence; low-performing systems may be infused with ambition to catch up. Where systems show meager resource allocations—e.g., low teacher salaries, low per-pupil spending, or inordinately large class sizes and teaching loads—districts may be embarrassed into providing more learning resources for their children, especially if performance results show concomitant shortfalls. Systems evidencing rich resource constellations and lackluster student performance may be induced to examine their resource utilization patterns for sources of inefficiency.

Helping School Systems Assess Their Performance

Outcome data across the full spectrum of institutions may be of little relevance to particular systems. A given state or school system may have a legitimate interest in comparing itself with states or systems that benefit from similar resources. For instance, states that pay high teacher salaries may wish to compare their class sizes, teaching loads, and pupil outcomes with those of states bearing similar teacher costs. States in the deep south, where parent education levels tend to be lower than elsewhere in the nation, may wish to enlist each other as reference points for certain comparisons. States with high concentrations of nonwhite minority children may want to look to each other for specific assessments. Schools with demonstrated commitments to small mathematics classes may wish to compare themselves with other schools that have similar commitments.

Enabling Fair Comparisons

An indicator system that includes resource measures may produce fairer comparative evaluations. Outcome measures alone cannot be used to make fair comparative assessments of a school's or school system's performance. For example, it is unfair to draw inferences from outcome data about the relative effectiveness of schools in the absence of information about the family educational backgrounds of students. An inner-city high school whose pupils come from poor families may perform at unprecedented heights for schools with such characteristics. Yet, its test scores may not even approach those of flagship suburban schools. If monitoring data inspire fair comparisons in the eyes of school systems, educators are likely to accept and use monitoring information more frequently and are more likely to provide critical cooperation in collecting and reporting information in the first place.

The importance of fair comparisons is evidenced by the cries of "foul" heard when the U.S. Department of Education (ED) published state-by-state comparisons of student performance on the Scholastic Aptitude Test (SAT) and American College Test (ACT) for college admissions in its Wall Charts of education statistics (U.S. Department of Education, 1984b, 1985, 1986). At least two lessons regarding fairness emerged from the Wall Chart saga. First, the SAT and ACT scores were clearly sensitive to the extremely divergent proportions of students in each state taking these tests (Powell and Steelman, 1984), but even publishing these data as a context for interpreting the test scores did not quiet objections from the field. Second, there is a fundamental problem in using a test designed to gauge aptitude for college (and not geared specifically to high school curricula) as a school system performance indicator.

Reflecting the Growing Interest in Resource Measures

Recent activities producing or contemplating education quality comparisons suggest—not surprisingly, in view of the arguments above—that resource measures will be included in forthcoming monitoring schemes. ED incorporates the following resource measures in its Wall Charts of education statistics (U.S. Department of Education, 1984a, 1985, 1986):

Indicators Used in All Four Years
    Current expenditures per pupil
    Expenditures as a percentage of per capita income
    Average teacher salary
    Pupil/teacher ratio
    Federal funds as a percentage of school revenues
    Per capita income
    Percent poverty, ages 5–17

Indicators Excluded in 1986 and 1987
    Median years of education, adults

Indicators Used in 1986 and 1987 but not 1984
   Pupil/staff ratio (added in 1985)
   Performance-based teacher incentive (added in 1985)

In addition, the Council of Chief State School Officers is developing suggestions for nationwide elementary and secondary education monitoring that will include recommended resource and context indicators, according to preliminary reports (*Education Week*, 1985).

SELECTING RESOURCE INDICATORS

Developing a Conceptual Model of Resource Measures

Given the need for including resource measures in an indicator system, what resources should be monitored, and why? The answers must be based on a conceptual model of how various elements of the educational system interact and affect outcomes. The comprehensive model of schooling shown in Chapter 1 included several resource constructs as inputs. Figure 2.1 suggests an elaborated scheme of education inputs consistent with that comprehensive model.

In Fig. 2.1, the critical resources contributing to processes of education (and, implicitly, outcomes) are *educational resources,* comprising personnel, curriculum materials, and facilities, and the *students* themselves. An unquestionable determinant of the educational resources available to a school or school system is the *fiscal allocation,* or budget. Budgets are the result of public decisionmaking processes that are influenced by the *capacity* of a community (e.g., state or school district) to support its schools, which in turn corresponds to available public revenue-raising bases. Actual budgets for schools and other public services reflect the willingness of communities to levy taxes or fees for those services.

Educational resources also materialize through the contribution of outside inputs, such as volunteer classroom aides and local booster foundations—resources provided by others in the community. In addition, the students represent a resource that interacts with other resources in the processes of education, a set of activities beyond the scope of Fig. 2.1 but discussed at length in other chapters of this volume.

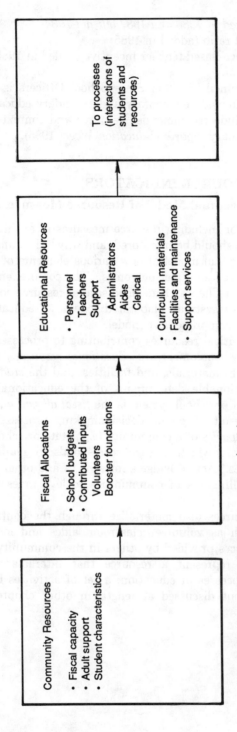

Fig. 2.1—Resource inputs for a comprehensive educational system model

Some Constraints on Selecting Resource Indicators

The simplicity of the model masks a number of complexities which underlie the relationships, but which are not elaborated here. For instance, the linkage between fiscal capacity and fiscal allocations for schools is subject to a variety of influences, particularly levels of competing needs for public services and overall preferences for private versus public goods. And the linkage between fiscal allocations and educational resources could be embellished with detailed cost indices for the various ingredients enumerated as educational resources. A comprehensive resource indicator system could conceivably account for dozens of explanatory or interpretive variables of these types.

While school finance researchers have shown much interest in detailed understanding of such relationships (e.g., Carroll and Park, 1983; Chambers, 1980, 1978; Ladd, 1975), we assume that the designers of indicator systems for science and mathematics education will not choose to proliferate arrays of indicators. The costs of such attempted perfection are not only monetary; the insufferable detail it requires often leads to ultimate rejection by monitoring audiences.

Parsimony is thus an important consideration in choosing specific indicators. A monitoring scheme should not be overburdened with labyrinthine concepts of resource inputs, but rather should concentrate on an efficient set of indicators that describe the core resource contexts of school processes and outcomes and also advance the goals of motivation, local utility, and fairness of comparison. Monitoring schemes must also consider their own budgets, which determine the degree to which they can generate original information and the extent of their reliance on current data collection activities of agencies or associations.

A second consideration affecting the nature, availability, and attainability of resource data is the level within the system of schools for which comparisons are sought. State, school district, school, and classroom-level measures present varying opportunities and constraints to would-be monitors of resources, as well as other characteristics of schooling processes. Many state-level resource indicators are presently collected and reported in forms useful for state comparisons. School district, school, and classroom resource data are more likely to require original data collection, particularly where comparisons across systems (e.g., school districts in different states or schools in different districts) are desired.

A third consideration is the balance of interest in general resources supporting education versus resources specifically devoted to mathematics and science education.

Finally, a simple scaling principle should apply to resource measures for schooling. Since states, school districts, schools, and classrooms vary in the size of the populations they serve, most resource measures should be considered on a per-pupil or per-capita basis to make cross-unit comparisons meaningful.

Recommended Indicators

With the concept of resource inputs to education shown in Fig. 2.1—and the constraints discussed above—the following classes of indicators seem most important and feasible. These indicators are discussed in order of their importance and according to the interpretive relationships among them.

Direct Indicators of Fiscal Allocation. The most fundamental resource measure of fiscal allocation to schools is per-pupil expenditures. Per-pupil expenditure measures are readily available for both school districts and entire states; but they are practically never available for individual schools within districts—some districts, in fact, appear to take precautions which assure that such measures are not generated and circulated publicly. Thus, generating per-pupil expenditures for mathematics or science instruction would require dedicated studies.

The National Center for Education Statistics (now the Center for Statistics (CS)) has reported school spending per pupil by state for years. State departments of education have accessible records of each school district's per-pupil spending, since state foundation aid and other fiscal assistance for school districts are commonly determined with particular distributions of total per-pupil expenditures as central objectives.

Informative but not essential classification schemes could refine reports of per-pupil expenditures. For example, per-pupil revenues from local, state, and federal sources could be reported separately. The shares in each category, particularly the state and local components, vary from state to state because the tax systems that support education are diverse. But since the central interest of a monitoring scheme is in overall levels of support for schools, such information is not likely to be valued. Alternatively, funds could be classified as general or categorical. Categorical funds are appropriated by states and the federal government with specific intended target populations. Examples include the federal Chapter 1 program, which is intended to support services for children from economically disadvantaged backgrounds, and federal assistance to special-needs youngsters through Public Law 94–142. Levels of support for education net of categorical programs would be a desirable indicator of resources available for regular instructional purposes, including instruction in mathematics and science. Obtaining this information would appear to require special runs of data at state education agencies; we know of no systematic reporting of expenditures in this format.

Educational Resources: Interpreting Resource Allocation. Overall fiscal allocations in per-pupil terms are a first building block of an indicator describing resources available to schools. Real comparisons of system resources demand consideration of what budget allocations are actually able to purchase, which will vary across locales and systems. The educational resources obtained through budgets (shown in Fig. 2.1) include personnel, curriculum materials, and facilities and support services. For several reasons, this chapter concentrates on fiscal resources for teachers. First, other curricular indicators (e.g., materials and facilities) are addressed elsewhere in this volume (see Chapter 5). Second, teacher inputs occupy an overwhelming share of education budgets—80 to 90 percent of the typical school district's budget is allocated to salaries and wages, with 70 to 80 percent used for teacher salaries (Guthrie and Reed, 1985). And third, the teacher-headed classroom is the principal locus of instruction.

Three indicators of teacher resources are tightly linked to budget allocations. The number of teachers a given budget will support is tied to the distribution of teacher salaries and is summarily reflected in the *average teacher salary*. Average teacher salary is thus suggested as a fundamental resource-related indicator. An indicator of how intensively teaching resources could be distributed across enrolled students is reflected in a system's *pupil/teacher ratio*. Pupil/teacher ratios are thus a key indicator of the potential availability of teacher resources to students (independent of questions of the *quality* of teacher resources, discussed in Chapter 4 of this volume). And finally, the way teachers are actually deployed by schools and systems is reflected in *average class sizes* and *teaching loads* (i.e., the total number of pupils assigned to each teacher).

Two of these indicators, average teacher salaries and pupil/teacher ratios, are regularly collected at the state level by state departments of education (SDEs). The National Education Association (NEA) publishes average teacher salaries by state, both overall and for elementary and secondary teachers separately, along with other SDE statistics, in a series entitled *Estimates of School Statistics*. Since much mathematics and science education takes place in secondary schools, secondary teacher salaries would be a desirable resource indicator.

Pupil/teacher ratios are shown in two ways in the NEA reports: according to pupils in average daily attendance (ADA), and according to pupils in average daily membership (ADM). The former refers to counts of pupils actually attending (or with valid excuses for nonattendance) each day; the latter refers to numbers of pupils on the rolls. As a resource indicator, pupils in membership per teacher would be preferred because it reflects the total number of pupils that teaching resources must serve. Having fewer students per day because of absences may, in fact, make the teachers' job more difficult, since helping individual students catch up can be time-consuming.

Neither average class size nor teaching loads are reported in common compendia of school statistics; we have not determined whether individual states collect such data, and if so, whether the data are comparable. Teaching loads for mathematics and science teachers would seem to be a highly desirable resource indicator. As Sizer (1984) has suggested, the teacher with 150 pupils has little time to devote to any individual student's work. Spending 10 minutes per week on individual student products adds up to 25 hours outside of class time. The algebra teacher with 80 pupils is more likely to offer regular and concrete feedback on student assignments.

Students as Resources. The effects of student family background characteristics on educational performance are profusely documented, and for this reason, students themselves should be considered a resource in the processes of education. Indices of family socioeconomic status, which comprises parental education, job status, and income, show strong links to measured educational achievement and performance (Coleman et al., 1966; Jencks et al., 1972). In the interests of fairness, a monitoring system that displays student educational performance statistics should also report some representation of pupil family background.

Pupil family education and income levels are not routinely reported by states or school systems, although some statewide systems of pupil testing, such as the California Assessment Program, generate schoolwide estimates of pupil socioeconomic status from teacher or student reports on individual test forms. Reports of parent education or income levels for education monitoring schemes would generally have to be based on original data collection. A weak proxy for state-by-state comparisons would be median education levels of the adult population, which are estimated and reported by the U.S. Census Bureau, but they of course include many adults who do not have children in school. Additional indicators of student background characteristics are the percentage of nonwhite minority pupils within schools, a statistic collected by CS for states, and the percentage of students from families receiving Aid to Families with Dependent Children (AFDC), a statistic that is available for most schools and systems through SDEs.

Fiscal Capacity. If school systems are to be compared according to their resource allocations to schools, some index of their communities' capacities for spending should be included. Recent ED Wall Charts have included the percentage of per-capita income devoted to education in each state as an approximation of this. Analyses published in 1986 by the Advisory Commission on Intergovernmental Relations (ACIR), however, suggest that per-capita income, despite its simplicity and intuitive appeal, is deficient as an index of revenue-raising capacity. The ACIR argument is straightforward: The ability of governments to raise revenues depends on a full complement of bases subject to taxes and fees, including all statutory revenue bases, e.g., property value, business activity, and various licensing operations, as well as personal income. The ACIR (1986) presents and discusses several indices, the best of which appears to be the calculation of revenue-raising capacity under what it calls the Representative Revenue System (RRS). State-level data on tax capacity per capita based on the RRS are routinely available through ACIR with a two-year lag time. These figures could be compared with per-pupil expenditures in a scheme of state resource comparisons.

Individual school district fiscal capacity is calculated for school finance system operations in some states (Carroll and Park, 1983). Although the methods and figures may be consistent for districts within a particular state, measures of school district fiscal capacity are not consistent across states because the tax systems supporting schools differ widely. Some state school systems, such as Oregon's, are highly reliant on local property taxation. Some, such as California's, depend heavily on state tax collection from diverse sources.

Contributed Inputs. The model in Fig. 2.1 shows contributed inputs to education, such as volunteer time and community foundations, which provide funds to some schools and districts. No central data source appears to report on these systematically, either for states or for school systems within states. Although intensive examination of selected individual schools could provide such information with small marginal costs, its likely insignificance in relation to overall levels of resource inputs suggests that it is not likely to be included in monitoring schemes. Thus, contributed inputs are not included among the recommended indicators in Table 2.1.

AVAILABILITY OF DATA ON THE RECOMMENDED MEASURES

Table 2.1 lists the resource indicators described above and some alternative measures for them. The availability of each for states as a whole, for school districts, and for mathematics and science education specifically is shown.

Some of the indicators in Table 2.1 are suggested for minimalist monitoring schemes—minimally adequate representations of resource contexts that can be assembled or calculated from available data. Additional statistics that could be provided by additional analysis of existing data files or original data collection strategies could improve on the minimal model. For example, current per-pupil expenditures (ADM basis) are a recommended indicator, but the alternative, per-pupil expenditures net of categorical funds, would be a better indication of resources available for regular instruction. Readily available community adult education levels are a weak substitute for parent education or SES levels, which are not systematically recorded across American schools. Class size and teaching load information are also desirable, but resource-demanding, supplements to ready-made statistics.

As Table 2.1 indicates, the ready availability of data declines sharply below the state level and also diminishes as specific curricular targets are introduced. The table shows which indicators are regularly collected and published; which ones are expected to be available in existing databanks at CS or at SDEs and could be extracted through specific processing requests; which ones appear to require original data collection through surveys or other strategies; and which ones will be especially difficult to acquire. Some of the indicators, such as the fiscal-capacity estimates of the ACIR, are available only at the state level.

It is apparent in Table 2.1 that few resource indicators are universally and readily available for school district comparisons; per pupil expenditures, average teacher salaries, and pupil/teacher ratios exhaust the list. Others have been generated from special surveys that are not replicated on a regular basis, but these do not constitute even an acceptable minimal set for a monitoring scheme, particularly since student family background is not included. At the school district level, family background appears to require original data collection; a proxy, percent of students from AFDC families, is generally available because districts may qualify for federal programs on the basis of that percentage. Generally comparable fiscal capacity and fiscal effort indicators for school districts are difficult to collect because of idiosyncratic revenue-raising schemes across states.

Table 2.1

RECOMMENDED RESOURCE INDICATORS FOR EDUCATION MONITORING SYSTEMS

Indicator	Availability for Comparisons		
	State Level	School District Level	Science/Math Specific
Direct indicator of resource allocation			
Current per-pupil expenditures (PPE)	1*	1*	3
PPE net of categorical funds	2	2	NA
Indicators aiding interpretations of resource allocations			
Average teacher salary	1*	2*	3
Average secondary teacher salary	1*	2*	—
Pupil/teacher ratio	1*	1*	3
Average class size	3	3	3
Average teaching load	3	3	3
Specific curriculum materials, facilities[a]	3	3	3
Students as resources			
Parent SES or education	3	3*	3
Community Adult Education level (median achievement)	1*	3	3
Percent minority students	1*	2*	3
Percent students receiving AFDC	1*	2*	3
Fiscal capacity			
ACIR RRS tax capacity	1*	NA	NA
Per-capita income	1	NA	NA
Within-state measures of school district fiscal capacity	—	4	—
Fiscal effort for schools			
PPE as percent of RTS tax capacity per capita	1*	NA	NA
Within-state measures of fiscal effort	—	4	—

1 = Available through existing data collection and reporting practices
2 = Available through special runs of existing data
3 = Available through original surveys
4 = Available from some states; little comparability across states
* = Recommended indicator for minimal systems
[a]See Chapter 5 of this volume.

The availability of school district data varies from state to state, since reporting requirements and protocols differ. In some states, school district resource profiles may be easily attained, but the degree to which they can be justly compared with those of other states will vary depending on the states involved.

Table 2.1 also shows an unpromising profile of the availability of resource indicators for specific activities in science and mathematics instruction. Some of those shown could provide interesting assessments of how a state, district, or school attends to these curricula. Class sizes and teaching loads, salaries of mathematics and science teachers, and family backgrounds of students in their classes all represent desired resource profiles. They are also statistics for which specifically tailored inquiries would have to be designed.

SUMMARY AND CONCLUSIONS

Resource measures are essential for an indicator system intended to monitor science and mathematics education. Such indicators may improve understanding of observed performance differences, since certain resource differences are thought to be related to pupil outcomes. By including resource information, an indicator system may also motivate education providers to reassess their resource allocations and may facilitate comparisons requested by consumers of the system's products.

We have presented a model of resource inputs for schooling that traces community fiscal capacity to school budget allocations, and these allocations in turn to the purchase of educational resources. The model also includes students as a central resource in educational processes. Based on this conceptual model, the following indicators would be the minimum required to represent the resource context of school systems:

- Current per-pupil expenditures (PPE)
- Average teacher salary
- Average secondary teacher salary
- Pupil/teacher ratio
- Educational background of families
- Percentage of minority students
- Percentage of students receiving AFDC
- ACIR RRS tax capacity
- PPE as a percentage of RRS tax capacity per capita

An adequate set of resource indicators for state comparisons can be generated from available data. However, a considerable amount of original data must be collected to make resource comparisons for school districts and schools and for mathematics and science education. This effort will be necessary because data on some important indicators are not generated by existing efforts and because data collection practices vary from district to district and from state to state.

Chapter 3

SCHOOL CONTEXT AND ORGANIZATION

Jeannie Oakes

WHY SCHOOL-LEVEL INDICATORS?

Systems that monitor the nation's progress in science and mathematics education should include indicators of schooling processes. Such indicators can help policymakers, educators, and the public better understand the conditions under which students participate and achieve in science and mathematics. This chapter is concerned with the school as a whole: how resources are allocated among classrooms, what general policies construct and constrain teacher behavior, and general schoolwide attitudes, values, and morale. These features of school context and organization mediate (in the broadest sense) the influence of public expectations, resources, and state and local district policies, and they shape classroom teaching and learning.

In addition to providing a more complete picture of the educational system, school-level indicators can help policymakers and educators design effective improvement strategies. The school context is a potent target for effective policymaking, since changes at the school level promise to be potent and long lasting. Unlike classroom-level interventions, school reforms do not depend on the willingness and ability of individual teachers to alter their practices in isolation. Moreover, reforms at the school level can outlast the inevitable turnover in teaching.

If increasing concern about the quality of mathematics and science learning is to result in lasting improvement, educators and policymakers need explicit information about the schools in which this learning takes place. This chapter recommends a set of specific indicators that would provide that kind of information. A later chapter will discuss what goes on within individual classrooms.

CONTEXT INDICATORS

Despite the need for context measures in indicator systems, real stumbling blocks stand in the way of their development. Deciding which school characteristics to include in an indicator system poses problems. We have only limited understanding about which school features most influence the quality of classroom experiences. Most studies of schools have concentrated on those features that might relate to how well students score on general measures of verbal and mathematics achievement. Yet even within this rather narrow focus, research on school effects does not point unequivocally to a set of school characteristics that matter.

The task of specifying what school characteristics deserve attention is further complicated because we have no "strong" theory that links various elements of the educational system to the accomplishment of school goals. Moreover, we have little empirical data that suggest which school characteristics function as the most important mediators between school resources and student results. Additionally, like many of the schooling results we seek, many of the school characteristics researchers hypothesize as influences on achievement (and many of those parents and educators value highly) lie beyond our current measurement technology.

Part of the difficulty stems from the fact that our knowledge base is grounded largely in a concept of schooling as a production process—a series of inputs, processes, and outcomes. The straightforward nature of this concept is appealing, but more complex nonlinear and systems models of schooling suggest that an input-process-outcome model may account for only a fraction of what happens in schools.

In an attempt to identify promising school-level indicators, I have reviewed several strands of research on schools. The review was directed at answering the following questions:

1. What school characteristics have clear empirical links with highly valued educational experiences and outcomes?
2. What school-level indicators could help specify the central role of school characteristics in the educational process?
3. What school-level indicators could press schools toward emphasizing the full range of desired educational experiences and results?
4. What school-level information might policymakers and educators find useful for understanding schooling problems and shaping school improvement efforts?

The first question led to an unsurprising conclusion. Most school studies have attempted to identify features associated with how well students score on tests of basic verbal and mathematics achievement. Even with this narrow focus, the research has not pointed unequivocally to characteristics that account for more than a small fraction of the variance in outcomes. We know even less about how school characteristics influence broader schooling goals. Thus, the relative absence of empirical research complicates the task of specifying which school characteristics to measure as indicators.

Nonetheless, the literature does provide clues about answers to the remaining three questions. It provides some *limited* evidence about the effects of specific school features on commonly measured student outcomes. It also identifies other characteristics that are conceptually or logically related to a fuller range of desired goals and experiences. We can conclude that school characteristics are important to the quality of mathematics and science education because decisions about school organization, activities, and procedures set conditions for teaching and learning in classrooms. They create the conditions that *enable* learning to take place.

Looking at the literature through these lenses, we can identify three global school conditions as ideal targets for indicator development. The first condition is *access to knowledge*, the extent to which schools provide students with opportunities to learn domains of knowledge and skills in mathematics and science. The second is the institutional pressure the school exerts in order to get students to work hard and achieve in these subjects (i.e., *press for achievement*).[1] The third is *professional teaching conditions*, those conditions that can empower or constrain teachers and administrators as they attempt to create and implement instructional programs.

These three conditions meet important indicator criteria. They can help specify the central role of schools in the educational process, thereby providing a more complete picture of the performance of the educational system. These constructs, on their face, may seem to focus on intangible school climate characteristics. However, each results from concrete decisions about how to distribute resources, what structures to create, and what processes, norms, and relationships to establish at a school. As such, they are *alterable characteristics* of interest to educators and policymakers. Composite or multiple indicators of these three characteristics could encourage schools to broaden their emphasis beyond raising test scores. And, finally, such indicators are likely to

---

[1]The concept of *institutional press* has been more fully developed in studies of higher education and non-educational organizations than in studies of elementary and secondary schools.

help policymakers and educators better understand the conditions under which other experiences and results accrue. This understanding should help inform decisions about which improvement initiatives will be most fruitful.

In the next section, I explicate more fully the concepts of access, expectation, and teaching efficacy as conditions linked to the quality of mathematics and science education. I also attempt to demonstrate how existing research supports the importance of these ideal school-level indicators. Following that discussion, I suggest how we might go about measuring these somewhat intangible constructs by assessing realistic proxies for them.

ACCESS, PRESS, AND PROFESSIONAL TEACHING CONDITIONS: INDICATORS GROUNDED IN RESEARCH

The schooling literature does not warrant a claim that indicators of access, press, and professional conditions fully specify the role of schools in determining educational quality. Nonetheless, it does support the importance and usefulness of these constructs, and there is some empirical evidence that links these characteristics with student outcomes. However, they are more useful as indicators if we consider them *enabling* conditions rather than as being important primarily for their possible direct effects on outcomes. That is, to the degree that access, press, and professional teaching conditions exist in schools, they appear to promote high-quality teaching and learning.

The specific evidence supporting the importance of these factors as context indicators comes from a wide range of research on schooling. In the following, representative studies are cited to support the importance of access, press, and professional conditions as school conditions worth monitoring.

It is well known that the nearly two decades of work on identifying school effects on student learning have turned out to be largely frustrating. The most salient finding has been that school resource differences account for little variation in students' achievement scores (e.g., Coleman, 1966). The findings are as consistent as they are discouraging. One early review (Averch et al., 1972) concluded that "research has not identified a variant of the existing system that is consistently related to students' educational outcomes" (p. 154). A more recent review is similarly pessimistic: "The available evidence suggests that there is no relationship between expenditures and the achievement of students" (Hanushek, 1981, p. 19).

It has been consistently demonstrated that a school's resources have less influence on its ability to bring about learning less than do its students' background characteristics—their race, their economic status, their parents' expectations and involvement with the school. Also, the range of achievement within any one school is far greater than the differences in achievement across schools. Of course, this finding has been widely interpreted to mean that differences among schools don't matter. These findings have been as consistent as they have been discouraging to those seeking alterable school features that influence students' learning.

However, many critics of these early studies of school effects (including those conducting more recent research on "effective schools") have refused to see these studies as discounting the importance of school differences. Some have attributed the discouraging findings to methodological and conceptual difficulties (e.g., Wiley and Harnischfeger, 1974). Others have blamed the nearly exclusive focus on average effects (Klitgaard and Hall, 1973). Still others cite the often poor fit between a school's curricular goals, content, and materials and standardized achievement tests in basic subjects (Madaus et al., 1979). Finally, a number of researchers have blamed the "no-effects" finding on the restricted range of resources available to schools (see Barr and Dreeben, 1983; Bidwell and Kasarda, 1975; Spady, 1976). These analysts point to the limited usefulness of using school as the single unit of analysis—as if all students in a school have access to the same level of resources (Burstein, 1980; Murnane, 1982).

An important second area of inquiry, then, is how schools *use resources* to create educational programs and establish policies. Policies distributing resources to groups of teachers and students shape a school's organizational structure (Brown and Saks, 1980). Curriculum priorities dictate how much time and/or how many courses schools can set aside for various subjects. Decisions about what particular knowledge and skills will best meet students' needs influence the selection of course content. Counseling and placement policies combine students into instructional groups, recommend particular course-taking patterns for various groups of students, and assign teachers to various classes. Such organizational policies set the boundaries around students' exposure to content, their participation, and their accomplishments. School policies also set standards for homework and attendance, and establish promotion and graduation requirements.

A substantial literature suggests that these structures are important for student learning. But while schools have some discretion in allocating resources, they are clearly constrained by the resources provided them by states and local districts and by policies governing the use of those resources. Moreover, just as schools are relatively similar in the resources they are provided, they appear to be quite similar in the structures they create. The length of school year and day, age-grade structures, subject-area divisions and course titles, selection of books and materials, etc., do not differ dramatically from school to school. Unlike the case of resources, however, *rather subtle differences in the structures among schools appear to have a substantial impact on the quality of education that takes place.*

Finally, traditions govern the quality of day-to-day school experiences. What people expect, how they think they should act, and how they relate to one another stem from school norms. Complex and unique, this set of norms reflects basic beliefs, values, expectations, and relationships that make up the school culture.

The school culture influences whether teachers are able and willing to provide mind-stretching learning opportunities and whether students are willing to take advantage of them. It helps to determine whether students and teachers feel satisfied with their schools. It influences whether they believe that the school provides a good education and whether or not students are learning (e.g., Anderson 1982; Hamilton, 1983; and Rosenholtz, 1985). Perhaps even more than resources and school organizational structures, the norms and relationships in the school culture affect the access and press schools provide students. Additionally, cultural attributes of schools influence how schools function as workplaces for teachers. Measures of commitment to student learning, the primacy of teaching, teachers' opportunities to participate in program improvement and staff development activities, and the type of administrative leadership are all central. Each influences access, press, and professional conditions for teaching. Each affects the quality of what happens in school.

Studies supporting the importance of school culture and climate, including the recent "effective schools" literature, abound (see, for example, Edmonds, 1979; Clark, Lotto, and Astuto, 1984; Glenn and McLean, 1981; Mackenzie, 1983; Purkey and Smith, 1983; and Rutter, 1983). Even though many critics have attacked this work on conceptual and methodological grounds (see Cuban, 1984; Purkey and Smith, 1983; Rowan, Bossert, and Dwyer, 1983), the literature on effective schools is not easily dismissed. However, the importance of school culture does not rest solely on evidence from effective-schools studies. Earlier work, conceptually and methodologically distinct, has also produced consistent and supportive findings. Notable survey research supports the importance of schools' adolescent subcultures (Coleman, 1961) and the salience of teacher-student relationships in the schools' social systems (Gordon, 1957). This early work clearly established the importance of the prevailing value system or normative climate for academic achievement, aspirations, and other outcomes. Further, quantitative and qualitative studies of schooling ecology have shown culture to be of central importance to the quality of life in schools (Goodlad, 1984; Hamilton, 1981; Sarason, 1982). Also important are studies assessing the influence of global school climate characteristics on academic opportunities and student outcomes (see Anderson, 1982, for an extensive review).

Because of its centrality to schooling and teaching, knowledge of the cultural characteristics of schools can provide insights into schools both as educational organizations and as workplaces for teachers. Measures of commitment to student learning; the primacy of teaching; opportunities for program improvement, skill development, and renewal; parent involvement; and administrative leadership can provide important and useful information for policymakers and educators interested in understanding the school conditions necessary for high-quality science and mathematics education. Moreover, despite its close connection with perceptions and feelings, school culture is a policy-relevant concern. Policies shape the dimensions of school culture that are consequential for student learning and teacher productivity—policies distributing time, energy, and resources for student achievement and professional teaching.

ACCESS TO SCIENCE AND MATHEMATICS KNOWLEDGE

Because students' learning is influenced by the knowledge and skills they have an opportunity to acquire, we can link access to mathematics and science knowledge with student outcomes. Furthermore, access is a matter over which schools have considerable influence and control. This clear connection between access and policy makes access an appropriate focus of monitoring.

Access is a function of school resources, structures, and culture combined. Basic resources are the time, facilities, materials, and staff necessary to bring students in contact with mathematics and science concepts, processes, and skills. Curriculum structure at the elementary level determines the classroom time available for learning mathematics, science, and technology, and the way students are grouped for instruction. In secondary schools, the curriculum structure includes the number of courses offered in mathematics, science, and technology and the criteria used for enrolling students in those courses.

Schools govern the opportunities available to students not only by the courses they offer but by the exclusiveness of courses. If a school restricts participation in challenging courses or academic programs, its access is more circumscribed than that of a school that includes a wide range of students. Indicators of access should consider both depth and breadth of opportunities.

Other structures that enhance access are advanced courses in mathematics, science, and technology, and programs offering remediation, tutoring, and extra academic support for students in these subjects. Access is also provided through extracurricular enrichment activities—participation in science fairs, field trips, visiting experts, cooperative programs with museums and universities, etc. Also important are the opportunities the staff has to develop skills for working with diverse groups of students and the extent to which schools involve parents in the teaching and learning process.

Taken together, these resource, structure, and climate characteristics of schools determine the amount of access students have to science and mathematics knowledge. These characteristics either afford or deny students the opportunity to gain particular knowledge and skills. In itself, of course, access to science and mathematics knowledge does not produce student outcomes. Access is an enabling condition. It provides the structure to translate school resources into classroom teaching and learning.

Resources and Access

We can be fairly certain from the work attempting to link resources and student outcomes that resources, while critical to a school's ability to create an instructional program, are not *in themselves* the factor that ultimately determines school quality. How resources translate into access to learning opportunities is what appears to make a difference for students (Bridge, Judge, and Moock, 1979; Centra and Potter, 1980; Glasman and Bimiaminov, 1981; Hanushek, 1981; Murnane, 1982; Spady, 1976).

Resources are enablers. If schools had substantially fewer resources, students' access to mathematics and science knowledge might be reduced dramatically. Conversely, if schools had substantially greater resources, students' access might dramatically increase. This effect is demonstrated in the research on class size. When the number of students drops below 15, researchers find consistent positive effects (see Glass and Smith, 1978). Unfortunately, the narrow range of school resources does not facilitate investigating these possibilities.

Data on resource levels, then, indicate what schools have available to them. On the most basic level, we need to know how much financial support schools have. But at a second level, information is needed about how schools spend educational dollars to enhance students' access—by providing teaching and administrative staff, reducing class sizes, providing facilities and equipment, funding staff development, and purchasing curriculum materials. The resource levels provide the parameters in which schools operate; they define the outer limits of what is possible. Whether or not schools provide the equipment and materials necessary for essential instructional activities conveys important information about their potential for educational quality. And when resource levels are coupled with measures of resource use, their power to indicate school quality is likely to increase dramatically.

Resources also indicate the level of public commitment to schooling, and they provide tangible evidence to teachers, parents, and students that the community values good schooling. Resources that promote access to quality mathematics and science education are well-qualified teachers; class sizes small enough to permit intensive engagement in mathematics and science process work; up-to-date textbooks and curriculum materials in sufficient quantities; laboratories equipped and supplied for hands-on activities and experimentation in the mathematical, biological, physical, and computer sciences; support staffs to manage and maintain laboratories; and monies for field experiences. These resources signal a school's potential to offer quality education in mathematics and science.

Time and Access

The way schools spend time also merits attention as an indicator of access to knowledge. There are gross measures of time that suggest how schools differ in access to knowledge—the number of hours in the school day, the number of days in the school year, the average percentage of students attending school. Elementary schools in the Study-of-Schooling sample, for example, reported a range of 19 to 27 hours of instruction per week (Goodlad, 1984). Other national data also show time variations among secondary schools (Schmidt, 1983; NCES, 1985b). Data from the High School and Beyond (HSB) study show that students typically spend 5 hours per day in credit-earning classes, but the range in average time is considerable. Students in the top 10 percent of the nation's school districts spend 5.8 or more hours per day in credit classes, while students in the bottom 10 percent spend only 4 hours or less (NCES, 1985b).

Researchers have linked these time differences to scores on measures of verbal ability, reading comprehension, and mathematics achievement. Students in the HSB sample who attended high schools with longer school days and/or academic years performed better on the

HSB achievement tests (Peng, Owings, and Fetters, 1982). However, not all studies have found the same relationship between time and achievement (see, for example, Wiley and Harnischfeger, 1974; Karweit, 1976).

The amount of class time actually spent in instruction also appears to vary considerably among schools. The amount of time spent in instruction in elementary schools in the Study-of-Schooling sample ranged from 64 to 84 percent; in the secondary schools, it ranged from 68 to 87 percent (Goodlad, 1984). Clearly, the time students spend in academic pursuits in high school affects their achievement (Rock et al., 1985). Schools whose students attend more regularly and whose students spend more of their out-of-school time doing homework or participating in academic clubs and activities consistently show higher levels of academic achievement (Coleman, Kilgore, and Hoffer, 1982; Rock et al., 1985).

Recent work emphasizes the primacy of within-classroom time (see Chapter 6 of this volume). This time is particularly important for learning in some subject areas and is most influential on learning in those subjects that are not often taught at home—mathematics, science, and literature (Husen, 1967; Schmidt, 1983).

Curricular Emphasis and Access

The curricular emphasis of schools also tells a great deal about students' access to mathematics and science knowledge. Studies done as long ago as 1915 have found that schools differ considerably in the time they devote to various subjects (Borg, 1980). More recently, Goodlad (1984) found considerable variation in the school time devoted to various subjects in self-contained elementary school classrooms and the number of teaching resources allocated to different subject areas in secondary schools. The most significant variation in curricular emphasis noted at the high school level was the overall division of curricula into academic and vocational subjects.

In the 13 Study-of-Schooling elementary schools, the percentage of time in mathematics ranged from 3.8 to 5.5 hours per week. Science typically occupied far fewer hours in the elementary school day, but the variation among schools was greater, from 1.3 hours to 5.3. In departmentalized secondary schools, there was considerable variability in allocation of teaching resources to science and mathematics. Among the Study-of-Schooling junior high schools, for example, the average full-time teaching equivalents devoted to mathematics ranged from 13 to 22 percent. In science, the range was 7 to 20 percent. There was slightly less variability in emphasis at the senior high school level. The 13 senior high schools in the sample devoted an average of 13 percent (a range of 9 to 20 percent) of the teaching resources to mathematics and 11 percent (a range of 8 to 15 percent) to science (Goodlad, 1984).

What makes variation in curricular emphasis worth noting is the connection between students' exposure to subjects and their achievement. Schools that persuade students to take more courses in academic subjects show better results on academic tests. Using the number of mathematics courses students took as a measure of the time spent learning mathematics, Welch, Anderson, and Harris (1982) found substantial mathematics achievement differences in the National Assessment of Education Progress (NAEP) sample. Students who took more mathematics classes learned more. Schmidt (1983) obtained similar results from analyses of data from the 1972 National Longitudinal Study (NLS), as did Jones et al. (1986) from the HSB study.

Differences in curricular emphasis among schools can lead to considerably different learning opportunities in various subject areas because students are unlikely to learn things that are not taught. Thus *the school students happen to attend affects their chance to learn science and mathematics.* We could undoubtedly link the differences to what and how much students actually learn. Curriculum emphasis is also important because it is an alterable school feature. Current reforms setting new high school graduation requirements attest to the sensitivity of curricula to policy decisions. Monitoring schools' curricular emphasis will provide important and useful information about schools (see Chapter 5 of this volume).

Curricular Differentiation and Access

Grouping and tracking policies determine which students will have access to particular curricula within science and mathematics. When schools place students in different groups or curriculum tracks, the students have different learning opportunities in these subjects.

Schools in which large numbers of students are in academic programs offer more courses in mathematics and science and provide greater opportunities to learn these subjects (NCES, 1985b). Moreover, track placement affects the overall educational quality that students experience and has specific effects on their science and mathematics opportunities. There is a growing body of evidence indicating that tracks and groups identified as academic or "high" are advantaged in their access to school resources—instructional time, teacher quality, exposure to content, and classroom learning environment (McKnight et al., 1987; Oakes, 1985). On the other hand, students in low-ability or non-college-preparatory tracks in junior and senior high schools are likely to have fewer learning opportunities. Enrollment in these lower groups typically results in less mathematics instructional time, lower quality of mathematics instruction, less exposure to mathematics concepts, and more negative learning environments. There is also some evidence that curriculum differentiation policies can either widen or restrict students' opportunities for learning content related to scientific literacy (Guthrie and Leventhal, 1985). Some schools provide a number of "entry options," offering several entry-level courses and considerable student choice. Other schools have fewer offerings and rigidly structured courses with prerequisite requirements.

Like secondary school tracking, ability grouping in elementary schools is likely to affect the quality and quantity of learning opportunities. Students in lower groups spend less time than others in instructional activity, and teachers expose them to fewer concepts (Barr and Dreeben, 1983; Hallinan and Sorenson, 1985).

Extra Support and Access

Programs providing academic support beyond the regular classroom can enhance access and achievement of students exhibiting poor academic performance, especially in the elementary grades. However, not *all* extra support programs increase access. Many pull-out, compensatory programs simply add a second set of instructional tasks to the workload of students who are already struggling with tasks assigned in the regular classroom. Supplementary tasks often bear little relationship to the regular curriculum and do little to help students perform well in the regular classroom. Many programs remove low-achieving students from the classroom during the time when they would normally be learning the regular curriculum with their high-achieving peers (Wang and Walberg, 1986). These programs can actually limit access. But other out-of-classroom programs have avoided these pitfalls and have increased elementary students' access to and performance in mathematics. A recent review suggests that two types of programs are most promising: programs that provide adult or peer tutors who work one-on-one helping students with their classwork, and computerized programs that direct remedial work toward the specific difficulties students are having (Madden and Slavin, 1987).

The links between science experiences and science achievement found in the NAEP also suggest that schools that provide students with enrichment opportunities (field trips to museums, science club activities, etc.) may enhance access to knowledge (Hueftle, Rakow, and Welch, 1983). Such activities seem particularly important to students who lack such experiences outside of school.

Parent Involvement

Research on parent participation is relatively undeveloped. However, some types of family involvement with a child's schooling evidently can be critical in the amount of effort students put into their schoolwork and in how much they learn. But there is little evidence that parent involvement in non-instructional ways directly affects learning. One consistent finding from studies of parent involvement, primarily at the elementary level, is that children learn more when their parents actually participate in instructing them (see Clark, Lotto, and McCarthy, 1980; Clark, Lotto, and Astuto, 1984; Fantini, 1980; Gordon, 1980; Walberg, 1984). Parental involvement in instruction at home and programs using joint teacher-parent planning for learning sessions are particularly effective (Barth 1979; Epstein and Becker, 1982). Parent involvement in instruction clearly increases students' access to knowledge.

PRESS FOR ACHIEVEMENT IN MATHEMATICS AND SCIENCE

In schools with a strong press for mathematics and science achievement, teachers and students take teaching and learning very seriously. They expect and value high achievement. Underlying this disposition is the belief that all students are capable of learning the important mathematics and science knowledge and skills schools want to teach. While most research supports the link between expectations and student learning, students are helped or hindered most by the educational structures and processes that schools establish based on their expectations. Press is also manifest in how schools spend their resources and how they organize their time and activities.

We can judge the press for mathematics and science achievement at a school partly by the importance administrators, teachers, and students place on learning these subjects. Where press is strong, students learn a rich and rigorous curriculum, and they have the support they need for success. Such schools recognize, highlight, and reward achievement. These practices influence the press for achievement that exists at the school. When schools create structures that focus student time and energy on academics, they may foster more than academic achievement: Aspirations, attitudes, and behavior also appear to improve.

However, not all efforts at making schools more academic guarantee a positive press for achievement. Emerging evidence on some negative effects of minimum competency requirements and increased course requirements for graduation raise essential concerns. We should monitor these features of schools, not because they will reveal which schools are best, but because they reflect assumptions about school goals, student capabilities, and the power of schools to bring about significant learning.

Commitment to Student Learning

Even though all schools say that learning comes first, not all schools' cultures make intellectual endeavors and academic accomplishment their top priority. In some schools, students and teachers clearly understand that academics drive the school, occupy the most time, consume the most energy, and provide the most meaningful source of success and rewards. In other schools, quite the opposite is the case. The focus of the adults may be on "keeping the lid on"; student life may be overwhelmingly dominated by concerns of social life, sports, or even gangs. In these schools, academics clearly take a back seat (Goodlad, 1984).

The degree of school commitment to academic learning has an important relationship to student outcomes. High schools at which faculty and students stress academic accomplishment and student intellectualism foster higher academic achievement and encourage more students to make college plans (Madaus et al., 1979; McDill and Rigsby, 1973). Elementary schools at which students achieve well are consistently characterized by teacher expectations for academic success, student support for academics, systems for monitoring and rewarding academics, greater time focused on learning, and protection of classroom time for teaching and learning (Brookover et al., 1979; Clark, Lotto, and Astuto, 1984; Glenn and McLean, 1981; Hawley et al., 1985; Mackenzie, 1983; Purkey and Smith, 1983; Rutter, 1983). Moreover, commitment to academic learning appears to have these effects in all types of schools, regardless of student socioeconomic status or ability (Goodlad, 1984; McDill and Rigsby, 1973).

Why is schoolwide emphasis on academics so powerful? Some work suggests that a strongly articulated academic mission energizes teachers toward student achievement and pushes students toward academic success (Brookover et al., 1979; Rutter, 1983). Apparently, the values prominent in the larger school culture permeate the classroom, creating classroom climates strongly directed toward learning (Goodlad, 1984; Moos, 1979). Other studies have also documented that whether students turn toward or away from academics is not solely determined by their background characteristics, but is partly a response to the structure and culture of the school (Hamilton, 1981).

There is also some evidence that schools that value academic learning engender greater satisfaction among students, parents, and teachers. In the Goodlad schools that focused on academics, all groups reported more often that their school provided a good education, the curriculum related to their lives, the ambiance was academic, and the school was a safe place (Goodlad, 1984).

Curriculum Differentiation and Press

Curriculum differentiation is also part of assessing schools' press for achievement in science and mathematics. Patterns of student assignments and the proportion of students participating in academic programs in secondary schools are policy-sensitive data that can show what proportion of students the school expects to learn high-level mathematics and science. At the elementary level, classroom assignment practices provide information about the extensiveness of press.

The HSB data indicate that the percentage of students in the academic track at a school is exceptionally powerful in explaining average achievement test scores (Rock et al., 1985). Schools with more students in the academic track seem also to have lower rates of misbehavior and absenteeism, and their students have higher expectations (Peng, Owings, and Fetters, 1982). These findings are consistent with other analyses that suggest that tracking systems promote the achievement of those in college-preparatory programs, accelerated classes, and gifted programs (Gamoran, 1986; Kulik and Kulik, 1982). However, these positive effects are not universally found. Controlled studies of students taking similar subjects in mixed and tracked groups have shown that high-ability students rarely benefit from being separated (Esposito, 1973; Kulik and Kulik, 1982; Noland, 1986). In contrast, achievement and aspirations are negatively affected by participation in low-ability and non-academic tracks (see Alexander and McDill, 1976; Heyns, 1974; Alexander, Cook, and McDill, 1978; Rosenbaum, 1980). And some work even suggests that low-track placement has a depressing effect on I.Q. (Rosenbaum, 1976).[2]

We can explain these effects partly by the influence of grouping on access to knowledge, noted above. But effects of the peer composition of groups and tracks on press for achievement may also be a factor. Track membership in high schools influences students' associations with their peers in classrooms and in extracurricular activities, and also their friendship choices (e.g., Alexander and McDill, 1976; Rehberg and

---

[2]The effects on I.Q. scores were found in a longitudinal study of students at a single high school. Caution should be exercised in applying these findings broadly.

Rosenthal, 1978; Rosenbaum, 1976). These associations influence academic press, since peer relationships relate to school effort and academic aspirations (e.g., Coleman, 1961). Student achievement increases when peers are oriented toward academics (McDill and Rigsby, 1973). Because track placement follows from attitude, behavior, and motivation, as well as ability, low tracks are particularly impoverished in peer dispositions toward achievement. However, the presence of able students in heterogeneous groups can contribute to the achievement of low-ability students without depressing that of high-ability students (Dar and Resh, 1986; Spady, 1976).

The effects of between-class ability grouping in elementary schools are similar to those of secondary school tracking—lower achievement for average- and low-ability students and no important effects on the achievement of high-ability students (Slavin, 1986). In contrast, some studies have found mixed ability grouping to be particularly useful in promoting the achievement of students with mild academic handicaps (see, e.g., Madden and Slavin, 1983, for a discussion of mainstreaming). Some studies have found negative effects for within-class grouping, but the evidence here is less conclusive (Sorensen, 1970; Filby et al., 1982; Hallinan and Sorensen, 1983; Good and Marshall, 1984; Slavin, 1986; Sorensen, 1970).

Exit and Promotion Criteria and Press

Minimum competency examinations and increased course requirements for graduation are two popular ways to set higher school-completion standards and even grade-to-grade promotion criteria. Analysts have yet to find significant relationships between minimum competency requirements and student achievement (see, for example, NCES, 1985a). Evidence from some studies suggests, in fact, that minimum competency requirements may actually backfire and work to lower the quality of teaching and learning. For example, in some states, minimum competency requirements apparently promote instruction that emphasizes low-level skill learning and may lead teachers to neglect concepts, topics, and skills that are not tested (Darling-Hammond and Wise, 1985).

The effects of increased graduation requirements are similarly little known. One recent study attempting to link increased course requirements with student achievement found no consistent relationships (NCES, 1985b). These findings are inconclusive, however, since they rely on SAT and ACT test scores. Only students intending to go to college take these tests, and these students are the sector of the student body that is least likely to pattern course-taking after a school's graduation requirements. Here too, other evidence is emerging about possible negative effects of increasingly stringent graduation requirements. For example, some analysts suggest that increased school requirements may be a factor in the rising dropout rate in secondary schools (ASCD, 1985; McDill, Natriello, and Pallas, 1986). Further, grade-to-grade promotion requirements may also affect students adversely. There is substantial evidence, for example, that being held back may serve to retard some students' progress rather than remediate academic deficiencies (see Labaree, 1984) and may lead to increased dropouts (Hess, 1986).

In contrast, however, some studies provide support for higher standards. The number of courses in mathematics, science, and foreign language required for graduation can have a positive influence on students' selection of an academic curriculum. In the cases studied, this selection led students to take more rigorous courses and to show higher achievement (Newfield and Wisenbaker, 1985). One might conclude from this work that higher standards for graduation lead to academic gains. However, it may be that raising graduation requirements serves to drive a deeper wedge between high and low achievers in school. High achievers may be spurred on to take more rigorous courses, while low achievers may become discouraged and, at worst, leave school altogether.

Administrative Priorities and Press

Principals' own goals and objectives focus the school's time, attention, and energy toward or away from academic achievement. When principals become involved in matters of curriculum and instruction, they communicate clearly that teaching and learning constitute the important work of the school (Mackenzie, 1983; Rosenholtz, 1985).

Principals can send a clear message that student accomplishment is the most valued school goal by basing teacher supervision on substantive discussions of learning goals, frequent observations and involvement in classrooms, and monitoring of student achievement (Armor et al., 1976; Brookover et al., 1979; Rutter, 1983). Supervision so conducted may enhance school quality because it clarifies teachers' responsibilities and centers rewards squarely on teaching. This may enhance teachers' ability and interest in teaching. Additionally, the principal keeps the primacy of school goals active in the minds of students and staff and can set criteria for schoolwide decisions, establish standards for judging the accomplishment of goals, and promote guidelines for successful work based on student achievement (Rosenholtz, 1985). All these are likely to influence academic press.

PROFESSIONAL TEACHING CONDITIONS

Professional teaching conditions are also manifest in the way schools use resources to develop programs, particularly in the relationships between school administrators and teachers concerning mathematics and science teaching and learning.

A professional teaching environment is an important school characteristic, since it encompasses the working conditions most likely to attract high-quality teachers and to encourage those already in the teaching force to remain. Teachers at schools that provide professional teaching conditions are more likely to be committed and energized, permitted to teach well, and willing to learn to teach better. Staff turnover is likely to be low, so the schools can make and carry out long-range plans. Professional teaching conditions cannot be directly linked to student outcomes, but there is evidence that a "professional" staff will work toward implementing strategies and programs that will produce better results. Because of its importance to teacher commitment, satisfaction, and, albeit indirectly, teacher effectiveness, the professional climate for teaching is an important indicator.

Primacy of Teaching

Few would dispute that good teachers are the single most important educational resource, but the school conditions that can enhance or impede good teaching should not be overlooked.

Teachers' Responsibilities. Schools where administrators act as a buffer and nurture teaching are more likely to attract, develop, and retain good teachers (Darling-Hammond, 1984; Rosenholtz, 1985). In schools where the administration views teachers as professionals and regards and protects teaching as professional work, teachers are able and willing to provide quality instruction. In schools where teachers are heavily occupied with paperwork, bureaucratic requirements, controlling student behavior, and other non-teaching tasks, far less time and energy are available for teaching. Most teachers will do a better job in a supportive climate.

Time. The time teachers have available within their professional day to plan for and think about teaching sets clear limits on their work. If teachers spend all of their school time with students and performing non-teaching duties, they cannot participate in the creative, energizing lesson preparation, subject area reading, and work with colleagues that result in better instruction. Schedules that do not include time for these activities invite the domination of classrooms by packaged lessons, last year's plans, and "fail-safe" curriculum guides from the district.

Like other school resources, time, in itself, is not enough. Strong cultural norms for professional work must direct the use of teachers' time toward involvement in important schoolwide decisions, development and adaptation of classroom practice, and collaboration (see, for example, Little, 1982; Rosenholtz, 1985). Teacher involvement leads to consensus about school priorities and practices and consistency among school goals, grade-level and classroom objectives, instructional content and activities, and assessment of results (Cohen, 1983; Rosenholtz, 1985). Without teacher influence, what goes on behind individual classroom doors is likely to be disconnected from articulated goals and policies.

Autonomy and Flexibility. Teachers need considerable autonomy in making classroom curriculum and instructional decisions, as well as flexibility in implementing schoolwide programs and innovations (Clark, Lotto, and Astuto, 1984; Purkey and Smith, 1983; Mackenzie, 1983). When schools deny teachers influence and autonomy, they relegate them to merely carrying out administrative directives and implementing curriculum and instruction designed by "experts." Under these conditions, teachers are, to a large extent, stripped of their professional expertise and prohibited from exercising professional judgment about what and how to teach. The balance of teacher influence and autonomy seems central to teacher commitment and effort (Levin, 1980; Lightfoot, 1983).

Collaborative Norms and Collegial Work. Effective schools are characterized by collaborative staff planning, intellectual sharing, and teamwork (Armor et al., 1976; Rutter et al., 1983). Collaborative planning and collegial work develop and support shared goals and school norms; good teaching becomes a shared responsibility (Little, 1982). A schoolwide commitment to student learning can develop when groups of teachers work together toward agreed-upon academic goals. Opportunities for collegiality, collaboration, and decisionmaking decrease teacher absenteeism and teacher turnover—both surely critical "bottom lines" in the educational system. (See Rosenholtz, 1985, for an extensive review of this literature.)

Opportunities for Program Improvement, Skill Development, and Renewal

The degree to which school staffs plan and implement new structural arrangements, programs, and instructional approaches is also central to the school culture. Because improvement efforts are essentially attempts to develop teaching skill and more effectively accomplish school goals, schools engaged in processes conducive to change and improvement are likely to have better student achievement, participation, attitudes, and other desired student outcomes. Engagement in improvement activities is also likely to heighten teachers' certainty and professional commitment (Rosenholtz, 1985).

Cultural elements critical to school improvement and skill development are the leadership role of the principal, the relationships among teachers, and teacher attitudes (Fullan, 1982). The principal's active support and involvement are crucial, particularly in the substantive, instructional aspects of innovations. Critical to teachers' peer relationships in the process of change are collegiality, open communication, trust, support and help, interaction, and morale. The essential teacher attitude for generating and sustaining improvement efforts is efficacy—teachers' belief that they can accomplish the goals of the school (see, for example, McLaughlin and Marsh, 1978). Consistent themes in research on this dimension of school culture include collaborative planning, opportunities for collegial work, a school administrative atmosphere that encourages experimentation and evaluation, and leadership and active involvement of the school administration in improvement efforts (see, for example, Berman and McLaughlin, 1975–79; Crandall et al., 1983; Fullan, 1982; Goodlad, 1975; Heckman, Oakes, and Sirotnik, 1981; Sarason, 1971, 1982).

Administrative Leadership

The elements of school climate that promote quality education must be carefully nurtured, supported, and protected by a strong school leader. Typically, but not always, this leader is the principal. Effective school leaders take the initial steps to establish school norms—e.g., the primacy of academic achievement and regard for the professional work of teachers (Clark, Lotto, and Astuto, 1984; Purkey and Smith, 1983). They use their discretionary resources to create time and opportunities for teacher involvement in school planning and collegial work (Rosenholtz, 1985). Schoolwide norms about the nature of parent involvement often begin with the principal or with the principal's endorsement of teachers' initiatives. The types of staff interaction and staff development structured by school administration can either promote or stifle a renewing school climate (Bentzen, 1975; Goodlad, 1975; Heckman, Oakes, and Sirotnik, 1983; Sarason, 1982).

Buffering. Principals who buffer the work of teaching provide teachers with support in organizational and routine matters and protect classroom time from interruptions and low-priority matters. The buffering of teachers from non-teaching tasks creates favorable conditions for increased skill acquisition, certainty, commitment, and rewards for teachers (Rosenholtz, 1985). Buffering can include the establishment by the principal of a schoolwide climate of good student behavior (Edmonds, 1979; Purkey and Smith, 1983; Clark, Lotto, and Astuto, 1984). The creation and maintenance of an orderly school environment lowers teacher frustration and frees classroom time for teaching and learning.

Leadership Style. The way school principals use their administrative authority is also central. Schools that are rated most effective have principals with the ability to build a strong, cohesive teaching team, encourage a free flow of information, support new ideas and risk-taking, and provide access to expert advice and guidance. In short, effective schools have mutually supportive professional environments where collaborative processes are the norm (Daly, 1981). Principals contribute to such environments by providing opportunities for teacher decisionmaking influence, collaborative planning, and collegial work. This helps both to create a professional climate for teaching and to establish receptivity to school improvement, with all the attendant benefits. Principals who encourage teachers' professional work are most likely to provide flexibility regarding school procedures, rules, and regulations. In the process, they enhance teachers' commitment, sense of ownership, and skill development (Rosenholtz, 1985). Schools with participative management (important decisions reached through consensus), with good collegial communication, and with good information flows are those that have the greatest staff satisfaction, the best educational performance and student attendance, and the lowest dropout rates (see Daly, 1981; Seibert and Likert, 1973).

ACCESS, PRESS, AND PROFESSIONAL TEACHING CONDITIONS: OPERATIONALIZING "IDEAL" INDICATORS

The research literature supports the intuitive sense that several school characteristics influence school quality; some characteristics even have notable links to commonly measured student outcomes. Because of these links, data about school characteristics should be included in educational indicator systems. However, the school serves primarily to mediate between its social and political context and classroom teaching and learning, so measures of school conditions that appear to *enable* teaching and learning in mathematics and science will be better indicators of educational quality than isolated features that may show some direct relationship to student outcomes.

Moreover, what happens in schools is nearly always different from the sum of individual school characteristics. What actually happens is also influenced by subtle interrelationships within a school. Therefore, it is important to measure distinct school characteristics—use of time, course offerings, parent involvement, etc.—within the context of larger school conditions that will better capture important differences among schools.

Research on many dimensions of schools has produced two main conclusions for the development of school-level indicators:

- School resources, structures, and culture are not discrete school characteristics; they interact. While the development of an effective school context cannot be attributed to the level of resources provided to it, neither can it be separated from it. The presence or absence of resources (e.g., non-teaching time) can make cultural norms (e.g., collegial work) easy or nearly impossible to establish. Similarly, particular organizational structures (e.g., many rigorous course offerings) will interact with and reinforce particular elements of the school culture (e.g., a commitment to student learning).
- Ideally, school-level indicators will provide descriptive information about important combinations of school characteristics. The challenge is to construct indicators that will inform policymakers and educators about how schools use their resources to establish policies, organizational structures, and cultures that promote high-quality teaching and learning.

Based on these conclusions, the concepts of access to knowledge, press for achievement, and professional conditions for teaching become good candidates for composite school-level indicators. As Fig. 3.1 illustrates, they integrate our knowledge about the effects of school resources, policies and organizational structures, and culture on teaching and learning. The specific variables that can be used as indicators of these three important school conditions are listed below.

Operationalizing Access to Knowledge

Assessment of the access to knowledge a school provides would include measures of the following tangible school characteristics:

- Use of mathematics and science subject-area specialists or resource teachers.
- Overall instructional time (length of school year and hours of class time per day).

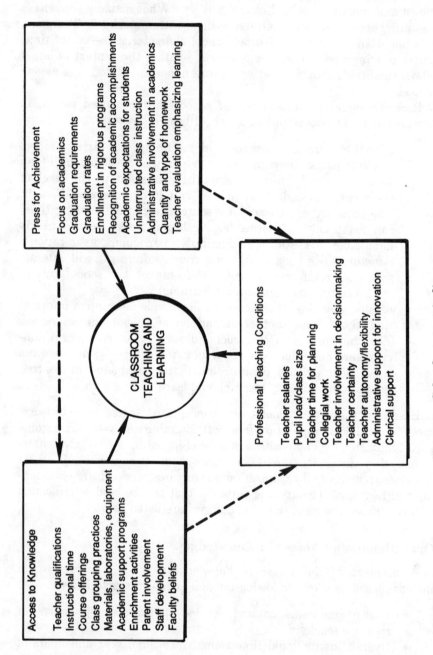

Press for Achievement

Focus on academics
Graduation requirements
Graduation rates
Enrollment in rigorous programs
Recognition of academic accomplishments
Academic expectations for students
Uninterrupted class instruction
Administrative involvement in academics
Quantity and type of homework
Teacher evaluation emphasizing learning

CLASSROOM TEACHING AND LEARNING

Professional Teaching Conditions

Teacher salaries
Pupil load/class size
Teacher time for planning
Collegial work
Teacher involvement in decisionmaking
Teacher certainty
Teacher autonomy/flexibility
Administrative support for innovation
Clerical support

Access to Knowledge

Teacher qualifications
Instructional time
Course offerings
Class grouping practices
Materials, laboratories, equipment
Academic support programs
Enrichment activities
Parent involvement
Staff development
Faculty beliefs

Fig. 3.1—School context indicators

- Instructional time in various subject areas (at the elementary level).
- Course offerings in academic subjects and the number of sections of each course (at the secondary level).
- Classroom or course assignment practices (ability-grouped classes or mixed instructional groups) and the curriculum associated with each ability group.
- Student mobility among groups and tracks (e.g., percentage of students moving upward from non-academic or low-ability classes or course sequences).
- Availability of instructional materials, laboratories, computers, and equipment.
- Teachers' qualifications and experience (and, at the secondary level, the match between teachers' backgrounds and their current teaching assignments).
- Availability of academic support programs (tutoring, after-school remediation, etc.).
- Academic enrichment and support (science fairs, field trips, museum programs).
- Parent involvement in instruction at home or at school.
- Opportunities for staff development.
- Staff beliefs about the importance of challenging academic study for all students.

Operationalizing Press for Achievement

Assessing a school program's press for achievement, then, would entail measuring the following characteristics:

- Staff emphasis on academic achievement.
- High school graduation requirements.
- High school graduation rates.
- Students' participation in challenging academic work (at the secondary level, for example, participation in advanced courses).
- Schoolwide recognition of academic accomplishments.
- Faculty expectations about students' ability to learn (e.g., whether all students are capable of high-level cognitive processes and mastering rigorous curriculum content).
- The degree to which non-instructional constraints interfere with classroom activities.
- Administrative advocacy and support for challenging curriculum and instruction.

- The type and amount of academic homework assigned.
- The extent to which teaching and learning is central to teacher evaluation.

Operationalizing Professional Teaching Conditions

Assessing a school's professional conditions for teaching would entail measuring the following more tangible characteristics:

- Teachers' salaries.
- Teachers' pupil load and class size.
- Teachers' time available for professional, non-teaching work.
- Teachers' time spent on school-based, collegial goal setting, staff development, program planning, curriculum development, instructional improvement, collaborative research, etc.
- Teachers' participation in schoolwide decisionmaking.
- Teachers' certainty about their ability to influence and achieve school goals.
- Teachers' autonomy and flexibility in implementing curriculum and instruction.
- Administrative support for professional risk-taking and experimentation.
- Administrative provision of clerical support for teachers' non-instructional tasks.

PROMISE AND LIMITATIONS OF SCHOOL INDICATORS

Access to science and mathematics knowledge, the press for science and mathematics achievement, and professional teaching conditions appear to be school characteristics that, if measured, can provide policymakers and educators with central, policy-relevant information about schools. Although these three are best thought of and measured as distinct, they are likely to function synergistically. Broad access to science and mathematics knowledge and high expectations for achievement in these subjects undoubtedly are most powerful in combination—important knowledge and skills extended to the broadest range of students and a powerful force that compels and supports teachers' and students' attention to learning. Without the expectation of achievement, schools providing broad access to mathematics and science knowledge might fall into a pattern of trivializing these important subjects, perhaps by providing a smattering of topics and skills in a smorgasbord of course offerings and classroom activities. On the other hand, expectations without broad access might result in schools with elite science and mathematics programs for only a few students and a vacuum of learning opportunities for the rest. Perhaps worse, such schools might increase the dropout rate among students who do not learn quickly and easily. (See Powell, Farrar, and Cohen, 1985, for striking examples of these circumstances in American high schools.)

However, access to knowledge and press for achievement for learning are unlikely to be found at schools where the level of professional teaching conditions is not high. Unless the school climate is characterized by a belief in the staff's ability to produce high achievement in students, academic expectations and access are unlikely to follow. High expectations for themselves may be a necessary precursor to teachers' high expectations for students. Conversely, expectations and access are certain to feed a school staff's sense of efficacy and nourish professional commitment. This likely synergy among access, expectations, and efficacy requires monitoring of all three indicators.

The most salient message from this search for school-level indicators, however, is that schools are complex and intricate places. We must temper the development of school-level indicators with this caveat: We cannot adequately understand any item, attribute, or condition outside a larger context. That context is, at the very least, the culture found at the school level, although it probably extends beyond that. The summing and averaging of school attributes and then relating them only to individual student achievements obscures rather than highlights the effects of schools. School features produce different effects within schools and classrooms, and these ultimately have a powerful influence on what children learn. To appreciate the importance of school-level variables, it is necessary to understand their chain of influence through their effects on lower levels of schooling such as the classroom, student-teacher interaction, etc. These effects directly influence student outcomes. It is not easy to understand—or even to describe—the events themselves, and there is little in the theory and research on schooling to guide us.

The bottom line of school research for the development of indicators is the paradox that those school features that are most easily recognized, measured, and reported are the least likely to provide useful insights into school quality. The most important features are elusive, complex, and intangible conditions that are closely tied to everything that goes on in schools. In view of this reality, those involved in specifying indicators and conceiving educational monitoring systems face an important social and scientific challenge: developing measures that accurately capture important alterable school conditions.

Chapter 4

TEACHERS AND TEACHING

Linda Darling-Hammond and Lisa Hudson

INTRODUCTION

Ultimately, the quality of mathematics and science education rests on the quality of instruction that students receive. This, in turn, is largely determined by the qualifications of mathematics and science teachers and the conditions under which these teachers work. Although many other factors mediate the nature of the student-teacher interaction, none can fully overcome the consequences of inadequate or poor-quality teachers. Thus, indicators of teacher quality are fundamentally important to assessing the state of mathematics and science education.[1]

For a monitoring system, indicators of teacher quality should include not only those characteristics of teachers that are related to teaching effectiveness, but also information about how these and other characteristics are related to teachers' assignments, practices, and career decisions. This chapter therefore discusses features of teachers and teaching that are (1) predictive of effectiveness (e.g., preparation and years of experience), (2) policy-relevant (e.g., working conditions, certification status), (3) problem-oriented (e.g., characteristics related to supply and demand), and (4) descriptive of who teachers are and what they do in classrooms (e.g., demographic information and teaching assignments). A well-constructed monitoring system should allow analyses that provoke hypotheses for further research, even if it cannot itself support complete testing and resolution of difficult research and policy problems. Thus, a comprehensive monitoring system should incor-

---

[1] It would be more precise to use the term *teacher qualities* rather than *teacher quality* to reflect our view that the characteristics that contribute to good teaching are many, and that no single configuration of traits, qualifications, or behaviors unvaryingly produces optimal student outcomes in all situations. Furthermore, as there is no single agreed-upon measure of teacher quality (see e.g., Rumberger, 1985), we find it more fruitful to discuss the variables generally subsumed under the rubric of teacher quality in terms of the characteristics of teachers and teaching, rather than as a single, ultimately undefinable construct. When we refer to teacher quality, this should be interpreted as a shorthand label for the many characteristics that, in many different combinations, produce effective learning.

porate indicators of who is teaching what to whom, as well as how the teaching force is changing over time.

The issue of teacher quality is particularly important and particularly problematic in mathematics and science education. Even as demands for more rigorous, comprehensive, and equitably provided mathematics and science education intensify, the ability of school systems to provide such education is declining, and current shortages of mathematics and science teachers have profound implications for the extent and quality of teaching (see Darling-Hammond, 1984; ASCUS, 1984; Johnston and Aldridge, 1984). When teacher shortages occur, school districts often adopt strategies that may create suboptimal learning experiences for students. These strategies include the assignment of teachers not trained in mathematics or science to teach courses in these fields, the enlargement of class sizes or expansion of teaching loads for mathematics and science teachers, and the cancellation of (usually upper-level) courses that cannot be even marginally well taught by untrained teachers. Thus, teacher supply and demand conditions have important effects on the quality of education that students receive and are important mediators of teacher quality.

Because teacher supply and demand exert such a substantial influence on who teaches and on the conditions of instruction, we urge the development of an indicator system that incorporates measures of the current and potential supply of qualified teachers, the assignment(s) of teachers with various backgrounds, and teacher satisfaction, commitment, and retention; these measures serve both as indicators of trends in the supply and composition of the teaching force, and as indicators of the current and prospective quality of mathematics and science instruction.

Another "missing link" in traditional studies of teacher quality is the relationship between teacher characteristics or competence and teaching practice. We focus on this area for two related reasons. First, the nearly indefinable construct called teacher quality may be seen as a function of both who teachers are and what they do. Aspects of performance—revealed behaviors and attitudes—apart from knowledge, intrinsic abilities, and other personal traits are generally assumed to be included in the definition of a "good teacher." That is, good teachers not only know or believe certain things, but can and do apply such knowledge and beliefs in their work. Second, although researchers have explored the relationships between teacher *characteristics* and student outcomes, and between teacher *behaviors* and student outcomes, they have devoted little attention to the implicit, often assumed, relationship between the attributes of teachers and attributes of their teaching.

As policymakers struggle with new standards for certification, and with the implications of alternative and emergency certification as well, they must make judgments about what kinds of training teachers need; that is, they must assess what preparation makes a difference in what teachers actually do, and by implication, what kinds of qualifications define (or at least contribute to) teacher quality. To make these judgments, the policymakers must have data on both teachers' attributes and teaching practices.[2]

However, even an examination of teacher qualities and teaching practice ignores another important mediating factor. What teachers actually do depends not just on their competence, but also on the conditions under which they must provide instruction. A fully competent teacher may perform less than adequately in the classroom, if he or she is working in a disorganized and unsupportive environment for teaching and learning. On the other hand, teachers with only minimal competence can perform fully adequately, given supportive, favorable working conditions. Thus, the *occupational support structure* for teaching must be examined in any effort to monitor or assess "teacher quality." Since the occupational support structure mediates how well teachers can provide instruction, we discuss indicators of this structure below, referring to them as enablers of *teaching quality*.

We start from the premise, then, that a monitoring system should include indicators of who teaches mathematics and science, what these teachers do in the classroom, and what conditions affect their work, their attitudes toward their work, and the probability of their staying in the teaching profession. The distribution of teachers across students and subjects is also an important dimension of overall teaching quality, as is the current and potential supply of qualified teachers.

The following sections discuss our approach to identifying potential indicators, including a model of how teacher and teaching quality interact with other educational processes; identify the teacher characteristics and teaching conditions useful for a comprehensive monitoring system; and, finally, present a few caveats regarding the use of the indicators we have identified.

A CONCEPTUAL MODEL

The literature on school and teacher effectiveness views student learning as the result of numerous nested and interacting educational

---

[2]Indicators of teaching practice are discussed more fully in Chapter 6, which discusses instruction. This division is somewhat unnatural, however, as teacher characteristics and teaching practices are necessarily interrelated in classroom situations, and as the nature of teaching cannot be fully examined or understood without knowledge of both of these factors.

influences (e.g., Barr and Dreeben, 1983). One variation of this model is detailed below (see Fig. 4.1). This is a compressed version of the more comprehensive model outlined in Chapter 1, reflecting the focus of this chapter on teacher quality. For example, this model subsumes school and pupil quality variables under the category "Mediating Factors," as they mediate the effects of teacher quality variables on teaching quality and student outcomes.

We are primarily concerned with the two boxes in Fig. 4.1 labeled "Teacher Quality" and "Teaching Quality," and with their relationship to student outcomes and teacher commitment and retention. The model shows that teacher quality and teaching quality can be distinguished by the directness of their effect on student learning. Teaching quality, along with school and pupil factors, has a direct effect on student outcomes, while teacher quality affects student learning only through its effect on teaching quality, which is determined both directly by teacher factors, and jointly by teacher, school, and pupil

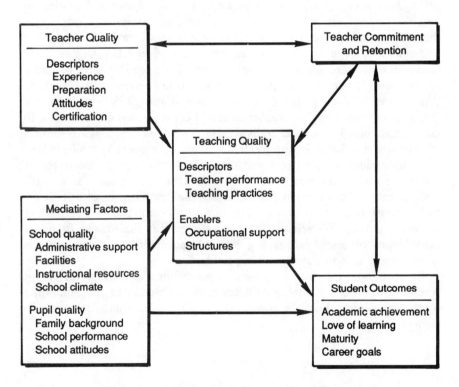

Fig. 4.1—Model of teacher quality effects

factors. Thus, school and pupil characteristics can be viewed as mediating, or intervening, variables for the effects of teacher quality on teaching quality, and for the effect of teaching quality on student outcomes.

Occupational supports are presented in the center box as enablers of teaching quality, although they are in a sense also mediating factors. Enablers are conditions that are presumed necessary, to some degree, for effective teaching, and for which we can say, "All other things being equal, the more the better." These conditions include high-quality materials and facilities, opportunities for professional development and discourse, time for teaching and for preparation, and favorable classroom characteristics (appropriate assignment, class size, teaching load). As will be shown below, these kinds of enablers are related to teacher effectiveness, satisfaction, and retention; they are clearly vital to a full understanding of mathematics and science teaching.

Finally, teacher commitment and retention are directly affected by all other variables in the model, including the attributes of the individual teacher and the kind and quality of teaching he or she is able to provide. These retention patterns, in turn, determine the quality of the subsequent teacher force, by specifying who will remain in teaching and who will leave for other endeavors. Recent evidence suggests, for example, that more academically able individuals tend to leave teaching sooner and in greater proportions than other recruits to teaching (Vance and Schlechty, 1982; Schlechty and Vance, 1983)—a tendency that is encouraged by the greater range of occupational choices open to more academically talented individuals. These factors make retention of qualified mathematics and science teachers especially problematic, since individuals trained in these disciplines fall disproportionately at the upper end of the academic ability spectrum (Berryman, 1983; College Entrance Examination Board, 1983), making them most at risk for early attrition from teaching. Further, the occupational alternatives for mathematics and science teachers are greater than those for most other types of teachers, making it even more difficult to retain the academically able in these teaching fields.

In sum, retention patterns, which are determined by a variety of teacher and school factors, also determine the quality of the remaining teacher pool and, thus, the continuing quality of mathematics and science education.

INDICATORS OF TEACHER QUALITY

Who Is a Teacher?

A basic issue for developing indicators of teacher quality in mathematics and science is how one defines a mathematics or science teacher. The definition of "teacher" will establish the unit of analysis for the indicators selected and will determine what questions the indicators can address. For example, is someone who is certified to teach mathematics but is teaching only home economics considered a mathematics teacher? Is someone who is teaching science but is certified only in physical education a science teacher? Are part-time or substitute teachers included as "teachers"? And how does one define a teacher who provides instruction in both mathematics and science?

How one resolves these issues depends on the reasons for examining teachers. If the goal is to evaluate and describe the supply of qualified mathematics and science teachers, one might include only individuals who are certified—or qualified by some other objective standard—to teach in these fields, regardless of what they are currently teaching.

On the other hand, if the goal is to understand the quality of educational instruction that students receive, the definition of "teacher" should include all those who teach mathematics and science, regardless of their formal qualifications or full-time teaching status. If out-of-field teachers are less qualified (in terms of subject-matter knowledge) than teachers assigned to classes in their area of certification or preparation, it is important to know what and whom they are teaching. If a non-trivial amount of instruction is conducted by part-time or substitute teachers, it is important to know who they are and where (whom) they teach. There is evidence, for example, that not only do substitute teachers occasionally provide a substantial amount of the instruction students receive, but that this occurs more often in certain types of schools (for example, inner-city schools) than in others (Meara et al., 1983). Thus, the distribution of part-time, substitute, and misassigned mathematics and science teachers, as well as their qualifications, is of practical importance in understanding the nature and quality of instruction.

In a national indicator system for mathematics and science education, the major questions pertain to the individuals who teach mathematics or science, regardless of their certification or other status. Thus, one measure of teacher quality is whether the teachers' certification status and educational background are appropriate for the area(s) they are teaching; another might be the extent of experience in a particular area. This is an especially important issue in mathematics and science, as misassignment frequently occurs in these areas, especially in physics and chemistry courses (Johnston and Aldridge, 1984; Rumberger, 1985).

These concerns suggest that a mathematics and science education monitoring system should include information on teachers' educational background—including, but not limited to, area(s) of certification and college coursework preparation—*linked with* information on assignment, to provide a more reliable means of determining each classroom teacher's qualifications. In addition, a focus on the students' educational experiences suggests considering all teachers who provide instruction in mathematics and science, including part-time, itinerant, and substitute teachers.

With this in mind, we turn now to an examination of teacher quality indicators, including indicators of teachers' characteristics and competence, and teacher supply and demand.

Teacher Quality: Teacher Characteristics and Competence

A variety of teacher competence measures have been examined for their relationship to student learning. These include teachers' years of education, recency of educational enrichment, years of teaching experience, and academic ability. Studies of these relationships have had equivocal results, primarily because of (1) an inability to specify and take into account the effects of variables that mediate between teacher characteristics and student performance, and (2) the lack of adequate student attainment measures that reflect a wide range of content and modes of performance. Under these conditions, measures of association are likely to be weak if they appear at all; therefore, findings of no relationship should not be viewed as conclusive evidence of the independence of a given teacher characteristic and student achievement. On the other hand, where relationships between fairly gross measures of teacher quality and student learning have been found, these measures should be viewed as especially promising avenues for indicator development.

Educational Background. It is widely assumed that subject-matter knowledge is related to teacher competence. While there is some support for this assumption, the findings are not as strong or consistent as one might expect. Byrne (1983) summarized the results of 30 studies relating teachers' subject knowledge to student achievement. The results of these studies were mixed, with 17 studies showing a positive relationship and 14 showing no relationship. However, many of the "no relationship" studies, Byrne noted, had so little variability in the teacher knowledge measure that insignificant findings were almost inevitable. Studies of teachers' scores on the National Teachers

Examination (NTE) area tests have found no consistent relationship between this measure of subject-matter knowledge and teacher performance, as measured by either student outcomes or supervisory ratings (Summers and Wolfe, 1975; Ayers and Qualls, 1979; Andrews, Blackmon, and Mackey, 1980; Quirk et al., 1973).

On the other hand, Druva and Anderson (1983), in a meta-analytic study of science teachers' characteristics and behaviors, found that student achievement was positively related to the teacher's background in education, biology (for biology teachers), and science. Although the correlations were small, they were consistently positive. Also, Casserly found that girls perform relatively better in mathematics when taught by teachers with backgrounds in science, mathematics, or engineering (Kolata, 1980).

Comparisons of teachers having degrees in education with teachers having subject-matter degrees usually show no relation between educational training and teacher performance. This finding may indicate that certification requirements result in teachers with different degrees having very similar educational backgrounds (see Murnane, 1985). It could also be that the small, positive effects of subject-matter knowledge considered alone are offset or augmented by knowledge of how to teach a particular subject. That is, the degree of pedagogical skill may interact with subject-matter knowledge to bolster or reduce teacher performance.

Glaser's (1983) work suggests that how one teaches mathematics or science (i.e., knowing how to teach problem-solving, reasoning from evidence, checking one's procedures, and checking for understanding) is as important as what is taught. Also, in a review of findings of the National Longitudinal Study of Mathematical Abilities (NLSMA), Begle (1979) found that the strongest indicator of preparation as a correlate of student performance was the number of credits in mathematics methods courses.

This evidence suggests that teacher knowledge of subject matter and content-specific methods may be a better predictor of student achievement in mathematics and science than in some other subject areas. (Even the small effects reported in the above-mentioned studies are more substantial than those found in other teaching areas.) Why this should be so was recently discussed by Brophy and Good (1986, p. 369):

> Research in mathematics and science instruction has shown that many concepts are counterintuitive or otherwise difficult to grasp and retain, not only for students but also for teachers and other adults. Consequently, teachers with limited backgrounds in certain subject matter areas may teach incorrect content or fail to recognize and correct their students' distorted understandings. . . . Clearly, the

effectiveness of lessons will vary with teachers' interest in and knowledge about the content being taught.

Area of Certification. While certification presumably reflects a teacher's area of expertise, this measure is of limited utility for a national indicator system, since state requirements for certification vary substantially and the relationship of certification to particular kinds of preparation is uncertain. An uncertified teacher may lack pedagogical courses, subject-area preparation, or student teaching experience, each of which has different implications for a teacher's knowledge and experience base. Given the vagaries of certification standards, an uncertified teacher may even be better prepared than one who is certified. For example, Carroll (1985) found that most teachers with less than a college minor in their teaching field were nonetheless certified in that field, and that nearly three-quarters of those with *no* college training in their field had still received certification.

The inadequacies of certification as an indicator of a teacher's competence can best be overcome by a detailed accounting of the teacher's educational history, including course credits in subject matter and pedagogical courses; these provide indicators of both qualifications and the effects of policy changes on certification standards.

Thus, we would argue that the usefulness of certification as an indicator of teacher quality depends on its link to these other, more standardized and powerful measures.

To assess subject-matter knowledge, we propose collection of the following information:

- College major and minor.
- College/university attended.
- Undergraduate grade-point average (GPA).
- Number of course hours in mathematics, life and physical sciences, computer science, and pedagogical courses, specifically mathematics and science education courses.
- Post-secondary degrees and coursework (types and numbers of courses; whether mandated or voluntary; recency of educational training/enrichment).
- Certification status (areas of certification).

These measures will provide more-reliable information about teachers' academic ability (through university ranking and reported GPA), as well as about the adequacy of their training in mathematics and science and mathematics and science education.

Other Indicators of Teacher Knowledge. *Teaching experience* is clearly a major means by which teachers learn how to teach. Years of teaching experience have been found to correlate with teacher effectiveness (Murnane and Phillips, 1981; Klitgaard and Hall, 1974). Penrick and Yager (1983) and Druva and Anderson (1983) both found that more-effective science teachers tended to be older and more experienced than their less-effective peers. However, it is unclear whether this relationship is linear or curvilinear, with too many years of experience resulting in "burnout" or a drop in performance.

Some studies have found that effectiveness may level off after about five years of experience, particularly in non-collegial work settings (Rosenholtz, 1985). Others have suggested that these findings in cross-sectional studies are really the result of cohort or attrition effects—i.e., cohorts of teachers hired in the past in times of teacher shortage may be less well-qualified than more recent cohorts; disproportionate early attrition of more-able teachers may suggest that experienced teachers are *on average* less capable, although for individuals, experience produces better performance. In any event, at least up to some point, experience improves teachers' performance.

The *recency of educational enrichment* has also been used as a proxy measure for teacher knowledge. Penrick and Yager (1983) found that teachers in exemplary science programs had more years of education and more recent educational experiences (despite being older than the average science teacher). Hanushek (1970) found that the recency of *voluntary* educational experience is related to teacher performance. As Murnane (1985) notes, these findings suggest that it may not be only the knowledge acquired with a higher degree that is important, but also the enthusiasm for learning that leads the teacher to seek new knowledge that relates to increased student learning. Thus, educational enrichment is a measure of both commitment and qualifications.

Involvement in professional associations and activities may also relate to teacher quality. Penrick and Yager (1983) found that teachers in exemplary science programs were more likely to be actively involved in professional organizations. This involvement not only provides additional learning opportunities, it also signifies a commitment to continual learning and to the field itself. To measure this kind of involvement, an indicator system should include at least some of the following:

- Mathematics/science professional organizations to which the teacher belongs.
- Professional conferences attended per year (and presentations made at conferences).
- Professional (school and non-school) committees on which the teacher serves.

- Professional journals and subject-area magazines read regularly.
- Journal articles and curriculum materials published by the teacher.

Teacher Traits and Attitudes. The indicators of teacher quality we have discussed to this point all relate to training, certification, and experience, as indicators of teacher knowledge of subject matter or pedagogy. However, as our model indicates, some teacher attributes may serve as enablers of teacher quality—that is, they make teachers' knowledge efficacious. These characteristics, e.g., *verbal ability, interest, flexibility, sense of efficacy, enthusiasm,* and *satisfaction,* are not strong candidates for inclusion in an educational indicator system, for several reasons. For one thing, policymakers are less likely to be able to influence them directly, in the way they can such factors such as teachers' educational backgrounds. Moreover, they are difficult to measure cost-effectively. Nevertheless, they bear consideration because they continue to be a major focus of the research literature on teachers and teaching.

Several studies have found that teachers' *verbal ability* is related to student achievement (e.g., Bowles and Levin, 1968; Hanushek, 1970), although this finding may be differentially applicable for teachers of different types of students (e.g., Summers and Wolfe, 1975). Verbal ability may itself be an indicator of teachers' ability to convey ideas and to convince others.

The ability to persuade and inform students may also depend on teachers' *interest* in a subject. If teachers are not very interested in or comfortable with mathematics or science, these subjects may be less likely to be taught well or extensively. This is particularly important at the elementary level, where both the kind and *extent* of instruction offered in mathematics and science are highly variable. Elementary school teachers tend not to have taken many mathematics or science courses in college (Galambos, 1985), and are often not required to do so to receive certification (NRC, 1985), so it is not surprising that some second-grade teachers devote an average of only 15 minutes per day to mathematics instruction (McDonald and Elias, 1976).

It is possible that some personality traits improve teachers' performance. Although research on personality characteristics has produced few encouraging findings (Schalock, 1979; Druva and Anderson, 1983), studies of teachers' *flexibility* (alternatively labeled "adaptability" or "creativity") consistently show strong, positive effects on student learning (Darling-Hammond, et al., 1983; Walberg and Waxman, 1983; Schalock, 1979).

Given the multidimensionality, simultaneity, and immediacy of classroom events (see Chapter 6 of this volume), it is not surprising that teachers who are flexible, adaptable, and creative should be more effective in encouraging student learning. The positive findings of research based on various creativity/flexibility scales and personality ratings (see Schalock, 1979) suggest that valid indicators of this construct do exist and can feasibly be included in an indicator system.

Teachers' attitudes—specifically, *feelings of efficacy*, a belief in their ability to help students learn—are also strongly and consistently related to teacher performance and to student outcomes (Armor et al., 1976, Brookover et al., 1979; Rutter et al., 1979). Efficacy also appears to influence teacher satisfaction and teachers' more generalized feelings about their work (Rosenholtz et al., 1985); teachers who lack confidence in their teaching skills have higher rates of absenteeism and attrition (Chapman, 1984; Litt and Turk, 1983).

Enthusiasm is also consistently and positively related to student achievement (Walberg and Waxman, 1983), perhaps because it is related to other teacher traits (e.g., knowledge and love of subject matter) and/or because it increases engagement in the lessons at hand. It is unclear how efficacy and enthusiasm affect instructional practice; however, the existence of these effects suggests that these attitudes and the conditions that may produce them are worth including in an indicator system. Information on both could be acquired through teacher self-reports. They could also be inferred indirectly, but perhaps more objectively, from absentee rates. While a certain percentage of any teacher's absences are due to unavoidable illnesses or personal/family problems, dissatisfaction or frustration with one's work can lead to a greater susceptibility to some illnesses and a greater willingness to remain home for a "marginal" illness or a "mental health day."

Finally, teacher *satisfaction* is a natural concomitant of interest, enthusiasm, and efficacy. Teacher satisfaction is, of course, partly determined by how well the teacher's own goals, knowledge, and experience fit with the formal and informal goals and policies of the school. It may also be related to teachers' preparation for the courses they are assigned to teach and to other conditions of teaching work. Satisfaction is likely to be a determinant of continuation in the profession, but at the moment, we can only speculate about the links between teacher satisfaction, teaching conditions, and resulting performance and retention. Our understanding could be increased by including in an indicator system some measures designed to assess teachers' satisfaction with their work settings, with teaching generally, and with their assigned courses or students.

Implications of Supply and Demand for Teacher Quality

The quality of mathematics and science education is determined not only by the characteristics and competence of current teachers, but also by teacher supply and demand, which indirectly influence what qualifications mathematics and science teachers will have, and what teaching conditions (course offerings, teaching load, class size) will prevail. These concerns are especially germane to mathematics and science education, which suffers from some of the most severe shortages of qualified teachers (Howe and Gerlovich, 1982; Darling-Hammond, 1984). As a result of these shortages, fewer than half of the newly hired mathematics and science teachers in 1981 were certified or eligible for certification in the subjects they were assigned to teach (NCES, 1982) (see Fig. 4.2). Further, the National Science Teachers Association (NTSA) estimates that approximately 30 percent of all secondary mathematics and science teachers are either "completely unqualified or severely underqualified" to teach these subjects (Johnston and Aldridge, 1984).

Ironically, these discouraging statistics are in part the result of an increased demand for better mathematics and science education. As

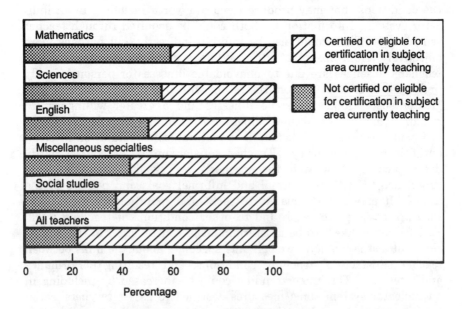

Fig. 4.2—Qualifications of new teachers for the subject area
they are currently teaching (1981)

high school graduation requirements have been raised, schools have added more required technical courses, creating new teacher demand (ASCUS, 1984; NCES, 1985a). Because fully trained mathematics and science teachers are in such short supply, however, schools must often resort to hiring or reassigning teachers trained in other fields to teach these courses (National Research Council, 1985; Johnston and Aldridge, 1984).

The inadequacy of the supply of mathematics and science teachers is a growing problem, both because there are fewer new entrants to these areas and because many of the teachers hired to teach the baby boom generation 20 years ago are now approaching retirement. Between 1970 and 1980, the number of mathematics and science majors who chose to become teachers declined by 65 percent (McBay, 1986). In 1981, the nation's colleges granted fewer than 1,400 bachelor's degrees in the fields of mathematics and science education combined, and only about half of these graduates took teaching positions (NCES, 1983). In the following school year, about 8,300 mathematics and science teachers left the teaching profession altogether—for every newly trained entrant, about twelve mathematics and science teachers left teaching (Aldrich, 1983). The future may not be much brighter: the NSTA estimates that over 40 percent of the current mathematics and science teachers will retire by 1995 (Aldrich, 1983) (see Fig. 4.3).

Why is it so difficult to attract and retain qualified individuals to mathematics and science teaching? As our economy has shifted from a manufacturing to a technological base, people with mathematics and/or science training have had more job opportunities than most other education majors. This "problem" has been exacerbated by expanding labor market opportunities for minorities and women—the groups that have traditionally entered teaching when barred from other professional careers. Between 1970 and 1980, the proportion of women receiving bachelor's degrees in education decreased by half, while the proportion of degrees granted to women in the biological sciences, computer sciences, engineering, and law increased tenfold (Bureau of the Census, 1973, 1983). The number of new candidates for teaching has steadily declined since 1970, from about 300,000 annually to just over 100,000 in 1984. And most of the "defectors" from education have been those who are most academically able and well-prepared (Vance and Schlechty, 1982; Wagenaar, 1984).

While some of these individuals may still go into teaching, for most, the change in college major represents a change in occupational choice. Moreover, teachers with academic majors who do go into teaching tend to be more dissatisfied than education majors with the lack of administrative support, bureaucratic interference with their work, lack of

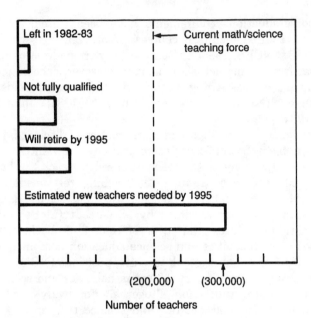

Fig. 4.3—Status of the mathematics and science
teaching program

autonomy, other unfavorable working conditions, and salaries (Darling-Hammond, 1984), and more likely to say they plan to leave teaching. This latter tendency is especially disheartening, since academic majors appear to be better prepared in their subject areas than education majors. A recent study by the Southern Regional Education Board noted that education majors tend to take fewer mathematics and physical sciences courses than do arts and sciences majors, and teacher candidates are often segregated into remedial or lower-level college mathematics and science courses (Galambos, 1985).

In addition to the loss of the more academically trained teachers, current and impending teacher shortages may detract from teaching quality in other ways. First, projections of increasing teacher demand suggest that one (or both) of two hiring patterns for mathematics and science teachers may become more prevalent. There is likely to be even more reassignment of teachers from other subject areas to mathematics and science courses. While these individuals may be competent teachers, mathematics and science teachers trained in their area of instruction are generally considered preferable to those trained in other subject areas (especially if inservice retraining programs are weak or nonexistent). On the other hand, hiring a full complement of newly trained mathematics and science teachers—even if it were possible, given the short supply of such individuals—may have other drawbacks, as *new* teachers are generally less effective (Rosenholtz, 1985) and more likely to leave teaching than are more experienced teachers (Schlechty and Vance, 1983; Pederson, 1970; Murnane and Phillips, 1981). To the extent that supply falls short, a final set of options for dealing with a lack of qualified mathematics and science teachers is to simply offer fewer courses or to increase class size or teaching load. While these options solve the dilemma of reassigning versus hiring teachers, none of them is optimal for mathematics and science education.

To examine how these influences affect the quality of mathematics and science education, an indicator system must include data on the interrelated factors affecting the supply of and demand for mathematics and science teachers. In addition to detailed information on teachers' educational preparation and current assignments, indicators concerning teacher supply and demand require several other important elements:

- Estimates of demand based on school enrollments, student coursetaking trends, and teacher/pupil ratios.
- Estimates of supply, based on numbers of new entrants from teacher education institutions, other college majors, and other sectors of the workforce, including reentrants from the "reserve pool."
- Estimates of attrition (necessary to project both continuing supply and future demand).

Data on the components of demand are easily collected from Census data and from other national and state data collection systems. However, data on sources of supply and on attrition are markedly absent from current national data collection efforts and are therefore discussed more specifically here. To enable policymakers to understand the implications of supply for teacher quality, an indicator system should include demographic characteristics of teachers, their educational backgrounds (discussed above), their assignments, their work history, and attrition patterns.

Demographic Characteristics. While not directly related to teacher quality, demographic characteristics of the teaching force have a great deal of policy relevance. The age composition of the teaching force is a key component of teacher supply, as it determines the proportion of teachers who will soon be eligible to retire and describes the proportion of young, inexperienced teachers, a group known to have high attrition rates. Monitoring of the sex and race composition of the teaching force helps assess the degree to which expanding occupational opportunities draw women and minorities away from teaching, or conversely, the degree to which changing sex roles encourage more women to enter the more male-dominated fields of secondary science and mathematics education.

Assignment. Appropriate assignment (or, conversely, "misassignment") is defined in terms of a teacher's educational preparation and the type of class or classes he or she is teaching. Labor market imbalances can prevent the close correspondence between a teacher's educational background and course assignments that defines an "appropriate" or "in-field" assignment. For example, when relative demand for teachers shifts among fields, school systems tend to shift senior teachers from low-demand courses (e.g., physical education) to high-demand courses (e.g., physics), rather than hiring more highly qualified newcomers for these vacancies (Johnson and Aldridge, 1984) or letting the courses go untaught. Although such misassignment appears to be especially prevalent in mathematics and science, there is no consensus on how to estimate its extent. Data from the Center for Education Statistics and the National Education Association (NEA) have provided three different estimates of the prevalence of misassignment—estimates that vary depending on who is asked to estimate the degree of misassignment (school administrators or teachers) and on how misassignment is defined:

- Not certified in area of primary assignment: 9 to 11 percent, by teacher report; 3.4 percent, from central office administrators' estimates (NEA, 1981; NCES, 1985d).
- Not certified for some classes taught: 16 percent, by teacher report (NEA, 1981).
- Less than a college minor in area of primary assignment: 17 percent, by secondary school teacher report (Carroll, 1985).

While these definitions take into account certification or undergraduate educational background, none includes inservice retraining or later degrees. While these statistics are useful indicators of supply and demand imbalances, they provide no insight into the educational consequences of misassignment. As mentioned above, certification standards vary so widely that "area of certification" is an insufficient measure of teacher qualification in a subject area. And teaching fields are so broadly defined that the fit between a teacher's educational background and the actual courses taught cannot be ascertained. To define and interpret the consequences of misassignment, we must have more detailed information on teachers' specific educational preparation and their actual teaching assignments.

Work History. Detailed work histories from current teachers would provide data useful for monitoring teachers' experience and career paths. In addition to allowing a fuller assessment of teacher qualifications for their teaching assignments, these data would provide more complete information than currently exists for monitoring the sources of teacher supply and the routes that individuals take into teaching (i.e., entrance from a college teacher preparation program, through an alternative certification route, reentrance from the teacher "reserve pool," or entry from another occupation). Work history information would also provide indicators of teacher mobility (across locations, teaching fields, and sectors), thus illuminating the dynamics of the teacher labor market.

For work history indicators, we propose that in-depth information be collected on:

- The type and extent of teachers' preservice training.
- Inservice training, especially training to upgrade mathematics/science knowledge, or retraining to teach mathematics and science.
- Other occupations held (in past and currently), including movements into and out of the teaching force.
- Teaching experience, broken down by grade level, subject matter, and location of school/district.

This information could be collected from a nationally representative sample of mathematics and science teachers. Or data on source of entry could be gathered from school principals on the previous year's new hires. Either of these strategies would provide estimates of sources of new supply in any given year as well as reentry rates of "reserve pool" members by type (age, sex, field, etc.).

Attrition. Aside from student enrollments, the prime factor that determines teacher demand is teacher attrition. It is impossible to accurately monitor or predict teacher labor market conditions without some knowledge of this important component of both the demand for and the continuing supply of teachers.

Estimates of attrition can be obtained in several ways, which vary in their cost-effectiveness depending on whether the primary purpose is to estimate attrition *rates* or *patterns*. If the goal is to estimate the rates at which mathematics and science teachers leave (or can be expected to leave) teaching, then data from large, "representative" samples of schools on the number of teachers leaving, by where they are going (i.e., another teaching job versus out of teaching), can be used as the basis for such estimates. These data would also allow examination of attrition patterns from schools or districts of different types, but would not allow exploration of attrition patterns by *teacher* type (e.g., age, qualifications, sex, race). At a minimum, data on the age distribution of the mathematics and science teaching force would allow more accurate estimates and projections of attrition than currently exist.

If the primary purpose is to understand attrition *patterns*, current longitudinal databases (e.g., the National Longitudinal Studies, High School and Beyond) could be used to analyze which members of the teacher subsamples in particular cohorts leave teaching, but these analyses would not reveal the overall attrition rates of mathematics and science teachers. An alternative, but more costly, approach to understanding the attrition patterns of mathematics and science teachers would be to follow longitudinally a large, nationally representative sample of mathematics and science teachers to examine both the rates of attrition and the characteristics of leavers, as well as their destinations and reasons for leaving teaching. This kind of data is extremely important for understanding what forces influence teacher attrition and what policies might promote greater retention of well-qualified mathematics and science teachers.

Summary of Teacher Quality Indicators

We have identified and argued for the inclusion of a number of potential indicators of teacher quality, including:

- Educational background (college and graduate-level courses in subject-matter areas and teaching methods).
- Areas of certification.
- Basic demographic information (age, sex, ethnicity).
- Assignment (courses taught) and length of time teaching each course.
- Career histories.
- Attrition rates and patterns.
- Years of teaching experience.
- Recency of educational enrichment.
- Involvement in professional associations and activities.

Teacher Quality Priorities for an Indicator System

If design constraints make it impossible to consider all these teacher quality variables, the highest priority should be given to obtaining (1) demographic data, which provide the most basic and easy-to-collect information on teacher characteristics; (2) detailed educational background and work history data, which provide the most relevant information on teacher qualifications, including subject-matter knowledge, academic ability, and teaching experience; and (3) current teaching assignments, which can be used to assess the degree of out-of-field assignment occurring in mathematics and science, and the kinds of courses taught by teachers with various kinds of preparation. Data on teacher attrition are also vital for monitoring changes in the nature of the mathematics and science teaching force. Linkages among these data elements will allow analyses of the relationships among teachers' characteristics, their teaching assignments, and their career paths into and out of teaching. Lower priority should be given to measures of teachers' professional associations and activities, and of their satisfaction and future plans. The former is a less-well-validated indicator of teacher qualifications; the latter are less-well-supported proxies for teachers' labor market behavior.

TEACHING QUALITY IN MATHEMATICS AND SCIENCE

The proximal goal of obtaining good teachers is to ensure good teaching. However, what constitutes good teaching is a matter of extensive research and theoretical debate. This literature is too extensive to be reviewed here. See Brophy and Good (1986); Centra and Potter (1980); Medley (1979); and Peterson and Walberg (1979) for comprehensive reviews of teaching behavior and its relation to student outcomes. Chapter 6 of this volume also reviews this literature in the context of the development of mathematics and science education indicators.

One major outcome of research on teaching effectiveness deserves special mention here: Effective teaching behaviors are found to vary consistently for students of different psychological, developmental, and socioeconomic characteristics (Brophy and Evertson, 1974, 1977; Cronbach and Snow, 1977; Peterson, 1976) and for different grade levels and subject areas (Gage, 1978; McDonald and Elias, 1976). Druva and Anderson (1983), for example, found that while teachers' background in science was positively related to students' science achievement, this relationship became stronger at progressively higher grade levels. Crocker, Bartlett, and Eliott (1976) found that in elementary science classes, a structured model of teaching was more effective, overall, than an unstructured model, but that the model's effectiveness varied by student type. Also, a student-structured approach to learning has been found to improve males' attitudes toward science, while females' attitudes are more enhanced by a teacher-structured approach (Abhyankar, 1977). As a final example, Webb (1980) found that group problem-solving is more effective for middle-ability students when the groups are uniformly middle-ability, but is more effective for high- and low-ability students when the groups are of mixed ability levels.

Furthermore, the effectiveness of different teaching behaviors seems to vary depending on the goals of instruction. For example, many of the behaviors that seem to result in increased achievement on standardized tests of rudimentary skills are dissimilar, indeed nearly opposite, to those that seem to increase complex cognitive learning, problem-solving ability, and creativity (McKeachie and Kulick, 1975; Peterson, 1979; Soar, 1977; Soar and Soar, 1976). Moreover, desirable affective outcomes of education—independence, curiosity, and positive attitudes toward school, teacher, and self—seem to result from teaching behaviors that are different from those prescribed for increasing student achievement on tests requiring factual recall and routine applications of lower-order skills (Horwitz, 1979; McKeachie and Kulick, 1975; Peterson, 1979; Traub et al., 1973). As Brophy and Good (1986) pointed out in the most recent edition of the *Handbook of Research on Teaching*:

> Effective instruction involves selecting (from a larger repertoire) and orchestrating those teaching behaviors that are appropriate to the context and to the teacher's goals, rather than mastering and consistently applying a few "generic" teaching skills (p. 360).

For our purposes, the most significant implication of this literature is that teaching—even in specific subject areas such as mathematics and science—is too complex and multifaceted to be adequately assessed by one discrete, easily tallied set of behavioral indicators. However, sets of indicators can be developed to describe "important" features of teaching (i.e., those of some theoretical and practical interest), regardless of the directness of their effect on particular measures of student achievement. Indicators of what is taught and how it is taught provide information that is useful not only in monitoring progress in mathematics and science education and in describing the teaching environment, but also for providing analysts with data for developing, and perhaps testing, hypotheses on teacher effectiveness in mathematics and science education. These types of indicators are discussed in Chapters 6 and 8. In this section, we are concerned with the teaching conditions and occupational support structures within schools that contribute to teacher quality by setting the context in which teaching occurs.

Occupational Support and Teaching Quality

To work most effectively, teachers must have support from the institution in which they are working. This occupational support includes the working conditions and atmosphere established within the school (or school district) that enhance or impinge on teachers' ability to provide adequate instruction and that influence their likelihood of remaining in the teaching workforce. Adequate facilities, materials, and supplies, administrative and clerical support, inservice training programs, peer support and assistance networks, and opportunities to influence decisionmaking all facilitate quality teaching by enhancing teacher commitment. Commitment then increases effort, thus helping the teacher to reach and maintain effectiveness (which in turn reinforces the teacher's commitment) (Blase, 1982; Rosenholtz, 1985).[3]

Not only do the conditions under which mathematics and science teachers work affect their ability to provide high-quality instruction, they also affect the ability of education to attract and retain the best-qualified mathematics and science teacher candidates. The occupational conditions of teaching, including salary levels and the lack of opportunities for advancement, are often cited by academically able students as reasons for *not* considering teaching as a career (Berry, 1986).

One major occupational support feature, the material resources available for teaching, is discussed in other chapters in this volume; here, we focus on time for instruction, class size and teaching load, administrative buffering, collegiality (opportunities for collaboration), decisionmaking ability, and monetary rewards.

Time for Instruction. The most fundamental resource available to teachers is time for instruction and for those activities that enhance the productivity of time spent directly with students—preparation, planning, providing written feedback to students, and consulting with colleagues. Though the profitable use of time is clearly critical, the availability of time for key teaching functions sets absolute limits on what can be accomplished during a school day, week, or year. How schools structure time, then, is an important determinant of how teachers can use their knowledge and energies on behalf of students.

---

[3]The authors wish to thank Susan Rosenholtz for her contribution to the portions of this discussion related to organizational influences on teacher commitment.

Allocation of Classroom Time. Aside from the nuances of teaching activities and methods, teachers' effectiveness appears to increase as they spend more time actively engaged in subject-matter teaching (McDonald and Elias, 1976; Brophy and Evertson, 1977; Stallings and Kaskowitz, 1974). This level of engagement is influenced by both the allocation and use of classroom time (the latter is discussed in Chapter 6). Available teaching time is determined by the length of the school day, school year, and class period (at the secondary level), and by the amount of class time devoted to subject-matter coverage.

The extent and use of teaching time in different subject areas varies among teachers, schools, districts, states, and even nations. For example, American elementary teachers spend an average of only 15 minutes per day on science instruction (Blank and Raizen, 1985), and less than four hours per week on mathematics instruction (Flowers, 1984), but the range of time allocations across schools and teachers is quite large. The relatively lower mathematics achievement of American students, compared with that of Japanese and Taiwanese students, has been partially attributed to the shorter school year and smaller amounts of daily time devoted to mathematics instruction typical of American schools (National Science Board, 1985). In fact, Wiley and Harnischfeger (1974) concluded that schools with 24 percent more school time produce gains of over 33 percent in mathematics achievement. There is also evidence that increased exposure to mathematics may be particularly beneficial for the lowest-achieving mathematics students (e.g., Stallings, 1976).

The amount of time devoted to mathematics and science teaching is, when prescribed by schedule or curricular mandate, a constraint under which teachers operate. When time allocations are a product of teachers' own decisions (as is the case in many elementary schools), they may reflect teachers' interest in or comfort with particular subject matter, as well as teachers' perceptions of student outcomes that are valued by the school or district. In either case, time available for mathematics and science instruction is a measure of how teacher qualifications are utilized in schools, and it shapes the extent and nature of teaching students receive.

Indicators of the use of classroom time include the amount of time spent on mathematics and science instruction per week (across students, schools, and districts) and the length of the school day and school year.

Allocation of Teachers' Time. How schools structure and teachers use their total occupational time is also relevant to teaching quality, because it describes the occupational supports for translating teachers' knowledge into instructional activities and may influence the nature of instructional processes within the classroom. A teacher's duties and responsibilities are many and varied; the amount of time a teacher devotes to activities related to classroom teaching (planning, preparation, grading), faculty meetings, curriculum planning, tutoring students, parent meetings, administrative paperwork, and non-teaching duties reflects both the enabling conditions for teaching and the degree of teacher commitment to teaching. The time provided for teaching-related activities within the school day (as opposed to non-teaching duties) reflects the school's emphasis on instruction and may relate to teacher commitment and attrition as well.

Possible indicators of time use include:

- Amount of time within the school day allocated to classroom instruction, preparation, non-teaching duties (bus duty, hall duty, etc.), meetings with colleagues, and meetings or conferences with parents and students.
- Amount of time outside the school day teachers spend on planning and preparation, grading classroom assignments, contacting parents, working with students, completing administrative paperwork, and reading professional journals or participating in other professional development activities.

Class Size. Closely related to the availability of time is the distribution of that time across students and courses. The amount of time and attention a teacher can devote to the needs of particular students or the demands of specific courses depends in large part on how many students and courses the teacher must attend to.

Class size has not always been found to be related to student outcomes, in part because of restricted sample class sizes and failure to control for other teaching variables. But there is some evidence to suggest that smaller class sizes are related to higher student achievement levels, particularly in the primary grades, in reading and mathematics classes, and for low-achieving and economically disadvantaged students (ERS, 1986). Glass and Smith (1978) found a threshold effect for class size—large gains in student achievement were found when class size was reduced to 15 students or less. Klitgaard and Hall (1974) also found that schools with achievement levels higher than would normally be predicted tended to have smaller class sizes. Summers and Wolfe (1975) found that at the junior high school level, larger classes had lower levels of student achievement, a finding that was especially strong among classes comprised of low-socioeconomic-status (SES) students.

The relation between class size and teacher satisfaction and commitment has been, apparently, too obvious to warrant much study. Certainly, few teachers would claim that their teaching effectiveness would be improved by larger classes, and many claim that reducing class size would improve their teaching. Smaller class sizes can increase the individual attention each student receives and the possibilities for teacher effectiveness, by increasing one-on-one contact and by reducing managerial chores and paperwork. Small class sizes are likely to be especially beneficial in classes utilizing "hands on" instruction (e.g., chemistry or biology labs), where individual attention is particularly important.

Teaching load—the number of different subjects and classes a teacher is responsible for—is both an indirect measure of the amount of time a teacher can devote to preparation and instruction and an indicator of teachers' working conditions. It is reasonable to expect that heavy teaching loads may influence teacher satisfaction, commitment, and retention as much as they may affect performance. Measures of class size and teaching load not only serve as indicators of the quality of education in the classroom, they are also potential indicators of teacher shortages, since one response to increased demand for mathematics and science teachers in the face of decreased supply is to increase teaching loads and/or class size.

A monitoring system should thus provide indicators of how many classes teachers have each day in each subject area they teach, and what their mathematics and/or science class sizes are. It is also important to collect information on the "demography" of specific classes. This includes information on what course is being taught (e.g., geometry, biology, chemistry), on the ability level and extent of ability grouping in the class, and on the SES, racial, and sex mix of students in the class. These data would permit analysis of whether and how teacher (and teaching) qualities and conditions vary by class and student type. For example, the extent to which lower-level versus upper-level mathematics courses are taught by teachers assigned out-of-field could be determined, as could the extent to which teachers' qualifications and teaching practices differ for classes serving different types of students.

Administrative Buffering. Working conditions that help individuals concentrate on their central tasks also enhance their commitment to the job (Locke, 1976, Rosenholtz et al., 1985). Teachers' tasks that are unrelated to teaching and learning—such as non-teaching duties and administrative paperwork—contribute to teacher dissatisfaction (Darling-Hammond, 1984; Bredeson et al., 1983; Lortie, 1975; Raschke et al., 1985; Rosenholtz et al., 1985), as well as reducing the time available for teaching or planning. Teachers work more effectively if they can be "buffered" from such intrusions (Rosenholtz, 1985).

Opportunities for Collaboration and Decisionmaking. Most schools are characterized by isolated working conditions, where colleagues seldom see each other teach and teachers have few opportunities to engage in discussions about teaching practices (Bishop, 1977; Glidewell, 1983; Lortie, 1975). Where collaboration is encouraged, teachers are more likely to discuss their teaching, to try new ideas, and to seek help in solving teaching problems (Armor et al., 1976; Little, 1982; Mann and Fenwick, 1985; Rutter et al., 1979; Venezky and Winfield, 1979; Rosenholtz et al., 1985). Collaborative, as opposed to isolated, settings seem to increase not only teacher learning, but also commitment to teaching, as there is substantially lower teacher absenteeism and turnover in schools that encourage and provide time for teachers to work together (Bridges and Hallinan, 1978; Litt and Turk, 1983; Sizemore et al., 1983; Rosenholtz et al., 1985).

Teachers' participation in instructional decisionmaking also reduces absenteeism and turnover (Azumi and Madhere, 1983; Chapman and Hutcheson, 1982; Rosenholtz et al., 1985). This mechanism probably promotes collaboration among faculty, with its positive effects on teachers' commitment to teaching (Armor et al., 1976; Glenn and McLean, 1981; Rosenholtz et al., 1985; Rutter et al., 1979; Cruickshank, 1985; Mann and Fenwick, 1985). Involvement in decisionmaking may also augment commitment by increasing teachers' sense of ownership of the educational enterprise.

Opportunities for Professional Development. The connection between teachers' sense of efficacy and their commitment to teaching suggests that chances for teachers to enhance their knowledge and skills should also enhance their effectiveness and attachment to the profession. We noted earlier that the recency of teachers' educational enrichment seems related to teaching effectiveness; opportunities to engage in such activities are an important feature of the school environment which mediates teacher performance. This is consistent with teacher reports that the absence of opportunities for professional development contributes to their dissatisfaction and attrition (Darling-Hammond, 1984; Bredeson et al., 1983; Mann and Fenwick, 1985; Rosenholtz, et al., 1985). The importance of such opportunities for teacher commitment seems logical—opportunities for professional growth enhance teachers' mastery of instructional practice, their sense of efficacy, and ultimately their commitment to teaching (see, e.g., Huberman and Miles, 1984; Rosenholtz et al., 1985).

Monetary Rewards. The literature on monetary rewards yields limited information on the role of those rewards in securing teachers' commitment. Existing studies do not indicate that increased pecuniary benefits by themselves increase teachers' performance (Mann and Fenwick, 1985; McLaughlin and Marsh, 1978) or retention (Bredeson, Fruth, and Kasten, 1983; Bruno 1981; Chapman and Hutcheson, 1982; Frataccia and Hennington, 1982). However, low salaries and low occupational prestige are important factors cited by those who do not choose teaching as an occupation (Rosenholtz and Smylie, 1983; Page and Page, 1982; Roberson et al., 1983). And low salaries influence teachers' propensity to take second jobs for supplemental income, thus decreasing the time they can devote to teaching. In fields such as mathematics and science, where alternative occupations offer substantial wage differentials, teachers' salaries may more strongly affect early attrition. Salaries may especially influence the entry and retention of subgroups that are particularly attractive to schools, such as talented women who are currently choosing other occupations (Waite and Berryman, 1984).

Teacher Quality Priorities for an Indicator System

Of the occupational support indicators discussed here, highest priority should be given to those easy-to-collect measures with the most direct relation to teacher performance, satisfaction, and retention. The most directly available of such indicators are class size, teaching load, and time use. These data are easily operationalized and are available on a number of current national-level educational survey instruments. Salaries and other monetary incentives should be given the next level of priority, since they are related to both teacher supply and demand and to the propensity of teachers to take second jobs to supplement their income. The supports provided by collegiality, buffering, and opportunities for collaboration and decisionmaking are more difficult to operationalize and less directly influenced by policy. While they also bear an important relation to teacher quality, they should be given a lower level of priority.

CONCLUSIONS

At this point, it would be useful to discuss how indicators of teacher quality fit into a monitoring system of mathematics and science education, and some of the constraints on these indicators.

Students can fail to learn for a multitude of reasons, at any level in the educational system. One potential cause of students' insufficient learning is that they have not been taught well enough. And one cause of poor teaching is the use of unqualified or underqualified teachers, or teachers who are rendered less effective in other ways, such as by misassignment or by being overburdened with too many students, classes, or non-teaching duties. Therefore, to comprehensively monitor the status of mathematics and science education, these teacher and teaching factors must be considered as relevant aspects of educational quality.

The need for data on teacher quality has recently been emphasized by many groups, including the National Research Council in its Research Agenda on Mathematics, Science and Technology (1985):

> Whatever its effect, little is known about the subject matter preparation of the 2.37 million teachers in the current pool . . . much less about their competence for teaching science and mathematics. (p. 16)

> The committee recommends the development of a national database on teacher preparation and qualifications sufficiently detailed and appropriately stratified to reflect conditions in different types of school districts and for varying student populations. (p. 18)

Filling this gap in our knowledge of the qualifications of current mathematics and science teachers should be a top priority in a prototype monitoring system. We propose the incorporation of a wide range of information on teachers, including (1) demographic characteristics, (2) educational and occupational backgrounds, (3) teaching assignments, and (4) teaching conditions.

The list of indicators proposed here is based on two assumptions: First, the use of specific, discrete teaching behaviors (e.g., wait-time, types of questions asked, etc.), while of some use in research studies, is too context-specific to provide useful information for a monitoring system. The classifying and counting of discrete teacher behaviors is not only costly and time-consuming, but also overlooks many important, interactive and/or dynamic aspects of teaching.

Second, given that we are far from being able to specify the particular qualities of effective teaching, in mathematics and science or in general, teaching "quality" is best assessed by teacher qualifications, general patterns of teaching practices, and the presence of enabling conditions for effective teaching. In developing our list of indicators, we have relied as heavily on logical analysis as we have on empirical evidence for determinants of effective teaching. This strategy seems justifiable, given both the indirect relation of many of these indicators to teaching "quality" and the goal of *monitoring* the status of mathematics and science education. Even so, each indicator we have proposed has either been empirically related to teacher effectiveness or bears such a compelling logical relation to effective teaching that its omission would be difficult to justify.

It should be kept in mind, however, that most of the proposed indicators are only *indirect* measures of teacher "quality": A teacher may be fully qualified for teaching mathematics and may work in a school with favorable conditions for effective mathematics instruction, yet still be only a mediocre mathematics teacher. Likewise, a teacher with less academic training and ability and less favorable conditions may have the "intangible" (i.e., as yet unmeasurable) characteristics that make her or him an effective mathematics teacher. The types of indicators that are most feasible to collect, such as those proposed here, are useful and informative, especially at the aggregate level and over time. However, they should never be mistaken as "proof" of a teacher's ability or inability to teach. They are more accurately viewed as measures of an individual's *potential* to be an effective teacher.

Another limitation of some proposed indicators is that they are most easily collected by asking teachers for self-reports, which may introduce social desirability biases. This is especially likely to occur if teachers realize the questions are designed to assess some dimension of teacher "quality." Referring to the indicators as part of a monitoring system of the *status* of mathematics and science education will help alleviate, but will not eliminate, this problem. The potential for social-desirability response effects should be considered in the selection, design, and interpretation of all data gathered from self-reports.

Finally, the effects of the various proposed indicators on policy decisions should be considered. As McDonnell points out in Chapter 10, if the information provided by an indicator system is not useful to policymakers, it will have failed to benefit its primary intended audience and will not survive as a publicly supported endeavor. The indicator system we envision would provide important additional information about teachers and teaching and would permit the linking of this information to other educational factors. However, because policy effects are difficult to trace, overambitious claims for findings that may result from a monitoring system should be resisted.

On the more positive side, an indicator system has the potential for providing information on mathematics and science teachers and teaching that can be constructively used to improve the quality of mathematics and science education. Attempts to improve that education *without* a comprehensive monitoring system can be, as most policymakers will attest, a highly frustrating task—evidence of educational quality that is sporadically collected, usually in noncomparable form across studies, provides information that is far inferior to what *could* be available from an integrated, comprehensive, consistently administered monitoring system. In spite of the caveats that accompany it, such a monitoring system would vastly improve our understanding of current educational conditions and of the effects of various policies on these conditions.

Chapter 5

CURRICULUM

Jeannie Oakes and Neil Carey

Curriculum is the *what* of science and mathematics education. Curriculum is content—the topics, concepts, processes, and skills that students learn in science and mathematics classes—but it includes more than that. It includes the depth to which students explore content; the way teachers organize, sequence, and present it; and the textbooks and materials schools use. Perhaps most important, curriculum encompasses the substantive goals teachers intend to accomplish with the content they present (e.g., to have students gain basic facts and skills or to have them develop problem-solving strategies). Despite their obvious overlap with the domains of teaching and instructional processes, all of these dimensions are also legitimately part of curriculum. They all help define *what* the subjects are, and they all influence what science and mathematics students actually learn.

Indicators should describe all the domains of the mathematics and science curriculum so that policymakers and educators can make judgments about curricular quality. The indicators should be constructed so that these judgments can be based on comparisons among states and localities, comparisons over time, comparisons with curriculum standards set by subject-area experts (e.g., the Conference Board of Mathematical Sciences), and comparisons with what states and local districts want their students to learn. Additionally, curriculum indicators should permit analysts to track the effects of various policies on curriculum.

Few would dispute the importance of such curriculum indicators. Without them, there would not be enough information available to monitor mathematics and science education. Well-constructed outcome measures may reveal what students learned, but curriculum indicators are needed to convey what students had the *opportunity to learn.* Moreover, a "curriculum-free" indicator system might send the erroneous message to educators, parents, and students that the specifics of *what* science and mathematics knowledge schools offer do not matter very much as long as students do well on tests.

Despite their importance, curriculum indicators are not easy to develop. In this chapter we identify five curricular domains that warrant indicators: (1) breadth of content coverage, (2) depth of content coverage, (3) mode and sequence of content presentation, (4) textbook and materials used, and (5) curricular goals. We argue that indicators need to present information about each of these domains from several perspectives. We suggest four types of indicators that promise to be robust across curriculum variations. We believe these indicators will provide descriptions that policymakers and educators can use to guide curriculum policy decisions. Before we discuss the indicator development process, though, we briefly describe two of the obstacles that make this task particularly difficult.

OBSTACLES TO CURRICULUM INDICATOR DEVELOPMENT

Several different mathematics and science curricula exist, a situation that makes it difficult to get useful and comparable descriptions of what students actually experience. Students in different schools (and even different students within the same school) are taught different mathematics and science curricula. Moreover, mathematics and science curricula differ at different points in the educational system: The ideal conceptions of curriculum developers may bear little resemblance to the nitty gritty of actual classroom lessons. Two political issues exacerbate the problem of multiple curricula: a lack of national consensus about *what* the ideal curriculum should be, and a lack of agreement about *who*, if anyone, should prescribe curricula.

A second problem is posed by the limits of existing empirical evidence. The research literature provides only a limited basis for deciding what curriculum indicators would be most valid and useful.

The Multiple Curricula Problem

Schools provide different curricula for different students according to their ages, abilities, and interests. Thus, measuring the curriculum offered to one group of students at one point in time will capture only a small fragment of the total mathematics and science curricula in any school system. Indicator developers, then, must address the question of how to monitor the curricula offered to all students and the related, and perhaps more difficult, question of how to judge the appropriateness of the different curricula.

Curriculum exists in a number of different forms within the educational system—in the recommendations of subject-area experts, in state curriculum standards and requirements, in local district curriculum guides and course outlines, in textbooks and curriculum materials, in teachers' instructional plans, and in the content of classroom interactions. Since there is considerable slippage between these levels, deciding how to monitor curriculum requires careful consideration of which level or levels can provide the most important and useful information.

Differentiated Curricula. Schools differentiate their mathematics and science curricula according to students' age, abilities, and previous achievement. Age and grade differences are particularly important at the elementary school level, and ability-level distinctions become increasingly evident in secondary schools. There is considerable empirical evidence that curricula differ substantially in the concepts, topics, and skills taught, in the materials used, and in the kinds of learning tasks they include (Becker, 1983; Guthrie and Leventhal, 1985; Goodlad, 1984; McKnight et al., 1987; Oakes, 1985).

Differentiation complicates curriculum monitoring. Measuring the curriculum schools offer to one group of students will not provide accurate or useful information about the way schools parcel out their curricula to different groups. Neither would it accurately represent the content experienced by more than one segment of the student population. Yet collecting and aggregating curriculum data across all the groups in the school would produce a description of a curriculum that no student experiences.

The only entirely satisfactory solution is to develop indicators that describe separately the mathematics and science curricula that all groups of students in the school experience. The indicator system must collect and analyze data separately at more than one elementary grade level (to capture likely differences between primary and upper-grade curricula) and in secondary school courses for students on a variety of academic tracks. Even so, these indicators will not provide easily interpretable information. Just as there is considerable diversity of opinion regarding the ideal overall curriculum, there are no agreed-upon standards regarding what curriculum is most appropriate for students of different ages and different abilities.

Curricular Levels. At each point in the educational system where decisionmakers make recommendations about what science and mathematics should be offered to students, a curriculum is generated. At one level—often far removed from the actual practice of schooling—scholars and experts in the pedagogy of various subject areas conceptualize ideal curricula. These ideals often appear in scholarly publications, and they influence the ideas of educators and the content of textbooks and commercially produced curriculum materials. At a policy level, legislators, state education agency staff, accreditation associations, university admissions offices, and local district school boards formulate regulations, standards, and guidelines regarding course offerings and subject-area content. These policies usually appear in official curriculum documents. Within local school systems, district office administrators and curriculum committees typically flesh out the mandated curriculum framework into a scope and sequence of topics and skills in subjects, specific course outlines, and suggestions for lessons. At the level of lesson planning, teachers operationalize the curriculum by deciding what specific content, modes of presentation, and materials they will present to particular groups of students. Finally, at the level of the classroom, teachers create curriculum on their feet in response to the exigencies of the moment. (See Goodlad, Klein, and Tye, 1979; and Griffin, 1979, for an elaborated discussion of curricular levels.)

These different levels have consequences for monitoring, primarily because of the slippage that can occur among them. That is, the substance of the curriculum can differ significantly from one level to the next. Therefore, measuring curriculum at one level will not necessarily provide accurate or complete information about the curriculum at other levels. Course titles and official descriptions from schools may tell little about what students actually study. Teachers using the same textbooks may teach considerably different content. Unless all levels are monitored, indicators will produce an incomplete description of the curriculum.

Some observers hypothesize that knowledge about "level" differences can be useful in policymaking. Cuban, for example, argues that the different curricular levels vary in their permeability. That is, some levels are quite susceptible to change through policy initiatives, while others are more resistant (Cuban, 1979). For example, probably because states develop curriculum frameworks at some distance from actual teaching and learning, these formal frameworks change readily in response to new policy. State documents often quickly incorporate new content and approaches and emphasize new curriculum conceptions or national recommendations. At the level of the school district, curriculum is also fairly responsive. Districts fairly readily develop new courses, adopt new text materials, and establish new teacher guidelines that try to respond to new state policies or national priorities. Curriculum at the classroom instruction level, on the other hand, is quite stable. The curriculum teachers plan and implement persists over time. Even when course titles, content guidelines, and texts change, many teachers continue with what and how they have taught in the past. Curriculum behind the classroom door proves to be quite difficult to change (see Berman and McLaughlin, 1977; Fullan, 1982; Goodlad and Klein, 1970; Sirotnik, 1986).

To describe the curriculum completely, indicator systems should provide measures of all of these curricular levels. No one level provides the single key to unlocking what content teachers teach or how curriculum changes. We have some evidence that teachers make curricular choices based, more than anything else, on their own background and experience, and on their views of their students' interests and abilities (Klein, 1980). Yet teachers make these content decisions within the parameters of the institutional, formal, and ideal curricula. These other levels undoubtedly constrain the decisions teachers make, since it is probably not often that science and mathematics teachers introduce content *outside* of district and state curricula. More likely, they choose to include, emphasize, or exclude particular content from that available in textbooks, materials, and formal guidelines. Unfortunately, we have little information to document these curriculum decisionmaking processes or the extent of curriculum slippage from one level to the next.

Multilevel curriculum monitoring could document the effects of various curriculum sources on classroom practice and could answer the following kinds of questions: What curriculum represents the officially adopted policies of states and local districts? What curriculum do adopted texts and materials include? What curriculum characterizes classroom practice? Where are there consistencies and inconsistencies among various curricular levels? Where is the slippage most likely to occur? These data could lead to well-informed curriculum policymaking.

Operationally, however, an ideal monitoring system would have to include parallel measures for state curriculum frameworks and standards, district curriculum guides, adopted textbooks, teachers' instructional plans, and classroom instruction. Data collection and analyses would require different methods at different levels. For example, data about curriculum development and planning can be collected through interviews and questionnaires from officials in state agencies, local district administrators, and teachers, but state and district curriculum frameworks and textbooks require content analyses. Observation and journal-keeping are probably the best methods for collecting data at the point of instruction in classrooms. Moreover, given the age and tracking differentiations of the curriculum noted earlier, all of these data would be needed for several groups of students within each system. Complicating matters further, few adequate measures exist for measuring the curriculum at any level.

We will not pursue further the requirements for developing a *comprehensive* set of curriculum indicators. By now, the point must be clear: Substantial new measures and procedures for assessment will have to be developed. However, even a quite elaborate monitoring system will require compromises about the curriculum indicators to include. Even with the best measures, a system including indicators of all of the above would be costly and likely to collapse under its own weight. We suggest later what those compromises might be.

Multiple Curricula and Curriculum Politics. Indicator developers acknowledge two critical and interrelated political issues as they contend with the problems of multiple mathematics and science curricula. The first is the lack of a national consensus about what (and for whom) science and mathematics curricula ought to be. This is a major concern, since the definition of what curriculum should be is inextricably linked with views of what education itself should be. The second issue is the problem of who should have the responsibility for developing indicators, given the diversity of views about what they ought to be.

There is considerable disagreement about what the mathematics and science curricula should be. While nearly all educational professionals and concerned citizens will rally around calls for better course content, for updating textbooks to reflect scientific advances, or for placing greater emphasis on higher-order thinking, when it comes to the specifics, there is a substantial lack of a consensus about ideal curriculum (Hurd, 1986). Moreover, conceptions of the best curriculum change over time. For example, from the mid-1950s to the mid-1960s, the perceived Soviet threat to American scientific prowess led to calls for a heavy emphasis on basic science and mathematics disciplines—that is, teaching science and mathematics as scientists and mathematicians performed them at the time. Yet, in the more domestically focused decade that followed, self-actualizing (e.g., minicourses, exploratory experiences) and socially relevant approaches (e.g., ecologically, ethnically, and culturally focused studies) became major curricular influences. Now, we see a trend toward a cognitive-processes approach partly in reaction to disappointing achievement scores in problem-solving and critical thinking. Some reformers embrace this approach as they look to recent work in cognitive science as a basis for developing curricula (e.g., National Science Board, 1983). One study, however, *Project 2061: Phase I, "What understanding of science and technology will be important for everyone in tomorrow's world?"* (American Association for the Advancement of Science, 1985), is an example of a current curriculum project reflecting a social-relevance perspective, in that its central question is, What science should all citizens know to function well and make good public decisions in the future? The diversity of conceptions of the ideal curriculum, how conceptions of the ideal change over time, and the implications for science and mathematics have been the topic of considerable scholarly work (Berliner, 1979; Eisner and Vallance, 1974; Gay, 1980; Prakash and Waks, 1985; Shane and Tabler, 1981). Essentially, however, the lack of curricular consensus and changing emphases affect the development of curriculum indicators in two important ways. First, judgments about what to measure are inextricably related to how values-based questions such as, What is worth knowing? are answered. Second, a deeply-rooted national tradition supporting local control and curricular diversity makes any federal involvement in answering these questions problematic (Boyd, 1979; Noddings, 1979).

Paralleling the problem of the lack of consensus about what the science and mathematics curriculum *ought to be* are conflicts about the appropriate role of the federal government in influencing school curricula. The implementation of a set of national science and mathematics curriculum indicators will undoubtedly raise the specter of a national science and mathematics curriculum. The prospect of federal development of *any* single set of curriculum indicators is particularly troublesome.

Historically, states and localities have cherished their constitutionally protected right to determine the content of schooling and preserve their differences—even though the differences may be largely illusory. Matters of textbook selection and course development are usually left to local districts—sometimes within a set of state-approved choices. Moreover, there is considerable individual school and teacher discretion in how materials are used and courses designed. National curriculum indicators threaten the exercise of local discretion and the local control that maintains it.

Given this sensitivity to local interests (compounded by the lack of national consensus about ideal curriculum content), it would be unwise to adopt any set of curriculum indicators without careful consideration of the political implications of doing so. Many will see curriculum indicators as reflecting arbitrary federal preferences and will interpret their development as an effort to impose a nationalized curriculum in mathematics and science. If state and local policymakers or educators challenge the legitimacy of indicators, they may resist—and even subvert—indicator development and implementation.

Determining Effective Curricula: The Limits of Empirical Studies

There is very little research literature that attempts to identify effective curricula. Typically, expert opinion and tradition, rather than empirical findings, have guided choices about what curricula to offer students. Moreover, in those studies that have compared the effectiveness of specific curriculum designs (sequenced steps toward skill mastery, or individualized learning approaches in mathematics, for example), researchers have found few advantages to particular designs. A more typical conclusion is that there are both strengths and weaknesses in any curriculum design or structure (Fey, 1982).

However, some empirical work has demonstrated that "new science curricula" (those developed after 1955) have a more positive effect on student achievement and attitudes than traditional approaches (Shymansky, Kyle, and Allport, 1983). The new curricula (including many sponsored the National Science Foundation (NSF)) emphasize the structure of science, integrate laboratory activities with knowledge acquisition, and stress better cognitive skills. Their creators have tried to diverge from traditional science curricula's emphasis on facts, laws, theories, and more tangential laboratory work.

The existing empirical studies are of limited use for indicator development. First, their focus has generally been on the effectiveness of *the total curriculum* rather than the contribution of particular curricular elements (e.g., content, emphases, or design features) to student results. Also, few of the studies controlled for the fidelity with which the new curricula were implemented. Most often, the only criterion for inclusion in these evaluation studies was whether or not a pre- or post-1955 curriculum was adopted; there was no consideration of whether curricula were being implemented in new or traditional ways. While there is undoubtedly some overlap, the studies can tell us only about outcomes related to the formal curriculum level, not to the curriculum actually experienced in classrooms.

However, a more fundamental and obvious problem is that the *form and content of the outcome measures used in studies linking particular curricular dimensions to student outcomes will nearly always dictate which curriculum emerges as most effective.* In other words, the curriculum identified as most powerful for particular results will almost invariably be the curriculum that is most closely aligned to the content and processes assessed. Therefore, even if a wealth of curriculum effectiveness studies existed, they would offer little more than circular arguments for means of achieving one or another set of science and mathematics results. This would not be a major problem if there were universal agreement about what science and mathematics results are most desired. But, as noted earlier, opinions vary.

Curriculum indicator selection and development, then, must begin at a more primitive level. We must determine what the central domains of curriculum are, make judgments about the value of reporting these domains as indicators, and then suggest which specific curriculum variables should be measured to provide indicators of these central domains. In the process, indicator developers must recognize the pluralism of the curriculum in American schools and select indicators that allow for legitimate differences in curricula. The data should provide comparable, descriptive information about key curricular elements common to all schools—no easy task.

DEFINING CURRICULUM DOMAINS: TARGETS FOR INDICATORS

The conventionally accepted definition of curriculum is *content.* Typically, the content of a subject area includes the concepts, topics, and skills that make up the substance of the subject. Science, for example, includes broad content subdivisions (e.g., earth science, physical science, biological science); mathematics typically includes such major subdivisions as number theory, arithmetic, algebra, geometry, probability and statistics, and calculus. Within each of these major subareas, extensive sets of concepts, topics, and skills constitute the content of these subjects. Content, then, is a central and easily agreed-upon domain of curriculum.

But students experience science and mathematics differently depending on the depth to which they explore particular content, the mode and sequence of teachers' presentations, and the materials teachers use to help convey subject matter. Perhaps most important, teachers' goals drive the curriculum—what they hope to accomplish as they present science and mathematics content. A system of curriculum indicators must account for all these important domains if policymakers are to better understand *what* science and mathematics students are given an opportunity to learn, and whether reforms should be targeted at particular curricular elements.

Breadth of Content Coverage

One target for an indicator system, then, is to describe the range of science and mathematics topics and skills being offered to students. We can justify indicators of this aspect on both empirical and logical grounds. Considerable empirical research reinforces our intuitive sense that what teachers teach influences what students learn (Crosswhite et al., 1985; Husen, 1967; McKnight et al., 1987; Wolf, 1977).

At the most basic level, elementary and secondary students' science and mathematics achievement depends on whether schools expose them to these topics and skills (e.g., Welch, Anderson, and Harris, 1982). The International Association for the Evaluation of Educational Achievement (IEA) showed that U.S. students fell progressively further behind those of other countries as their opportunities to learn the topics covered on a science test diminished (e.g., Wolf, 1977; McKnight et al., 1987). At the secondary school level, both the *number* and *type* of courses students take are related to achievement. Horn and Walberg's (1984) analysis of mathematics achievement data for 1,480 seventeen-year-olds who participated in the National Assessment of Educational Progress (NAEP) provides ample evidence of the influence of coursetaking. For example, students taking a relatively advanced course such as analytic geometry exhibited greater achievement than those taking classes in elementary algebra. A Wisconsin Center for Education Research analysis of High School and Beyond data (cited in Raizen and Jones, 1985) showed that the number of mathematics courses taken influences achievement even when race, sex, previous mathematics achievement, and socioeconomic status (SES) are controlled for.

These findings imply that curriculum indicators should include measures of the range of mathematics and science content schools offer to students. At the grossest level, these indicators will give an overview of students' "opportunity to learn" these subjects.

Depth of Content Coverage

However, measuring the range of content covered will not measure students' opportunity to learn various dimensions of mathematics and science. More problematic, indicators that simply report whether or not students have covered particular content will provide policymakers with few clues about why some schools, districts, or states that cover the same topics achieve quite different results. Consequently, indicators should also report the depth to which teachers have students explore mathematics and science content. This can help policymakers judge whether the curriculum can help students develop an *understanding* of mathematics and science.

The apparent simplicity of developing content coverage indicators (e.g., checklists of whether students are taught particular topics and skills) disappears when we attempt to assess and report the depth of content. The task becomes exceedingly difficult if we wish to juxtapose the depth of coverage offered with the depth that particular students need to *understand*.

The central problem of developing indicators of whether the curriculum provides the depth of coverage required for understanding is the constructive nature of knowledge in science and mathematics. Students do not just absorb information, but actively construct an understanding of the concepts presented to them (Osborne and Wittrock, 1983; Wittrock, 1974). Students compare what they see and hear in class with their previous conceptions (Fig. 5.1), so when science and mathematics concepts differ from pupils' previous understanding, instruction can fail miserably: Students may read the textbook or perform the experiment without constructing a correct understanding of the concepts being covered. Anderson and Smith (1986) cite the answers of four fifth-grade students on a test administered before and after a widely used six-week unit on "producers." In this unit, students participated in a series of experiments and discussions designed to teach them that plants do not consume food, but produce it through the process of photosynthesis. Only 7 percent of 213 students correctly learned the idea that plants get food solely by making it themselves (Roth, Smith, and Anderson, 1983). The students' previous conceptions that all living things ingest food was in conflict with the point of the science unit—and the misconception clearly prevailed for the majority of the students.

Results such as those reported by Anderson and Smith (1986) are common. Students experience conceptual difficulties at both secondary and elementary levels in many scientific fields (e.g., Driver and Easley, 1978; Driver and Erickson, 1983; Gilbert and Watts, 1983). For example, pupils have misconceptions concerning the concepts of force (Champagne, Klopfer, and Gunstone, 1982; Clement, 1982), gravity (Watts, 1982), electricity (Osborne, 1981), and living (Brumby, 1981).

The research cited above primarily involves students' understanding of scientific concepts, but students can also have difficulty understanding procedures. For example, Erlwanger (1975) conducted a case study with "Benny," an elementary school child whose classroom had adopted an individualized curriculum. Students moved at their own pace, taking instructional units that began with a pretest, followed by instructional materials and a posttest. Benny was making superior progress in this program, and his teacher considered him to be one of the best pupils in the class. But Benny said that 2/1 plus 1/2 equals 1, and 2/10 expressed as a decimal was 1.2. Further discussions with Benny revealed that Benny had idiosyncratic and erroneous ideas

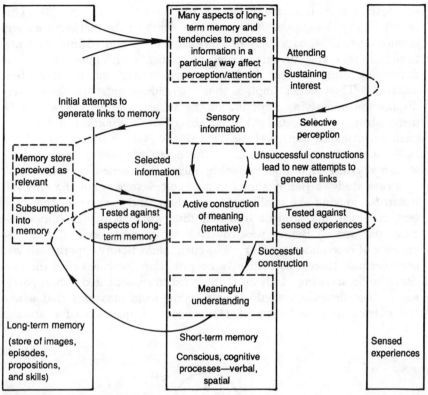

Source: Osborne and Wittrock, 1983.

Fig. 5.1—Representation of how children learn science concepts

about mathematics which he believed worked like "magic, because really they're just different answers which we think they're different but really they're the same" (p. 173). Although he used these ideas to justify results such as $1 = 4/4$ or $1 = 1/2 + 1/4 + 1/4$, he also used them to justify $4/11 = 1.5$ or $11/4 = 1.5$. The finding that children develop their own maladaptive understandings and procedures in mathematics is not unique to Erlwanger's work. Brown and associates (Brown and Burton, 1978; Brown and Van Lehn, 1980) demonstrated that children's errors in subtraction are rule-governed and might be considered analogous to faulty computer algorithms.

Resnick (1976) proposed a model of covering arithmetic concepts by bringing together the "structure of the task as defined by the subject matter, the performance of skilled individuals on a task, and a teaching or acquisition routine that helps novices learn the task" (p. 73). This model (Fig. 5.2) suggests that we cannot think of the mathematics and science curriculum as a body of knowledge to be poured into students' heads. Rather, the curriculum presents students with opportunities for developing bridges which lead to mature understandings of content material. This model implies that curriculum must (1) adequately display the underlying structure of the subject matter, (2) be easy to demonstrate or teach, and (3) be capable of transformation into an efficient performance routine (Resnick, 1976, p. 74).

What do these observations on the depth of coverage required for students' conceptual understanding mean for curriculum indicators? The case study of Benny shows that topic coverage is not the only criterion for judging the quality of curriculum, and it suggests that content coverage and student understanding are not always compatible curricular goals. Benny was covering topics quite well, but at the expense of true understanding. The curriculum Benny experienced was poor because there was evidently no provision for checks on the students' understanding. Indicators intended to report the depth of coverage in the curriculum would have to come from measures that assess the curriculum's inclusion of (1) conceptual questions for student

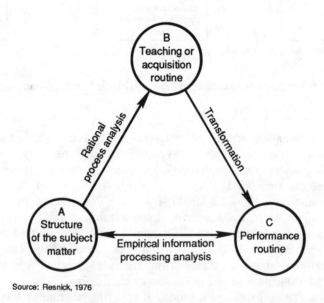

Source: Resnick, 1976

Fig. 5.2—Relations among teaching routines,
performance routines, and structure of subject matter

exploration, (2) a variety of concept interpretations, and (3) challenges to students' current misconceptions about science and mathematics.

Mode and Sequence of Presentation

A third central element of the mathematics and science curriculum is how content is sequenced and the mode in which teachers and texts present it to students. This dimension is critical to whether students have an opportunity to learn mathematics and science as simply series of facts and rules, or as tools for solving problems in the real world. For example, Schoenfeld (1983) suggests that many teachers present science and mathematics content-related tasks to children as mere exercises, rather than as problems they can solve. For example, a problem is only a *real problem* (as mathematicians use the term) if you don't know how to go about solving it. A problem that holds no surprises and that students can solve comfortably by routine or familiar procedures (no matter how difficult!) is an *exercise*. This latter description applies to most of the "word problems" that students encounter in elementary school, and to "mixture problems," "rate problems," or other standard parts of the secondary curriculum (Schoenfeld, 1983, p. 41).

Even if students are being exposed to real problems, indicators are needed to show the degree to which students have opportunities to learn to use heuristics and an organized approach to solving problems. Polya (e.g., 1957, 1962, 1965) has proposed that mathematics students need to learn heuristics or actions that assist in the discovery of a problem solution, stating that "heuristical reasoning is reasoning not regarded as final and strict but as provisional and plausible only, whose purpose is to discover the solution of the present problem" (Polya, 1965, p. 113).

Suydam (1980) has reviewed the literature on teaching heuristics and writes that "research evidence strongly concurs that problem-solving performance is strongly enhanced by teaching students to use a wide variety of strategies or heuristics, both general and specific" (p. 43). Lester's (1980) review provides a less positive interpretation of the evidence, while Schoenfeld's (1982) summary suggests that the better-controlled studies provide evidence favoring heuristic training. He proposes that students need not only a group of problem-solving heuristics, but also a "managerial strategy" to budget time efficiently and prevent "wild goose chases."

Schoenfeld's conclusions suggest that an important indicator of curriculum would report the degree to which mathematics and science content includes presentation modes that emphasize heuristics and managerial strategies—strategies used by experts. In a study that sheds light on this type of indicator, Larkin et al. (1980b) compared the problem-solving strategies and managerial skills of novices and experts in solving physics problems. The experts differed from the novices in their *perception* of the problem. The novices were bound to the concrete characteristics of particular questions, while the experts developed more abstract representations which allowed them to disregard irrelevant aspects of the problems and prevent "wild goose chases." The experts looked at the particular problem by reference to its structural properties, which also allowed them to use less of their memory capacity in remembering relevant aspects of the problem (e.g., Simon, 1979).

This review suggests that curriculum indicators should provide information about the degree to which students experience the curriculum in a problem-solving mode rather than as exercises that are relatively straightforward translations of procedures. A curriculum emphasizing problem solving would have a rather flexible approach to the sequencing and pacing of topics. The implication is that rather than having students proceed through a preset series of topics and skills, teachers should view those who are "stuck" as in an honorable state—a state that provides an opportunity to bring in other ideas, and a major avenue for improving one's understanding and thinking.

If a monitoring system is to provide information about the mode of presentation and sequencing of curriculum, particularly in relation to students' development of problem-solving abilities, the following might be useful indicators: (1) the number of problems presented that are not straightforward applications of the textbook; (2) the number of problem-solving heuristics presented to students; (3) the number of times students redo homework problems to learn them in a more optimal manner; (4) the number of times students are expected to explain the managerial strategies they use in solving problems; (5) opportunities for hands-on, learning-by-doing engagement with content; and (6) teachers' flexibility with the sequencing of content.

Textbooks and Materials Used

A fourth central element of curriculum is the array of textbooks and other curriculum materials used by teachers to convey subject matter. Textbooks and curriculum materials both offer explicit suggestions for science and mathematics lessons, and they influence teachers' content selection. Of all the sources of subject-matter knowledge (e.g., treatises by subject-area scholars, recommendations of professional organizations, state and district curriculum guides, etc.), texts are closest to the classroom. Moreover, mathematics and science teachers cite textbooks and other commercially produced curriculum materials as important influences on content selection (Klein, 1980; Stake and Easley, 1978; Weiss, 1978). Consequently, they should be targeted for indicator development. Some work in this area provides models and concepts to guide analysis (Armbruster and Anderson, 1981; Deese, 1981; Kuhs et al., 1979; Walker, 1981). However, most efforts to assess textbooks do not produce sufficient quantifiable information for useful indicator development.

Goals

The final central element of curriculum that we recommend for indicator development is the goals teachers have for their students in science and mathematics. Despite the variations in curriculum noted earlier (e.g., among different age and ability levels), recent studies suggest that the actual range of topics schools present in the mathematics and science curricula may be quite narrow (Freeman et al., 1983a; 1983b; Goodlad, 1984). Other work suggests that students in most schools may spend most of their time in both subjects studying low-level terminology, facts, and operations (Romberg, 1983; Rowe, 1983).

Despite the similarity in content coverage, schools and individual teachers appear to disagree about the goals of science and mathematics education: Should students study mathematics and science to gain fundamental concepts and master basic skills? Should students study these subjects to become more interested in them? Should students learn knowledge that will help them prepare for further study in science and mathematics? Should these subjects help students develop problem-solving or inquiry processes? Should they help students to better understand and solve the problems of daily life? And so on. Which of these goals are most important will affect decisions about the other curricular elements. For example, a recent analysis of fourth-grade textbooks and standardized achievement tests in mathematics found the degree of emphasis on conceptual understanding, skill mastery, and applications to be quite different (Freeman et al., 1983a), and teachers using the same texts or curricular guidelines emphasized quite different aspects of the included material (Freeman et al., 1983b; Berliner, 1979). Therefore, indicators of curricular goals will provide useful clues to policymakers about influences on other curricular elements.

TOWARD A USEFUL AND MANAGEABLE SET OF CURRICULUM INDICATORS

Ideally, curriculum indicators should provide information about the range of content covered, the depth to which each topic is presented, the mode and sequence of presentation, the text and materials teachers use, and teachers' curricular goals. These indicators should span the range of curricular levels—from ideal conceptions, to curriculum policy, to formal planning by schools and teachers, to classroom experiences. Additionally, indicators at different ages and for students of differing abilities should provide information about the age at which various curricula are taught, and what curricula schools offer to students identified as more and less able in these subjects.

The intent of this section is to specify what indicators would provide the most useful information about the curricular domains identified above. First, we will define a comprehensive set of indicators that would capture a great deal of useful information. Then we will suggest a more limited set that, given the current limited "state of the art" of curriculum measurement, can provide the most useful and manageable benchmarks about the science and mathematics curriculum.

Ideally, we recommend the following four types of curriculum indicators:

- *Curriculum policy indicators* to provide information about the curricula states and local districts are attempting to implement.
- *Curriculum practice indicators* to describe the range of curricula covered in classrooms.
- *Curriculum materials "quality" indicators* to assess the match of extant curriculum with expert opinion.
- *State- and locally-developed indicators to augment national indicators with specific curriculum information of local concern*—e.g., matters of content coverage, approaches, depth, sequence, and emphasis related to local goals.

Curriculum Policy Indicators

The first set of curriculum indicators will provide quantitative data about generic curricular policies in all states and local districts, and at the state, local education agency, and school levels. They will describe the general nature of those policies (as reflected in state, LEA, and school legislation, regulations, guidelines, or other formal curriculum documents) and can serve as indicators for national description and comparisons.

- **Content:** The extent to which states, districts, and schools set policies regarding the content of mathematics and science education and the emphasis placed on the following types of content: (1) number and types of courses required (at the secondary level); (2) time on subjects at the elementary level; (3) specification of major content areas and/or concepts, processes, and skills. The following are examples of major content areas:

  - *Science*: life science, earth science, physical science.
  - *Mathematics*: whole number arithmetic, spatial relations, measurement, fractions, coordinate geometry, algebra, and statistics.
  - *Technology*: awareness (literacy), use (word processing, etc.), and instructional aids such as computer-assisted instruction (CAI).

- **Sequencing:** Policies regarding sequencing of courses and within-class content—e.g., whether content is sequenced according to behavioral psychological learning principles (e.g., Gagne, 1968), historical development (Tyler, 1949), or spiraling of organizing elements and themes (Bruner, 1960; Goodlad, 1979), or is presented as real problems (Schoenfeld, 1983; Polya, 1965).

- **Mode of presentation:** What policies states, districts, and schools set regarding the mode of mathematics and science education (e.g., presented as facts students should learn or as problems they can solve) and the extent to which lectures, texts, and activity-, field-, or laboratory-based experiences are mandated.

- **Textbooks and materials:** The extent to which states, districts, and schools set policies or guidelines for the adoption of textbooks and curriculum materials and the type of policies used. Two types are particularly relevant: (1) the extent to which written materials (textbooks, activity cards, work sheets, student writing) and laboratory or manipulative "hands on" materials) are used, and (2) the extent to which teachers and/or curriculum specialists use subject-area experts, curriculum guides, textbooks, other materials, and their own background and experience as content sources in planning and implementing curriculum.

- **Goals/objectives:** The policies states and districts set regarding the goals and objectives for mathematics and science education, and the extent to which they include (1) understanding fundamental science and mathematics concepts and procedures, (2) coverage of basic knowledge and skills, (3) the development of problem-solving skills, (4) awareness of the role of science in contemporary life, (5) developing positive attitudes, (6) encouraging involvement and participation, and (7) awareness of and opportunities to pursue science-, mathematics-, and technology-related career options.

- **Curriculum differentiation:** The policies that are set regarding prerequisite course requirements, the use of ability-grouped classes, and the provision of remediation and enrichment opportunities. These indicators would describe the extent to which *all* students have access to the mathematics and science curriculum, and also the extent to which the core curriculum is buttressed with advanced materials and experiences for students with special interests, and supplementary materials and experiences for students needing additional support in science and mathematics.

Curriculum Practice Indicators

Curriculum practice indicators are global indicators of the curriculum *actually in place* at the classroom level; they report the same elements as the policy indicators above. These descriptive data are also appropriate for national descriptions and comparisons.

- **Breadth of content coverage:** Teachers' coverage of particular topics, processes, and skills.
- **Depth of content coverage:** The depth to which teachers cover particular topics, processes, and skills.
- **Sequencing:** The order in which topics are presented in the classroom or the ordering of courses available to students.
- **Mode of presentation:** The frequency with which teachers employ factual presentation and/or problem-solving strategies in science and mathematics (e.g., lecture, paper-and-pencil, problem-solving, or learn-by-doing activities such as lab-based, activity-based, or field-based approaches).
- **Textbooks and materials:** The textbooks and materials teachers use; the recency of curriculum materials; the percentage of the text covered during the course or year; and teachers' judgments of the suitability of the texts.
- **Goals and objectives:** The extent teachers emphasize various curriculum goals and objectives in science and mathematics classes.

These curriculum policy and curriculum practice indicators are likely to be robust across diverse conceptions of the curriculum and across local variations in curricular emphasis and should remain relevant even as specific content and emphases change over time. As such, they permit description and comparison of sustaining curricular elements and allow tracking of non-trivial changes in what science and mathematics students are learning and of changes that follow the adoption of new policies.

Policymakers and educators could also use these indicator data to determine where curricular consensus exists and where there is diversity in judgment and practice. However, we must exercise considerable caution when using these data for comparing curriculum *quality* in states and local schools. The indicators will not capture essential curriculum details, so they can compare and track only the most general curricular differences and policy effects.

Second, because these data would report the inclusion of particular curriculum specifics, their comparative use could encourage a counterproductive quantitative view of curriculum quality. That is, results could easily be interpreted to mean "more is better"—i.e., the curriculum that covers the *most* topics and skills is the *best* curriculum. Administrators and teachers could be pressed by these comparisons into emphasizing content coverage rather than depth of understanding, a trend that is already of considerable concern to many science educators (see, for example, Rowe, 1983; Yager, 1981a).

Models for some curriculum practice indicators exist in the Classroom Process Questionnaires developed for the Second International Mathematics Study (IEA, 1980) and in measures developed by the Ontario Assessment Instrument Pool (McLean, 1985). (See Blank and Raizen, 1985, for a more detailed discussion of curriculum content measures.) The IEA also used questions about the number of problem-solving approaches in its Second Study of Mathematics.

Most of these indicators, however, require much developmental work. For example, no current indicators measure the depth of coverage in a way that reveals whether students are likely to develop conceptual understanding. Such indicators would probably need to focus on the curriculum's inclusion of (1) a focus on conceptual questions, (2) presentation of a variety of concept interpretations, and (3) challenges to students' misconceptions. Their development will require considerable pathbreaking work. Similar difficulties will plague the development of most of the indicators suggested here.

Curriculum Quality Indicators

Curriculum quality indicators would report expert assessments of the quality of the formal curriculum as represented in state, district, and school curriculum guides, and in the most widely used commercially produced textbooks and curriculum materials. These data would permit assessing the match of the extant curriculum to a consensus of expert opinion of the ideal. Three quality indicators are proposed:

- **Scientific accuracy of curriculum content:** How well the curriculum reflects scientific and mathematical knowledge as judged by an expert panel of scientists and mathematicians, science and mathematics curriculum scholars, cognitive psychologists, educational policymakers, and practitioners.
- **Congruence of curriculum with "expert" judgment:** How well the curriculum reflects the opinions of an expert panel of scientists and mathematicians, science and mathematics curriculum scholars, cognitive psychologists, policymakers, and practitioners regarding the inclusion of and emphasis given to various goals and objectives, concepts, processes, and skills.
- **Pedagogical appropriateness of curriculum content:** How well the curriculum matches the cognitive needs of students as judged by an expert panel of scientists and mathematicians, science and mathematics curriculum scholars, cognitive psychologists, educational policymakers, and practitioners.

Textbook quality stands out as a particularly crucial curricular domain. Textbooks are arguably the single most important influence on many teachers' choice of exercises (e.g., Freeman et al., 1983a,b); National Advisory Committee on Mathematics Education, 1975). Thus an essential consideration is whether textbooks present conceptually correct explanations. Warren (1979, App. 2) includes several pages of inaccurate or misleading quotations from physics textbooks.

The congruence of texts with experts' views of the science and mathematics curriculum can provide an important evaluative framework for selecting texts. This is particularly important, since textbooks vary greatly in the degree to which they overlap with standardized achievement tests on the intent of the problems they present (conceptual understanding or application), the topics covered, and the operations required (Freeman et al., 1983a,b); see Table 5.1.

In addition to knowing the content and procedures covered by textbooks, it would also be useful to know the degree to which a particular text stresses thinking skills. Akers (1984) suggests that the following

Table 5.1

PERCENTAGE OF TEST OVERLAP WHEN TEACHER USES VARIOUS METHODS OF DELETING MATERIAL FROM TEXTBOOKS[a]

Test (items)	Total Book (209/69)	Textbook, Bound (157/47)	Selective Omission (168/52)	Basics With Measurement (167/59)	Basics Without Measurement (150/54)	Management by Objectives (23/13)
CTBS-I (98)						
S_1	86.7	83.7	86.7	82.7	79.6	45.9
S_2	62.2	61.2	62.2	61.2	60.2	40.8
CTBS-II (98)						
S_1	86.7	75.5	79.6	81.6	76.5	31.6
S_2	50.0	39.8	40.8	48.0	46.9	24.5
Iowa (104)						
S_1	79.8	74.0	74.0	76.0	75.0	40.4
S_2	53.8	50.0	50.0	52.9	51.9	35.6
Metropolitan (50)						
S_1	88.0	70.0	68.0	82.0	72.0	18.0
S_2	60.0	48.0	60.0	58.0	46.0	18.0
Stanford (112)						
S_1	63.4	60.7	59.8	58.0	57.1	23.2
S_2	35.7	31.3	31.3	32.1	30.4	17.9

SOURCE: Freeman et al., 1983.

[a]Numbers of S_1/S_2 items are shown in parentheses; S_1 = test items that focus on *topics that satisfy the minimum standard* (i.e., topics covered by 3 or more textbooks; S_2 = test items that focus on *emphasized topics* (i.e., topics covered by 20 or more textbook problems).

questions be asked of textbooks:

1. *Are there problems that require students to think about and analyze situations?* Aker suggests that as an alternative to word problems that require simple computations, textbooks should include some thought problems. For example, texts might ask students who are learning fractions to evaluate statements according to whether they make sense, such as, "One-half of the students are boys, and two-thirds of the students are girls," or "One-half of the students are boys, and two-thirds of the students are wearing jeans."

2. *Does the text feature sets of problems that call for more than one arithmetic operation?* Textbooks often ask for repeated applications of the same operation without requiring students to choose which operations are actually appropriate.

3. *Are there problems that contain extraneous and/or insufficient information?* For example, very large proportions of 9- and

13-year-olds can be confused by the question, "One rabbit eats 2 pounds of food each week. There are 52 weeks in a year. How much food will 5 rabbits eat in one week?" Apparently the addition of the irrelevant information about the number of weeks in a year made the problem difficult for students.

4. *Are problems with more than one correct solution included?*
5. *Are there opportunities for students to use their own data and create their own problems?*
6. *Are students encouraged to use a variety of approaches to solve each problem?*
7. *Does the textbook encourage students to estimate their answers and to check their results?*
8. *Is a problem-solving approach used to teach all strands of the mathematical program?* (Akers, 1984, pp. 34–35).

Finally, curriculum materials quality indicators will help to evaluate the pedagogical appropriateness of the curriculum, i.e., how well the content presented matches the cognitive and other (e.g., motivational, cultural) needs of students. In particular, do the selection and presentation of content take into account students' mental models of science and mathematics concepts and processes? As noted earlier, the degree to which students are able to understand scientific concepts is affected by their previous understandings of these concepts. If their prior conceptions are quite different from those being presented, students may learn to answer questions about concepts correctly or perform experiments accurately, without understanding the meaning of what they are "learning." Unless curriculum explicitly confronts students' current conceptions, their faulty understanding of propositions and procedures is likely to persist. Thus, the degree to which the curriculum builds bridges that lead the student from naive or erroneous conceptions to mature understanding is of paramount importance.

Local Emphasis Indicators

A fourth set of indicators would assist state and local policymaking and improvement efforts. This set would include "empty slots" that states and local school districts could develop into indicators of their own curriculum priorities and special emphases. This would signal national support for and legitimacy of curricular diversity and would provide curriculum-relevant data for comparison of local programs with local standards, as well as the monitoring of local curricula over time. Locally generated data are likely to be *used* for program improvement. A model for local indicator development is California's Quality

Indicator project, where districts select local indicators to fill out the information provided in the state profile (California State Department of Education, 1984b).

Curriculum evaluation work suggests that national, state, and local collaboration can generate accurate and useful data collection and allay worries about the imposition of national indicators. (See Baker, 1984, for a discussion of a combined "top-down/bottom-up" approach to educational evaluation.) However, without a great deal of support and technical assistance, local educators are unlikely to develop indicators or use them productively. The federal government could identify models to guide state and local indicator development, and states could provide the technical assistance required to actually produce the desired indicators.

Curriculum Indicators: First Priorities

The indicators recommended above should be minimally implemented as follows. First, while all of the curricular levels are essential for understanding what mathematics and science schools teach, the "implemented" curriculum is the most important, since that is what students experience. Whether state and district policies are directed at particular sequences of concepts, processes, topics, and skills makes relatively little difference *if students are not experiencing that curriculum in classrooms*. The danger, of course, is that assessing only the implemented curriculum may lead the unsophisticated to assume that teachers are the sole determinants of content quality and that they make decisions independent of other curricular levels. Nevertheless, monitoring the curriculum in classroom lessons will provide the most useful information about what content students have an opportunity to learn.

Operationally, curriculum practice indicators must have top priority. Observation would provide the most accurate data about the curriculum of the classroom, but it is not practically possible to observe the curriculum in schools across the nation. The resources required to conduct observational data-collecting for an entire school year in more than a very small sample of schools would be staggering, and data analysis would be an equally horrendous task. A more reasonable approach, then, would be to ask teachers to report what curriculum they teach during the year. Teachers are a better data source than students in this regard, since students can report only what they have already experienced (if they recognize it in the terms we might ask them) and cannot project to the end of the school year.

Developing curriculum practice measures will require considerable new research, since these constructs have not been the focus of data collection efforts. An essential component will be validation studies to determine the accuracy of teacher reports. The IEA instruments (IEA, 1980) include examples of items asking teachers about specific content coverage and depth that provide good models. A more elaborate monitoring system could supplement teacher surveys with observational data during a specified time period in a smaller sample of classes.

Curriculum materials quality indicators should also be a top priority for monitoring, even though they will require extensive developmental work that is likely to be costly, cumbersome, and time-consuming. Most previous textbook analyses have attended only to the scope and sequence of content and skills and stylistic features of texts, ignoring the other essential issues outlined earlier. Curriculum materials quality indicators will provide information that can assist policymakers in selecting textbooks and in linking textbooks in use, teaching and instruction, and student outcomes.

Finally, curriculum practice and curriculum quality indicators must be measured at more than one elementary grade level (perhaps one grade each in grades K-3 and 4-6) and for various secondary ability and achievement levels. No composite picture can accurately describe the differentiated mathematics, science, and technology curricula in the nations' schools. Information is needed about (1) mathematics and science curriculum at the primary (K-3) and intermediate (4-6) elementary grade level; (2) mathematics and science experienced by students in high-, average-, and low-ability classes at the junior high school/middle school level; and (3) the content of college-preparatory and non-college-preparatory courses at the senior high school level.

Our recommendations for indicators do not resolve these concerns. However generic the indicators, specific items will measure whether or not certain content areas are covered, the extent to which they are covered, how they are presented, etc. These will not be open-ended items that might convey an equality among responses. Rather, they will more likely be checklists. For example, questionnaire items like the following could be used for gathering quantifiable data:

- Please indicate which of the following topics you taught this year (followed by a list of topics).
- Please indicate for each of the following skills taught, whether you (a) introduced students to the skill, (b) expected students to exhibit mastery of skill, or (c) expected students to apply the skill in novel circumstances.

- Please list the number of laboratory experiments students conducted in this class during the past month.

Such questions (even if developers intend them to produce descriptive, non-evaluative data) send messages about what curriculum is valued.

SUMMARY AND CONCLUSIONS

Historically, curriculum evaluation has been performed at the local level and rests on the assumption that some consensus exists about curricular goals and processes. That consensus comes either from expert judgments or from stakeholder preferences. But although curriculum evaluation usually focuses on the identified areas of agreement (see Hamilton, 1981), few grounds exist for assuming national consensus regarding the *most critical* content, sequences, and modes of presentation. Nor can we be confident that we could easily reach such a consensus or that reaching it would be perceived as a legitimate federal activity. A nationwide consensus of expert opinion would probably diverge considerably from local practice; further, many would view it as an imposition of a national curriculum. While a consensus might be developed among local practitioners regarding some curricular areas, those areas might not be the most critical for comparing curricula over time or with some standards of curricular quality. Further, stakeholder consensus is likely to exist only at such a general level that the information gained would be of little use in monitoring.

Despite the apparent inappropriateness of any individual approach, together the approaches described in this chapter provide a useful guide for curriculum indicator development. Although there is little national consensus about curricular specifics, there are some generic dimensions of curricular *policies and practices* that, if measured in states, districts, and schools could provide a core of descriptive information about curriculum *without assuming any particular evaluative stance.* These policies include broad curricular parameters—content breadth and depth (topics and skills covered); content sequencing; modes of presentation; textbooks and materials used; and goals. The information gained from these indicators will be useful for broadly describing the science and mathematics curricula *in use* and for monitoring the effects of policy.

To get some sense of how mathematics and science curricula measure up to informed ideal concepts, we recommend a limited set of curriculum materials quality indicators. These can be based on the collective judgments of panels representing a variety of areas of expertise: mathematicians and scientists; curriculum scholars in these fields; cognitive psychologists; educational policymakers; and practitioners. The indicators could enable evaluation of the importance, accuracy, and pedagogical appropriateness of the official, documented curriculum being offered to students.

Because assessing curricula is complicated by the existence of both differentiated curricula in science and mathematics and multiple levels of curriculum decisionmaking within the educational system, we believe that teachers and textbooks are the most useful and feasible data sources, that the most appropriate units of analysis are classrooms at various grades and ability levels, and that curriculum indicators can be used best for providing a comprehensive picture of the science and mathematics being taught in the nation's schools. Finally, to capture the curricular details that are crucial to state and local assessments of curricular quality and that can be useful for monitoring the effects of local policy efforts, we also recommend that states and local districts develop their own indicators to use in conjunction with national curriculum indicators.

The multiple approach to curriculum indicators seeks to provide descriptive and comparative data about important curriculum policies and practices nationally, without threatening the values of diversity and local responsibility. Undoubtedly, many will see such an approach as a considerable compromise compared with a system that might directly measure the quality of the science and mathematics curriculum according to a set standard. Some may find this approach a woefully incomplete means of determining what science and mathematics curricula students are experiencing in school. But despite these and other difficulties with identifying and developing curriculum indicators, knowledge about the curriculum is fundamental to understanding the health of the educational system.

Chapter 6

INSTRUCTION

Neil Carey

OVERVIEW

Instruction is the "how" of science and mathematics education—it consists of the policies, practices, and social climate in particular classes. Instruction results from the interaction of the teacher, the students, and the curriculum (the "what" of science and mathematics education). Furthermore, instruction depends crucially on teacher quality and working conditions, including class size, classroom resources, occupational support, schoolwide standards, and relationships among teachers. It is, ultimately, the quality of the curriculum, teachers, and instruction that affect student learning in classrooms.[1]

Considering the decisions made at the classroom level, it is clear that instruction must be addressed separately in a fully specified monitoring system. The teacher is the one who makes policies reflecting the goals of the class (Shavelson, 1983), the inclusion or exclusion of topics in the syllabus (Schwille et al., 1981), grouping methods (Webb, 1980), standards for evaluating pupil progress (Slavin, 1978, 1980), and task structures (Doyle, 1977). The teacher also makes decisions that affect the efficiency of time usage, such as whether students have learned enough to progress to new topics (Barr and Dreeben, 1983) and methods of presentation (Brophy, 1986). It is not surprising that variation in academic achievement of U.S. students may be largely due to classroom differences within the same school (Alexander and McDill, 1976; Shea, 1976).

Information on instruction provides a context for interpreting data on curriculum, teachers, and teaching conditions. For example, information on depth and breadth of curriculum coverage would be supplemented by data on teachers' policies regarding student standards and

---

[1]Because all three factors interact simultaneously in the classroom, it is impossible to separate indicators of curriculum, instruction, and teaching completely—to do so would be artificial. However, to avoid excessive overlap in this volume, "teaching" is used to refer to teaching conditions, the teaching assignment, and indicators of teaching quality; these are discussed separately in Chapter 4. "Curriculum practice" is defined as the content actually delivered in classrooms and is discussed in Chapter 5.

the perceived difficulty of a class. Information on teacher characteristics would be interpreted in light of the policies teachers set and what actually occurs in the classroom. Data on teacher working conditions would be supplemented with data on whether those conditions interfere with instructional processes in class.

This chapter examines indicators of the quality of mathematics and science instruction in terms of their relevance to policy and student outcomes. Two major questions are addressed: (1) What aspects of instruction should be monitored in a comprehensive indicator system? (2) What indicators of instructional quality should be given highest priority, in view of the fact that not all aspects of instruction are equally policy-relevant, and present measurement capabilities and resources are limited?

Although a comprehensive system for monitoring instructional quality would include detailed data on the policies, processes, and climates of classrooms, a variety of political, educational, and practical considerations argue against detailed monitoring of instruction at the national level. Not all aspects of instruction are relevant to state and national policymakers, and attempts to measure all potentially important aspects of classroom instruction would burden respondents far more than is practically or economically feasible. Many crucial aspects of instructional processes currently defy measurement.

Because of these constraints, this chapter argues against a *comprehensive* set of instructional indicators, but suggests, rather, that a set of national indicators should be parsimonious, focusing on relatively few generic features of instruction. Priorities are suggested among variables that might be collected in each domain of instruction. Among *instructional policies*, time allocation, student standards, the scientific and mathematical experiences given students, and grouping policies are most important to monitor. *Instructional processes*, while clearly relevant to an indicator system, currently defy our abilities to measure them adequately or in a cost-efficient manner. However, items on a questionnaire may provide very crude indicators of certain aspects of instructional process (e.g., number of pages covered in the textbook). Similarly, measures of classroom climate should be used experimentally as indicators of instructional characteristics, because of their limited policy relevance. Further research on indicators of process and climate might contribute to development of more comprehensive indicators for the future, but it is unlikely to contribute to their development in the near term.

This review concludes that an initial national indicator system should monitor relatively few aspects of instruction, and that the selection of a small, undeniably important subset of instructional indicators

should result in a data set that is measurable, administratively manageable, and useful to policymakers.

APPROACH

Instruction is a difficult phenomenon to monitor, given the speed,
complexity, and variety of classroom interactions. Furthermore,
instructors have the dual responsibilities of teaching subject matter and
enforcing classroom discipline. To simplify the myriad ways classrooms could be analyzed, the instructional constructs dealt with in this
chapter will include the following groups of instructional indicators
(see Fig. 6.1):

- *Policies*, such as allocation of time, within-class ability grouping, and student standards. These are the rules and structures
  set by the teacher within which educational activities proceed.
- *Processes*, such as teachers' management efficiency during class,
  interactive instructional decisions, and teaching behaviors.
  These are the events and activities that occur during instruction which cannot be fully anticipated by policies or rules set by
  the teacher.
- *Classroom climate*, such as students' views of class standards
  and the ease of getting help when it is needed.

Each successive feature of instruction is less controllable by the
teacher and more influenced by students. Classroom policies are
analyzed first, because they are relatively static and are the most easily
measured features of instruction that can be altered by the teacher's
conscious planning. Teacher policies "set the stage" for instructional
processes and classroom climate. Processes are reviewed next, since
they cannot always be anticipated by the teacher, are more difficult to
measure, and are greatly influenced by the classroom's policies.
Nevertheless, during class, the teacher can make conscious decisions of
what to do next and how to do it. Classroom climate is analyzed last
because it is least within the control of the teacher. It is influenced by
many factors, including student characteristics, classroom policies, and
classroom processes.

This chapter reviews relevant research in the policies, processes, and
climate domains and suggests a number of considerations which might
be included in a comprehensive system of instructional indicators.
Then, on the basis of research and practical considerations, priorities
are assigned to those aspects of instruction that are most logically compelling and concluded on the basis of instructional research to be the

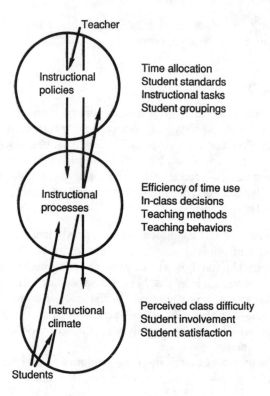

Fig. 6.1—Domains in an instructional monitoring system

most important. Major aspects of instruction that currently defy our abilities to monitor are also noted. The chapter concludes with a brief consideration of (1) what a parsimonious set of instructional indicators would look like, and (2) the value decisions involved in selecting such a set.

INSTRUCTIONAL POLICIES

The goals of the classroom (see Chapter 5) and teachers' working conditions (see Chapter 4) partially determine instructional quality. But the teacher must also make class-level rules ("policies") that can enhance or inhibit students' learning. Because these policies can be developed prior to class or decided after class has ended, they are more under teachers' control than are other aspects of instruction. Teacher policies concerning time allocation, student standards, instructional tasks and activities, and student grouping are reviewed below.

Time Allocation

Elementary teachers must allocate the time available for instruction among various content areas. Teachers can vary enormously in their time allocations—Berliner (1984), using observations, found that one second grade teacher allocated 16 minutes a day to mathematics instruction, while another teacher with the same amount of time available allocated 51 minutes to mathematics. Goodlad (1984) found that, by teachers' own estimates, elementary school children's average exposure to science in one school was more than three times that in another. The average school differences Goodlad found mask even larger differences between classrooms—Schwille et al. (1981, cited in Berliner, 1984) found that one teacher who enjoyed science taught 28 times more science than did a teacher who said she did not enjoy it.

At both the high school and elementary levels, time allocation could be measured crudely by whether certain topics are covered at all. Content coverage is related to student achievement, whether measured in pages covered or percentage of test items taught (Brophy, 1986; Borg, 1980; Good, Grouws, and Beckerman, 1978; Cooley and Leinhardt, 1980). The IEA's studies have found that U.S. secondary students achieved comparatively less in areas in which teachers stated their students had covered less of the material on the test (e.g., Husen, 1967; Murnane and Raizen, 1988). Therefore, indicators of instructional policy can and should assess both time allocations and content coverage.

Student Standards

Student standards comprise those policies related to teacher expectations of individual students. Thus, homework policy can be considered an area of student standards. Homework is also relevant to time allocation and content coverage, since it allows students more opportunity to practice skills and to develop understanding of concepts. Walberg and Fraser (1986), using National Assessment of Educational Progress (NAEP) data, found homework to be a significant predictor of 17-year-olds' science achievement; other research has shown that homework also correlates positively with achievement in elementary mathematics (Brophy, 1986; Good and Grouws, 1977, 1979). While research suggests that topic coverage is the most important instructional influence on achievement outcomes, homework has shown a weaker but rather consistent relationship to student learning

(Coleman, Hoffer, and Kilgore, 1982; Horn and Walberg, 1984; U.S. Department of Education, National Center for Education Statistics, 1985d). Measures of amount of homework could easily be obtained by having teachers estimate the amount of homework assigned, completed by students, and graded by the teacher.

Another important, but more difficult to measure, aspect of student standards is the grading system adopted by teachers. Doyle (1983) has argued that the "immediate task of teaching in classrooms is that of gaining and maintaining the cooperation of students in activities that fill the available time" (p. 179). One of the most powerful ways teachers have of gaining that cooperation and demonstrating what is truly important in class is to say that it will be graded. In fact, the classroom can be thought of as a marketplace where students exchange performance for grades (Becker, Geer, and Hughes, 1968; Doyle, 1977, 1983; Shulman, 1982). This suggests that measures of content coverage should include questions about whether assignments were given and graded on particular topics. At a minimum, data collection instruments should include a question about how often assignments are graded.

Another aspect of grading which might be monitored is the set of comparative criteria by which assignments are graded. Slavin (1978, 1983) found that a traditional grading system can contribute to declining motivation of students who get poor grades. He notes that the grading system is particularly deficient for lower- and middle-ability children's motivation because it encourages students to adopt norms relative to excellence. For example, students may dislike those who try hard in class because such behavior affects the standards by which all class members are evaluated. In addition, the grading system promotes student attempts to lower the standards by which they will be evaluated by negotiating decreases in the risk and ambiguity of assignments (Doyle, 1983). This research suggests that we would want to know whether a student's performance is compared with an ideal standard, with other students' performance, or with the student's own performance earlier in the year (i.e., he or she is given credit for improvement).

Instructional Tasks

A crucial dimension of student standards is the nature of the tasks that are assigned. The tasks and experiences of pupils who are learning mathematics and science can vary considerably. Pupils who learn taxonomic classification solely by memorizing names from a book have had, in some sense, completely different instruction from that of pupils who cover the textbook in conjunction with experiences in dissection or taking field trips. Furthermore, exposure to mathematical and scientific experiences is thought to have a large influence on students' motivation and eventual achievement. For example, Kahle (1983; see also Chapter 7 of this volume) found that black students do not engage in as many science activities as other students. Consequently, they do not have the experience with which to formulate attitudes toward science. Possibly as a result of their lack of experience, the students in Kahle's research found science less useful out of school, were less aware of scientific methods, and were less confident in the ability of science to solve current or future societal problems.

Because of the potential importance of mathematics and science activities, they should be monitored in an instructional indicator system. For example, the 1981 NAEP asked students whether they had conducted an experiment that lasted more than a week, used a telescope, experimented with chemical reactions, or read science articles in magazines. These items could be modified to refer solely to in-class experiences.

Another important, but difficult-to-measure, indicator is the nature of the problems students must solve in the context of class activities. Doyle (1983) has proposed a distinction between the risk and ambiguity of student tasks. Risk is the degree to which the student is likely to fail once the problem is defined; ambiguity is the degree to which the student is required to discover the problem that needs to be addressed and then define it. Task ambiguity is important in teaching students "higher-order" thinking skills (Sternberg and Baron, 1985; Bransford et al., 1986). In a word problem appropriate for developing such skills, students need to define the nature of a problem by asking, "Is there a right answer?" "Is there enough information to solve the problem?" "Is there extraneous information?" "What approaches to the problem seem appropriate?"

The importance of including the risk and ambiguity of assignments in an indicator system is underscored by achievement findings which suggest that the assignments students receive are not ambiguous enough to demand certain important thinking skills. Results from the NAEP (Carpenter et al., 1980) indicate that students have difficulty identifying the unknown, determining whether the data given are sufficient or redundant for the solution of a problem, and devising a problem-solving plan.

The distinction between risk and ambiguity suggests that student assignments should not be classified solely according to topic covered or the experiences they require. Tasks should also be classified in terms of the problems they present for interpretation and completion of the assignment.

Another fundamental aspect of academic tasks is whether they require students to deal with concepts that have already been invented, rather than on the processes that truly comprise "knowing how" in mathematics and science (Romberg, 1983). For example, Romberg proposes that, regardless of the mathematical content covered, students should be given assignments that involve four activities common to all mathematics:

- *Inventing activities*, in which the student must create a law or relationship.
- *Abstracting activities*, in which students are required to develop conceptions further from concrete experience.
- *Proving activities*, in which students must prove a theorem with enough rigor that anyone who understood the proof would agree with it.
- *Applying activities*, in which students must practice using mathematics to solve a problem in other domains.

Romberg's notions suggest that consideration should be given to the development of indicators of classroom assignments that include not only coverage of material and ambiguity, but also the degree to which students are required to perform the essential activities of mathematicians and scientists.

It is probably infeasible to attempt to develop nationally useful measures of these aspects of assignments. For example, it would take expert judgment to determine whether a particular assignment was "ambiguous" or "risky"; an "application" or merely an exercise; or whether the teacher had given students enough help that they were really developing proofs "by themselves." A formula that might be quite difficult to prove for younger students might seem quite easy for older students who are mathematically more mature.

More important, the *number* of thinking assignments is not as important as whether thinking assignments are given at the correct time for students to make optimal use of them (i.e., in the so-called "zone of proximal development," Vygotsky, 1978). Thinking assignments given before students are mathematically ready could discourage students rather than promote their thinking skills. Judging whether teachers assigned the correct kind of task at the correct time would require enough skilled observers to stretch the financial capacity of an indicator system. Therefore, these indicators are not recommended at the present time, although they would be worthy of consideration if the measurement difficulties could be overcome.

Instructional Grouping Policies

Teachers' grouping policies should be included in a monitoring system, for a number of reasons. Teacher policy with respect to grouping determines which students will be involved in specific classroom interactions. Also, teachers' impressions of the groups they have formed influence other instructional policies concerning grading, homework assigned, and time allocation. Shavelson (1983) has found that once reading-ability groups are formed, the high groups may be paced as much as 15 times faster than the low groups. The resulting differences in content coverage can be enormous (Berliner, 1984).

There also may be qualitative differences between teacher expectations for different groups. For example, Oakes (1985) quotes several low-track mathematics and science teachers concerning goals for their students (from Oakes, 1985, pp. 80–83):

> That they [students] know that their paychecks will be correct when they receive them. Punctuality, self-discipline and honesty will make them successful in their job. They must begin and end each day with a smile. To be able to figure their own income tax [at the] end of the year. (Senior high low-track math)

> Self-discipline, cooperativeness, and responsibility. (Senior high low-track science)

> More mature behavior—less outspoken. (Senior high low-track science)

In comparison, teachers' expectations for high-track students were considerably different (from Oakes, 1985, pp. 80–83):

> How to think critically—analyze data, convert word problems into numerical order. (Senior high high-track math)

> Determine the best approach to problem solving. Recognize different approaches. (Senior high high-track math)

> Problem-solving situations—made to think for themselves. Realizing importance of their education and use of time. Easy way is not always the best way. (Senior high high-track science)

There are undoubtedly qualitative differences in expectations of teachers for high- and low-ability within-class groups as well, given the differences in pacing of these groups found by Shavelson (1983).

Another reason for including classroom grouping in a monitoring system is that grouping affects the kinds of processes that occur among students during class. Webb (e.g., Webb, 1980, 1982, 1984a, 1984b, 1984c; Webb and Cullian, 1983) has explored the group processes associated with benefits of mixed-ability grouping on student achievement in mathematics and computer courses. In a 1980 study, Webb compared the problem-solving processes and achievement of five "groups" of eleventh grade students—those uniformly high, medium, or low in ability, mixed-ability groups, and students working alone. The students were required to calculate a general expression for the total number of dots in an array of hexagons in which the outermost hexagon had $N - 1$ dots on each side. Webb then developed a model for those group interactions which were shown to influence the individual students' test performance (Fig. 6.2).

Whenever a student in Webb's study made an error that was corrected with an explanation, the student subsequently solved a similar problem on the posttest. Those who made errors and were corrected without an explanation did not solve the posttest question correctly. Likewise, students who asked questions and received correct explanations subsequently solved the posttest problem, whereas those who received no explanation failed on the posttest. This initial phase of Webb's research showed that in order to learn, students must expose their misunderstandings and be corrected with explanations.

A second aspect of Webb's 1980 study attempted to determine which groups were most likely to have the beneficial correction-explanation cycles associated with learning how to solve problems. She found that students in uniformly high- or low-ability groups rarely offered explanations to each other. Students in high-ability groups who understood the problem evidently assumed that everyone in the group was able to solve the puzzle. They attempted to challenge themselves by solving the problem in the shortest time possible. Students in low-ability groups, on the other hand, decided that they had no possibility of answering the question and merely wanted to get the task completed even if their answers were wrong (Webb, 1980, p.78):

> Student 1: "Do you understand it?"
> Student 2: "No."
> Student 3: "I don't either."
> Student 4: "I don't know how we got the four. But it's cool."
> Student 1: "Should we do the third one?"
> Student 2: "We don't know how to do the *last* one."
> Student 3: "We got a formula. Isn't that enough?"
> Student 2: "Okay."

The individuals who benefited most from group work were high- and low-ability students *in mixed-ability groups*. In these groups, the high-ability students apparently benefited from helping the lower-ability

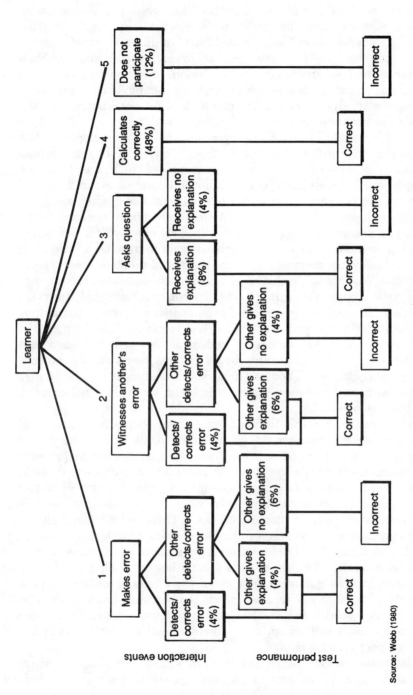

Fig. 6.2—Model of group process relations to test performance

Source: Webb (1980)

students, whereas low-ability students who received an explanation learned how to solve the problem. Somewhat surprisingly, middle-ability students benefited more from uniformly middle-ability groupings—perhaps they felt less inhibited about exposing their ignorance in these groupings. In conclusion, the important factors in increasing students' mathematical problem-solving ability was their willingness to expose their ignorance if they did not understand, and whether or not they received explanations.

There is further evidence to suggest that ability grouping should be monitored. Slavin (1983) concluded from a review of 46 experimental studies that mixed-ability groupings, combined with specific group rewards and between-group competition based on all group members' learning, can mitigate the tendency of the traditional grading system to discourage lower-ability students. Within-class games or tournaments between heterogeneous groups are particularly effective for low-ability students, because if all students' achievement contributes to the score of an entire group, members will care about and promote the academic performance of peers. In this case, students are motivated to help each other not merely get through the course, but actually learn the material. In one of several studies supporting Slavin's contention, Hamblin, Hathaway, and Wodarski (1971) found that the frequency of peer tutoring and the amount of student achievement increased as a proportion of students' rewards based on the lowest three members' scores. Sherman and Thomas (1986) also found that low-ability high school mathematics students performed better when they had cooperative in-class games.

In contrast to Slavin's findings, some investigators have found the effects of ability grouping to be positive. Kulik and Kulik (1982) analyzed findings from 52 studies of secondary school ability grouping and found small differences which suggested that secondary students generally achieve more in grouped classrooms. The results were clearer for high-ability students, especially when these students received enriched instruction in honors classes. There were essentially no achievement benefits to average and below-average students. However, Kulik and Kulik found that students in grouped classrooms develop more positive attitudes toward the subjects they are studying.

Although investigators disagree about the effects of ability grouping, it appears useful to ask teachers about the academic track of the particular class; whether within-class ability grouping is used; the amount of whole-class, small group, and individualized instruction used; and whether peer tutoring is used.

Classroom tracking status and types of within-class ability grouping should be included in even a minimal system of instructional indicators. Although these variables cannot be measured perfectly, a secondary school teacher should be able to tell whether the class is of mixed, low, or high ability; certainly an elementary teacher would be able to tell whether within-class mathematics and science groups are used. This information would provide useful indicators of trends that are occurring in the nation's mathematics and science classrooms.

Summary of Instructional Policies

A monitoring system should include indicators of time allocations and content coverage, student standards, the type of instructional tasks students are assigned, and grouping policies. While all of these aspects of instruction are difficult and expensive to monitor in comprehensive detail, all could be reported more generally via less burdensome questionnaire methods.

Although instructional policies are relevant to policymakers' concerns, it is the instructor who adapts them to the circumstances of particular classrooms. A skillful instructor can tell whether students in a class require more time or homework to master a particular topic or can handle ambiguous problem-solving activities. The process of adapting policies to the needs of students is an art that currently defies our ability to construct indicators. Thus, the indicators recommended here should be considered descriptive of central trends in instruction. More content coverage and more homework should not necessarily be interpreted as "better" in all classrooms.

The discussion of instructional policies has reviewed aspects of instruction that can be planned prior to class or dealt with after class has ended. There remains the question of whether indicators could be developed concerning what occurs during classroom time itself, when teachers are explaining concepts and dealing with student behavioral problems, and students are asking questions. Because classroom interactions are somewhat unpredictable, instructional processes are less under teachers' direct control. The next section deals with indicators of these aspects of instruction.

INSTRUCTIONAL PROCESSES

A classroom policy that calls for a certain amount of time to be allocated to a topic can be frustrated if the teacher allows distractions to eat up class time. A decision to have students work with laboratory equipment can be wasted if the teacher cannot efficiently deal with unanticipated misunderstandings about the purpose of the task assigned. This section on instructional processes considers three indicators of what occurs in class: (1) the efficiency of time usage, (2) the adequacy of teacher decisions, and (3) the behaviors and teaching methods displayed by teachers.

Efficiency of Time Use

Time must be structured properly for students to learn (e.g., Fisher et al., 1980). Teachers who schedule equal amounts of time for particular topics and who are equally adept at covering material may nevertheless differ in their abilities to get students actively engaged in the material. When students are not engaged in tasks of appropriate difficulty, time is wasted. For elementary schools, Berliner and associates (e.g., Berliner, 1979; Fisher et al., 1980) have distinguished among *allocated time*, which is the time teachers reserve for instruction, *engaged time*, which is the time students are observed actually working on academic tasks, and *academic learning time*, which is the time students spend engaged in tasks of appropriate difficulty (as evidenced by their getting a large percentage of problems correct). Since student achievement is most affected by the last two kinds of time usage (e.g., Berliner, 1979; Brophy and Good, 1986; Fisher et al., 1980; Good and Grouws, 1977; Stallings, 1980), teachers' ability to manage student activities and select exercises of appropriate difficulty for students has empirical support as an indicator of instructional process.

One implication of the research on academic learning time is that students learn more when teachers manage well and prevent distractions from academic tasks. Also, indicators should reflect how teachers manage time among in-class activities. Harnischfeger and Wiley (1980) propose that time allotment among activities in elementary classrooms can have a large influence on achievement. According to their model, it is important to know not only how much time students spend engaged in various topics, but also how long they spend in transition between academic activities.

Despite its importance, efficiency of time use is difficult to measure adequately without great expense. Research projects that include consideration of management efficiency (e.g., Fisher et al., 1980; Leinhardt and Greeno, 1986) have utilized observations over many days, videotaping, and pre- and post-interviews with teachers. These methods are particularly expensive, since multiple observations must be made for each classroom in order to obtain adequate reliability (Shavelson, Webb, and Burstein, 1986), and multiple observers are needed to assess interrater agreement. In addition, reliability and validity of observation schemes may vary depending on the kind of classroom observed

(Shavelson and Dempsey-Atwood, 1976). The multiple sources of error in observations (e.g., Shavelson and Dempsey-Atwood, 1976; Shavelson, Webb, and Burstein, 1986) and their high cost makes observations unwieldy for an indicator system. Similar problems exist for estimates of how much time is actually spent in activities such as whole-group or individualized instruction. Shavelson, Webb, and Burstein found that the level of detail needed to measure efficiency of time use adequately could be prohibitive.

The high cost of observation systems suggests that simple questionnaire indicators of instructional time might be used instead. For example, students, teachers, or observers could estimate the proportion of time spent in management routines, in disciplining students, or in academic tasks while in class (engaged time). Alternatively, they could estimate the proportion of time students spend practicing exercises for which they get a high proportion of problems correct (academic learning time). These measures can be used only as long as it is understood that research needs to determine sources of measurement error and degrees of bias. Teachers' memories of students' engaged time and academic learning time are not very reliable (Berliner, 1976), and students' memories of their engagement in class may reflect their aptitudes rather than how long they actually were engaged (Peterson et al., 1984).

These cruder indicators are recommended for inclusion in a monitoring system because management efficiency is related to student achievement, and because trend data could provide clues as to whether educational policies have had an impact on management efficiency.

Teacher Decisionmaking

Measures of the efficiency of time usage could provide an indication of the quality of instruction, but they would omit the importance of teacher decisions in determining instructional quality. Teachers must make relatively instantaneous in-class decisions about methods of presenting materials, how to answer student questions, and when to shift class activities. These decisions may have a large impact on student understanding, as they may affect the clarity of presentations and the time allocated to students for understanding the material.

It is difficult to evaluate teacher in-class decisions because there is no way to monitor the appropriateness of a teacher's judgments without reference to a myriad of highly context-specific circumstances. Doyle (1985) suggests that classrooms are marked by three characteristics:

- *Multidimensionality*, which refers to the large quantity of events and tasks in classrooms. A classroom is a crowded place in which many people with different preferences and abilities must use a restricted supply of resources to accomplish a broad range of social and personal objectives. Many events must be planned and orchestrated to meet special interests of members and changing circumstances throughout the year. Records must be kept, schedules met, supplies organized and stored, and student work collected and evaluated. In addition, a single event can have multiple consequences: Waiting a few extra moments for a student to answer a question can affect that student's motivation to learn as well as the pace of the lesson and the attention of other students in the class. Choices, therefore, are never simple.
- *Simultaneity*, which refers to the fact that many things happen at once in classrooms. While helping an individual student during seatwork, a teacher must monitor the rest of the class, acknowledge other requests for assistance, handle interruptions, and keep track of time. During a discussion, a teacher must listen to student answers, watch other students for signs of comprehension or confusion, formulate the next question, and scan the class for possible misbehavior. At the same time, the teacher must attend to the pace of the discussion, the sequence of selecting students to answer, the relevance and quality of answers, and the logical development of content. When the class is divided into small groups, the number of simultaneous events increases, and the teacher must monitor and regulate several different activities at once.
- *Immediacy*, which refers to the rapid pace of classroom events. Gump (1967) and Jackson (1968) have estimated that an elementary teacher has over 500 exchanges with individual students in a single day and, in a study of first and fifth grade classes, Sieber (1979a) found that teachers publicly evaluated pupil conduct with either praise or reprimands on the average of 15.89 times per hour, or 87 times a day, or about 16,000 times a year. In addition, Kounin (1970) found that order in classrooms depends in part upon maintaining momentum and a flow of classroom events. In most instances, therefore, teachers have little leisure time to reflect before acting. (Doyle, 1985, pp. 394–395).

Three other aspects of teacher in-class decisionmaking are the *unpredictability of events* such as interruptions and distractions, the *publicness of teacher decisions*, as students see how other students are treated, and *the history of classrooms*, as early meetings often determine the nature of the course for the rest of the year. These characteristics render teacher decisions difficult if not impossible to monitor on a nationwide basis. Nevertheless, there are a few indicators that might be used experimentally, such as pages of text covered in a typical day or number of student questions answered by the teacher. Because of the context-dependence of teacher decisions, it would not be possible to claim that for these indicators "more is better."

Teacher Behaviors and Teaching Methods

An alternative to monitoring classroom decisions would be to count those teacher behaviors or teaching methods that have been related to student achievement. This strategy has its own weaknesses. Whereas the research on classroom management suggests that the relationship between time in direct instruction and achievement is monotonically increasing, the research on specific teaching methods shows that some methods yield results that are curvilinear—in the range normally observed, more is usually better, but at a certain point, more of a certain behavior or process could be counterproductive. For example, the Beginning Teacher Evaluation Study found that in the classrooms that were observed, students did better if exercises given to them allowed for a high rate of success. This generalization is limited, however: Assignment of tasks on which all students get perfect scores would be wasteful. Other instructional variables known to correlate with achievement suffer the same flaw. For example, Brophy and Good's review (1986) suggests the following teacher behaviors as instructionally effective:

1. *Redundancy/sequencing.* Achievement is higher when information is presented with a degree of redundancy, particularly in the form of repeating and reviewing general rules and key concepts. The kind of redundancy that is involved in the sequential structuring built into the study reported by Smith and Sanders (1981) also appears important. In general, structuring, redundancy, and sequencing affect what is learned from listening to verbal presentations, even though they are not powerful determinants of learning from reading text.
2. *Clarity.* Clarity of presentation is a consistent correlate of achievement, whether measured by high-inference ratings or low-inference indicators such as absence of "vagueness terms" or "mazes." Knowledge about factors that detract from clarity

needs to be supplemented with knowledge about positive factors that enhance clarity (for example, what kinds of analogies and examples facilitate learning, and why?); in any case, students learn more from clear presentations than from unclear ones.

3. *Pacing/wait-time.* Although few studies have addressed the matter directly, data from studies of early grades seem to favor rapid pacing, both because this helps maintain lesson momentum (and thus minimizes inattention) and because such pacing seems to suit the basic skills learning that occurs at these grade levels. At higher grade levels, however, where teachers make longer presentations on more abstract or complex content, it may be necessary to move at a slower pace, allowing time for each new concept to "sink in." (Brophy and Good, 1986, p. 362)

Clearly, the value of these relationships is confined to a certain "normal" range—redundancy is helpful, but at a certain point it interferes with the pace of the class. Clarity may be useful in most circumstances, but spelling out too much of what is expected could interfere with students taking initiative or learning for themselves how problems should be approached. It might also require more time to be clear, again interfering with the pace of the class.

Because of the curvilinear and context-dependent nature of the relationships between student outcomes and the kind of teacher behaviors reviewed above, we recommend that most teacher behavior be excluded from the monitoring system at the present time.

Summary of Instructional Processes

Simple questions on efficiency of time usage, and to a lesser extent, teaching methods, should be used to develop indicators of management efficiency, the adequacy of teacher decisions, teacher behaviors, and teaching methods. In the short term, this leaves few measures of instructional process for a monitoring system. However, this recommendation is based on the considerations of policy relevance, cost, and the context-dependence of classroom interactions. Special studies might develop more useful measures of instructional process, in conjunction with efforts to create better indicators of teacher and curriculum quality.

CLASSROOM CLIMATE

As noted earlier, a major problem with traditional measures of classroom process is that the appropriateness of a particular behavior or decision depends on the context in which it is embedded and the type of students in the class. Furthermore, particular instances of classroom process are not as useful as tendencies that may build up over long periods of time. One strategy for circumventing these difficulties would be to ask students to make judgments about classroom processes based on their long-running experience with the classroom's "climate."

Two relevant lines of research have evolved concerning class climate. One set of studies, exemplified by the work of Walberg (e.g., Walberg, 1969a, 1969b), was conducted to evaluate a new physics curriculum and to identify correlates of student achievement. A second body of research, exemplified by the work of Moos (e.g., Moos and Moos, 1978; Trickett and Moos, 1973, 1974), examined the influence of environments on absenteeism and motivation.

Classroom Climate and Student Achievement

Walberg (1969a) analyzed data collected from classes of a sample of 57 physics teachers across the nation who had agreed to participate in a study of the Harvard Project Physics course. The study included data from the Learning Environment Inventory, personality scales, the Biographical Inventory (Taylor and Ellison, 1967), the Henmon-Nelson Test of Mental Ability (Lamke, Nelson, and Kelso, 1960), and data on the fraction of girls in the class and the number of students in the class. These independent variables were correlated with outcome measures such as science understanding (Cooley and Klopfer, 1961), science process (understanding of the "assumptions, activities, products, and ethics of science," p. 536), interest in science activities (Halpern, 1965), and a measure of voluntary activity in science (Cooley and Reed, 1961). Student perception of the difficulty of the class was the best classroom climate predictor of science achievement, whereas student satisfaction with the class was the best predictor of interest in physics. Further analyses (e.g., Walberg, 1969b) showed that these relationships held even after other variables were statistically controlled for. Walberg concluded that:

> To encourage high rates of growth in achievement and understanding in classes, the social environment must be intellectually challenging, a condition which does not inhibit affective and behavioral learning, since cognitive and noncognitive growth are independent. To encourage high rates of non-cognitive growth, classes must be satisfying and socially cohesive. (p. 448)

In later research using NAEP data on the science achievement of 13-year-olds, Walberg and associates (Walberg et al., 1981) found that a 21-item measure of classroom social-psychological environment was a strong predictor of achievement. Of the predictors used in this study (socioeconomic status, motivation, quality of instruction, social-psychological environment, and home conditions), social-psychological environment appeared as "the only unequivocal cause of science learning in the data" (p. 233). A subsequent review of the effect of social-psychological environments on learning (Haertel, Walberg, and Haertel, 1981) suggested that classroom climate may also be associated with mathematics learning. Although it is questionable whether Walberg and associates were justified in inferring cause from their data, this work underscores the potential importance of classroom climate as an indicator in a monitoring system.

Classroom Climate and Absenteeism

In a second line of research, Moos and Moos (1978) explored the relationship between classroom climate and absenteeism. Students absent from class are less likely to learn what is presented that day (Morgan, 1975), and those who attend class less receive lower grades (Kooker, 1976) and are at a greater risk of later dropping out of high school (Yudin et al., 1973).

Trickett and Moos (1973, 1974) found that students were more satisfied with classrooms perceived as having high student involvement, high affiliation, and clear rules regarding classroom behavior. Moos and Moos (1978) used the Classroom Environment Scale to further evaluate the relationships between high school classroom climate and other pertinent variables. They found that the relationship dimension (i.e., involvement, affiliation, and teacher support) significantly correlated with mean grade point averages. Classes with high absenteeism were perceived as high in competition and teacher control and low in teacher support. Causal connections should not be inferred from these data, however, because students who are better motivated or more academically able may also see their classrooms as having better relationships and more teacher support. In addition, the teachers in the more effective classrooms may have initially made clear the rules and expectations, which later encouraged students to try harder. Nevertheless, Moos and Moos believe that the Classroom Environment Scale could help identify classrooms that are "at risk."

In summary, research suggests that classroom climate could be a useful addition to a system for monitoring classroom processes. The Learning Environment Inventory would have the advantage of being validated for its usefulness in research in science classrooms, and it has been shown to be correlated with achievement.

Summary of Classroom Climate

As an indicator of *instruction*, classroom climate has the important advantage of providing an inexpensive way to monitor otherwise difficult aspects of classroom interaction, such as the relationship of teachers' expectations to student abilities. As an indicator of *instructional quality*, however, classroom climate has several important weaknesses. First, students often do not know or appreciate what science or mathematics really is, so they may prefer classes that provide inappropriate instruction (e.g., classes that emphasize memorization). Second, it is hard to pinpoint what a teacher could do to change the climate of a classroom for the better, since classroom climate includes students' relationships with each other as well as with the teacher. Therefore, the policy relevance of classroom climate is debatable. Finally, classroom climate measures are difficult to aggregate in a meaningful way, given the evidence that different types of environments may be optimal for different instructional purposes (e.g., Walberg, 1969b). We concluded that climate measures should be used experimentally, as proxies for more difficult-to-measure aspects of instruction, such as the appropriateness of teachers' expectations.

SUMMARY AND CONCLUSIONS

Priorities Among Instructional Indicators

The instructional indicators discussed here should be considered in terms of the larger indicator project of which this chapter is a part. This project has developed seven criteria for selecting features of schooling to incorporate into an indicator system: An indicator should (1) describe a central feature of the educational system, (2) provide information about current or potential problems, (3) provide policy-relevant information, (4) measure observed behavior rather than perceptions, (5) provide analytical links among important components of schooling, (6) generate data from measures generally accepted as valid and reliable, and (7) provide information that can be readily understood by a broad audience (Shavelson et al., 1987).

On the basis of these criteria, the following indicators of instruction have been recommended: Among *instructional policies*, time allocation, content coverage, student standards, scientific and mathematical experiences given to students, and grouping policies should be monitored. Each of these features is comparatively easy to measure objectively, and all are policy-relevant because they are largely in the control of teachers. Among *instructional processes*, efficiency of time usage and certain teaching methods should be monitored. However, the difficulties of measuring these aspects of instruction well and their comparative lack of policy-relevance suggest that these indicators are of less value to a monitoring system than are instructional policies. Among *classroom climate* indicators, perceived difficulty of the classroom, businesslike atmosphere, and the emotional warmth of the classroom could be monitored on an experimental basis, possibly in the context of cyclical studies designed to improve the quality of instructional indicators.

Lower priorities are assigned to instructional processes and classroom climate because these factors are less susceptible to policy interventions, more difficult to measure reliably and objectively (in fact, classroom climate is by definition a perceptual measure), and less readily understood by a broad audience. In contrast, instructional policies are easier to understand, influence, and measure.

A Final Word: Goals and Choice of Indicators

This chapter has proposed indicators of instructional policies, processes, and climate. Choices among instructional indicators require value judgments concerning which educational goals are most important. Three candidate goals would be (1) coverage of content, (2) encouragement of student understanding and problem-solving, and (3) promotion of positive attitudes and training for groups of students who have traditionally had difficulty in mathematics and science classes. Table 6.1 summarizes several indicators which would be most relevant to each of these goals. This is not meant to imply that a classroom that is successful in promoting one of these goals will necessarily fail to promote the others. Nevertheless, there certainly will be occasions when taking more time to make sure students truly understand a concept can slow the coverage of content, and other occasions in which overemphasis on promoting a warm classroom atmosphere could hamper other instructional purposes (e.g., Brophy and Good, 1985; Peterson, 1979).

If content coverage were considered the most important goal of instruction, then among policies, the classroom's time allocations, student standards, and grading policy would be crucial indicators. Among processes, management efficiency and classroom pace would be important indicators. Among features of instructional climate, perceived difficulty of the class and the businesslike atmosphere of the class would be important to monitor.

Table 6.1

INSTRUCTIONAL INDICATORS MOST RELEVANT TO PARTICULAR GOALS OF INSTRUCTION

Content Coverage	Understanding and Problem Solving	Positive Attitudes and Equitable Outcomes
Policies		
Number of assignments Student standards Grading policy Time allocations	Quality of assignments	Grouping policies Grading policies
Processes		
Management efficiency Classroom pace	Sensitivity to student understanding Challenges to student preconceptions Clarity of teacher's presentations	Enthusiasm and warmth of teacher
Climate		
Perceived difficulty Businesslike atmosphere	Atmosphere in which questions can be asked	Cohesiveness Competitiveness Student involvement, satisfaction

For those who view the goals of understanding and problem-solving as most important, the *quality* of assignments would count more than the number of topics assigned. For example, it would be important to know whether students were learning the mathematical processes of *invention*, *application*, and *proof* (Romberg, 1983). An emphasis on understanding and problem-solving would justify the exploration of classroom process considerations such as instructors' behaviors and methods, including sensitivity to student understanding, explicit challenges to student preconceptions, clarity of presentations, and encouragement of understanding. Clearly these are difficult processes to measure objectively. The climate variables associated with understanding and problem-solving would also be slightly different than those for content coverage. An atmosphere in which questions could be asked would be a crucial variable to monitor, but one for which it would be difficult to develop policy-relevant measures.

The goal of fostering positive attitudes in children and promoting equal outcomes for minority and lower-ability pupils would result in a third, slightly different set of indicator choices. In this view, grading and grouping policies would take on comparatively more importance. Among teacher behaviors and methods, the enthusiasm and warmth of the teacher should be particularly useful indicators if equity were the most valued goal of a monitoring system. Among climate variables, the classroom's cohesiveness, competitiveness, student involvement, and student satisfaction would be particularly important to monitor.

The recommended indicators would implicitly cover variables of import to all three of these instructional goals. Yet the recommended list gives considerably greater weight to indicators of relevance to the goal of content coverage, primarily because the features of instruction most relevant to student understanding, problem-solving, and attitudes are more difficult to measure objectively within reasonable cost bounds. Because of this, new efforts should focus on development of indicators of the "fuzzier" features of instruction, particularly those relevant to student understanding, problem-solving, and equity. These efforts might be conducted in conjunction with cyclical studies designed to create better measures of achievement, teacher quality, and curriculum quality.

Chapter 7

OUTCOMES, ACHIEVEMENT, PARTICIPATION, AND ATTITUDES

Neil Carey and Richard Shavelson

This chapter informs the design of an indicator system for precollege mathematics and science education by addressing two broad questions: (1) What individual-level indicators of outcomes, participation, and attitudes should be included? (2) Can these indicators be monitored adequately with present measurement capabilities?

The domain of individual outcomes includes students' (1) *achievement*, i.e., knowledge, understanding, and use of concepts and skills in mathematics and science; (2) *participation* within and outside of school in mathematical and scientific activities; and (3) *attitudes* and self-confidence concerning these subjects.

ACHIEVEMENT INDICATORS

When policymakers and the general public think about the quality of education—in science, mathematics, or any other field—they typically focus on achievement, as measured by scores on standardized tests. This focus ignores the influence of other elements in the education system, and their interactions, on achievement.

Nevertheless, achievement outcomes are generally seen as the final "proof" of an education system's quality, in terms of the larger goals that society has in supporting education. And achievement test scores are the most readily available and easily gathered indicators of achievement that we currently have.

The Relative Potential of National Achievement Tests for an Indicator System

Which national achievement tests seem most promising for a national indicator system in terms of their extensiveness, sampling, and relevance to mathematics and science curriculum? In this section we assess the strengths and weaknesses of the available tests on those dimensions. The tests are briefly summarized in Table 7.1.[1]

National Assessment of Educational Progress. The National Assessment of Educational Progress (NAEP) provides the most extensive, ongoing evaluation of the mathematics and science achievement of nationally representative samples of students. NAEP mathematics assessments have used a content-by-process matrix for organizing the achievement objectives covered (NAEP, 1981–82; see Appendix 7.1 for a list of objectives covered by NAEP). In the 1981–82 assessment, mathematical processes such as knowledge, skill, understanding, and application/problem solving were measured for mathematics up to, but not including, calculus. Numbers, variables and relationships, shape, size and position, measurement, statistics/probability, and technology were covered. NAEP's science assessments also use a process-by-content matrix to order their several hundred specific objectives. The 1976–77 matrix (reproduced in Appendix 7.2) provides an overview of how these objectives are organized.

Most of these objectives appear quite relevant for the purposes of developing achievement indicators for a monitoring system. The recently instituted balanced incomplete block spiraling design provides a method of student and item sampling for testing these many objectives without overburdening any single student. It also permits, for the first time, the estimation of relationships among the results of the hundreds of exercises (Messick, Beaton, and Lord, 1983).

Longitudinal Studies. Another important data source for monitoring mathematics and science education is the longitudinal studies sponsored by the Center for Statistics (formerly the National Center for Education Statistics, NCES). The National Longitudinal Study (NLS) tested a nationally representative sample of high school seniors in 1972 and periodically collects data on aspects of their career development and academic attainment. However, the utility of the NLS data is limited for monitoring mathematics and science achievement: Not only are the achievement data out of date, but science achievement was not tested.

The second of these longitudinal studies, High School and Beyond (HSB), is a survey of nationally representative high school sophomores and seniors. The first HSB survey was taken in 1980, and follow-ups have been performed every two years. A companion to the NLS, HSB was intended primarily to investigate trends in achievement between

---

[1]Private sector achievement tests such as the Stanford or California Achievement Tests are omitted from Table 7.1 because the development of a "crosswalk" between the various tests in the near future is highly unlikely, making them currently unsuitable for a national monitoring system.

Table 7.1

SUMMARY OF EXISTING NATIONAL ACHIEVEMENT TESTS

Test	Coverage	Assessment
NAEP	Math: Ages 9, 13, 17; 1972, 1978, 1985.	Strengths: Nationally representative probability sample; largest number of items used in any survey reviewed here. This gives it the potential to reflect school curricula. Weaknesses: Multiple-choice format hinders test's ability to assess depth of understanding or skills in in the process of doing math and science. Compromises made because of national scope lessen the degree to which NAEP reflects implemented or ideal curricula.
	Science: Ages 9, 13, 17; 1969, 1972, 1976, 1981, 1985.	See above. Multiple-choice format particularly unsuited for assessing process of doing math and science.
NLS	Math: Seniors, 25 items, 15-minute test of "quantitative skills." 1972.	Strengths: Longitudinal sample followed past high school. Weaknesses: Measures quantitative aptitude, not achievement, hence it does not reflect the curriculum. Too brief for indicator purposes. Has weaknesses common to all multiple-choice tests (see above).
	Science: none	
HSB	Math: Sophomores and seniors. Same as NLS, but 8 items added for seniors, 28 items added sophomores. 1980, 1982.	Strengths: Longitudinal and greater concern with achievement. Weaknesses: Too few items to reflect high school curriculum. Still mainly aptitude tests. Has weaknesses common to multiple-choice tests (see above).
	Science: 20 items, 10 minutes, 1980.	Strengths: Longitudinal and cross-sectional. Weaknesses: Too few items to reflect high school curriculum. Primarily a test of verbal ability. Has weaknesses common to multiple-choice tests (see above).

NELS	Math: 8th, 10th, 12th grade; 1988, 1990, 1992.	Strengths: Longitudinal and cross-sectional
	Science: 8th, 10th, 12th grade; 1988, 1990, 1992.	Weaknesses: May have too few items to reflect high school curriculum. Has weaknesses common to multiple-choice tests (see above).
IEA	Math: Ages 13, 17; 1964.	Strengths: Relatively large number of items. Compromises made because of international scope lessen the degree to which IEA reflects implemented or ideal curricula, but this problem is attenuated by the careful attention to teachers' responses concerning which exercises students should be able to do.
		Weaknesses: Not nationally representative. Evaluations not done at regular intervals. Has weaknesses common to multiple-choice tests (see above).
	Science: Age 14, final-year secondary; 1970, 1983.	Strengths: Relatively large number of items. Compromises made because of international scope lessen the degree to which IEA reflects implemented or ideal curricula, but this problem is attenuated by the careful attention to teachers' responses concerning which exercises students should be able to do.
		Weaknesses: Not nationally representative sample. Evaluations not done at regular intervals. Has weaknesses common to multiple-choice tests (see above).
SAT, ACT	Math: College-bound high school students, more than once a year.	Strengths: Sample of college-bound students.
		Weaknesses: Self-selected nature of sample makes SAT and ACT inappropriate for drawing inferences about students in general. Because the tests are meant to compensate for differences among high school curricula, they were deliberately designed not to reflect high school curriculum; they are thus primarily aptitude tests.

SAT, ACT (cont.)	Science: College-bound high school students; more than once a year.	See description of mathematics portions of SAT and ACT.
State-developed tests	Coverage depends on the state, and sometimes the district.	Strengths: Because these these tests are developed at the state level, they have the greatest potential for reflecting implemented curricula. States' responsibility for education makes it politically feasible for them to mandate more extensive testing. State data can be useful for illustrations of what is occurring nationwide.
		Weaknesses: Differences in content coverage and time of administration among states make state data, at present, unlikely in the near term for nationwide monitoring. Political and practical obstacles must be overcome if more homogeneity of achievement testing is to be accomplished.

1972 and 1980, and to "include curriculum-specific measures of achievement that, when given to the same students in 1982, would permit the computation of gain scores from the 10th grade to the 12th grade" (Heyns and Hilton, 1982, p. 91). However, the tests that were finally used (Appendix 7.3) were the result of compromises designed to preserve comparability with the 1972 battery while also introducing curriculum-sensitive achievement measures. There is strong evidence that regardless of their titles, they measure verbal and quantitative ability (Heyns and Hilton, 1982; Rock et al., 1985; Shavelson, 1985).

A third nationally representative longitudinal data set that might be useful for monitoring outcomes is the National Educational Longitudinal Study (NELS), which was first fielded in spring 1988. This longitudinal study began with a cohort of 26,000 8th graders who were tested in mathematics, science, English composition, and social studies. They will be tested again in the 10th and 12th grades, with follow-ups every two years, for a total of 10 years. The 8th, 10th, and 12th grade tests will include common items for bridging purposes; Item Response Theory (IRT) procedures will allow comparisons on the same scale for sets of items. Along with the achievement measures, further data will be collected from high school transcripts, students, teachers, parents, and school administrators. School dropouts will also be followed longitudinally at two-year intervals.

International Association for the Evaluation of Educational Achievement (IEA). The IEA conducts cross-national mathematics and science achievement assessments at irregular intervals. Mathematics achievement was assessed in 1964 and 1981–82. The most recent study covered arithmetic, algebra, geometry, statistics, and measurement for 8th graders, classified according to whether the assessments measured computation, comprehension, or application and analysis. These classifications were also used for the 12th grade items, which covered sets and relations, number systems, algebra, geometry, elementary functions/calculus, and probability/statistics (see Crosswhite et al., 1985; McKnight et al., 1987).

The IEA also conducts assessments of 9-, 13-, and 17-year-olds' biology and physical science achievement. For the two assessments, 1970 and 1983, 26 items for grade 5 (9-year-olds) and 33 for grade 9 (13-year-olds) are the same. The utility of these data are diminished by the fact that only 50 percent of the schools in the 5th grade sample and 36 percent of the schools in the 9th grade sample responded in 1983 (Raizen and Jones, 1985).

The infrequency and irregularity of the international assessments, the difficulties with gaining U.S. schools' participation for the science assessment, and the possible lack of curriculum validity of the tests (since they must be sensitive to international curricula guidelines) make the IEA studies of somewhat less value than the NAEP for a national mathematics and science monitoring system. Nevertheless, the IEA is an invaluable resource for cross-national achievement comparisons and for the extensive data collected on the content of courses in the U.S. sample.

College Entrance Examinations. The American College Testing (ACT) program and the Scholastic Aptitude Tests (SAT) were developed to assist colleges in selecting students—a process that would be difficult without standardized tests because of the diversity of curricula and grading practices across the nation's secondary schools (e.g., Braswell, 1978; Haney, 1984, 1985; Jones, Rowen, and Taylor, 1977).

The SAT is taken by about 1 million students each year. Along with the aptitude portion, which provides mathematical and verbal scores, students take three achievement tests, one in mathematics (usually level 1), one in English composition, and one in another subject area, usually history and social studies. However, there are also achievement tests in biology, chemistry, and physics.

Each of the SAT mathematics examinations contains 50 questions and requires 60 minutes. The Mathematics Level I examination covers questions in "algebra, geometry, trigonometry, elementary functions, mathematical reasoning, logic, and number theory" (Jones, Rowen, and

Taylor, 1977, p. 206). Thirty percent of the test covers algebra, 20 percent deals with plane geometry, and 16 percent requires knowledge of coordinate and solid geometry. Only 12 percent covers trigonometry, and 22 percent covers miscellaneous topics (Jones, Rowen, and Taylor, 1977). The Level II test contains 20 percent algebra, 20 percent coordinate, solid, and transformational geometry, 20 percent trigonometry, 25 percent functions, sequences, and limits, and 15 percent logic, probability, and elementary number theory (Jones, Rowen, and Taylor, 1977).

Smaller proportions of students take the ACT and the SAT's science achievement tests. The SAT and ACT achievement tests have been designed to be brief and curricularly neutral. These features are advantageous, at least in principle, since they do not disadvantage students due to curriculum content. Moreover, the tests were designed to supplement, rather than supplant, information on students' transcripts. However, these advantages for college selection are corresponding weaknesses for a national monitoring system: The tests include relatively few items, so that there is little breadth or depth of topic coverage. They also fail to provide nationally representative data on the college-bound population, let alone the broader population of interest to a monitoring system.

State-Developed Tests. A final alternative for monitoring achievement is to "piggyback" onto state-developed tests. However, the close relation of state tests and curricula makes cross-state comparisons very difficult (Burstein et al., 1985).

Mathematics appears to be the most promising subject in which to piggyback on existing state tests, since there is less diversity in mathematics than in science curricula (Guthrie and Leventhal, 1985). Furthermore, whereas virtually every state operates a testing program in reading and mathematics, considerably fewer states test for science achievement (Burstein et al., 1985).

Based on actual state tests, test manuals, and other details such as dates of test administration, Burstein et al. (1985) concluded that few mathematical topics were tested widely enough across states to be candidates for cross-state comparisons or national monitoring. They found that the best candidates for an exploratory study of the use of state mathematics data for national monitoring would include either numeration or measurement at grades 7 through 9. Even this most promising candidate might be somewhat difficult to implement: Of the 40 states that test at grades 7 through 9, only 25 administer their tests in the spring, so 15 states would have to change their schedules.

Burstein and his colleagues concluded that the feasibility of using state data for state-by-state comparisons "depends" (p. 6–1), particularly on whether expansions in state testing programs result in greater overlap in testing conditions among states. Their discussion implies that linking state data would be feasible if greater overlap were to occur as states continue to modify their assessment programs.

The potential for piggybacking on existing testing efforts is considerable. NAEP stands out as particularly useful because of its nationally representative samples of students, large item pools, and extensive experience in developing and validating items for use in its assessments. Unlike IEA, NAEP has a reasonably short and dependable assessment cycle. Unlike the college admission tests, NAEP does not collect data from a self-selected sample. While state-developed tests could prove useful, the practicality of using them depends on greater homogeneity of testing practices.

Our discussion to this point has focused on the virtues of tests defined in terms of the depth and breadth of topic coverage and the adequacy of the student sample tested. To decide which tests are potentially most useful, we must establish the criteria that tests must meet to provide valid indicators of mathematics and science achievement.

Criteria for Measuring Achievement in Mathematics and Science

Test scores can provide valid, unambiguous indicators of achievement only if the tests measure more than students' aptitude for mathematics and science. Effective tests must also capture, in some way, students' conceptual understanding and problem-solving skills, that is, their ability to apply their knowledge and understanding. As Fig. 7.1 indicates, to capture all of the relevant dimensions (and allow for other influences on test performance), tests must have: *cognitive fidelity, process relevance, curricular relevance,* and *aptitude relevance.*

For the purposes of an indicator system, we consider the criterion of *cognitive fidelity* particularly crucial, since it requires that tests be able to assess students' knowledge and conceptual understanding. Research on learning in mathematics and science suggests why *understanding* and *knowledge* are central to achievement:

- Conceptual understanding influences students' *attention* to various aspects of lessons. For example, students may listen to a presentation on photosynthesis but fail to attend to the implication that plants produce their own food (e.g., Anderson and Smith, 1986).

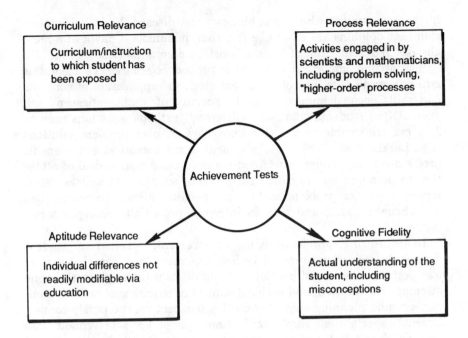

Fig. 7.1—Criteria for evaluating achievement tests

- Conceptual understanding influences students' *judgments* about phenomena in laboratory work. For example, students may have difficulty "seeing" that objects of different mass fall and hit the ground at the same time because the students believe that heavier objects should fall faster (Champagne, Klopfer, and Gunstone, 1980).
- Conceptual understanding may influence *planning and use* of concepts and skills, as when lack of understanding of scientific method inhibits students' abilities to do the logical manipulations necessary to design a controlled experiment (e.g., Feibel, 1978).
- Conceptual understanding can influence the *goals* students set for themselves, as when students believe the goal of solving physics problems is to find an appropriate formula and solve the equation, rather than reasoning from first principles (e.g., Clement, 1979a,b; Larkin et al., 1980a; Heller and Reif, 1982).

Research also indicates that mathematics and science learning often involves a fundamental restructuring of previous conceptions. For instance, a student who learns biology must discard the initial impression that dolphins are more like fish than mammals in favor of a more abstract representation of the relationships among species.

The second important criterion is *process relevance*. To meet this criterion, tests must be able to assess students' application of concepts and skills deemed important in the practice of mathematics and science. Often students who can understand textbook equations such as $F = ma$ are unable to use this knowledge to plan problem solutions (e.g., Larkin et al., 1980a). Achievement in mathematical and scientific problem-solving involves sustained reasoning and a great deal of attention to planning and organizing a problem solution, as well as determining what the problem is, how the problem should be represented and thought about, and how to interpret potentially ambiguous evidence.

In measuring problem-solving achievement, whether a student derives the correct answer may be less important than how that answer was derived. Successful problem-solving often involves more than one attempt at a solution, and each attempt may require goal setting, comparison, and planning steps. From this perspective, the purely computational aspects often emphasized in multiple-choice achievement tests may be the easiest and least important parts of many mathematical and scientific exercises, because they do not require representing the problem, goal-setting, and planning which make real-world problems so difficult. Instead, these exercises involve relatively routine substitutions of numbers into formulas. We argue that these problem-solving steps and the conceptions underlying them should be assessed more fully and efficiently than is presently done because of their importance in mathematical and scientific activities.

Curricular relevance, while an important criterion, is not quite as crucial as the first two—tests should measure achievement on important mathematical and scientific topics even if they have not been covered completely in all curricula. Nevertheless, curricular relevance is desirable because an indicator system should reflect changes influenced by schools, that is, by the curriculum to which students are exposed (Heyns and Hilton, 1982; Shavelson, Webb, and Burstein, 1986; Welch, Anderson, and Harris, 1982; Wolf, 1979). Abilities developed outside of class are important for individuals, but they tell us little about the system of education.

Aptitude relevance is the final, and least crucial, criterion. Aptitudes should be considered because they facilitate achievement, and are thus contextual variables for understanding why some classrooms have higher achievement than others. However, aptitudes should be given second priority in the outcome portion of an indicator system because they are less responsive to educational intervention than achievement and are therefore not instructional outcomes.

It is important to note that a test which meets one criterion might not necessarily meet another. For example, a *process-relevant* test will lack *curricular relevance* if students have not been taught problem-solving skills. Our multiple criteria lead us to suspect that monitoring outcomes may involve a series of achievement tests rather than a single one.

Assessing the Current and Potential Usefulness of the Tests

Although NAEP appeared to be the most obvious test to use for a national indicator system, it shares certain weaknesses with the other tests, judged by the criteria we have just discussed. The tests generally fail to meet the criteria of cognitive fidelity, process relevance, and curricular relevance. Analysis of these shortcomings may help to identify potential means of addressing the weaknesses.

Cognitive Fidelity. All of the achievement tests surveyed have a certain degree of cognitive fidelity because, other things being equal, students who have a deep understanding of mathematics and science concepts will perform better than others. Nevertheless, despite the best efforts of the test makers, the cognitive fidelity of present-day tests is limited primarily because they were not designed to measure students' understanding directly. Furthermore, the ability of the tests to determine whether students can understand and apply mathematical and scientific concepts is hampered by their reliance on multiple-choice formats.

Scores on multiple-choice tests often suggest that students have greater conceptual understanding than they actually have. For example, the 1972–73 NAEP used the problem shown in Fig. 7.2 to assess the ability of 9- and 13-year-olds to "understand and apply the fundamental aspects of science in a wide range of problem situations." A student could answer this question correctly without having an accurate conception of the relationship between water displacement and the weight of an object. For example, the student might merely reason that a brick placed on a pillow pushes further than a light piece of wood, thus arriving at the "correct" answer. Moreover, students might be able to answer this question correctly but not be able to predict which of two objects of the same weight, but different displacement, would be more likely to float (Feibel, 1978). Students often confuse weight and density in a variety of ways when asked questions like this.

One aspect of mathematical knowledge that is becoming increasingly important to monitor is the ability to estimate (e.g., Usikin, 1980).

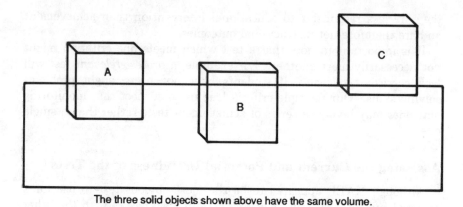

The three solid objects shown above have the same volume.
If they float as shown in the diagram, which one weighs
the most?

☐ Object A

☐ Object B

☐ Object C

☐ They all weigh the same

☐ It is impossible to tell without additional information

☐ I don't know

Source: NAEP (1976-77),p. 10.

Fig. 7.2—Question from the 1972-73 NAEP designed to assess
understanding and application of the fundamental aspects
of science in a wide range of problem situations

Multiple-choice tests might be deficient in measuring this ability as
well. For example, the 1981–82 NAEP included the following problems
relating to estimation:

5. Estimate the quotient for each of these division problems. Do
    not take time to calculate the answer using paper and pencil.
    Choose the answer closest to your estimate.

    A. 20/207   — 0.1   B. 300/5   — 60
                 — 0.01   — 600
                 — 1   — 6,000
                 — 10   — 1,500
                 — I don't know   — I don't know

Students might decide that they would rather work out the problem, taking more time. In this case, the problem ostensibly measures an important aspect of understanding mathematics, but there is no control over whether students are actually doing what the problem asks. Furthermore, in real-life mathematics, it might be important for a student to be able to evaluate whether a particular answer seems "about right," rather than choosing among a set of alternatives.

The least expensive alternative for improving the cognitive fidelity of current multiple-choice achievement indicators would be to add items to NAEP that have distractors keyed to various misconceptions (e.g., Messick, Beaton, and Lord, 1983). For example, the question in Fig. 7.3 presents alternatives, developed as a result of interview research by Clement (1979a, 1979b), that would clearly demonstrate whether students have misconceptions about force. Choice of answer A would demonstrate a misunderstanding of both the relationship between force and acceleration and the First Law of Motion.

This recommendation has had precedents. Messick, Beaton, and Lord (1983) also recommend this as a direction for NAEP to follow. The practice of reporting common student misconceptions based on multiple-choice test results has been followed in Australia, where the yearly report of examiners includes not only the percentage of students getting each item correct, but an analysis of the commonly chosen distractors and the conceptual difficulties indicated by these choices.

Testing for understanding and keying multiple-choice alternatives to misconceptions has several advantages. It demonstrates to students and to the public the need to understand and not merely calculate answers. Also, teachers can use test results to justify spending more time training students to think rather than merely to insert numbers into formulas. Finally, if students are encouraged to develop correct conceptions of sometimes counterintuitive aspects of science, they are likely to become more expert in solving physics problems. Experts spend more time thinking of an appropriate problem representation than on the computational aspects of problems (e.g., Larkin et al., 1980b; Heller and Reif, 1982).

Using computers may provide a more costly but possibly more useful long-run approach to improving the cognitive fidelity of tests. As an alternative to the paper-and-pencil, multiple-choice format with four or five misconceptions as distractors (exemplified in Fig. 7.3), Brown and Burton (1978) have developed computer models of dozens of "bugs" in students' understanding of subtraction. Others (e.g., McArthur (1985); Sleeman, 1982; Sleeman and Smith, 1981) have been developing computer modeling capability for additional topics in mathematics and science. If efforts such as these are successful, the knowledge of

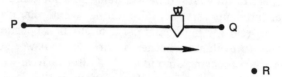

A rocket is drifting sideways from P to Q in outer space.
It is not subject to outside forces.

When the rocket reaches Q, its engine is fired to produce a constant
thrust at right angles to PQ. The engine is turned off again when it
reaches R.

Question 4

Which of the folowing (A,B,C,D,E, or F) best represents the path of the
rocket?

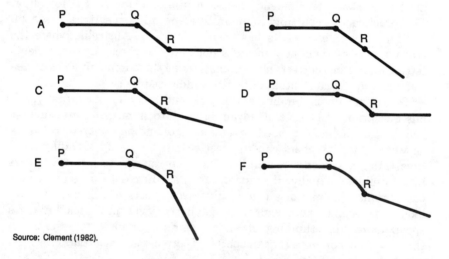

Source: Clement (1982).

Fig. 7.3—Problem with alternatives keyed to student misconceptions

misconceptions and "sticking points" could be used to (1) generate
better multiple-choice distractors or (2) allow the computer to test
achievement interactively. These efforts may be particularly important
for problem areas that students can misunderstand in a great number
of ways.

The computer may be particularly useful for improving the cognitive relevance of achievement tests because of its ability to almost instantaneously create new representations of a problem (Shavelson and Salomon, 1986). For example, in NAEP's flotation problem (Fig. 7.2), the computer could enable several representations of the problem to be used, each one based on the answer the student gave earlier. Pupils who chose Object B might be asked whether this would be a reasonable choice under certain conditions, such as (1) when all the objects have the same weight, but B has twice the volume of the others, (2) when all the objects have the same volume, but C has twice the weight of the others, or (3) when the liquid is oil rather than water.

Pursuing the reasoning of students who answered correctly might show that some of them have less complete understanding than their original answer indicated. Conversely, students who answer erroneously might be shown to know more than their original answers indicated.

The ability to condition the test's next action on the student's response could have other advantages as well. For example, response alternatives concerning why the student gave a certain answer could be conditioned on the student's previous response. Or questions based on incorrect responses could be included that would allow the students to discover their mistake.

Another major advantage of the computer for increasing the cognitive fidelity of tests is its ability to time student responses and present alternatives in a planned sequence. For example, in the NAEP estimation problem cited above, the computer could time students' responses and combine time and accuracy to measure their estimation ability. In another variation of this problem, students might be given each alternative and be asked whether it "seems right" for the problem.

A related development is computerized adaptive testing (e.g., McBride, 1985). Although not keyed to specific misconceptions, this technique promises to enable students' abilities to be assessed with fewer questions because the computer can choose items that are generally closer to the ability level of the student. The ETS is currently developing this technology for individualized diagnostic testing (e.g., Ranbom, 1985).

Process Relevance. Process relevance refers to the degree to which a test assesses students' ability to use concepts and skills to state and solve problems. A student might understand a scientific or mathematical concept but still be unable to solve significant problems. Various studies suggest that multiple-choice items, while adequate for monitoring some important aspects of the use of concepts and skills (cf. Aiken, 1982), cannot indicate enough about students' abilities to solve problems. Consequently, existing tests generally fail to satisfy our criterion of process relevance.

One serious weakness of the multiple-choice format is that distractors can inadvertently make a question easier or more difficult by simplifying the respondent's task to a choice among alternatives. The item makes the student's job easier if it suggests an approach he or she would not have thought of independently. Even when a test has been carefully edited, clever students can often get several answers correct via a process of elimination, thereby limiting the amount of information we actually gain in giving tests that purportedly measure problem-solving ability. Conversely, since students work under time pressure, the presence of attractive (but erroneous) distractors in an item might make the problem more difficult than it would have been if it were presented in free-response format.

Another serious problem with multiple-choice questions is that they do not tell how the student derived an answer. In problem-solving, it may be just as important to know that students performed reasonable steps as to know that they got the correct answer. Sometimes students carry out procedures correctly but make small computational errors; sometimes students respond correctly through fortuitous but erroneous reasoning.

Perhaps the worst problem with multiple-choice items is that they encourage test writers to devise questions that involve few steps or only knowledge of facts. Sternberg and Baron's (1985) recent analysis of problem-solving suggests that, in general, "higher-order thinking" includes recognizing that a problem exists and defining the nature of the problem. This is particularly true in mathematics and science. But the multiple-choice test format usually provides a representation of the problem to enable the student to solve it in a reasonable amount of time. Furthermore, by providing answer alternatives, the test developer implies many of the basic problem-solving steps to be taken. Consequently, it has been contended (e.g., by Frederiksen (1984)) that multiple-choice tests do not measure problem-solving abilities, and that when they do, they do not measure thinking processes completely. Frederiksen notes that the multiple-choice format influences the developer's task selection, which in turn influences the cognitive processes required to perform the tasks.

It is difficult to overcome the tendency of multiple-choice items to assess factual knowledge rather than the ability to use concepts and skills. For example, Levine, McGuire, and Nattress (1970) gave explicit instructions to item writers to create items that measured problem-solving skills in orthopedic medicine, such as interpretation of data, application of principles, or evaluation. Despite these efforts, most of the test items were judged to require mainly recall. Ward, Frederiksen, and Carlson (1980) compared multiple-choice and free-response measures of ability to formulate scientific hypotheses. They concluded that "the free-response and machine-scorable versions . . . clearly cannot be considered alternate forms of the same test, since the correlations between corresponding scores from the two forms are low" (p. 26).

Recognizing these difficulties, the National Science Board (NSB), in *Educating Americans for the Twentieth Century*, urged that greater emphasis be placed on developing "standards for achievement in basic problem-solving skills and in science content" and also on "evaluation of achievement by testing process skills and integrated knowledge as well as facts and concepts" (p. 36).

There are several ways to develop tasks that demand more realistic problem-solving skills than are required in present-day tests. One alternative is exemplified by an experimental section of the 1972–73 NAEP. The section required students to participate in a number of individualized activities administered by a trained interviewer, including "the use of scientific apparatus to conduct testing procedures and simple experiments, the application of knowledge to the observation of materials in order to make generalizations and the demonstration of principles by using models" (NAEP, 1975).

A number of other methods have been developed to measure problem-solving processes in the past few decades, including clinical interviews (Piaget and Inhelder, 1969), process tracing (having subjects "talk aloud" as they solve a problem), tab items (where the subjects must choose from a series of predetermined steps how they would respond), and stimulated recall (in which the respondent views a videotape of his or her problem-solving behavior and explains why steps were undertaken in certain ways) (Shulman and Elstein, 1975). Schoenfeld (1982) has developed methods of assessing mathematical problem-solving based on detailed analysis of students' written solution attempts, including counts of the number of potentially successful methods tried and the degree of success in performing the steps required in each method. Frederiksen and Ward (1978) have reported some success in developing a test of creativity in designing and analyzing psychology experiments.

All of these procedures for measuring problem-solving ability are costly, because they require trained interviewers or extensive protocol analysis. Advances in cognitive science and computer technology may allow many of these procedures to be performed inexpensively with the use of a computer. For example, in the chemicals task reproduced in Appendix 7.4, designed to assess experiment-building skills, the problem is to find which combinations of chemicals make a color, and to determine the role of each chemical in creating the color. Students "run experiments" to see the results of any combination of chemicals, until they feel they have enough information to solve the problem. ETS has also recently pilot-tested some computer-based simulation problems (ETS, May 1987).

Variations on the chemicals task could also be developed. For example, a computer might simulate the effect on a pendulum of changing its mass, height, and length. Students could "run experiments" in the computer simulation, changing these variables until they felt they had enough information to decide on the relationship between these factors and the period of the pendulum.

The chemical and pendulum exercises meet McGuire and Babbott's (1967) criteria for useful simulation tasks by requiring multiple data-collection steps and avoiding clues that are artifacts of the test technique. They satisfy the criteria upon which multiple-choice items were evaluated, in that they would avoid artificiality, allow monitoring of solution processes, and involve more than factual knowledge (presuming the student was new to the task). These tasks would appear amenable to scoring according to whether (1) the results of all possible combinations were requested, (2) redundant information was requested, and (3) appropriate conclusions were drawn.

These computer tasks also have essential properties required for assessing problem-solving skills more successfully than is possible with present-day multiple-choice tests: The computer tests keep track of the students' problem-solving processes while allowing them to design their own experiments and draw their own conclusions. The computer version of the chemicals task, for example, has many of the advantages of the experimental "hands-on" tasks given by NAEP in the 1972–73 Principles and Procedures science tests, without the disadvantages of requiring trained interviewers, expensive protocol analysis, or time-consuming setups of actual equipment. Although it would take time to devise tasks that have the same advantages for assessing other kinds of mathematical and scientific skills, the fact that some useful tasks have been devised suggests that others could be created.

Three arguments can be raised against the methods we have proposed for increasing the process relevance of achievement indicators. One argument is that computer-based methods are too expensive to develop and use on a nationwide scale. The cost of computing has dropped dramatically in recent decades, however, and it continues to drop, so cost considerations should probably be explored only after pilot projects and fundamental research have determined whether useful computer items can be developed on a small scale. We should be more concerned about the likelihood that the lack of better measures of problem-solving ability could be an excuse for not teaching it (e.g., Frederiksen, 1984).

A second argument is that the correlation between multiple-choice tests and more valid tests is so high that we might as well use the less-costly alternative (e.g., Whimbey, 1985). This argument is based in large measure on "higher-order thinking tests" which require substantial reading ability. But reading ability is not problem-solving *per se*. Some good readers might do well on a multiple-choice test and still be unable to solve significant problems in the real world.

A final argument against supporting research into better measures of the use of concepts and skills is that students are already having so much trouble with present-day measures of problem-solving (as demonstrated by the NAEP problems already cited) that creating more realistic and difficult problems would be fruitless. But some of the trouble might be associated with current testing technology itself.

We believe that the greatest benefits to be derived from the development of new testing technologies will be that they will encourage schools to teach and students to learn how to solve problems. The NSB's *Educating Americans for the 21st Century* recognized the power and influence of standardized tests: "Properly modified, these can have considerable effect in hastening the hoped-for improvements in teaching of mathematics in grades K-12" (p. 5).

Curricular Relevance

State-developed tests and NAEP most successfully meet the criterion of curricular relevance. College admission tests are primarily aptitude tests designed to supplement information in the student's transcript. Moreover, the self-selected nature of the test takers makes these tests poor candidates for a national indicator system. The national longitudinal studies are also limited in their curricular relevance, since they attempt to measure student achievement with brief tests in different academic areas, and the assessments for mathematics and science are necessarily too brief to reflect much about the curriculum to which a student is exposed. They, too, are better measures of verbal and quantitative aptitude than of mathematics and science achievement.

State-developed tests appear to have the greatest curricular relevance because they reflect a surer sense of the curricula to which students have been exposed. This is fine for in-state indicator systems, but it has a serious drawback for a national indicator system in that there is little overlap in the content areas that are stressed in different states' tests (Burstein et al., 1985). The viability of this option depends on future developments in coordinating state assessments, which may not take place.

This leaves NAEP as the most promising short-term alternative in terms of curricular relevance. But because NAEP continues to be altered, the data from past and subsequent assessments may not be dependably comparable. Further, NAEP's efforts at improving its curricular relevance are constrained by the fact that it is a national assessment and there are large differences in content coverage among textbooks, (Freeman et al., 1983) and by wide variations in the portion of the curriculum that is not text-governed (Freeman et al., 1983).

Designers face two important challenges in trying to improve the curricular relevance of a national assessment. First, such attempts will necessarily involve value judgments concerning the choice of the "core" knowledge and skills to be emphasized in the assessment. Chapter 5 of this volume details some of the perils of trying to decide on "core" knowledge. While the content of tests could be influenced through various means (e.g., blue ribbon panels), the political implications raised are beyond any one agency's complete control. Second, control of education is delegated to the states and local districts, and they might resist being compared on the basis of a test into which they had little or no input. The political considerations involved here are beyond the scope of this chapter. Oakes and Carey provide a fuller discussion of them in Chapter 5.

With these constraints in mind, we can identify three options for improving the curricular relevance of achievement tests. The first would be to include, in each assessment, a questionnaire that asks teachers to specify which topics on the test had been covered in class. This option, exemplified by IEA's latest mathematics assessments, seems to be a workable means of assessing curricular relevance, although the accuracy of teacher reports has not been well-established.

A second option would be to include an analysis of student transcripts and grades in the achievement indicators. Transcript analysis is costly because of the differences in course sequences in school districts, but rough classifications could be made.[2] However, even if the cost of transcript analysis could be justified, there are no general standards for assigning grades: "While grades may provide some sense of the different performances of students within the same class, the meaning of a specific grade is likely to vary from class to class, from school to school, from region to region, from year to year . . . identical

---

[2]Adelman (1983) used a classification system developed by Evaluation Technologies (1982) to study transcripts from the Study of Academic Prediction and Growth and the New Youth Cohort of the National Longitudinal Study of Labor Market Experience (High School Classes of 1975–81).

grades clearly do not imply identical performance" (Raizen and Jones, 1985, p. 113).

As Raizen and Jones (1985) point out, some university admissions offices maintain databanks with comparative data on high school grades and university performance, which they use to adjust grades from particular high schools. Because staffing and grading patterns change at schools, we are uncomfortable with the assumptions of such a system, even if this data source could be applied to more than a small sample of schools.

Given the difficulties with the two options, we would consider teacher reports to be the best available alternative in the near term for monitoring, if not improving, the curricular relevance of achievement tests.

PARTICIPATION INDICATORS

Participation refers to outcomes such as choice of students to enroll in mathematics and science courses and become involved in extracurricular mathematics and science activities. We include these indicators because increased participation in mathematics and science is a goal in its own right. In addition, participation indicators predict subsequent achievement and foreshadow longer-term phenomena such as choice of college major or career, and they probably reflect attitudes toward mathematics and science to some degree. We do not discuss longer-term phenomena such as career choice, because these are highly influenced by factors outside of precollegiate mathematics and science education. Engineering, for example, may become a less desirable career option if a slumping economy or change in government policy causes engineers to be laid off in large numbers.

We recognize that participation is also influenced by student background and social context. The choice to enroll in elective mathematics and science courses may be influenced, for example, by college entrance requirements and parental and community expectations. We label participation as an outcome because it reflects choices of students to gain certain mathematical and scientific experiences.

Within-School Participation Indicators

Course enrollment is an important participation indicator because coursework determines, in large measure, how much science and mathematics content students are exposed to. In their review of the literature on the relationship between course-taking and achievement,

Raizen and Jones (1985) found that mathematics achievement scores are related to the number of mathematics courses taken, even when adjusted for race, sex, socioeconomic status (SES), and students' earlier mathematics scores (see also Horn and Walberg, 1984; Welch, Anderson, and Harris, 1982). Coursework is important for determining achievement in science, as well. For example, school effects on achievement are considerably larger for science than for reading (Welch, Anderson, and Harris, 1982; Wolf, 1979).

There would be difficulties in using course enrollment as a sole indicator, however, because course titles are not standardized across schools, and the content of identically titled courses can vary dramatically. Nevertheless, analyses of course data from High School and Beyond and NAEP (cited earlier) show that when rough course categories are used, this indicator can be used to gauge relative progress in mathematics and science education.

Just because a student goes to class does not necessarily mean he or she pays attention in class. Thus, attention while material is being covered might be considered an important aspect of participation. For elementary schools, Berliner and associates (e.g., Berliner, 1979; Fisher et al., 1980) have distinguished among *allocated time* (the time teachers reserve for instruction), *engaged time* (the time students are observed actually working on academic tasks), and *academic learning time* (the time students are observed to spend engaged in tasks of appropriate difficulty, as evidenced by their getting a large percentage of the problems correct). Since student achievement is most affected by engaged and learning time (e.g., Berliner, 1979; Fisher et al., 1980), there is empirical support for using student attention in class as an indicator of participation.

The difficulty with using engaged time as an indicator is that it has traditionally been measured by observer judgments. One alternative would be to use student reports of their own attention and what they think about in class. Peterson et al. (1984) found that students' reports of attention, understanding, and thinking about class material were predictive of classroom learning, whereas observers' judgments of student attention were not. However, we do not recommend student reports of attention in class as an individual indicator because those reports are highly related to the students' aptitudes (see also Peterson et al., 1982). Until or unless research clarifies the nature of that link, student reports will provide ambiguous and possibly misleading indicators. And, of course, students might lie about how much they pay attention in class.

A final indicator of within-class participation would be whether students have had particular mathematical and scientific experiences. For example, the 1981 NAEP asked students whether they had experimented with something for more than a week, used a telescope, experimented with chemical reactions, or read science articles in magazines. Although NAEP's phrasing does not limit these activities to within-class or outside-of-class participation, this kind of data might be useful because it has been proposed that females and ethnic minority students are disadvantaged by not being exposed to the same quantity and quality of science experiences as are white males (Kahle, 1983; see also Chapter 8 of this volume).

Extracurricular Participation

An indicator system that includes only class-taking and attention in class would be missing the importance of extracurricular science and mathematics activities. Research suggests a relationship between such activities and achievement and has also found that these activities are sometimes more indicative of later-life accomplishment than classroom successes are (Munday and Davis, 1974).

Shavelson's (1985) study of Department of Defense Dependent Schools found that students in academic programs, who generally achieve better than other students in mathematics and science, were most likely to participate in intellectual extracurricular activities (e.g., school newspaper or mathematics clubs). Similarly, Munday and Davis (1974) found consistent but weak correlations between high school extracurricular activities and later career achievements.

Other research suggests that extracurricular activities increase students' "time on task" on mathematics and science activities, a construct which is central to theories of the influence of education on achievement (e.g., Harnischfeger and Wiley, 1976). Besides increasing time on task, these activities may help students acquire problem-solving abilities that are not taught in class, such as deciding on a topic to address, on the nature of the problem, and on relevant ways to address the question. Finally, outside activities may help students develop physical intuitions for certain subjects such as physics. For example, Steinkamp and Maehr (1984) suggested that boys' experience with hobbies such as repairing cars may help explain why some of them understand physics better than many girls do.

Just as extracurricular participation may affect achievement, it may also affect attitudes. Extracurricular activities provide an opportunity to experiment with ideas or projects in a nonevaluative environment, allowing students to take risks they might avoid if they knew they were going to be graded on their work. Such activities may also help students gain self-confidence and develop specialized interests not emphasized in the general mathematics and science curriculum. The fact that one has voluntarily participated presents a powerful motive for convincing oneself that mathematics and science are fun and that one is proficient in them (Festinger, 1957).

Extracurricular participation may not only affect attitudes, it could also be considered an indicator of attitudes. It may be especially useful in determining which high-ability students are most enthused about mathematics and science.

Despite the studies suggesting that extracurricular activities might be important for achievement and attitudes, the nature of this relationship is not fully understood. It could be that achievement and attitudes influence participation, rather than vice versa. Further analytical research is needed in this area to enable monitoring the health of the system, and to gain a better understanding of the influence of various mathematical and scientific activities.

Overall Assessment of Participation

Participation can be measured by course enrollment, attention in class, within-class mathematics and science experiences, and extracurricular mathematical and scientific activities. Because of the problems with measuring attention in class, however, we would suggest that only the other three be given serious consideration as indicators. Course-taking deserves highest priority because of its curricular relevance and relative ease of measurement. Additionally, course-taking data are already collected by NAEP, IEA, and the Center for Education Statistics' longitudinal studies. Indicators of whether students have had various mathematical and scientific experiences, such as those included in NAEP, would also be worth including in an indicator system. Finally, extracurricular mathematical, scientific, and technical activities appear to be an important indicator, both of additional learning opportunities and of attitudes.

We must note one caveat: Education is not the only important influence on participation in mathematics and science. Student background, economic conditions, parental expectations, and community support undoubtedly play a large role in determining the degree to which students elect to take classes or participate in extracurricular mathematical and scientific activities. Nevertheless, participation is an important construct because it is crucial to later achievement and eventual career choice. Elective participation in courses might be particularly crucial, since there is evidence that for the average student mathematics and science are less amenable to learning on one's own than are subjects such as English or social studies (Welch et al., 1982).

ATTITUDE INDICATORS

Attitudes must be considered in a monitoring system because it is widely believed that (1) attitudes can foreshadow students' decisions about whether to continue taking mathematics and science courses, particularly females and minority students; (2) attitudes influence student achievement; and (3) possession of certain attitudes can assist in mathematical and scientific problem solving. Despite the weak evidence for these claims and the difficulties of measuring attitudes, an indicator system must include some attitude indicators because otherwise it would be widely perceived as incomplete.

The domain of attitudes includes a large number of potential indicators. In the following sections, we consider three broad categories: (1) attitudes toward mathematics and science; (2) self-confidence in one's ability to be successful in mathematics and science; and (3) "scientific habits of thought." Each category will be reviewed for its potential importance to a monitoring system, and for the adequacy of our present ability to measure it. We conclude with recommendations about the attitude measures that should be included in an indicator system.

Attitudes Toward Mathematics and Science

Attitudes toward mathematics and science consist basically of students' attraction to these fields, i.e., opinions about the desirability of a scientific career, the perceived usefulness of mathematics and science to one's career, interest in and enjoyment of these subjects, and beliefs about the capacity of mathematics and science to alleviate important social problems.

One primary rationale for including measures of attitudes toward mathematics and science is that positive attitudes result in increased enrollments in relevant coursework. In turn, increased enrollment results in a larger pool of mathematicians and scientists and a more scientifically literate public (Welch, 1983). However, the validity of this assumed chain of causality has not been systematically evaluated in any major reviews of the literature. Instead, reviews have evaluated the relationship between attitude measures and achievement (e.g., Haladyna and Shaughnessy, 1982; Raizen and Jones, 1985; Welch, 1983), the results of past attitude surveys (e.g., Hueftle, Rakow, and Welch, 1983), the reliability and validity of measures of attitudes (e.g., Munby, 1983a), and ways to improve attitudes (e.g., Haladyna, Olsen, and Shaughnessy, 1983).

However, results of research on attitudes toward mathematicians and scientists have suggested reasons why some students do not pursue scientific careers. Roger Johnson (in Ward, 1979) cites a 1956 nation-wide poll of high school students in which 30 percent of the respondents stated that you cannot expect to raise a normal family if you become a scientist, 27 percent said that scientists are willing to sacrifice the welfare of others to further their own interests, 25 percent expressed the belief that you have to be a genius to be a good scientist, 25 percent said that scientists are "more than a little bit odd," and 28 percent said that scientists do not have time to enjoy life.

These student responses concerning their stereotypes of scientists and mathematicians largely reflect the influence of society rather than the educational system (e.g., Blosser, 1984; Gardner, 1975), so we suggest that attitudes about mathematicians and scientists should have low priority in a system of educational indicators.

We think considerably more effort should be devoted to developing measures of students' *descriptive perceptions* of the fields of mathematics and science. Assessments of students' qualitative impressions of "what mathematics and science are like" would provide clues concerning the nature of the mathematics and science instruction that students are exposed to in school, and as such, would be more indicative of precollegiate coursework than would students' impressions of scientific careers.

The second NAEP mathematics assessment used a scale for 13- and 17-year-olds called "Mathematics as a Discipline," which asked students to state the degree to which they agreed or disagreed with statements such as "Mathematics is made up of unrelated topics," "Mathematics helps one to think logically," and "Doing mathematics requires lots of practice in following rules." IEA's Second International Mathematics Study's "mathematics as a process" scale showed that U.S. students believe mathematics helps them think logically, is a good subject for creative people, and is a discipline where new discoveries are being made. Nevertheless, the data also indicated that 8th grade students strongly tend to look at mathematics as a set of rules to follow and memorize, although 12th graders showed somewhat less of this tendency (Crosswhite et al., 1985).

There is controversy concerning the degree to which attitudes toward science as a discipline can be measured validly. Haladyna and Shaughnessy (1982) conclude that a few well-validated instruments of attitudes toward science exist (e.g., Neale, Gill, and Tismer, 1970; Haladyna and Thomas, 1979). However, Munby's (1983a) more extensive and focused review is considerably more critical. Munby analyzed 56 Likert-type attitude scales and found that 21 had no reported reliabilities, and only 21 had been used in more than one study. The analysis of tests' validities was even more critical—only 7 instruments had been validated by two or more psychometric methods, and only 4 instruments contained no cognitive (as opposed to attitudinal) items. Munby further concluded that even the 7 "survivors" of the analysis were suspect on one basis or another.

Another aspect of attitudes toward science is students' assessments of whether they enjoy mathematics and science classes in school. The rationale for including these attitudes is that enjoyment of mathematics and science classes foreshadows further course enrollment and influences eventual choice of careers. NAEP and IEA have both measured these perceptions. For example, the 1981–82 NAEP science assessment asked students whether science classes were fun, and how often classes made them feel happy, interested, or curious. Students also indicated how easy their classes were and how comfortable they felt in class. Hueftle, Rakow, and Welch (1983) compared these data with the earlier assessment and found that both 13- and 17-year-olds found science classes less easy, comfortable, and interesting than did respondents to the 1977 assessment. These negative trends were counterbalanced somewhat by 13-year-olds' virtually unchanged perception of the usefulness of science classes and 17-year-olds' more favorable opinions concerning the usefulness of science classes, their science teachers, and scientific careers, compared with respondents in the 1977 assessment. The fact that 17-year-olds were less positive toward their classes but more attracted to science careers suggests that enjoyment of science might not necessarily translate into higher likelihood of entering a science career.

Another rationale for including students' attitudes toward their classes is that positive attitudes contribute to student achievement. However, this claim is suspect. The generally weak correlation found between attitudes and achievement (e.g., Haladyna and Shaughnessy, 1982; Horn and Walberg, 1984; Welch, 1983) argues against a linear, causal relationship and may even support the interpretation that measurement difficulties preclude testing causal hypotheses adequately. Welch (1983) reports that the median correlation between achievement and science in the IEA studies was +0.20, a meta-analysis of 49 studies by Haladyna and Shaughnessy (1982) found a median correlation between achievement and attitudes of +0.15. Kahle's (1982) analysis of 1977 NAEP science data showed that minority students had positive attitudes toward science, science-related careers, and scientific research, which have not been accompanied by higher enrollment or achievement. Willson (1983, reported in Raizen and Jones, 1985) has suggested that even the weak relationships that exist between achievement and attitudes are due to achievement's effect on attitudes, rather than vice versa.

A third rationale for including students' attitudes toward their classes is that such attitudes influence their willingness to participate in subject-relevant extracurricular activities. However, Kahle's (1982) findings throw that interpretation into doubt. At age 17, more blacks than whites found science seldom or never boring (27 percent vs. 17 percent) and found it always or often fun (30 percent vs. 26 percent), and more blacks always or often liked to go to science classes (48 percent vs. 35 percent). Yet "these same black students had fewer science experiences, found science less useful out of school, and were less aware of scientific methods and how scientists work. Furthermore, they were less confident in the ability of science to solve current or future problems" (Kahle, 1982, pp. 541–542).

NAEP and IEA have also assessed students' interest in mathematical and scientific careers. NAEP's 1981 science assessment (Hueftle, Rakow, and Welch, 1983) found that 13-year-olds were more likely in 1981 than they were in 1977 to agree that working in a science-related field would be fun and something they would like to do; they also were more likely to agree that the education and training needed to enter a scientific field would be worth the effort in the long run and would open job opportunities. On the other hand, they were also more likely to state that such a career would take too much education and that scientific training would not be worthwhile if one did not go into a scientific field. Seventeen-year-olds in 1981 were also somewhat more favorable toward careers in science, although they also thought that such careers would be lonely. These results suggest that attitudes toward science classes may be somewhat independent of students' attitudes toward science careers: Whereas opinions of their science classes had generally declined during the 1977–81 period, students were becoming more interested in scientific careers.

Evidence on the importance of assessing students' feelings toward science and mathematics careers is promising, but equivocal. On the one hand, interest in careers might be an important indicator of further course participation. For example, Berryman (1983, cited in Chapter 8 of this volume) found that girls who *are* interested in mathematics and science careers are more likely to take classes in these subjects. On the other hand, being positive toward mathematics and science careers is not always enough to assure that students will get the experiences needed to pursue such careers. In the 1976–77 NAEP science assessment, for example, more 13- and 17-year-old blacks than whites expressed positive attitudes toward scientific careers, yet blacks were far below whites in science experiences and awareness of the scientific process (Ward, 1979).

A final aspect of attitudes toward science is the degree to which students believe science can help solve society's problems. Although questions on this issue are undoubtedly asked because they are thought to affect students' career choices, a less commonly expressed reason for measuring attitudes toward mathematics and science has been fear that negative attitudes could eventually result in lower levels of public support for research in these fields. This reason is reflected in the 1976–77 NAEP's questions for 13- and 17-year-olds which ask about the importance of "studying the size of large groups of stars," "studies about migration habits of bees," "research into better ways to produce fertilizer," and "research to develop vaccines for epidemic-type diseases" (ETS, NAEP Demonstration Package, Year 8, p. 16). Other questions that fall into this category include questions about whether science research has produced useful information about what foods to eat, how much the application of science can help prevent worldwide starvation, and the degree to which science is personally useful outside of class.

The rationale for including measures of students' view of the usefulness of science to society can be questioned. In the 1981 science assessment, for example, 17-year-olds, who were more positive about science careers than the same age group in 1977, were also less confident of science's ability to solve world problems (Hueftle, Rakow, and Welch, 1983). This suggests that career preference is more strongly influenced by factors other than whether the career will contribute to society.

Self-Confidence in Mathematics and Science

Self-confidence refers to students' perceptions that they have the capacity to achieve in mathematics and science and that they can participate in mathematical and scientific careers. Research suggests that students' feelings of confidence can have important influences on their participation and achievement. From the psychological literature, Bandura (1977) has suggested that expectations of success determine whether people will attempt to solve a problem, how much effort they will expend, and how long they will persist when there are obstacles to meeting their goals. Minority and lower-SES children may be particularly prone to debilitation resulting from low self-expectations (e.g., Gurin et al., 1969; Oakes, Chapter 8 of this volume). More generally, studies by Schunk (e.g., 1981) have found that perceptions of competence predict both persistence and performance in mathematics among previously low-achieving children.

Research suggests that self-confidence can be important in science classes, as well. Simpson (1977, cited in Kahle, 1982) states:

> As students move through various grade levels feelings towards themselves play an increasingly important role in how they do academically. These attitudes form gradually, and once formed tend to be stable. Success in Junior High School science, and to a greater extent in High School science, is thus a product of a set of complex, accumulative feelings derived from earlier success and failures. (p. 42)

It has not been established exactly how students come to have self-confidence in mathematics and science, but it is likely that children's attributions for their success or failure influence their later choices and their persistence in attaining goals (see Weiner, 1972, 1977, 1979; Stipek and Weisz, 1981). For example, children usually persist less when they believe their failures are due to lack of ability than if they attribute failure to lack of effort. Chipman and Thomas (1984) note that women are less likely to attribute success to their own abilities, and they suggest that this might make past success less likely to inspire them to expect future successes.

NAEP and IEA have included measures of students' self-confidence in mathematics and science. NAEP's Second Mathematics Assessment asked students to indicate whether mathematics made them feel nervous and how difficult they found topics such as estimating answers to problems. The 1981–82 science assessment asked whether working in a science-related field was something students felt they could do. Between the 1977 and 1981 assessments, there was an increasing tendency for 17-year-olds to think that working in a science-related field was "something I could do" (55.8 percent in 1977 vs. 64.5 percent in 1982) and to agree that there are science-related jobs that they could learn to do (77.0 percent in 1977 vs. 81.9 percent in 1982). These NAEP questions are ambiguous: They confound the perception that jobs in science exist with the student's perception that he or she is capable in science. The IEA's Second International Mathematics Study contained less ambiguous measures of self-confidence: Students were asked to agree or disagree with statements such as, "I am not so good at mathematics" or "Mathematics is harder for me than for most people." Although the IEA questions are more clearly relevant to self-confidence, their phrasing is not as relevant to students' perceived career choices.

Attitudes as an Approach to Thinking

Some attitudes, such as curiosity, perseverance, flexibility, objectivity, and open-mindedness are thought to facilitate achievement. Judging by educators' statements of their aims, the development of attitudes toward thinking has been and will continue to be an important goal of education. Gauld (1982) cites a multitude of statements that stress scientific attitudes as a major goal of education (e.g., Whipple, 1932; Henry, 1947; Henry, 1960; Educational Policies Commission, 1966; N.S.T.A., 1971). Burnett (1944) called this goal "scientific mindedness," Noll (1933) called it "the habit of scientific thinking," and the Educational Policies Commission (1966) called it "the spirit of science." The most recent reports of commissions have echoed earlier findings, such as the NSB (1983) call for the design of instruction that would contribute to the development of "students' capacities for problem-solving and critical thinking in all areas of learning," and "development of particular talents for innovative and creative thinking" (p. 44).

Researchers have also considered approaches to thinking as important. In their review of the large body of research on scientific attitudes, Gauld and Hukins (1980, cited in Blosser, 1984) identified three broad groups of attitudes in terms of an approach to thinking. One group, which they label "general attitudes toward ideas and information," refers to traits such as curiosity, open-mindedness, and creativity. The second group, "attitudes related to the evaluation of ideas and information," includes objectivity, intellectual honesty, and caution when drawing conclusions. The third group, "commitment to particular (scientific) belief," refers to loyalty to truth, belief in the understandability of nature, and belief in the existence of natural cause-and-effect relationships. Nay and Crocker (1970) developed an inventory of scientific attitudes which includes all three of these areas (Appendix 7.5).

Approaches to thinking have been emphasized largely because such attitudes are considered useful to students who later become mathematicians and scientists. Another rationale is that such attitudes help students understand the nature of science and mathematics and represent desirable traits for all people (Gauld, 1982). Scientific approaches to problems are also thought to be effective for solving problems in everyday life:

> As we consider the future responsibilities of citizens, we will probably agree that helping children to become more co-operative, more responsible, more "open-minded," and, at the same time, more "critical-minded" is certainly worth the effort. (Henry, 1947, p. 87)

Nevertheless, there has been little emphasis on approaches to thinking in recent national and international surveys of education. NAEP (e.g., NAEP, 1977–78) has tended to measure students' attitudes toward mathematics and science in school, self-confidence and enjoyment of these subjects, opinions about the worth of these disciplines to society, and beliefs concerning mathematics and science as disciplines. None of these attitudes could be considered relevant to approaches to thinking or scientific attitudes as described by Gauld and Hukins (1980).

The IEA's assessments have also deemphasized measures of attitudes. The Second International Mathematics Study (Crosswhite et al., 1985) included scales called "mathematics and myself" (which measured self-confidence in mathematics), "mathematics and society" (which measured students' views of mathematics as useful and important), "mathematics and gender" (which measured students' views of mathematics as a male domain), and "mathematics as a process" (which measured whether students thought mathematics was good for creative people, helped them think logically, or was a growing discipline). As with NAEP's attitude questions, none of these IEA measures directly emphasized approaches to thinking, such as students' attitudes toward information and the evaluation of ideas, or their commitment to logical thinking.

There appear to be valid reasons for NAEP's and IEA's lack of emphasis on attitudes as approaches to thinking. First, it is difficult to develop valid measures of students' approaches to thinking. For example, the IEA's first international assessment of science discarded 8 of 12 original attitude scales because only four had sufficient reliability (Comber and Keeves, 1973; Welch, 1983). Gauld (1982) suggests that there are few available measures of scientific attitudes, and attitude measures in general have been brought into question by critical analyses (e.g., Munby, 1983a).

A more important reason for deemphasizing approaches to thinking is the lack of a relationship between the image of the scientist espoused in goal statements and the nature of science as it is practiced. Gauld (1982) cites studies of the psychology of scientists (e.g., Roe, 1961; Mahoney, 1979) and case studies of scientific discoveries (e.g., Swenson, 1970) to argue that most taxonomies of scientific attitudes preserve a stereotypical conception of scientists that is far removed from the way successful scientists actually operate. For example, Mitroff and Mason (1974) studied 42 scientists doing research related to the Apollo moon missions and found that the best of them were *both* emotional and objective, open-minded and tenacious, depending on context:

> The single dimension which most served to differentiate between the scientists was that of "speculativeness" or "willingness to extrapolate beyond the available data." At one end of the spectrum were the extreme speculative scientists who in the words of the respondents, "wouldn't hesitate to build a whole theory of the solar system based on no data at all"; on the other extreme were the data-bound scientists who "wouldn't be able to save their own hide if a fire was burning next to them because they'd never had enough data to prove the fire was really there". . . . One of the most significant things about these differences is that the more outstanding a scientist was, as judged by his peers, the more he lay near the speculative end of the scale. Conversely, the more "mundane," "typical," or "run-of-the-mill" scientists fell toward the "data bound" end of the scale.
>
> At the same time the more speculative scientists are also the kinds of scientists who are more likely to become rigidly committed to their ideas once they have produced them. Contrary to popular misconception, it is the "lesser" not the "greater" scientist, who is more likely to have an "open mind." The greater the scientist the more likely he is to develop a line and to push it for all it is worth. (Mitroff and Mason, 1974, from Gauld, 1982, p. 113)

Overall Assessment of Attitudes

The wide variety of attitudes suggests that priorities should be assigned regarding which of them are most important for an indicator system. We would suggest that the system should include (1) interest in mathematics and science careers, (2) perceptions of the process of doing mathematics and science, and (3) perceptions of the students' own mathematics and science classes. Career interest could be an important indicator of whether students are getting "turned off" at an early age, although our findings suggest that changes in the economy probably affect career choice as much as do in-school experiences. Perceptions of the process of doing mathematics and science and perceptions of mathematics and science classes could reveal whether students feel they are profiting from the types of experiences they receive in their classes.

We would place lower priority on attitudes toward scientists and mathematicians because these attitudes in large measure reflect cultural stereotypes unrelated to the school system; in any case, these attitudes apparently have less relationship to career choices than does interest in mathematics and science careers itself. It would be more important to find out whether students plan mathematical and scientific careers than whether they admire mathematicians and scientists. In many students' opinion, "science is generally viewed as an important and critical endeavor, but it is one to be pursued by somebody else" (Welch, 1983). Lower priority should also be placed on perceptions of the worth of research or the usefulness of mathematics and science to society, since these do not appear to have a large impact on career choice or course participation.

Among self-confidence variables, both attitudes toward one's competence, such as those assessed by the IEA, and feelings that one can participate in mathematical and scientific careers, such as those measured by NAEP, appear to be relevant. If attitudes are to be included in an outcome indicator system, self-confidence should be monitored along with attitudes toward mathematics and science.

We believe that measures of attitudes as an approach to thinking should not be included in an indicator system. Our review suggests that the attitudes portrayed in measures of approaches to thinking are unrelated to the real activities of good scientists. Furthermore, if such attitudes are supposed to facilitate achievement, then achievement itself is what should be measured.

Finally, because of the difficulty of measuring attitudes, we believe that measures of participation in coursework and in extracurricular mathematical and scientific activities are essential to any indicator system. While measures of participation, particularly in extracurricular activities, are most sensitive to the attitudes of the gifted and highly motivated, we believe that these items provide important, concrete indicators of those students' attitudes. In contrast, paper-and-pencil questions concerning self-confidence and attitudes toward mathematics and science classes might be most useful for tracking changes in the feelings of lower- or middle-ability students.

SUMMARY AND CONCLUSIONS

The most important mathematics and science education outcome indicator is achievement. Achievement is widely considered by policymakers, politicians, and the public to be synonymous with educational "effectiveness," but we believe it encompasses far more than what is measured by traditional multiple-choice tests. Achievement indicators should include measures of student knowledge, understanding, and application of problem-solving concepts and skills.

In the short term, achievement outcomes could be monitored by using data collected through NAEP, the national longitudinal studies, IEA, college admission tests, and state-developed tests.

In the long run, the present reliance on multiple-choice tests limits the ability of nationwide achievement assessments to monitor student understanding and problem-solving skills. We recommend further research into improving the ability to assess student understanding and problem-solving skills. Because testing exerts a profound influence on education, the application of testing research in a monitoring system could improve education dramatically, and could also help to monitor those aspects of achievement that are most crucial.

Student participation is the second most important indicator of education outcomes. Participation indicators should include measures of student course-taking; extracurricular mathematical, scientific, and technological activities; and mathematical and scientific experiences. We recommend these indicators but note that participation is highly influenced by factors other than schooling and should be interpreted accordingly.

Although research has presented little evidence that attitudes are essential to an indicator system, a system without some attitude measures would be perceived as incomplete. The most important attitudes to include in a system are students' perceptions of the process of doing mathematics and science, interest in mathematical and scientific careers, liking of their mathematics and science classes, and self-confidence in their abilities to do mathematics and science or participate in mathematical and scientific careers. Each of these attitudes can be related to students' precollegiate education experiences or has a logical relationship to future career choices. In contrast, we recommend against including measures of students' attitudes as an approach to thinking, of their stereotypes of mathematicians and scientists, or of their opinions about the ability of mathematics and science to solve significant social problems.

Appendix 7.1

MATHEMATICAL PROCESSES INCLUDED IN THE 1981–82 NAEP MATHEMATICS ASSESSMENT

I. Mathematical Knowledge
   A. How well can students recall and recognize facts, definitions, and symbols?

II. Mathematical Skill
   A. How well can students perform paper and pencil computations, including computations with whole numbers, integers, fractions, decimals, percents, and ratios and proportions?
   B. How well can students perform algebraic manipulations?
   C. How well can students perform geometric manipulations like constructions and spatial visualizations?
   D. How well can students make measurements?
   E. How well can students compute statistics, probabilities, or combinations?
   F. How well can students perform mental computations, including computations with whole numbers, fractions, decimals, and percents?
   G. How well can students estimate the answers to computations and measurements?
   H. How well can students perform computations involving whole numbers, decimals, fractions, and percents using hand calculators?
   I. How well can students read flowcharts or basic computer programs?

III. Mathematical Understanding
   A. How well can students translate a verbal statement into symbols or a figure, and vice versa?
   B. How well do students understand mathematical concepts and principles?
   C. How well can students select an appropriate computational method such as paper/pencil, mental, estimation, or calculator?

IV. Mathematical Application
  A. How well can students solve routine textbook problems?
  B. How well can students solve nonroutine problems?
  C. How well can students apply problem-solving strategies?
  D. How well can students estimate the answers to application problems?
  E. How well can students interpret data and draw conclusions?
  F. How well can students use mathematics, including logic, in reasoning and making judgments?
  G. How well can students use the hand calculator to solve application problems?

Appendix 7.2

MATRIX OF SCIENCE OBJECTIVES
FOR THE 1976–77 NAEP

Hundreds of aspects of science in the forms of facts, concepts, laws, principles, conceptual schemes, inquiry skills, appreciations, attitudes, and opinions (some with no "correct" or "incorrect" answer) have been systematically selected to sample the various cells of the matrix. Aspects of science were judged by leading science educators to contribute to important goals of science education because they met the *criteria* below.

Criteria for Aspects of Science to Be Included in the 1976–77 NAEP Science Objectives

To be included in the science assessment, aspects of science must meet one or more of the following criteria. They must:

1. Contribute substantially to the understanding of the nature of a subject area (considered important by leading professionals), or
2. Entail key concepts for large bodies of knowledge (e.g., integrative concepts showing interactions and interconnections), or
3. Have broad application beyond the curricular science area, or
4. Be personally relevant and applicable—contribute to the survival, well-being, and quality of life of the individual, or
5. Be useful in potential career preparation, or
6. Contribute to an effective base for decisionmaking at all levels of society (i.e., regarding persistent societal problems), or
7. Contribute to the understanding of self, or
8. Contribute to understanding the nature, potential, and limitations of science.

	Knowledge generation					Knowledge use			
	A. Biological Science	B. Physical Science	C. Earth Science	D. Multi-Disciplinary Science	E. Processes & Methods of Science	F. Science & Societal Problems	G. Science & Self	H. Science & Technology (Applied)	I. Scientific Decision Making
Cognitive 1. Knowledge									
2. Comprehension (Understanding)									
3. Application									
4. Analysis									
Affective 5. Receiving									
6. Responding									
7. Valuing									

Appendix 7.3

ITEMS ON 1972 AND 1980 HSB SURVEYS

Test Items[a]		Testing Time (minutes)
1972	1980	
Senior Battery		
Vocabulary (15)	Vocabulary, Part 1 (identical with 1972 test)	5
	Vocabulary, Part 2 (12 new items with broader range of difficulty)	4
Picture Number (30)	Picture Number (15 of original 30 items)	5
Reading (20)	Identical	15
Letter Groups (25)	Omitted	
Mathematics (25)	Part 1 (19 items the same as 1972, 6 easier)	15
	Part 2 (8 more difficult items)	
Mosaic Comparisons (116)	Mosaic Comparisons (89 of original 116 items)	6
	Visualization in Three Dimensions (16 items)	9
Sophomore Battery		
None	Vocabulary (9 from 1972 test and 12 new items increasing range)	7
	Reading (8 from 1972 test and 12 new easier items)	15
	Mathematics, Part 1 (18 from 1972 test and 10 new items increasing range)	16
	Mathematics, Part 2 (10 emphasizing achievement)	5
	Science (20)	10
	Writing (17)	10
	Civics Education (10)	5

SOURCE: Heyns and Hilton, 1982.
[a]The number of items is shown in parentheses.

Appendix 7.4

EXAMPLE OF A COMPUTER SIMULATION FOR
TESTING HOW WELL A STUDENT CAN
PERFORM A CONTROLLED EXPERIMENT[1]

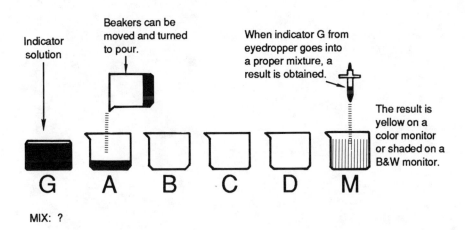

Indicator solution

Beakers can be moved and turned to pour.

When indicator G from eyedropper goes into a proper mixture, a result is obtained.

The result is yellow on a color monitor or shaded on a B&W monitor.

G A B C D M

MIX: ?

To discover to a certainty that only two of the mixtures would produce a color, the subject would have to try all 15 possible combinations of chemicals: GA, GB, GC, GD, GAB, GAC, GAD, GBC, GBD, played by the different chemicals—the indicator G, the neutral A, the reactants B and C, and the inhibitor D. Subjects who tried all combinations and identified the roles of the various chemicals were guided by a well-developed formal operational strategy. Subjects who did not achieve a color result, or who only got one color result, were not guided by formal operations.

This program is a computerized version of Piaget's task. It records and optionally prints out a hard copy of the solution strategy of the subject. The program also simulates Piaget's clinical or qualitative approach in that it is designed to permit identification of the problem-solving strat-

---

[1]From Life Science Associates.

egy used, rather than merely determine whether the subject got the answer correct according to the criterion of formal operations. This is accomplished by giving the subject the option of quitting the task whenever he is satisfied with the solution, and by asking why he is satisfied, and about confidence in this solution. At appropriate steps in the interview sequence, the subject is given the option to return to the task. These changes in satisfaction, confidence, or strategy are indicated on the hardcopy printout that describes the subject's behavior.

Appendix 7.5

AN INVENTORY OF SCIENTIFIC ATTITUDES[4]

1. Interests
   (The motivation for a person to become a scientist and continue to be one.)
   1.1 Understanding natural phenomena
       1.11 Curiosity
       1.12 Fascination
       1.13 Excitement
       1.14 Enthusiasm
   1.2 Contributing to knowledge and human welfare
       1.21 Altruism
       1.22 Ambition
       1.23 Pride
       1.24 Satisfaction

2. Operational adjustments
   (Primary behaviors which underlie competence and success in science, and performance at recognized standards.)
   2.1 Dedication and commitment
       2.11 Perseverance (persistence)
       2.12 Patience
       2.13 Self-discipline
       2.14 Selflessness
       2.15 Responsibility
       2.16 Dependability
   2.2 Experimental requirements
       2.21 Systematism (methodicalness)
       2.22 Thoroughness
       2.23 Precision
       2.24 Sensitivity
       2.25 Alertness for the unexpected
   2.3 Initiative and resourcefulness
       2.31 Pragmatism (common sense)
       2.32 Courage (daring, venturesomeness)

---

[4]From Nay and Crocker, 1970, pp. 61–62.

2.33 Self-direction (independence)
2.34 Self-reliance
2.35 Confidence
2.36 Flexibility
2.37 Aggressiveness
2.4 Relations with peers
2.41 Cooperation
2.42 Compromise
2.43 Modesty (humility)
2.44 Tolerance

3. Attitudes or intellectual adjustments
(Intellectual behaviors which are fundamental to the scientist's contribution to or acceptance of new knowledge.)
3.1 Scientific integrity
3.11 Objectivity
3.12 Open-mindedness
3.13 Honesty
3.14 Suspended judgment (restraint)
3.15 Respect for evidence (reliance on fact)
3.16 Willingness to change opinions
3.17 Idea sharing
3.2 Critical requirements
3.21 Critical-mindedness
3.22 Skepticism
3.23 Questioning attitude
3.24 Disciplined thinking
3.25 Anti-authoritarianism
3.26 Self-criticism

4. Appreciations
(Relative to the foundations, interactions, and dynamics of science.)
4.1 The history of science
4.11 The evolution of scientific knowledge
4.12 Contributions made by individual scientists
4.13 The exponential growth of science
4.2 Science and society
4.21 The social basis of the development of modern science
4.22 The contribution made by science to social progress and melioration

    4.23 The relationship between science and technology

    4.24 The interaction of the "two cultures"

    4.3   The nature of science

    4.31 The process of scientific inquiry

    4.32 The tentative and revisionary character of scientific knowledge

    4.33 The strength and limitations of science

    4.34 The value of one's own contribution and the debt owing other scientists

    4.35 The communality of scientific ideas

    4.36 The aesthetics and parsimony in scientific theory

    4.37 The power of individual cooperative effort

    4.38 The power of logical reasoning (rationality)

    4.39 The causal, relativistic, and probabilistic nature of phenomena

5. Values and/or beliefs
(In the realm of philosophy, ethics, politics, etc.)

    5.1 Philosophy

      5.11 The universe is "real"

      5.12 The universe is comprehensible (knowable) through observation and rational thought

    5.2 Ethical

      5.21 Science is amoral, but scientists have the responsibility to interpret the consequences of their work

      5.22 Humanism is the highest ideal

    5.3 Social

      5.31 Science must serve the needs of society

      5.32 Science flourishes best in a free and democratic society

Chapter 8

CREATING INDICATORS THAT ADDRESS POLICY PROBLEMS: THE DISTRIBUTION OF OPPORTUNITIES AND OUTCOMES

Jeannie Oakes

Throughout this volume we have stressed those generic features of schooling that will provide valid and useful information about precollege mathematics and science education. This chapter departs from that agenda to illustrate how indicators might shed light on a particularly critical policy issue and to suggest how the technical features of indicator systems can affect their ability to address policy problems.

Policymakers and the public have become increasingly concerned about the failure of women, the poor, and non-Asian minorities to participate or achieve as much as white males in mathematics and science education—a problem that has long worried educators. These differences manifest themselves early and become more pronounced as children proceed in school. Indicators have the potential for helping policymakers and educators to better understand this problem and to target reforms at those features of schooling linked to it. The data necessary to develop such indicators are described in other chapters, e.g., on resources, school context, curriculum, classroom practices, participation, and outcomes. However, these indicators can be useful only if we collect, analyze, and report data in ways that permit policymakers to examine and compare the experiences and outcomes of particular student groups. That will require designing sampling frames for new data collection efforts that permit estimates for important subpopulations and expanding the sampling frames of current data collection efforts so that they will also permit separate analyses of these groups. Additionally, indicators central to the participation of women and minorities should be reported separately to make information about the problem and potential solutions more accessible to decisionmakers.

This chapter outlines the policy problem in more detail, discusses the specific schooling conditions that may contribute to the group disparities we find, and identifies how indicators might provide useful information about this critical policy issue.

WHY DEVELOP INDICATORS ABOUT UNDERREPRESENTED GROUPS?

Public concern has been fueled by an outpouring of reports over the past ten years on improving elementary and secondary schooling. *Educating Americans for the 21st Century*, for example, linked the ability of American schools to upgrade the quality of mathematics and science education to the willingness and ability of the educational system to better educate the low-achieving groups. The report cautioned that their attainments will become an increasingly critical factor in the nation's scientific and technological strength.

That issue is one of the two major questions prompting policy attention: First, how will these groups' typically lower levels of achievement and participation affect the national welfare as the demand for a scientifically trained workforce increases? Second, does this phenomenon constitute evidence that women, the poor, and ethnic minorities do not have the equal educational opportunity that government policies have sought to ensure? Regardless of how great or little the effect addressed by the first question, the possibility of inequity remains a serious concern.

Evidence of unequal outcomes is, of course, of itself not enough to establish schooling inequities. However, persistent disparities in mathematics and science achievement do establish that schools have been considerably less successful with *some groups* of students than with others. The substantially unequal participation and achievement *among groups* (and the significant increases in outcome discrepancies over time in school) provide noteworthy signals that schooling factors may contribute to the inequities. Given current policy concerns, indicators are needed to monitor educational opportunity and the system's progress toward higher levels of educational achievement and participation among "at-risk" groups.[1]

THE POLICY PROBLEM

National statistics on academic achievement, high school completion, acquisition of college degrees, occupational status, and income all reveal substantial disparities among racial, ethnic, and socioeconomic groups. The most extreme disparities appear in science and mathemat-

---

[1]Confusion exists about the definition of "at-risk" students. Here, "at-risk" refers to female students, non-Asian minorities, and the poor—those groups whose established patterns of lower levels of school and adult accomplishments in scientific and quantitative fields put them educationally at risk in these subject areas.

ics, as has been eloquently detailed in several recent reports.[2] Further, in these subject areas, the disparities extend to gender as well.

The Larger Policy Context

These disparities are of increasing policy concern, given projected demographic changes in the United States over the next several years and changing demands in the nation's workforce (Levin, 1986). According to demographic projections, the youth cohort is decreasing and the poor and minorities will comprise a larger proportion of it. At the same time, the demand for a better-educated workforce continues to increase. For example, between 1976 and 1983, jobs for scientists and engineers increased at three times the rate of overall U.S. employment, and the annual employment growth in computer specialties during these years was 17 percent (National Science Board, 1985). And these figures may only scratch the surface of the *potential* for expansion in technological employment. Even as this sector of the workforce has increased, the proportion of the U.S. population trained in science and engineering has slipped markedly compared with our technological trading partners—Japan, West Germany, France, and the United Kingdom (Bloch, 1986).

The convergence of these trends brings new worries about how the typically low educational attainment of women, the poor, and minorities in science and mathematics may affect the national economy and security. Equally important, the educational attainment of these groups directly reflects upon the federal government's long-standing responsibility for ensuring the provision of equal educational opportunity.

The Extent and Implications of the Problem

It is clear that not all students (regardless of race, class, or gender) have sufficient aptitudes or interest to become scientists or mathematicians. However, the disparities for women and non-Asian minorities are so great that there can be no doubt that considerable science and mathematics talent is being lost from these groups. During the past two decades, women and, to a lesser extent, minorities have made important progress in narrowing these gaps. Nevertheless, the disparities are still great:

---

[2]E.g., American Association for the Advancement of Science (AAAS), 1984; Achievement Council, 1985; Berryman, 1983; Chipman and Thomas, 1984; Darling-Hammond, 1985; National Alliance of Black School Educators (NABSE), 1984; Scientific Manpower Commission, 1983.

- Women, blacks, and Hispanics consistently perform below the levels of white males on measures of end-of-high-school achievement in mathematics and science. Poor children do less well than their more affluent peers (NCES, 1985a). Not only is the overall pattern of differences disturbing, perhaps even more distressing is the persistence of the greatest disparities on measures of higher-level mathematical skills and problem solving (NCES, 1985a).

- Minority achievement is even lower, absolutely and relatively, than test scores imply, for two reasons: First, a disproportionate number of blacks and Hispanics are not in school and thus are not represented in measures of high school achievement. Second, those who drop out are typically among the lowest achievers, so their test scores would potentially widen the difference between minority and non-minority average scores (see Chapter 9 of this volume).[3]

- Although women and men enter college at relatively equal rates, black and Hispanic high school graduates are less likely than whites to enter college. Further, those who do enroll are more likely than whites to attend two- rather than four-year colleges. This pattern of disproportionate school attainment is reflected at every juncture in the educational pipeline. The gaps in the percentages of blacks, Hispanics, and whites completing four-year college programs and entering and completing graduate school continue to widen. Disparities between women and men appear at the highest levels—far fewer doctoral degrees are awarded to women (NCES, 1985a).

- Women, blacks, and Hispanics are underrepresented as college majors in science, mathematics, and engineering and as recipients of bachelor's, master's, and doctoral degrees in those fields. They decreasingly choose quantitative fields of study as they advance in school and are decreasingly represented as advanced degree holders (Commission on Professionals in Science and Technology, 1986).

- As a consequence of the above, women and non-Asian minorities are significantly underrepresented in the science,

---

[3]High School and Beyond (HSB) data reveal higher sophomore-to-senior dropout rates for blacks and Hispanics than for whites—16.8, 18.7, and 12.2 percent, respectively—and rates of 22.3, 13.2, 10.7, and 7.0 percent from the lowest to highest socioeconomic status (SES) quartiles (NCES, 1985a). These statistics underestimate the differences, since many minority youth leave school before grade 10. Census data from 1982, for example, show high school non-completion rates for then 20- to 24-year-olds as 23 percent for blacks and 40 percent for Hispanics, compared with 15 percent for whites (U.S. Department of Commerce, 1982).

mathematics, and technology workforce. In 1984, for example, fewer than 25 percent of the employed scientists and engineers were women. Fewer than 7 percent were Blacks, Hispanics, and American Indians (although these groups make up 20 percent of the total population) (National Science Foundation, 1986).

Patterns of lower achievement and underparticipation for women and minorities begin early in the educational process, and the discrepancies among groups grow larger the longer children remain in school. Race and SES differences in mathematics achievement are evidenced by age 9, are clearly in place by age 13, and continue to increase during senior high school (NAEP, 1980; Jones, 1984).

Small gender differences appear on some measures between the ages of 11 and 13 (Maccoby and Jacklin, 1974), with the earlier differences occurring among the most able students (Benbow and Stanley, 1980, 1982). Widespread gender differences are evidenced later in students' school careers, in senior high school. National Assessment of Educational Progress (NAEP) data on mathematics achievement support this pattern (even though they measure different student cohorts) (NAEP, 1980; Walberg, Fraser, and Welch, 1986).

Race, class, and gender discrepancies in *participation* in mathematics and science also increase over time in school. They become most evident in secondary school, when curriculum track differentiation and course choice become available to students: Women, non-Asian minorities, and the poor enroll in fewer courses and more lower-level courses than white males and Asians (NCES, 1985c).

The striking differences in college enrollments, choice of fields for study, and adult participation in the mathematics, science, and technology workforce pose serious challenges for all levels of precollegiate schooling. The possibility that educational policies and practices may actually play a role in these unequal results for various groups of students warrants the development of indicators of those schooling factors that may be related: (1) differences in educational resources and teacher quality, and (2) differences in actual school experiences for the at-risk and other groups. Disparities in these schooling inputs are of considerable policy interest in themselves. But, as shown in the discussion below, existing differences may, in fact, also be related to outcome disparities.

EDUCATIONAL RESOURCES FOR DIFFERENT GROUPS

Resource Disparities

Children living in communities with low levels of property wealth and personal income typically attend schools that spend fewer dollars on schooling (e.g., per-pupil expenditures). These relationships appear to persist even in those states where school finance reforms have attempted to equalize schooling resources (Carroll and Park, 1983). In some cases, in fact, per-pupil expenditures between neighboring high- and low-wealth districts differ by as much as a factor of two (see Chapter 2 of this volume).

Unequal funding patterns are particularly relevant to race- and class-equity concerns, since most minority and poor children attend schools in low-wealth communities or in central cities, where the competing demands for tax dollars are great. Resources available to central city schools are especially important because of the high proportion of non-Asian minorities who live in inner cities: In 1983, 71 percent of blacks and 58 percent of Hispanics lived in these areas (American Council on Education, 1983). The *proportion* of minority enrollments in large city school districts has increased dramatically in the past 15 years—in some cases, it has doubled—and current projections suggest that these trends will continue. As a result, the pattern of unequal funding in the nation's schools means that poor and minority children will have less access than their more advantaged counterparts to well-maintained school facilities, highly qualified teachers, smaller classes, and instructional equipment and materials—important educational resources that funding dollars buy.

Moreover, poor and minority children have been more negatively affected than others by recent changes in educational funding policies. First, the reduction of federal assistance to education over the past decade (including that for compensatory programs and impact aid to desegregating school districts) has reduced the resources available to poor and minority children (Levin, 1986). Second, changes in the means of distributing federal funds have further diminished programs and services to disadvantaged children. The Educational Consolidation and Improvement Act (ECIA) of 1981 lessened the regulation and monitoring of Chapter 1 compensatory funds with respect to both targeting aid for particular populations and ensuring comparable spending in target and non-target schools. Additionally, by combining the Emergency School Assistance Act program (aimed at assisting desegregating school districts) with a number of other programs into enrollment-based block grant funding, ECIA further reduced funds and programs for urban schools and minority children (Darling-Hammond, 1985).

At the state level, decreased public willingness to provide support for schooling (best exemplified by the "tax revolt" that began with the passage of California's Proposition 13 in 1978) has led to substantially fewer dollars being available for education overall. In many advantaged school districts, community groups have offset these reductions, at least in part, by establishing educational foundations to raise additional funds. These, however, are not the districts where most poor and minority children live. Even though we are now witnessing some increases in state funding in conjunction with educational reforms, few urban districts have been able to recoup their losses from the previous decline.

At the local level, declining enrollments, particularly in urban schools, have further reduced available tax dollars. Pressures for reducing educational budgets have caused many urban districts to cut back on the maintenance of facilities and purchases of textbooks and equipment, and some have closed schools altogether. Under these circumstances, the first item to be curtailed is likely to be spending for science-specific resources, including the equipment and supplies necessary to provide science laboratory experiences and participation in museum-sponsored programs and activities and the purchase of up-to-date science texts.

Recent studies have documented clear inequities in the number of microcomputers available for student use at different schools, and the ways computers are used vary for different subpopulations of children (Becker, 1983, 1986; Furr and Davis, 1984; Winkler et al., 1984). In 1986, only about 40 percent of middle schools in low-SES communities had as many as 15 microcomputers, whereas in high-SES communities, two-thirds of the middle schools had at least this number (Becker, 1986). The fewest microcomputers were available in elementary schools serving predominantly poor children and/or minority children, and at these schools, smaller percentages of children actually used the computers. Additionally, fewer poor and minority schools had teachers who were computer specialists. These schools were more likely to use their computers for "drill and practice" and less likely to use them for instruction in computer programming (Darling-Hammond, 1985). Gender differences in access enter the picture at this within-school level. In secondary schools, girls appear to have lower participation rates than boys (Furr and Davis, 1984), and boys outnumber girls by three to one in before- and after-school use of computers (Becker, 1986).

The distribution of educational resources is an essential indicator of schooling inequality for poor and minority students. School funding indicators must be analyzed and reported separately according to the racial and socioeconomic status of each school's student populations (see Catterall, 1986, for a discussion of educational finance indicators). Additionally, indicators of students' access to science laboratories, computers, and up-to-date science and mathematics textbooks, both across school types and within schools, are particularly important to monitoring equity in precollegiate mathematics and science education.

Disparities in Teacher Quality

Differences in the quality of teachers who provide mathematics and science instruction are another possible source of disparities in participation and outcomes. Most observers suggest that minority and poor students have less exposure to high-quality teaching because predominantly minority and poor schools are less able to attract qualified and experienced teachers. A recent report of the California Commission on the Teaching Profession argues that disproportionately high numbers of poor and minority students are taught during their entire school careers by the least qualified teachers (California Commission on the Teaching Profession, 1985).

Gaps in the distribution of teacher quality may be particularly critical in mathematics and science. In 1981, over half of the newly hired teachers in these fields were either not certified or lacked the qualifications for certification in the courses they were to teach (NCES, 1983). Because of the shortage of trained mathematics and science teachers and the particular difficulties urban schools face in attracting teachers, teacher quality in these subjects is likely to be particularly inadequate in predominantly poor and minority schools.

While there is little in the way of hard evidence to document the effects of teacher-quality differences on student achievement outcomes or rates of participation, few disagree that teachers are an important part of the educational process. Highly qualified teachers are perhaps the most critical educational resource (see Darling-Hammond and Hudson, Chapter 4 of this volume). Thus, the existence of a teacher-quality gap among schools serving different student population groups is, in itself, an important dimension of the distribution of educational opportunity. As such, it should be a primary target for monitoring equity in precollegiate mathematics and science education.

SCHOOL EXPERIENCES OF DIFFERENT GROUPS

Critical Factors

It is important to pay attention to both *what* conditions may erect barriers to the achievement and participation of at-risk groups and *when* these barriers first appear. Both aspects require an understanding of the typical paths to participation and end-of-high-school achievement.

Achievement and interest in mathematics and science in elementary school affect class placement in junior high or middle school, particularly in mathematics (Rosenbaum, 1980). Students who exhibit high levels of interest, prior achievement, and/or ability are often placed in classes that prepare for or even begin high school course sequences. For example, many junior high schools offer pre-algebra and algebra for high-achieving students, and a few even offer geometry (Oakes, 1985). On the other hand, students who exhibit substantial lack of interest and/or low levels of ability and achievement are often assigned to remedial, review, or practically oriented classes.

Achievement in junior high school influences high school course enrollments. High-achieving students enroll in college-preparatory or academic programs that require both a greater number of courses in mathematics and science and sequenced courses in these subjects that include advanced concepts and processes. Lower-achieving students enroll in vocational or general curricula that typically require fewer courses (Guthrie and Leventhal, 1985). Many non-academic mathematics and science courses are non-sequential, low-level, or remedial (Oakes, 1985).

After students complete high school graduation requirements, their enrollment in non-required science and mathematics courses depends on their interests, attitudes, and prior achievement (Lantz and Smith, 1981). Teacher and counselor encouragement (usually based on these characteristics) may influence students' decisions to persist (Cicourel and Kitsuse, 1963; Rosenbaum, 1976; College Entrance Examination Board, 1986).

High school mathematics and science course completion—both the number and level—is the strongest influence on students' end-of-high-school achievement and, for the college-bound, their preparation for college-level work (calculus-readiness in mathematics, for example) (Walberg, Fraser, and Welch, 1986; Welch, Anderson, and Harris, 1982). For college-bound students, end-of-high-school achievement is the strongest influence on choice of major. Mathematics preparation may be particularly critical, since admission to many science and quantitative fields requires readiness for college-level calculus (Sells, 1982).

Choice of college major leads directly to attainment of degrees in quantitative fields and participation in mathematics-, science-, and technology-related careers.

While these patterns may appear obvious, they hold the keys to successful schooling in mathematics and science. In particular, three seemingly interrelated factors are critical to high levels of accomplishment for all students: (1) access to mathematics and science instruction; (2) early achievement in mathematics and science which, in turn, leads to further instructional opportunities; and (3) the development of attitudes such as confidence, interest, and willingness to study mathematics and science. Moreover, high expectations and encouragement from parents and school adults and contacts with academically oriented peers are important influences on these factors. By looking more carefully at how girls, minorities, and the poor diverge from success patterns, we can identify pivotal targets for monitoring equity.

The Cycle of Access and Achievement

Curricular Paths. Growing evidence indicates that schools' judgments of students' intellectual abilities play a major role in differential allocation of learning opportunities (Guthrie and Leventhal, 1985; Lee, 1986; Oakes, 1985). As a result of these judgments, the access students have to mathematics and science knowledge is affected early in their school careers. In elementary schools, students who are slow to catch on to mathematics are often placed in "slow" groups or remedial programs. Students who learn more easily go to "fast" groups or high-ability classes. At the senior high level, judgments about students' ability influence decisions about curriculum track enrollment—whether students are placed in college preparatory, general, or vocational courses of study. Curriculum track enrollment, in turn, is a critical factor both in course-taking (Lee, 1986; Rock et al., 1984, 1985) and in the quality of the curriculum content, instructional practices, and learning environment (Oakes, 1985).

Schools usually explain these class and track placements and the subsequent differences in learning experiences as appropriate and necessary, given quite apparent differences in students' ability to learn. However, growing evidence suggests that the ways elementary schools respond to students may help to "fix" students' perceptions of their own ability to learn and, over time, may actually exaggerate initial differences among them (see Rosenholtz and Simpson, 1984). Moreover, the group a student is placed in will influence both the pace and the content of instruction he or she experiences, and these differences affect what and how much the student will actually learn (Barr and

Dreeben, 1983; Hallinan and Sorenson, 1983). In particular, students who are not in the "top" classes can be held back by their class placements (Slavin, 1986), with the result that some students leave elementary school ready to begin preparation for high school mathematics concepts and skills, while others still lack understanding and skill in basic facts and operations.

In secondary schools, tracking is most often found to work to the academic detriment of students in low-ability classes or non-college-preparatory groups (see, for example, Calfee and Brown, 1979; Esposito, 1973; Findlay and Bryan, 1971; Noland, 1985; Rosenbaum, 1980). Further, national data suggest that at the high school level, whether a student is enrolled in an academic (college-preparatory) or non-academic program has an *independent* effect on achievement. Placements in higher and lower tracks cause students who are initially similar in background and aptitude to exhibit increased achievement differences (Alexander and McDill, 1976; Alexander, Cook, and McDill, 1978; Gamoran, 1986). The net effect appears to be cumulative, since students' track placements are usually quite stable and long-term. Students placed in low-ability groups in elementary school are likely to continue in these tracks in middle schools and junior high schools; these students typically wind up in non-college-preparatory tracks in senior high school (Rosenbaum, 1980; Oakes, 1985).

These findings about curriculum tracking raise the possibility that in their efforts to accommodate differences in ability with different educational experiences, schools may actually exacerbate the differences among students by limiting some students' opportunities to learn.

Race, Class, and Curricular Paths. The first signs of black and Hispanic students' divergence from successful curriculum paths appear early in elementary school. By age 9, minority students score substantially lower than whites in both mathematics and science (Carpenter et al., 1984; Hueftle, Rakow, and Welch, 1983).

In elementary and middle schools, poor and minority students are more likely than whites to have initial difficulties and be placed in low-ability and remedial classes or in special education programs (Persell, 1977; Rosenbaum, 1980). Whites and upper-SES elementary students are more likely to be identified as able learners (and more often as "gifted and talented") and placed in enriched or accelerated programs (Darling-Hammond, 1985). As a result, the poor and minorities may have less access to the topics and skills that would prepare them for successful participation in academic sequences in senior high school mathematics and science.

The paths of many poor and minority children continue to veer off-course in junior high school. As a consequence of their poorer elementary school performance, these students are often assigned to remedial programs as they begin their secondary education. During these middle school years they have little access to the topics and skills that would prepare them for academic sequences in senior high school mathematics. Neither do non-Asian minorities (and most probably the poor as well) close the mathematics-achievement gap with whites, even in those low-level topics and skills that have been the focus of their remedial instruction (NAEP, 1983). This pattern appears in science as well, since junior high schools often differentiate science curricula for high and low achievers, frequently basing these grouping decisions on students' mathematics achievement (Oakes, 1985). Again, non-Asian minorities and the poor are more likely than others to end up in low-achieving groups.

These patterns continue into senior high school, with blacks, Hispanics, and poor students enrolling more frequently in vocational and general (non-academic) courses and whites and high-SES students more frequently in academic curriculum tracks (Rock et al., 1985) and high-ability classes (Oakes, 1985). These curriculum differences relate to differences in course offerings at various types of schools, to different course-taking patterns in mathematics and science for various groups, and to considerably different learning experiences within the classes the groups take.[4]

Different Course Offerings. The courses that high schools actually offer place limits on what students actually take. This obvious conclusion is an equity concern, since poor and minority students are more likely than others to attend schools with limited offerings in mathematics and science. HSB data show that, nationally, schools serving predominantly poor and minority populations offer fewer advanced and more remedial courses in academic subjects, and that they have smaller academic tracks and larger vocational programs (Matthews, 1984; NCES, 1985a; Rock et al., 1985). Schools that emphasize vocational and/or general track programs are less likely to offer advanced courses in science, mathematics, and foreign language than schools with extensive college-preparatory programs (Rock et al., 1985).

---

[4]Gender does not appear to have significant effects (independent of race) at the elementary level. Although there are some early warning signals, with boys slightly outperforming girls on some measures, achievement levels are relatively equal in both mathematics and science throughout the elementary grades (Carpenter et al., 1983; Hueftle, Rakow, and Welch, 1983). Gender differences in course participation do not appear in junior high school, and at age 13, girls' mathematics performance continues to equal that of boys (Carpenter et al., 1983). Girls, however, do fall behind boys in science, with significant differences found in their achievement (Hueftle, Rakow, and Welch, 1983).

These findings parallel NAEP data, which show that course-taking patterns vary among schools with the ethnic makeup of their student populations. At schools with substantial black populations, fewer mathematics courses are taken, on the average, than at schools with substantial white populations (Jones, 1984).[5]

These patterns of course offerings undoubtedly relate to the lower levels of achievement typically found at these schools. Minority and low-SES students are generally lower in achievement by the time they reach secondary school, and schools respond to those differences with programs they see as educationally appropriate. But what is of particular interest here is that placement in these programs continues a cycle of restricted opportunities, diminished results, and exacerbated differences between low-track students and their higher-track counterparts. The restricted courses available to students at predominantly poor and minority schools also severely limit the opportunities of the academically able students who attend these schools. Even if they represent a relatively smaller proportion of the student body, these students are denied mathematics and science opportunities simply because of the schools they happen to attend.

Variations in Course-Taking. For all students, course-taking is the most powerful school-related predictor of achievement, particularly in mathematics (see, for example, Welch, Anderson, and Harris, 1982). Precollegiate course-taking patterns are clearly related to fundamental race, class, and gender differences in science and mathematics attainment. However, the precursors of differential course-taking patterns are different for minorities than for girls. Until high school, girls appear to achieve in mathematics at levels that do not disproportionately disqualify them *academically* from taking advanced courses in mathematics and science. Blacks and Hispanics, on the other hand, fall behind in achievement early in their school careers and are less likely to enroll in academic tracks or to attend schools that require them to take classes that would prepare them for advanced work.

As Table 8.1 shows, substantially lower percentages of poor and non-Asian minorities complete academic courses of study in mathematics and science (either concentrating—i.e., completing several advanced courses—or completing four-year college-entrance requirements in

---

[5]It should be noted that recent analyses of HSB data reveal no discrepancies in course-taking when schools with 10 percent or greater black or Hispanic enrollment are compared with schools enrolling fewer than 10 percent minorities (NCES, 1985b). However, these HSB data are likely to be misleading, since 1980 data show that three-quarters of all black students attend schools where minority enrollments exceed 30 percent (Jones, 1984). Lumping together all schools with 10 percent or more minority enrollment may obscure important differences in course offerings and course-taking among those schools.

Table 8.1

**ACADEMIC COURSE-TAKING PATTERNS,
BY SES AND RACE**

(Percentages of students exhibiting pattern)

	SES			Race		
Course	High	Middle	Low	White	Black	Hispanic
Academic mathematics	69.1	45.7	25.1	51.5	28.1	28.9
Academic science	58.3	36.9	19.6	40.7	26.1	23.8
Computer science	17.4	12.4	8.4	13.8	10.5	8.0

SOURCE: National Center for Educational Statistics (1985b).

Table 8.2

ACADEMIC COURSE-TAKING PATTERNS, BY SEX

(Percentages of students exhibiting pattern)

Patterns in Science and Math Course-taking	Male	Female
Math		
Concentrator	9.3[a]	9.0
	(53.1)	(46.9)
Four-year college bound	34.7	38.5
	(46.8)	(52.3)
Science		
Concentrator	11.6	7.1
	(61.4)	(38.6)
Four-year-college bound	26.6	28.8
Computer science		
participant	13.6	11.4
	(53.8)	(46.3)

SOURCE: National Center for Educational Statistics (1985b).

[a]The upper figure represents the percentage within the entire sample of students; numbers in parentheses represent the percentage of students within each pattern with the designated characteristic (male or female). For example, 53.1 percent of all the math concentrators were male.

these subjects). Differences are also substantial in computer science course-taking.

Gender differences in course-taking follow a different pattern. While relatively equal numbers of high school boys and girls participate in academic and non-academic programs, the extent to which they *concentrate* or simply meet a more limited college-preparatory requirement varies. As Table 8.2 shows, boys are more likely than girls to concentrate in mathematics, science, and computer science. Therefore their course-taking outdistances that of girls.

While gender differences follow a consistent pattern, they are substantially greater in science than in other areas; within sciences, the greatest discrepancies exist in physical sciences. Differences in mathematics reflect differences in enrollment in the most advanced courses—trigonometry and pre-calculus (Fennema, 1984). Taken together, these differences in enrollment are likely to represent substantially less experience for girls in quantitative study.

The HSB data on gender differences parallel findings about differential course participation from NAEP. The NAEP data indicate that boys leave high school with one and one-half times more pre-calculus preparation than girls. And in 1980, only 15 percent of black and Hispanic students had completed trigonometry, compared with 27 percent of whites and 50 percent of Asians (Armstrong, 1981).

For both minorities and girls, considerable evidence supports the influence of lower levels of participation on achievement. Analyses of NAEP data have shown that the differences in the number of high school courses taken by black and white students account for a considerable part of the differences between black and white 17-year-olds' mean achievement scores (Jones, 1984). HSB data showed the strong relationship between course-taking and achievement to hold, even when students' prior achievement in mathematics is controlled for (Wisconsin Center for Educational Research, 1984).

The *level* of courses taken is also an important factor in subsequent achievement and postsecondary participation in mathematics and science (Sells, 1982; Peng et al., 1982). Analysts have found differences in the *level* of courses taken by minority and white students (Jones, 1984). Blacks and Hispanics (with lower achievement at high school entrance) are disproportionately enrolled in low-level high school mathematics and science courses; whites are disproportionately enrolled in advanced courses (NCES, 1985; Peng et al., 1982).

Sex-related achievement differences are also largely explained by greater course-taking by boys than girls (Pallas and Alexander, 1983). Again, this relationship appears to hold when analysts control for prior mathematics achievement (Wolfe and Ethington, 1986). This is consistent with evidence that boys' superior test performance is not matched by gender differences in classroom performance levels. When girls do enroll in mathematics courses, their course grades are as high as boys' (Pallas and Alexander, 1983; Benbow and Stanley, 1980, 1982; DeWolf, 1981). Some might argue, of course, that this occurs because only the relatively fewer high-ability girls actually enroll in advanced mathematics courses. NAEP data showing nearly equal mean mathematics achievement scores for 13-year-old boys and girls provide some evidence to counter this argument. NAEP scores suggest that it is only *after* differential course-taking patterns appear that girls and boys exhibit different mathematics "ability."

Failure to enroll in courses (for girls) and failure to achieve at levels that enable enrollment (for minorities) are critical areas for monitoring. Indicators should monitor race, class, and gender differences in curriculum paths (ability-group assignments, remedial program participation, assignment to programs for the gifted and talented, curriculum track placement, and course participation) in mathematics and science at several critical junctures in elementary and secondary schooling: early in the elementary grades; at the upper elementary level; during junior high and middle school; and at two critical points in senior high, 10th and 12th grades. Tenth-grade course-taking will assess early program assignments (academic or non-academic) and specific course enrollments; 12th grade assessments will capture participation in advanced and non-required courses.

Clearly, course offerings and course-taking patterns represent a critical interaction of student background characteristics (race, class, and ability as assessed by schools), schooling opportunities, and school performance. How these factors come together in poor and minority schools appears to restrict the chances these students have to learn science and mathematics. Because a bottom-line requirement for equity is that students have courses available to them, equity indicators should describe the mathematics, science, and computer science courses offered and the percentages of students of various groups enrolled in them, and should provide enough information to permit comparison with other schools. Even though we may not be able to disentangle all of the influences on course offerings, course-taking, and program placement, these clearly are *indicators* of both future achievement and the progress being made toward overcoming participation and outcome disparities among groups.

Uneven Classroom Opportunities. To understand students' actual opportunities to learn science and mathematics, analysts must explore classroom characteristics as well as school-level characteristics.

What students experience in their science and mathematics classrooms, from the earliest grades through senior high school, is likely to influence both what they actually learn and whether they continue along the precollege mathematics and science pipeline. The quality of students' day-to-day experiences is shaped to a large extent by factors such as the instructional goals and objectives teachers hope to accomplish; the knowledge and processes teachers make available for students to learn; the books, materials, and equipment used to aid student learning; the classroom learning activities teachers arrange; and the support and resources available to teachers. Understanding the quality of the science and mathematics experiences requires understanding how these several dimensions of schools and classrooms work together to create opportunities for students to learn and the extent of combinations of school program characteristics offered to various groups of students.

Considerable evidence suggests that classroom experiences are likely to differ both among schools and among students within the same school. NAEP data, for example, indicate that black students are involved in fewer science activities in their classrooms (Kahle, 1982). Further, some case-study evidence suggests that the curriculum content within subjects taught to students in predominantly poor and minority schools is essentially different from that taught to white and middle- and upper-class children. These content differences suggest that advantaged children are more likely to learn essential concepts (as opposed to isolated facts) and to be taught that academic knowledge will be important to their future lives (see, for example, Anyon, 1981; Carnoy and Levin, 1985). Even children who are identified as gifted but attend low-SES schools appear to miss out on the enriched curriculum offered their peers who attend high-SES schools (Hanson, 1986).

Further, there may be critical differences in the opportunities to learn *science and mathematics content* in classrooms of different groups of students within the same school. Recent studies of the distribution of classroom experiences among academic (college-preparatory or high-ability) and non-academic (general or low-ability) classes in science (Guthrie and Leventhal, 1985) and mathematics (Oakes, 1985) show considerable differences in the opportunities afforded these two groups.

A Study of Schooling (Goodlad, 1984), for example, found that teachers exposed students in mathematics classes at different levels to substantially different topics and skills. Students in upper-level classes focused primarily on mathematical concepts; low-level classes focused almost exclusively on computational skills and mathematical facts. Marked differences were also noted in the use of class time and the quality of instruction. Students in high-track classes were given more instructional time in class, and teachers expected them to spend more time doing homework. High-track teachers were more enthusiastic, their instruction was clearer, and they used less ridicule or strong criticism. Moreover, the climates of high- and low-track classes differed in ways that are likely to limit the opportunities of students in the lower groups. Students in lower-track classes were less friendly to one another; teachers were more occupied with matters of discipline and control. The pattern of classroom experience shown in these data seemed to enhance the possibilities of learning for those students already disposed to do well and to inhibit the learning of those students most likely to have difficulties (Oakes, 1985).

Minority students who are placed in low-ability classrooms have limited contacts with academically able peers. Track membership influences students' peer associations inside the classroom, in extracurricular activities, and in friendships (e.g., Alexander and McDill, 1976; Rehberg and Rosenthal, 1978; Rosenbaum, 1976). One important dimension of these friendship choices is the academic orientation of students' peers (Vanfossen, Jones, and Spade, 1985). Peer relationships are important for school effort and academic aspirations (see, for example, Coleman, 1961), and achievement gains are more likely in peer groups oriented toward academics (McDill and Rigsby, 1973; Persell, 1977).

A final factor related to classroom experiences is that teaching strategies in mathematics and science may have quite different effects on different groups. If this is the case and if the most commonly used instructional methods are those that advantage whites and boys, then unequal participation and performance might be linked to the use of these methods.

There is some evidence that boys are advantaged by conventional mathematics and science teaching strategies, such as whole class instruction and competitive reward structures, and girls and minorities benefit from strategies using cooperative and "hands-on" activities (Kaagan, 1980; Lockheed, 1984; Peterson and Fennema, 1985; Slavin, 1983). Moreover, there is some evidence that the latter types of strategies—e.g., stress on using mathematics to solve everyday problems, instruction based on work in projects, and emphasis on the utility of mathematics and its relation to future education and jobs—while often used in successful intervention programs aimed specifically at increasing minority and female participation in mathematics and science, are not typically found in regular classrooms (Malcom, 1986).

Because of the probable influence of classroom learning opportunities on achievement and participation, their distribution also warrants careful monitoring (see Chapters 4, 5, and 6). Indicator data must permit analyses of important teaching and classroom constructs, by the race, class, and gender of affected students. However, while these data will provide essential information on the *distribution* of classroom learning opportunities, considerable additional research is needed to establish the differential impact of classroom practices on girls, racial minorities, and the poor, and to explore practices that will lead to greater equity. Equity in science, mathematics, and technology curriculum and teaching should be a central focus of research accompanying and supporting the development and implementation of monitoring systems. Further, inquiry is needed into school and classroom *interventions* aimed at equalizing learning opportunities, achievement, and participation. Once characteristics of successful interventions are identified, we should develop indicators of them for monitoring classroom experiences.

Expectations and Treatment by School Adults. Teachers and counselors influence student participation and achievement with their expectations, advice, and encouragement. Teachers encourage or discourage future course-taking and higher achievement in their day-to-day interactions with students. Counselors provide or withhold important encouragement, knowledge about career opportunities, and knowledge of sources of financial support for college (Chipman and Thomas, 1984; College Entrance Examination Board, 1986).

Many studies show that expectations influence attainments (see the series of studies following Rosenthal and Jacobson, 1968) and that a student's track level and "track label" influence teacher expectations (see Persell, 1977). We also know there are important differences between school adults' expectations for boys, whites, and middle- and upper-middle-class children and those for girls, blacks, Hispanics, and poor children (Persell, 1977). The most successful groups of students (males) have been traditionally (although perhaps decreasingly) the object of higher expectations for mathematics achievement, and also the recipients of greater counselor encouragement (Casserly, 1979) and greater praise and reward for achievement (see Stage et al., 1985).

Some studies have found evidence of more subtle differences: Teachers interact with boys more frequently than with girls during mathematics instruction and provide greater encouragement for boys in science and mathematics. These differences have been particularly noticeable among groups of high-ability students (Parsons, Kaczala, and Meece, 1982). Some studies suggest that differential teacher treatment is partially responsible for differences in boys' and girls' participation and achievement in mathematics and science (see Stage et al., 1985). Work supporting this conclusion shows that teachers who actively encourage girls through exposure to role-models, give sincere praise, and support the value of mathematics for high-paying, high-prestige careers do have a positive influence on girls' attitudes toward mathematics (Casserly, 1979).

Subtle day-to-day school interactions, support-giving, and expectations may be impossible to monitor with indicator data. However, as in classroom instruction, we need research in this area to guide monitoring activities. This research might focus on differential school expectations and their effects and also investigate how school interventions can increase adult support and encouragement for the mathematics and science achievement and participation of girls, minorities, and poor students. These studies could enable the development of indicators of interventions that successfully attack the problem of differential expectations and encouragement. These indicators could then provide information about the extent to which the educational system is intervening to promote race, class, and gender equity.

INFLUENCES BEYOND SCHOOL

Much has been written about the very real disadvantages that poor and minority children bring to school with them and about the effects of gender stereotypes on women's education and career choices. This section discusses family and attitudinal influences on the achievement and participation of women, the poor, and minorities. While these factors do not alone *cause* low achievement and underrepresentation, they do interact with what students experience at school. The sources of any inequity are likely to lie in the nexus of student characteristics and school opportunities.

Family Influences

Social and economic factors are critically important to understanding lower achievement levels and underrepresentation of women, the poor, and minorities in mathematics and science. There is considerable evidence that minorities' and women's high school performance and postsecondary plans closely relate to their families' economic status (Chipman and Thomas, 1984; Dunteman, Weisenbecker, and Taylor, 1979). Family income relates to the level of education students' parents attained, and parent education is an important predictor of womens' and minorities' school success (Berryman, 1983; Malcom, George, and Matyas, 1985). We find this relationship, for example, in minority students' participation in mathematics and science. Unlike first-generation college students, minority college freshmen whose parents were college educated choose quantitative majors with about the same frequency as whites (Berryman, 1983). Closely connected to levels of parent education are parents' expectations and aspirations for their children and the encouragement they provide; the effects of these factors, too, are significant for women and minorities (Chipman and Thomas, 1984; Malcom, George, and Matyas, 1985). Primary language is another important factor. Hispanic students, especially those whose native language is not English, appear to do less well in mathematics and science (McCorquodale, 1983), but this probably reflects family income and education levels as well as primary language, since non-English-speaking Hispanics are among the (economically) poorest students in American schools.

Much of the educational difference between minorities and whites disappears when analysts control for family income and parent education. Nevertheless, SES does not *fully* explain achievement. There is some evidence of differences in science achievement between minority and white senior high students, for example, even with SES, school experiences, and prior achievement controlled (Walberg, Fraser, and Welch, 1986). A similar "unexplained" achievement difference exists between genders (Chipman and Thomas, 1984; Fennema and Carpenter, 1981; Maccoby and Jacklin, 1974; Stage et al., 1985; Walberg, 1986).

Attitudes and Self-Perceptions

Speculation about the relevance of attitudes and self-perceptions arises from research suggesting that individuals pursue areas they value and in which they expect success (see, for example, Chipman and Thomas, 1984). Among the hypothesized factors for women's and minorities' lower achievement and participation in quantitative fields are gender- and race-linked differences in (1) liking for math and science, (2) relative interest in people and things, (3) perceived utility of science and mathematics, (4) stereotyping of these subjects as the purview of white males, and (5) lack of confidence in abilities. Few of these factors have been researched extensively, however, and findings about most are as yet inconclusive. (Malcom, George, Matyas, 1985). Also, far less is known about these potential influences on minorities than on women. Nevertheless, a brief look at these factors is useful because of their possible interactions with student behaviors and school programs.

Interest, Liking, and Valuing. Early interest patterns appear to have some connection to differential race and gender participation in quantitative fields of study (e.g., choice of college major) (Chipman and Thomas, 1984). Some analysts reason that because students usually experience mathematics, science, and technology as abstract and disconnected from other people, they are more appealing to white males than to women or minorities. Closely related to this "people/things" dichotomy is the issue of cognitive style. Some studies have found evidence of gender and ethnic differences in field-dependence (i.e., learning highly influenced by the context in which knowledge and skills are embedded) and field-independence. These style differences are widely perceived as cultural in origin, with Hispanics most often characterized as field-dependent learners. It has been posited that lower Hispanic achievement in mathematics relates to a preference for more wholistic and less abstract learning conditions, conditions not typically found in mathematics classrooms (Ramirez and Castaneda, 1974; Valverde, 1984). Women, too, have been characterized as field-dependent learners.

Because there is some evidence that the students who enjoy mathematics and science are the ones who are most successful in these subjects (Antonnen, 1969; Bassham, Murphy, and Murphy, 1964; Schofield, 1982), researchers have also examined the connection between race- and gender-linked liking patterns and achievement. In these studies, boys consistently express more positive attitudes about mathematics (Sherman, 1980; Sherman and Fennema, 1977). This work offers some support for the association between gender and achievement because one finding has been that girls typically like these subjects less (Armstrong, 1980; Creswell, 1980). However, the direction of causality between liking and achievement has not been established. Although some evidence exists that for girls, changed attitudes toward mathematics accompany and sometimes precede a change in achievement (Fennema and Sherman, 1977, 1978), it would not be surprising to find that doing well in a subject leads to more positive attitudes.

However, "liking" may not be relevant to increased minority student performance, since even when minority students say they like mathematics, their performance and achievement do not appear to reflect this (Kahle, 1982). In contrast, the *value* placed on mathematics may have important links with later participation, for *both* women and minorities (Chipman and Thomas, 1984). Valuing and liking are not the same, of course. The first is probably indicative of the perceived importance of a subject; the second, of how enjoyable it is.

Perceived Utility. There is some evidence that minority students have less expectation than whites that mathematics and science will prove useful in jobs, schooling, or everyday life (Matthews, 1984).

Further, boys perceive mathematics as useful more than girls do; and these perceptions relate to differences in their course-taking patterns (Sherman, 1980; Sherman and Fennema, 1977; Hilton and Berglund, 1974). A relationship between perceived usefulness and participation is reinforced by data showing that girls who are interested in science- and mathematics-related careers are more likely than others to pursue study in these subjects (Berryman, 1983).

Stereotyping of Math, Science, and Technology. Girls who see mathematics and science (particularly physical science) as masculine, and therefore not particularly relevant to their lives, may be less determined to do well in these subjects (Stage et al., 1985). This perception of mathematics is related to achievement differences (Sherman, 1980; Fennema and Sherman, 1978; Dwyer, 1974), as girls sometimes lower their expectations for success when they see tasks as masculine (Lenny, 1977). This sex-stereotyping can occur as early as primary grades (Vockell and Lobonc, 1981). Girls may also be deterred by what they see as both current and future social costs in aspiring to mathematics and science careers (Chipman and Thomas, 1984). One such cost is anticipated additional conflict between male-dominated careers and child-raising (Ware and Lee, 1985). The relevance of sex-stereotyping is given some support from programs successfully using female role-models to increase girls' participation in mathematics (Brody and Fox, 1980; Tobin and Fox, 1980). These programs stem from evidence that girls have little exposure to adult women engaged in mathematics and science and who are confident about their mathematics abilities (see Stage et al., 1985, for a review).

We know less about the possible effects of minority stereotyping of science, mathematics, and technology as white domains. There is some evidence that this is the case (Matthews, 1984), but few analysts have explored the relationship between stereotyping and minority achievement. Further, there is considerable speculation that the lack of appropriate minority role-models in mathematics and science may be an important factor in minority underrepresentation (Johnson, 1984).

Confidence. Considerable evidence shows that while boys and girls are likely to be equally *motivated* to achieve, girls are less confident that their efforts will lead to successful performance (see, for example, Lantz and Smith, 1981; Hudson, 1986). Other work suggests that girls give up more easily than boys after experiencing failure or difficulty, are especially insecure about succeeding on tasks requiring high ability, and are less persistent on unfamiliar or difficult tasks.

Specifically, boys are more confident about their *mathematics* abilities than are equally able girls, and they exhibit more confidence while solving problems on mathematics achievement tests (Hudson, 1986).

Closely related are findings that girls are more subject to "math anxiety" than are boys (Stage et al., 1985). Sex differences in confidence levels emerge at junior high school, just prior to the appearance of enrollment and achievement differences (Stage et al., 1985), and at just about the time important gender-role decisions are being made. Not surprisingly, confidence relates consistently to differential course-taking (Stage et al., 1985). The links between minorities' confidence levels and mathematics and science learning have not been studied in depth.

WHAT WE DO NOT KNOW ABOUT RACE, CLASS, AND GENDER EFFECTS

While some theoretical work has suggested that race, class, and gender are inseparable and interactive influences on children's measured abilities and educational and occupational attainments (Grant and Sleeter, 1986), we know little about the combined effects of these characteristics. We have considerable data on the experiences of minorities and women, but rarely are data for subpopulations of these groups collected or analyzed separately. There is little data, for example, to document gender differences within minority groups—differences between black women and black men or differences among black, white, Hispanic, and Asian women, for example. There are even fewer studies of differences among subgroups in all three categories—differences among groups of low-, middle-, and upper-SES black women, for example.

The data are useful for monitoring, since some evidence suggests that subgroups may exhibit quite different patterns. For example, gender differences can operate differently among black and white students. While more white boys enroll in advanced high school mathematics courses than do white girls, some studies have found the opposite patterns among black students (e.g., Matthews, 1984). Moreover, even though more black women than men begin college studies in science and mathematics, fewer of them earn advanced degrees.

There are other important knowledge gaps. Little information is available on the experiences of important racial and ethnic subpopulations. Mexican-Americans, Central Americans, Puerto Ricans, and Cubans are typically lumped together as Hispanics, while the Asian category usually includes such culturally diverse groups as Chinese, Vietnamese, Japanese, and Hmong (Malcom, George, and Matyas, 1985). Further, some issues have received considerably less attention from researchers than others. We know less about the *science* participation and achievement of women and minorities than about their involvement in mathematics. We know less about racial minorities' mathematics and science participation and achievement than about women's. In fact, much of the information on minority achievement and participation has been extrapolated from studies of gender differences (Matthews, 1984). Among minority groups, we know less about Hispanics and other minorities than about blacks.

One of the most puzzling questions is whether children's opportunities for achievement and participation are affected more by race or by socioeconomic background. Race has received the bulk of the attention, since racial discrimination has been the subject of many court actions and federal programs. Moreover, the task of analyzing the educational status and experiences of poor and minority children separately is complicated, since many of the poorest children in this country are black and Hispanic. However, inferring the status of poor children in this country from the circumstances of black and Hispanic children grossly and stereotypically oversimplifies matters. Not all black and Hispanic children are poor; not all poor children are minorities.

Recent analyses of HSB data illustrate the importance of SES. With other school and home factors (including race and ethnicity) controlled for, students' SES (defined by education levels of parents, father's occupation, family income, and household possessions) accounted for a substantial amount of the difference in students' mathematics achievement (Rock et al., 1984). We find similar parallels in SAT scores (Darling-Hammond, 1985).

Despite our relative lack of knowledge about the interactions of race, class, and gender and their combined influence on schooling experiences and outcomes, the data do support one conclusion: Both in and out of school, those resources, experiences, and attitudes that encourage and support white boys in mathematics and science also appear to encourage girls, minorities, and poor students. Prior achievement, course-taking, expectations of parents and school adults, academically oriented peers, interest in science and mathematics, perceived future relevance of these subjects for career and life goals, and confidence in ability are inducements for achievement and participation among *all* groups of students (Lantz and Smith, 1981). Race-, class- and gender-related differences may be caused less by some *unique* needs of women or minorities than by the fact that these groups typically have less access to the positive factors that promote high achievement and continued participation. This is a critical caveat for understanding the causes of low achievement and underrepresentation and for developing indicators to monitor educational equity.

INDICATORS FOR MONITORING UNDERREPRESENTED GROUPS

A national monitoring system should be capable of reporting indicators of school processes and outcomes by gender, race, SES, and all their combinations. With this capability, equity indicators might provide some insights into how educational policy could weaken the influence of student background characteristics on mathematics and science outcomes.

The most important equity indicators will be those that monitor the progress of the schooling system in raising the current low levels of achievement of women, the poor, and minorities in mathematics and science and increasing their representation. An essential subset of these indicators, then, will be data that report the *distribution* of essential educational conditions (e.g., school, classroom, and teacher characteristics, curriculum content) for at-risk subpopulations as well as for currently more successful groups.

Given the state of knowledge about inequities in mathematics, science, and technology education, indicators must be reported by race, gender, and SES. The data should be collected by race, class, and gender of students at the individual level; and by race, class, and gender composition of their student population at the school and classroom level.

Equity in the Pool of Prospective Scientists and Mathematicians

Indicators should be disaggregated by at-risk groups to provide indices of the "bottom line" for equity monitoring. They should track by race, class, and gender the outcomes of schooling related to continued participation and success in mathematics, science, and technology—high achievement, successful course completion, and aspirations. They should report:

- School completion or dropout rates.
- Number and level (college-preparatory vs. general or remedial) of science and mathematics courses completed by high school seniors.
- Percent of high school seniors intending to pursue college majors in science, mathematics, and technology.
- Achievement of high school seniors in science and mathematics.
- College entrance exam (SAT/ACT) scores.

Equity at Critical Junctures in the Precollege Pipeline

Indicators should also capture educational participation rates, achievement, and attitudes at pivotal decision points on the path through school. The following indicators should be disaggregated by at-risk groups to capture information at critical schooling junctures— following earliest exposure and middle and high school grades where decisions about future course-taking occur:

- Achievement in science and mathematics at grades 4, 8, and 10, reported as means and the distributions of various groups in quartiles.
- Self-selection factors—interest in science, mathematics, and technology; confidence in abilities; parental encouragement at grades 4, 8, and 10.
- Attitudes toward further science, mathematics, and technology study in school and toward careers in these fields at grades 4, 8, and 10.
- Course participation—number of semester hours and levels of courses (ability track) in science and mathematics for various groups at grades 8 and 10.

Equitable Science and Mathematics Learning Opportunities

The following indicators should be disaggregated by at-risk groups to monitor those school conditions that relate to differential participation and outcomes for various student groups:

- Key resource indicators, by school type (e.g., schools serving different race and SES student populations): per-pupil expenditures, teacher salaries, pupil/teacher ratios, class sizes.
- Instructional time in science and mathematics at elementary schools of different types.
- Course offerings in science and mathematics at secondary schools of different types.
- Ratio of enrollment of students from various groups in mathematics and science courses of different kinds to their representation in the school population. (For example, black students represented x percent of the student population, but only x percent of the enrollment in calculus classes.)
- Science and mathematics resources available at schools of different types.

- Teacher quality at schools of different types.
- Curriculum in science and mathematics available to various groups of students (e.g., in districts, schools, and classrooms serving different race and SES student populations).
- Instructional processes in science and mathematics available to various groups (e.g., in classrooms serving different race and SES student populations).

School Interventions to Promote More Equitable Outcomes

Of secondary, but substantial significance is the monitoring of school efforts to interrupt typical patterns of low achievement and underrepresentation. These intervention indicators are considered secondary only because the primary indicators should reflect their *results*. The "true test" of a successful intervention lies in measures of quality school processes and outcomes; however, we do need indicators that document the extent to which schools, districts, and states are attempting to promote greater equity in mathematics and science. Data about the following dimensions of school interventions should provide useful information about the extent to which these programs are being used in schools:

- Supplemental programs to boost achievement of girls, minorities, or the poor in science and mathematics (e.g., after-school tutoring, parent involvement).
- Extracurricular programs to promote participation in science, mathematics, and technology (either school-based or in cooperation with museums, universities, etc.) and to increase interest, promote course-taking, provide information about careers, provide role models, increase student and parent expectations, etc.
- Staff development aimed at changing classroom science and mathematics instruction to better serve girls, minorities, and the poor.
- Curriculum development or adoption aimed at providing materials designed to increase achievement and participation of girls, minorities, or the poor.
- Special guidance programs aimed specifically at increasing interest, confidence, expectations, and career awareness or encouraging course-taking patterns that will permit college entrance and quantitative majors.

Until we have a more precise understanding of critical program features, these data will at least provide descriptive information about interventions now under way.

AVAILABILITY OF INDICATOR DATA

Developing equity indicators for an educational monitoring system would not require a new area of data collection. A number of current data collection efforts now gather information that could be useful. Some current sampling frames are not adequate for collecting data on important subpopulations, and sample sizes are likely to be too small to permit analyses of subgroups within race, class, and gender categories, but the following data sources should be examined for their potential usefulness in equity indicators and for their possible modification to permit subgroup analyses:

- The decennial census, which collects data about illiteracy, school enrollment, and educational attainment by minority group and gender.
- Data collected by state educational agencies about the resource allocations (per pupil expenditures) and the minority and SES composition of school districts.
- NAEP data, which provide information on achievement by gender and ethnicity and about teaching strategies.
- National longitudinal studies (NLS, NELS) at the school and teacher level, which can be used to assess school conditions and outcomes by minority and SES composition of student body— e.g., teacher quality, curricular quality (course offerings), and enrollment patterns. Student-level data collection efforts can also provide information about individual students' school experiences (counseling advice, teacher encouragement, etc.), attitudes, aspirations, enrollment, and achievement by gender, race, and SES.
- National Teacher Surveys (NCES), which can be used to identify teacher qualifications as well as the race, ethnicity, and gender of mathematics and science teachers (to measure the availability of role-models for women and minorities).
- National School Administrator Surveys (NCES), which provide data regarding school conditions by student body, race, and SES composition—course offerings; course requirements; mathematics and science laboratories; special programs (e.g., math-science magnets); and so forth.

- Data from the two NCES surveys (Teacher and School), which can provide information about teacher characteristics, qualifications, and attitude by school minority and SES composition.

RESEARCH NEEDED FOR DEVELOPING AN INDICATOR SYSTEM

The highest current priority for an indicator system is the ability to disaggregate data about all aspects of the educational system by race, class, and gender (and various combinations of those classifications). Disaggregation of the indicators recommended above should accomplish this goal. However, to develop disaggregated indicators that provide insights about how and why particular distributions occur and that can inform educators and policymakers about effective interventions, additional research in the following areas is required:

- Measurement of how *school* conditions influence differential patterns of student participation and achievement—curriculum offerings, facilities and resources, teacher quality, tracking systems, etc.
- The differential distribution and impact of classroom learning processes—teacher expectations, teaching methods, learning tasks, teacher/student interactions, curricular content, reward systems, classroom climate, peer interactions, etc.
- Guidance and counseling practices.
- Characteristics of school interventions that are successful in increasing the achievement and participation rates of women, poor, and minority students.
- Non-formal educational experiences that may provide out-of-school avenues to competence and related occupational attainment of at-risk groups (Ferris, 1981).
- Assessment of educational values, parent aspirations, stereotyping, perceived utility of science and mathematics education, and their interactions with schooling processes.
- Assessment of the dynamics of family schooling and occupations for race, class, and gender groups (Guilford and Hartman, 1981).
- Assessment of historical, social, and social psychological influences on students' motivation and persistence in schooling.
- Assessment of historical and social influences on schools' curricular, instructional, and guidance responses to diverse groups of students.

CONCLUDING REMARKS

For both ethical and practical reasons, monitoring educational equity is an essential focus of a national indicator system. Nevertheless, we must exercise caution with such a politically sensitive issue. While its overarching value is little disputed, the specifics of equity are controversial. Decisions about what constitutes educational equity and what government interventions represent appropriate policies for achieving it are highly charged. Equity implies fairness or justice, but little agreement exists about what educational conditions are fair and just.

Various conceptions of educational equity have emerged over the past 150 years, conceptions that translate into quite different educational policies: (1) providing equal access for all to the same schooling—free public education and common curriculum (e.g., the nineteenth century "common school" or more recent desegregated schools); (2) providing separate and different, but equal, educations to various groups (e.g., racially segregated schools, magnet schools, or different curricula within schools for students of different abilities); (3) providing equal educational resources to all groups—conditions likely to lead to equal outcomes for equally capable individuals (e.g., school finance reforms aimed at equalizing spending among schools and districts); and (4) providing equally *effective* resources to all groups— conditions likely to equalize results—by using additional resources to overcome the initial difficulties of disadvantaged groups (e.g., federal compensatory programs, bilingual education, and special education) (see Bell, 1972; Coleman, 1968; Levine, 1975; Gilmartin, 1981).

Each of these views implies quite different educational goals and educational processes. However, indicators must be relevant to equity more generally, since specific definitions and policy concerns may shift over time. Information is needed that will inform policy without predetermining what that policy should be. The most pressing need is for data that can assess the extent of the disparities in school processes and outcomes, ground the discussion of national goals for equity (and its specific definition), and track progress toward the attainment of those goals.

Chapter 9

SCHOOL COMPLETION AND DROPOUTS

James S. Catterall

INTRODUCTION

In the United States today, an average of 85 percent of high-school-age children attend school, and about 75 percent complete their high school education with their original classmates. Somewhere before or during high school, 25 percent drop out. Although a higher completion rate is clearly desirable, the numbers receiving diplomas place the United States far beyond most developed nations in the school attainment of its citizens. However, these national averages cloak the wide variation in completion and dropout rates among states, between urban and non-urban areas, and across racial, ethnic, and economic groups. In some areas, almost 50 percent of students fail to finish high school, and the dropout rates among different racial and ethnic groups can differ by as much as 30 or 40 percentage points. These rates and their unequal distribution raise a host of social, political, economic, and educational issues—including questions of equity.

Despite the general concern over these issues, we have very incomplete knowledge about the dropout phenomenon, its causes, and its effects. What we do know suggests that information on dropouts may prove important for interpreting other data about the state of mathematics and science education in this country. This chapter (1) explores the potential importance of dropout information for a national indicator system aimed at assessing that state and (2) weighs the need for such information against the difficulties of acquiring it.

By definition, school dropouts cease to participate in the science and mathematics education offered by the schools. Thus, the nature and extent of dropout behavior must be considered in any comprehensive assessment of achievement in mathematics and science education. However, the importance of these data for an indicator system appears to depend on the primary intent of the system. If concepts of general *literacy* in mathematics and science are the primary concern of the system's sponsors and audiences, then dropout indicators should be included. If the primary concern is education's potential for enhancing scientific and technological advancement, then dropout behavior is largely irrelevant, except for the effect that it might have on average achievement test scores.

If general literacy is the primary concern, gathering the necessary data will be a serious challenge. At present, we have few readily available or usable statistics on dropout behavior. There are several reasons for this paucity of data: no consensus exists on an operational definition of "dropout"; data collection practices are idiosyncratic; and uneven attention is paid to dropout information across the states and school systems. Consequently, needs must be weighed against the anticipated costs of acquiring dropout information. For some indicator system agendas, the costs of better data are probably not worth incurring.

The following discussion considers the possible justifications for including dropout statistics in an indicator system for science and mathematics education, reviews the relevant research, and describes the current state of dropout information collection by government agencies and school systems.

SHOULD AN INDICATOR SYSTEM INCLUDE DROPOUT STATISTICS?

Cutting-Edge Skills or Scientific Literacy

There are two obvious concerns that might motivate an indicator system. One is the degree to which students prepare themselves to participate in the scientific community: Are students undergoing training that makes them potential contributors to knowledge? Or are students receiving sufficient mathematics or science training to prepare them for careers as school mathematics or science teachers? The other is the degree to which students become scientifically literate: Can they, for example, appreciate the meaning and importance of scientific debates surrounding public policy issues, such as current deliberations regarding the AIDs epidemic?

We assume that increased public interest in science and mathematics training reflects concern about the United States' competitive position in the world economic and political arenas. Technological advancements contribute to military and defense capabilities and may foster the productivity essential to deliver goods at home and abroad at competitive prices. The health of major U.S. industries, such as automobile manufacturing, is perceived to be threatened by foreign nations, such as Japan, where scientific training and technological development are considered superior to that in the United States. Improved technology is also thought by many to be the critical ingredient in stemming the flow of U.S. manufacturing operations to countries where labor is abundant and less expensive. Technological advances can render American labor more productive.

Because we know that dropping out is concentrated among students who are academically "estranged" and low achievers, it seems logical that dropout data would be only marginally useful for indicator systems concerned with the advancement of knowledge, technological development, and the training of future teachers. The students who pursue science and mathematics as college majors are a subset of the 25 percent or so of all youth who attend four-year baccalaureate programs. Only a small fraction of this subset continues on to postgraduate training and research careers, or to careers as mathematics or science teachers. Since low achievers are rarely destined for such adult paths, whether a tenth or a third of them drop out has little bearing on the outcomes of interest.

However, all citizens can benefit from scientific and mathematical literacy. It can contribute to individual quality of life and greater social welfare by helping people manage personal finances, make informed purchases, understand personal and public health issues, know how machines and chemical processes work, avoid potential hazards in their use, and so on. Dropping out almost certainly affects the level and distribution of science and mathematics literacy in our society, because the underlying concepts are probably more available to those who stay in school than to those who quit. Dropout data should thus be of interest in indicator systems concerned with these outcomes of education.

Regardless of the primary intention of indicator systems, dropout data will probably be significant on one dimension: Scores on achievement tests will no doubt be scrutinized by science and education monitors (see Chapter 7 of this volume), and the interpretation of these scores should reflect any changes in the student populations being tested. Academic requirements for high school completion appear to be increasing in many schools, districts, and state systems (U.S. Department of Education, 1984b). At the margin, making school harder is likely to have the independent effect of pushing low achievers out. If fewer of them attend school, average results on schoolwide tests of science and mathematics achievement will probably show gains. This is a case where dropout information could help analysts interpret other indicators in the system and where its absence could lead to erroneous conclusions.

A Cautionary Consideration

The concern with dropouts takes as given that those who quit school will have lower science and mathematics literacy than those who stay. However, research is only beginning to produce any empirical basis for this. Arguments claiming deficits in the literacy of dropouts are grounded largely on reasoned intuition. The most important thing that can be claimed about the potential ties between dropping out and learning in mathematics and science is the obvious: Those who drop out do not have the same opportunity to learn whatever curriculum brings to those who stay in school.

The little research that has been done on dropouts' knowledge and skills supports this reasoning. However, the research results remain far from conclusive. Little attention has been paid (absolutely and relative to research on other domains) to dropouts' achievement in mathematics and science. The High School and Beyond (HSB) survey (discussed in more detail below) included a brief test of mathematics characterized as 8th grade level (Heyns and Hilton, 1982). This test yielded little insight into the effect of curriculum on the relative performance of dropouts and those who remained in school. The HSB test battery also included a brief test of scientific reasoning and concepts, but no analyses have emerged reporting the results of the science test alone for dropouts versus finishers.

The mathematics tests used for the earlier Project Talent study were also quite rudimentary (Combs and Cooley, 1968). Project Talent reported the few available academic achievement results that tie dropouts to mathematics learning, and these results did not yield anything surprising or distinguishing. Lower average achievement scores were reported for those who drop out, and the deficits were not markedly different for mathematics than for other areas tested. Lower composite test scores for dropouts (across multiple test domains) are also reported by Youth in Transition researchers (Bachman, Green, and Wirtanen, 1971) and by those analyzing HSB data (National Center for Education Statistics, 1985c; Alexander, Natriello, and Pallas, 1985).

Perhaps the best work in this area is a recently published analysis of the results from a battery of cognitive and vocational tests administered to a representative national sample (N = 12,000) of American 15- to 23-year-olds (Bock and Moore, 1986). In this survey and testing effort, called Profile of American Youth, subjects completed tests of mathematics knowledge, arithmetic reasoning, and general science, among others. Across the tests, subjects who had completed some high school generally scored about one-fourth of a standard deviation below subjects who completed high school but did not go on to college. A notable exception relevant to this discussion was that in tests of quantitative attainment, non-poor white and black high school completers showed the smallest score increments over those who had only some high school. The authors interpret this to be a result of "the concentration of general courses relevant to Arithmetic Reasoning and Mathematics Knowledge in the first two years of high school" (p. 69). The achievement profiles provided in that study also document basic differences across white, Hispanic, and black youth which suggest that for Hispanics and blacks, deficits caused by dropping out will compound existing achievement disparities.

The relatively smaller differences in scores for those who drop out and those who only complete high school suggest that dropouts may be forgoing fewer learning opportunities in mathematics and science than one would expect. It would appear that children in these two groups do not tend to enroll in what might be called the hallmark mathematics and science courses, namely two years of algebra, geometry, and advanced analysis or calculus in mathematics, and biology, chemistry, and physics in the sciences. Nor, one would surmise, do these youngsters study computer-related topics in any depth. The general and vocational tracks populated by dropouts and "terminal graduates" would probably not include such classes. For this reason, the difference, for science and mathematics literacy, between dropping out and staying to graduate is tied to the specific nature of general and vocational curricula. That is, the effect of dropping out on the quality and distribution of mathematics and science education depends on what dropouts would actually be doing in school if they, instead, remained to graduate.

This appears to be rather unexplored territory from the perspective of dropout research. Just what is the nature of the mathematics and science curriculum for the low achiever, i.e., for the general or vocational track student? And of interest to the sponsors of projects involving mathematics and science indicators is a related question: What should this curriculum contain if it is intended to promote scientific literacy?

A REVIEW OF RESEARCH ON DROPOUTS

This section presents the essential findings of the dropout literature, much of which has some bearing on what indicator systems might gain by incorporating dropout data.

Historical Perspectives

For 65 years following the turn of the century, the fractions of American adolescents attending and graduating from high school increased steadily, and a once elite enterprise became a mass institution. Just over 6 percent finished high school in 1900—by 1940, about half were finishing. Today about 75 percent graduate on schedule, and 85 percent of high-school-age children attend high school. The percentage graduating peaked in 1965 at just over 76 percent and has been very stable at about 75 percent for the past 20 years (National Center for Education Statistics, 1985d).

These assessments are generally based on counts of diplomas awarded each year in comparison with 9th grade enrollments for the same age group 3 to 4 years earlier. It appears that more than half of those who do not graduate with their classmates eventually secure a high school equivalency certificate under the General Educational Development (GED) program, or through state equivalency programs.[1] In the past two or three years, isolated claims of increasing dropout rates have been heard, but national data for this recent period are not available.[2]

This picture contrasts sharply with the experiences of other developed nations, where many students are diverted into specialized vocational programs by the time they reach age 14. In these countries, fewer than 30 percent typically graduate from secondary schools. Japan is a singular, comparative exception; about 85 percent of Japanese youngsters finish the equivalent of high school (Kirst, 1984, p. 8).

The national averages do not reveal the considerable variation in graduation rates from state to state and locale to locale. In 1979–80, when the national graduation average was about 72 percent, the fraction was as low as 60 percent in Florida and Mississippi and as high as 85 percent in Minnesota and Iowa (NCES, 1984, p. 58). Some states have extreme internal variations in dropout rates. In California, for example, analysts claim that the overall attrition rates exceed 50 percent for some school districts and are nominal in other districts (California Assembly Office of Research, 1985). It is also reported that the dropout rates in Los Angeles high schools (grades 9–12) alone range from about 5 percent to more than 50 percent (Los Angeles Unified School District, 1985).

---

[1]National Center for Education Statistics, 1984; see Table 1.24, p. 60.
[2]See Wheelage and Rutter, 1985; also California Assembly Office of Research, 1985.

Research on Dropouts

Research on school dropouts has been reported regularly but not voluminously over the past 20 years. Events of the 1960s turned major policy interest toward issues related to the equality of educational opportunity in the United States. A natural consequence was the growth of academic and professional curiosity about who completes school. It did not require research to establish that low achievers and economically disadvantaged minorities were comparatively likely dropout candidates. Research has focused on a more detailed understanding of the correlates, causes, and consequences of leaving school before graduation.

Researchers curious about dropouts have faced some daunting hurdles. There are limited primary databases available, and what exists tends to go little beyond idiosyncratic reports of school completion rates. Additional data that might distinguish school leavers from persisters, such as individual characteristics and school program information, are not built into the counting exercises conducted by most government agencies and school districts.

Probing large samples of dropouts is simply beyond the means of any but the most generously endowed research efforts. When pupils are in school, they can be sampled and queried efficiently, given a modicum of cooperation on their part and on the part of school officials. When dropouts leave school, they are difficult and expensive to follow. This has meant that most of what qualifies as generalizable research on dropouts has depended on a few very large-scale data collection efforts—surveys large enough in scope to catch dropouts along with others in their nets.

A small amount of this broad-based work derives from Census Bureau activities, particularly the 1976 Survey of Income and Education (discussed below). The core research on dropouts has utilized a handful of national longitudinal surveys of adolescents, which were conducted generally for the purpose of probing transitions between youth and adulthood in our society. These surveys are Project Talent, 1960 to 1964,[3] the Youth in Transition Survey, 1965 to 1970,[4] the Survey of Youth Labor Market Experience (YLME), 1979 and ongoing,[5] and the High School and Beyond (HSB) survey, 1980 and ongoing.[6] A fifth well-known survey, the National Longitudinal Survey of the High School Class of 1972, has not yielded information on high school

---

[3]See Combs and Cooley, 1968.
[4]See Bachman, Green, and Wirtanen, 1971.
[5]See Rumberger, 1983.
[6]See Jones et al., 1983.

dropouts, chiefly because the initial sample was surveyed in the winter of the senior year in high school—too late to capture much of the drop-out phenomenon. In addition to the core of dropout research based on these studies, researchers have mounted numerous smaller-scale efforts which when considered in the large, tend to echo the dominant themes of the more ambitious studies.

The large-scale surveys differ from more modest dropout data collection efforts in their systematic follow-up of those who drop out. Many of the less-intensive efforts have succeeded in gathering arrays of baseline information on subjects but were confined to linking this antecedent information to dropping out decisions because the researchers did not hear again from the dropouts involved. As a result, this research has tended to concentrate almost exclusively on the individual characteristics associated with dropping out—and not on what dropping out has meant in the subsequent lives of dropouts. However, more intensive follow-ups have recently begun to be made of those who dropped out.

A second important note is that in the longitudinal-design research a "dropout" is generally defined as anyone who was no longer enrolled in school at the time of a follow-up survey and who also had not at that time received the high school diploma. For a variety of reasons, this definition may not correspond to that used by states or school districts in cataloguing their own student behavior.

General Findings of the Research

Background Factors. The socioeconomic status (SES) of the pupil's family is chief among the characteristics associated with dropping out. Reporting on Project Talent, Combs and Cooley (1968) found that more than half of both male and female dropouts came from the lowest SES quartile. They also found that less than a fourth of the male dropouts and less than a fifth of the female dropouts came from the upper half of the SES distribution. About 60 percent of the dropouts in the Youth in Transition Survey hailed from the lowest two of six socioeconomic levels identified for the sample (Bachman, Green, and Wirtanen, 1971).

The core of research on dropouts also documents the ties between minority status and dropping out, although the independent effect of minority status or ethnicity is not firmly established because of its collinearity with low SES. Analyzing data from HSB, Peng, Takai, and Fetters (1983) report sophomore-to-senior-year dropout rates of 18.0 percent for Hispanics and 17.0 percent for blacks, in comparison with 12.2 percent for whites and 3.1 percent for Asians or Pacific islanders.

Steinberg, Blinde, and Chan (1984), in their work with data from the 1976 Survey of Income and Education, observed that ethnicity, apart from SES, is a more important factor in dropping out for Hispanics than for children from other ethnic or racial backgrounds. They also reported that language minority status is an important independent contributor to dropping out, especially for Hispanic children. Here, rates of "not completed and not enrolled in school" among a national sample of 14- to 25-year-olds were 11 percent for the total sample, 18 percent for all with non-English background, and 40 percent for those whose dominant language use was not English (p. 117).

Other pupil background factors that appear to be consistently tied to dropping out (with intuitively predictable coefficient signs) across the core dropout literature are specific home-environment measures, such as the presence of books (negatively related to dropping out), the presence of both parents in the home (also negatively related), and the number of siblings (positively related).

Academic Achievement. Various negative academic performance indicators have been associated with subsequent dropout decisions in these studies. Low achievement test scores, low grade-point averages, and prior grade retention have all shown substantial correlations with dropping out. In a multivariate analysis with YLME data, Rumberger (1983) found that race and ethnicity had no effect on dropping out when academic achievement was controlled. This finding was replicated in Pallas' (1984) extensive treatment of HSB data.

Based on the earliest of the major surveys, Project Talent, Combs and Cooley (1968) reported that 55 percent of the male and 40 percent of the female 9th graders who dropped out had scored in the lowest quartile on a composite measure of academic ability. The academic ability test battery used in that study had 19 sections covering such skills as reading comprehension, mathematical computation, abstract reasoning, mechanical reasoning, memory, and visualization (p. 355). For each of 19 subtests administered in the 9th grade, students who subsequently dropped out scored significantly lower (p < .01) than a comparison group of students who finished high school but who did not go on to college. Eighty percent of the male dropouts and 74 percent of the female dropouts scored in the bottom half of all students taking the test battery.

The Youth in Transition survey probed a nationally representative panel of 10th grade males beginning in 1966 (Bachman et al., 1971). Among its subjects, more than half of the eventual dropouts had been held back for one or more grades prior to the start of grade 10. This compares with a prior grade retention rate of 24 percent for school finishers in the sample. Primary grade retention and absenteeism were also found to be tied to dropping out (Howell and Freese, 1982; Stroup and Robbins, 1972).

Additional indicators of academic performance were also considered by Bachman. About half of the students reporting D grade averages for the 9th grade eventually dropped out, compared with 2 percent of those reporting A averages. The students also took tests of reading (the Gates reading test) and vocabulary (the GATB-J test of vocabulary). Mean student scores on these tests differed significantly and predictably among groups: Dropouts had the lowest scores, with progressively higher scores for dropouts who eventually finished high school, high school finishers with no additional schooling, and graduates continuing on to college. Bachman also reported that the dropouts are less distinguishable from "finishers" than from students who go on to postsecondary education. This pattern is replicated in the more recent HSB data.

The HSB study is the most comprehensive data collection effort for analysis of dropout-related issues in the United States (Jones et al., 1983). Sponsored by the National Center for Education Statistics, HSB surveyed approximately 30,000 high school sophomores and 28,000 seniors beginning in 1980. Follow-up surveys were conducted in 1982 and 1984, and further follow-ups are planned. A very rich array of information was collected for each student—student background characteristics, attitudes, school characteristics, in-school experiences, beyond-school experiences, and so on. Students also were tested using a battery of six short tests covering verbal and mathematical domains, writing, science, and civics (see Heyns and Hilton (1982) for a description of the HSB tests).

The HSB survey is unique in its attention to dropouts. About half of those who dropped out after they were surveyed in the spring of their 10th grade year were found and surveyed as part of the 1982 follow-up. (About 14 percent of the original sophomore sample dropped out.) In addition to completing comprehensive follow-up surveys, both dropouts and those remaining in school were retested in 1982, using the same battery of tests.

A variety of observations concerning academic performance and dropouts have been generated with HSB data, and many more will undoubtedly emerge as analyses of these data proceed. Not unexpectedly, dropout rates among HSB sophomores varied inversely with test performance. Of those scoring in the lowest composite test score quartile, the dropout rate was about 25 percent. Dropout rates decreased to 15.3 percent, 8.6 percent, and 3.7 percent for students in successively higher test performance quartiles. (Recall that these rates apply to a two-year period only—late sophomore to late senior year.) Self-reported class grades were also related to dropping out. Students respectively reporting mostly As, Bs, Cs, and Ds experienced corresponding dropout rates of 2.9 percent, 8.1 percent, 18.5 percent, and 42.5 percent.

Alexander, Natriello, and Pallas (1985) have presented the most comprehensive discussion and analysis to date of relationships between cognitive performance and dropping out, based on HSB data. Their stringently controlled models provide evidence that dropping out has independent negative effects on cognitive growth (as measured by the six-test battery). They further suggest that these effects tend to be larger in test domains that are linked to high school curricular offerings (among the HSB tests, civics and writing), and that the negative effects of dropping out are more pronounced for both Hispanic-origin and economically disadvantaged students. This last result corresponds interestingly to the research of Heyns (1978) which found that summer learning losses are greater for the same disadvantaged groups.

Reasons for and Consequences of Dropping Out. Two additional themes are apparent in research on dropouts. The first concerns the reasons why youngsters leave high school before graduation. The best systematic inquiries in this area are based on two of the surveys described above, which asked large numbers of dropouts why they left school (HSB, reported in Peng, Takai, and Fetters, 1983; and the Survey of Youth Labor Market Experience, reported in Rumberger, 1983).

A wide range of self-reported reasons emerges in these surveys. Dislike of school and having poor grades head the list of volunteered reasons and stand apart as the most frequent responses. As many as 45 percent of dropouts cite such reasons. Pregnancy or marriage plans influenced about one-third of the female dropouts in both samples, with pregnancy more frequently mentioned by minority females and marriage plans by white females. Inability to get along with teachers was cited by 16 percent of HSB 1980 sophomores. Having to work to support a family was offered by only 11 percent.

Another major research theme is the effect of dropping out on the individuals involved and on society. A number of recent studies have documented a variety of disadvantages accruing to school dropouts in their lives beyond school. On average, dropouts work less, earn less, and occupy lower-status occupations than their school-finishing peers. The labor market performance of dropouts has been associated with social costs, in terms of forgone economic activity and forgone government revenues. Dropouts also appear to be more involved in a variety of socially burdensome and personally costly behaviors—higher dependence on public assistance and public health services, more involvement in crime and crime-related services (such as courts and correctional systems), and lower rates of political participation. The causal relationships between dropping out and these outcomes are debated. Levin (1972) and Catterall (1986) provide extensive discussions.

THE STATE OF DATA ON DROPOUTS

This section addresses the questions of how dropouts are defined in practice, what data are currently available on dropouts, who generates them, and how useful they might be for purposes of science and mathematics indicator systems.

Defining Dropouts

Our working, implicit definition in this essay has been that a dropout is simply a student who leaves school without obtaining a high school diploma. The various agencies that gather data on dropouts have defined the term in different ways.

Louisiana legislation defines the dropout as:

> Any student who exits school, for any reason except death, before graduation or completion of a regular curriculum which leads to a high school diploma, and without transferring to another school. (Louisiana, Revised Statutes 227–330)[7]

In California law,

> Dropout rate means the percentage of pupils enrolled in any of grades 7 to 12, inclusive, who stop attending school prior to graduation from high school and who do not request, within 45 days of leaving high school, that their academic records be forwarded to another school. (California, Senate Bill 65, 1985)

The denotation of dropout is straightforward and causes little confusion—the dropout has left school and is not progressing toward a diploma. In practice, schools, districts, and states implicitly define dropout behavior in various ways, and their reporting of dropout behavior presents knotty problems for an indicator system.

Some locales and states seldom collect or report information at all, but when they do, the collection reflects highly variable decision rules, illustrated by all of the following:

---

[7]This definition was provided by officials in the Office of the Superintendent of Education.

- The grade levels tracked vary. Dropout rates may be reported for particular grade levels and are alternatively shown for grades 10–12, or 9–12, or 7–12, depending on local requirements or preferences.
- Schools may or may not require transcripts of previous school work for new enrollees, particularly at lower grade levels such as grades 7 and 8. This results in abandoned schools not knowing that a pupil has reenrolled elsewhere.
- There is no standard length of time between a pupil's initial absence and the declaration of dropout status. Does a week's absence constitute dropping out? Is a pupil who enters a high school equivalency test preparation program six months after leaving school considered a dropout?
- There is no standard length of time that a student must be enrolled and attending a particular school prior to dropping out so that he/she is considered a dropout from that school. Is a student who enters and then leaves a school within a week this school's dropout or a dropout from his or her previous school?

Research on dropouts raises other definitional issues as well. Most of the relevant published research and analysis does not depend on institutional reporting, but rather is based on the major surveys described above. In longitudinal research surveys, dropouts are generally defined as individuals enrolled in school at one wave of a survey, who are subsequently not enrolled in school and not in possession of a diploma in a later wave of the survey. This approach generates different levels of attention to just how long a survey subject has been out of school, to subsequent reenrollments, and to the individual's pursuit of alternative "completion" arrangements. And dropout rates generated in longitudinal surveys are, of course, sensitive to the timing of survey waves.

Most analyses of Census Bureau data classify dropouts as respondents who report eleven or fewer years of schooling completed. We would suspect that individuals responding to Census surveys might tend to overstate their attainment levels and also to equate the completion of a General Educational Development (GED) certificate with twelve years of formal schooling. In fact, Census Bureau estimates of dropout percentages in the young adult population are considerably lower than observed dropout rates (Rumberger, 1986).

A final implicit definition of dropouts is assumed by recent reports of state-level data. The three Wall Charts of comparative state education statistics issued by the U.S. Department of Education (1984a, 1985, 1986) include state high school completion rates that were calculated by comparing the numbers of graduates in each state in one year with 9th grade enrollments four years earlier. Dropout rates can be calculated by subtracting the completion rate from 1. (Of course, not all non-completers are dropouts—some take equivalency diplomas, some leave the country, some are deceased, and so on.)

National Data

The quality of dropout information in the United States corresponds to its level of collection. National school completion figures are the most dependable and regularly generated. They are based largely on the efforts of the Census Bureau to catalogue school enrollments. It is important to note that national-level data are not derived from upward aggregations of state and local figures. Instead they are drawn from major censuses, a variety of one-time surveys,[8] and annual national surveys that probe school participation. Tabulations of these annual surveys are issued in Series P-20 of Current Population Reports and are now titled, "School Enrollment: Social and Economic Characteristics of Students." They have been published for each October for more than 30 years.

Dropout rates are not specifically reported in these documents, but the total enrollments by grade level from year to year allow us to deduce overall attrition rates and are used by the National Center for Education Statistics (NCES) when it reports school completion data periodically in its compendia of school statistics.[9] The translation of overall attrition patterns to national dropout rates involves a small amount of error because of the data's sampling basis and also because of migration of school pupils across national boundaries. No suggestions of particular bias in these national data have been raised in the literature. Full reports for each October are published about three years after the surveys. Advance reports based on the October surveys are issued a year or two following each survey in the same P-20 series.

Data on national-level school completion are also included in the more comprehensive population counts conducted for each decennial census. We are able to catalogue the education levels of individuals at various age levels on the basis of their responses to Census inquiries. Reports of these data include distributions of educational attainment for adults (fractions completing various amounts of education, includ-

---

[8] E.g., the 1976 Survey of Income and Education.

[9] See particularly various issues of the *Digest of Education Statistics and the Condition of Education*, published annually by the National Center for Education Statistics, Washington, D.C.

ing the categories "8 or fewer years of school" and "1 to 3 years of high school," and so on).

State and Local Data

State and local data on school dropouts are piecemeal at best. The figures reported above for several states were based on a specific NCES effort to analyze 1980 Census data along with results of attrition counts. Only in decennial census material can we discern the fractions of the most recent should-have-graduated school cohort that were granted diplomas across the 50 states. Data for local districts are based primarily on studies sponsored by district officials. These studies are idiosyncratic in their methods and purposes, as well as their regularity. Some school districts do not collect or report dropout data.

The U.S. Department of Education currently draws state-by-state comparisons of school completion, the comparisons represented in the Wall Charts mentioned earlier (1984a, 1985, 1986). For these 50 state comparisons, completion rates were calculated on the basis of 9th grade enrollments in each state versus numbers of diplomas granted four years later. The reported completion rates range from about 60 percent to over 90 percent.

The generally spotty nature of state-level data is apparent in a recent survey that assessed the nature and extent of information collection and public policy attention to school dropouts at the state level across the 50 states (Catterall, 1988). An immediate conclusion of this work is that one-fourth of the state departments of education develop no regular information on school dropouts at all and do not have immediate sources to turn to for such information (other than comparative grade level enrollment figures). Another is that steps are under way in some states to improve dropout data collection.

Several technical hurdles have inhibited the development of better state-level information on dropouts, and many of these problems also extend to local efforts. First, the states do not engage in the sort of census activities carried out by the federal government, nor do they benefit individually from the Census Bureau's annual October surveys. These efforts are designed to construct a national picture, but their sampling strategies do not result in representative state-level profiles. Four regions of the country and three community types constitute the geographical units of analysis for these reports.

States and local districts have additional problems keeping track of the attainment levels of their own school-age youngsters. Schoolchildren are geographically and institutionally mobile. In a recent year, between 10 and 20 percent of school-age youngsters, depending on region of the country, changed domiciles (Bureau of the Census, 1983, p. 20). The west and south recorded high mobility rates, and the midwest and northeast had comparatively low rates. Fewer than half of these movers remained within the same metropolitan area. In addition, some pupils change schools while retaining the same residence.

All this mobility means that both the states and individual school districts have large numbers of students leaving and entering schools at various grade levels, including their high schools, each year. (A high school principal interviewed by the author reported 4,000 different students attending a 2,000-student school in a single academic year.) Some, but not all, of the leavers are dropouts. Simple attrition figures, which are frequently the only basis of local reports, and school enrollment data generally do not describe dropping-out patterns in an individual state or district very well.

This situation implies that if states and localities wanted to generate comprehensive and accurate portraits of dropping out from year to year, they would have to follow school-leavers intensively to determine whether they have in fact dropped out. This might involve active searching for leavers, which is an individual, labor-intensive, and expensive prospect—and a practice that is not regularly carried out anywhere. The most being done now is some sort of record-keeping on the expressed destinations of pupils (which are in various ways and to varying degrees recorded) and on requests for transcripts from the subsequent schools of school-leavers. When a pupil departs and no transcript request follows, he or she may be classified as a dropout.

These data have a hit-or-miss quality, since transcripts are not always sought when a leaver enters another school, and some leavers wait a great while before reentering. Further, making district-level sense of such data would require additional reporting and aggregating procedures, as would state-level compilation beyond that. For data generated from the bottom up in this manner to be comparable across districts and states, uniform definitions of dropouts would have to be adopted—an issue many districts have not even settled for their own informational purposes.

Most states and districts have not been prompted to allocate the substantial resources it would take to collect data for addressing dropout issues. And whether they should allocate them is a reasonable question. How much effort should a school or system put into classifying those who are gone? And from which ongoing activities should the needed resources be reallocated?

Implications for an Indicator System

The most important implication is that if developers of science and mathematics indicator systems want dropout information, they will have to collect it themselves. There is some, but not much, data on dropouts of interest to indicator system developers and their audiences that are simply awaiting collection and reporting. A minimal prototype indicator system that relies on compiling existing data in useful ways will not attend very precisely to issues of school completion across states, schools, or districts. State-by-state figures can be approximated from enrollment counts at various grade levels compared with counts of diplomas awarded (the Wall Chart approach). But existing district and school data cannot lead to a representative picture because of extreme idiosyncracies in methods and incidence of collection. Annual national completion rates can be ascertained, but these have limited utility for any comparison purposes.

The U.S. Department of Education is in the process of improving its dropout data collection practices. The Department's Center for Statistics and the Council of Chief State School Officers have convened a joint task force for this purpose. Certainly the desires of known monitoring efforts for dropout information are likely to be rather similar; their sponsors could speak with a concerted voice to the Department of Education on this issue, and all could benefit from the results. However, we have seen no indication of commitment to a wholesale restructuring of dropout data collection across the nation.

Alternatively, and if resources allow, projects might build specific data collection strategies into their own prototype schemes. Because the data problem is rooted in every school and district, it is doubtful that a single indicator system will inspire or fund the large-scale changes required to effect systematic dropout reporting. An alternative approach would be to identify a limited sample of schools or districts across the nation that are surveyed thoroughly and regularly for dropout data, along with other desired information. These "Neilson schools"[10] could become the basis of year-to-year tracking on a number of indicators. For these schools, steps could be taken to ensure uniform pupil follow-up procedures, uniform definitions of dropouts, and other standardized assessments. The costs of such a scheme would of course depend on the numbers and locations of schools involved, the intensity and sorts of data collection, the degree to which local cooperation would yield inputs to the effort, and so on.[11]

---

[10]Named for the television ratings scheme of the A. C. Neilson Company.

[11]The Center for Statistics has proposed such a school sampling scheme, tentatively titled "The Elementary/Secondary Integrated Data System" (see Center for Statistics, 1986).

CONCLUSIONS

The relevance of school dropout data to an education indicator system depends on the purposes of the system. If monitoring the upper bounds of mathematics and science achievement is the purpose, the system will have little need for dropout information: Few high achievers leave school without graduating. However, dropout information is important for monitoring average levels of achievement. Because dropouts tend to be low achievers, dropout rates will influence average achievement scores.

Dropout indicators would seem to be even more important if the system is intended to assess general scientific literacy. We assume that people who leave school will have less chance than people who finish school to learn the underlying concepts of mathematics and science that may be practically useful in life. However, that assumption may be questionable. Some analyses of test scores have found fairly small differences in achievement between high school dropouts and non-college-bound graduates. These results suggest that to judge the effect of dropping out on scientific literacy, an indicator system would need rather specific information on the kinds of curriculum to which dropouts and "terminal" graduates are exposed.

If a monitoring system is concerned with distributions of science literacy across racial, ethnic, and economic groups in the United States, information on dropouts would be germane. If dropping out results in deficits in scientific literacy, the effects are not evenly distributed across U.S. society. There appears to be a much higher incidence of dropping out among Hispanics and blacks, and any dropout deficits are added to consistently evident differences in achievement across these groups, when grade levels attained are controlled.

Any education indicator system that requires good state or school district comparisons on dropout behavior faces an expensive challenge. Existing data collection practices cannot provide adequate information, and it is reasonable to presume that improving the current state of dropout information would require a substantial allocation of resources. The education policy community in general has not reached the conclusion that better dropout statistics are worth the price. It is not clear that specific efforts, such as one aimed at assessing the state of mathematics and science education, will find independent reasons or resources to take up the challenge.

Chapter 10

THE POLICY CONTEXT

Lorraine M. McDonnell

INTRODUCTION

Unlike concepts such as curriculum content, student achievement, or even school climate, "policy context" seems quite nebulous in relation to a national system for monitoring mathematics and science education. Yet the policy context—the political system's articulation of policy goals and their translation into concrete actions through either the allocation of resources or the imposition of regulations[1]—is a critical factor in designing a national indicator system.

The policy context, in fact, provides the major rationale for developing an indicator system. When a commission of the National Science Board recommends that all students should acquire a set of specific mathematics and science skills or a state legislature requires that all high school students take two years of mathematics and science courses, they signal what outcomes need to be measured and establish standards against which reported outcomes should be judged. Unless an indicator system can generate information that aids the process by which such policy choices are assessed, it will not survive as a publicly supported endeavor. But the policy context influences more than just the types of data to be collected; its actions can also affect the direction that different indicators take over time. When policymakers adjust teacher salaries, select textbooks, or pursue a variety of other initiatives, these actions may be one of the factors that helps explain observed changes in schooling outcomes.

The policy context, then, plays two distinct roles in the design of an indicator system. First, it provides the major *rationale* for developing and operating such a system. Meeting the information demands of policymakers is a primary function of indicator systems, one that shapes

---

[1]This definition includes both the political process that generates policy decisions and the output of that process, the policies themselves. It also recognizes that education policy is enacted and implemented in a federal system where each governmental level has its own set of policy needs and interests. As the discussion in this chapter demonstrates, this characteristic has major implications for the design of a national indicator system.

what information is collected, how it is reported, and in turn, the level of political and financial support available.

Second, the policy context constitutes a key *component* of any educational indicator system, because specific policies can change the major domains of schooling in ways that affect educational outcomes. For example, federal, state, and local policies largely determine the level and type of resources available to education. Although their effects on most other components of schooling are less direct, these policies can also influence who is allowed to teach, what content is taught, and even how it is taught. What is perhaps most striking about the education reform policies of the past few years is that they have moved the influence of policy further down into the educational system than has traditionally been the case. In the past, policy typically focused on how schools were financed and governed; now its scope also includes what is taught and who teaches it. Consequently, the larger policy context needs to be included as an integral part of any indicator system measuring the condition of mathematics and science education.

This chapter analyzes the information preferences of policymakers at the national, state, and local levels and suggests how these can be accommodated in the design of an indicator system. It then discusses the ways that policy actions may affect the contours of mathematics and science education. The purpose of this discussion is to demonstrate how important these factors may be in explaining observed changes in educational outcomes, and also to acknowledge how difficult it is to measure the independent effect of any single policy or even the aggregate effect of several policies.

INDICATOR SYSTEM RATIONALE: PRODUCING USEFUL POLICY INFORMATION

The Lessons of Past Experience and Research

The current interest in developing educational indicators is not new. The U.S. Office of Education was established in 1867 "for the purpose of collecting such statistics and facts as shall show the condition and progress of education . . . and of diffusing such information [to] promote the cause of education throughout the country" (cited in Warren, 1974, pp. 204–205). Interest in the development of social indicators revived in the 1960s and early 1970s, but despite a flurry of scholarly and governmental activity, the movement quickly died. Its history, however, provides some important lessons for current efforts to create a national indicator system in mathematics and science education.

In the early 1960s, officials at the National Aeronautics and Space Administration (NASA) recognized that manned space flight might have a profound effect on American society. Consequently, a number of researchers explored the possibility of developing social indicators to monitor the effect of space flight, on the grounds that "for many of the important topics on which social critics blithely pass judgment, and on which policies are made, there are no yardsticks by which to know if things are getting better or worse" (Bauer, 1966a, p. 20). The NASA project spurred an indicator movement that featured social statistics and was expected to play "the same role in depicting the social state of the nation as the economic indicators depict its economic health" (Hauser, 1975, p. 17). The movement found a friendly home in Lyndon Johnson's Great Society and in Richard Nixon's vision of the "science of government" in the planning process for the twenty-first century. It was further stimulated by the Department of Health, Education, and Welfare's *Toward a Social Report* (1969), the Office of Management and Budget's *Social Indicators* (1974), the National Science Board's Special Commission on the Social Sciences, and the enthusiasm of the social science community (see Hauser, 1975; Sheldon, 1975; Sheldon and Moore, 1968; Sheldon and Parke, 1975).

Despite this early enthusiasm, however, the social indicators movement soon died. Nevertheless, it contained an important lesson about the relationship between policymakers' needs and the process of indicator development. The social indicator producers of the 1960s and 1970s failed to "deal with the style, objectives and constraints of decisionmakers," and information users failed in "not establishing the systems which would permit them to choose information they needed to make use of it" (de Neufville, 1975). This experience demonstrated that education indicators must be developed iteratively with decisionmakers to ensure that the information produced meets their needs.

A second lesson learned from the social indicators movement is that the expectations of both information providers and users were overly optimistic. Given a general lack of theory about the determinants of many social conditions and a limited ability to measure those conditions reliably, it was unreasonable to expect that a balance sheet such as that produced with economic indicators could be developed. Similarly, the measures included in an indicator system are too broad in scope to be used in the evaluation of individual policies or programs. As the other chapters in this volume indicate, the limitations of theory and measurement apply in much the same way to the development of educational indicators. Research about schooling is not sufficiently advanced to support a strictly predictive or causal model. Existing measures, particularly of student achievement, teacher quality, and the instructional process, are seriously inadequate.

In sum, past indicator efforts have shown the need to accommodate both the technical requirement that indicators be reliable and valid and policymakers' needs for them to be useful. Without the former, the system will lack credibility and analytical power; without the latter, it will lack political and financial support. Past efforts also showed the need for reasonable expectations about what an indicator system can and cannot do. At this point, an indicator system can realistically provide a broad picture of the status of mathematics and science education, identify emerging problems, and suggest possible options for addressing those problems. It cannot, however, document a clear, causal link between different policy interventions and the desired outcomes of mathematics and science education.

Just as past experience provides lessons for the design of an educational indicator system, so does a body of research that has examined the conditions under which policymakers are likely to use research-based information (e.g., Lynn, 1978; Lindblom and Cohen, 1979). Knowledge utilization research has indicated quite clearly that those who assumed that a knowledge-driven model of research application derived from the physical sciences would also be valid for public policy were naive. Research and the information it produces do not progress in a linear fashion from basic to applied and on to practical policy applications. The information generated from an indicator system or any other type of research endeavor becomes just one more resource that policymakers can use as they attempt to balance competing interests in an essentially political environment. Weiss (1979) characterizes what is probably the most valid depiction of knowledge utilization by policymakers as an "enlightenment" model:

> Here it is not the findings of a single study nor even of related studies that directly affect policy. Rather it is the concepts and theoretical perspectives that social science research has engendered that permeate the policymaking process. (1979, p. 429)

The notion of information influencing the terms of political discourse is particularly important for an indicator system. One of the most critical functions such a system can serve in the policy context is to provide a common framework and set of concepts that policymakers can use in considering mathematics and science education policy. Members of the policy community are beginning to talk about changes in SAT scores in ways that resemble their discussions of economic indicators. However, the sophistication with which economic policymakers use information is not yet matched by education policymakers. A major reason for this is the absence of a comprehensive system of educational indicators—the information that is typically available now consists largely of unrelated pieces. An ongoing, widely used indicator system could help introduce into policy discourse more sophisticated notions of student outcomes and a better understanding of the relationships among those outcomes and aspects of the schooling process over which policymakers have some control.

Usefulness to the policy community depends on much more than just the availability of research results. It hinges on many factors, including which indicators are included in a monitoring system, how they are conceptualized and measured, the level to which they can be disaggregated, and the way they are analyzed and reported. How these issues are addressed in the design of a monitoring system depends on prior decisions about the audience to be served and the purpose the system is to fulfill.

Indicator System Audiences

The question of audience revolves around (1) the extent to which a monitoring system should serve policymakers, as compared with a technical community, and (2) who within the policy community should be served.

Technical vs. Policymaker Audiences. Earlier attempts to build social indicator systems demonstrate how critical policymaker use and support are to the survival of an indicator system. At the same time, it is the technical community that will generate and interpret indicator data. Therefore, any indicator system must meet the needs of both groups.

Yet those needs are not entirely similar. One of the most important differences lies in the kind of models each community requires. In assessing the underlying model for an indicator system, the criterion for the scientific community is, Does it explain? Researchers want a model that specifies indicators with theoretical relevance and causal impact. The criterion for the policy community, on the other hand, is, Does the model work as a predictive device? Policymakers have less need to know why certain factors are related to each other; they just want to know whether or not the factors they can influence consistently alter the direction of valued outcomes. The time frame for the two communities differs also. Scientific canons require that researchers perfect their models over what may sometimes be a long time period. The short-term demands of pressing policy problems and electoral cycles require that policymakers proceed on the best available information, even though that information may not be fully predictive or theoretically elegant.

Needless to say, these two approaches are not dichotomous, but rather represent two ends of the same continuum. The areas of commonality between the two communities are usually greater than the differences. And at a very pragmatic level, straying too far in either direction on this continuum can cause serious problems: Without policy-relevant indicators, such a system will not survive; without a theoretically sound model, policy prediction will be flawed and may result in politically costly mistakes. What is important, then, is that the needs of both audiences be considered in designing a monitoring system.

The needs of both audiences can be addressed in a number of ways. For example, the system can incorporate the best currently available data on key indicators to provide timely information for policymakers. At the same time, developmental work can be conducted in those areas where reliable indicators are not yet available. As better indicators are developed, they can be incorporated into the operational system. This two-track approach would accommodate both the short-term needs of policymakers and the desire of the technical community to produce more valid indicators. Similarly, institutionalizing an indicator system with a predictable collection and reporting cycle would allow the production of time-series important to research endeavors and would also ensure that policymakers receive information on a schedule suited to their needs.

Different Policymaker Audiences. Even within the policy community, however, information needs are not completely similar across governmental levels. Consequently, the level of the policy system that should be addressed becomes an issue. A national indicator system would be financed by federal funds and would have to meet the needs of federal policymakers (e.g., Congressmen and staffs of Executive Branch agencies such as the National Science Foundation (NSF) and the Department of Education (ED)). Yet the role of the federal government in mathematics and science education is very limited. Whether the outcomes the federal government values in this area are to be achieved will depend on what states and localities do. Therefore, at least to some degree, all three levels need to be addressed. However, because each level has different information needs, significant opportunity costs are likely to be incurred in trying to meet all the needs with a single indicator system.

Defining Expected Outcomes

The issue of different policymaker audiences with different interests and needs is also manifested in the identification of outcomes that an indicator system should measure.

To a large extent, the expected outcomes of mathematics and science education are defined by practitioners and researchers within the education community itself. The outcomes they specify are typically quite precise and cover the full range of mathematics and science-related knowledge. For example, in its 1980 Agenda for Action, the National Council of Teachers of Mathematics made eight general recommendations that were then divided into 48 more specific ones, outlining in detail the desired outcomes of mathematics instruction (viz., specific kinds of problem-solving skills, the mastery of ten basic skills, and computer literacy) and the curriculum and pedagogical approaches to achieve those outcomes. Similarly, researchers studying science and mathematics education make explicit assumptions about desired instructional outcomes (e.g., science education should produce changes in students' conceptual thinking rather than the learning of specific facts) (Anderson and Smith, 1986).

However, when educators pressure the political system to translate their goals into policy objectives, or when political and business leaders themselves articulate goals related to mathematics and science education, the policy context begins to play a role in defining expected outcomes. This role is important not only because of its implications for identifying the educational goals that are likely to receive financial and political support, but also because the policy community's definitions of expected outcomes help delineate the parameters within which the educational system will be accountable to its constituents. How these expected outcomes are translated into policy objectives may affect the relative emphasis accorded possible outcomes (e.g., postsecondary attainment vs. basic-skills achievement, subject-matter competence vs. problem-solving skills) over time and in different places. The policy context may also play a role in defining the amount of change expected in mathematics and science outcomes.

Policymakers may influence not only the type and level of outcomes selected, but also the way those outcomes are expected to be achieved. However, in contrast to the precision with which the education community typically defines desired outcomes, the objectives articulated by the policy system may often be quite vague and diffuse.

If we look beyond Congressional and Executive Branch policymakers to the larger federal policy community that includes the NSF, we find that expected outcomes for mathematics and science education have been defined quite specifically at the federal level, in comparison with most state policy. This fact, combined with the very limited role the federal government is currently playing in education policy, presents a serious dilemma for the designers of a national mathematics and science indicator system. On the one hand, the recommendations coming from NSF, ED, and other federal agencies about what mathematics and science education should be accomplishing and how those goals can be achieved are quite precise. At the same time, the federal government's limited, and now even more diminished, role in education means that whether these goals are even pursued depends almost entirely on state and local policy action. But because the concept of a national indicator system is at least implicitly derived from federal expectations about what mathematics and science education should accomplish (National Science Board (NSB), 1983), this disjuncture between the precision with which policy goals are articulated and how they are to be met must be considered quite carefully in deciding the functions an indicator system can play, how expected outcomes will be defined and measured, and the extent to which the policy context can be adequately captured.

Federal Definitions of Expected Outcomes. Over the past five years, various federal agencies have stated explicitly what they believe the outcomes of mathematics and science education should be. *A Nation at Risk* (National Commission on Excellence in Education, 1983) argued that high school mathematics and science instruction should equip students with the following skills:

- In mathematics, [the ability] to (a) understand geometric and algebraic concepts; (b) understand elementary probability and statistics; (c) apply mathematics in everyday situations; and (d) estimate, approximate, measure, and test the accuracy of their calculations.
- In science, [an elementary understanding of] (a) the concepts, laws, and processes of the physical and biological sciences; (b) the methods of scientific inquiry and reasoning; (c) the application of scientific knowledge to everyday life; and (d) the social and environmental implications of scientific and technological development.
- In computer science, [the ability] to (a) understand the computer as an information, computation, and communication device; (b) use the computer in the study of the other basics (subjects) and for personal and work-related purposes; and (c) understand the world of computers, electronics, and related technologies. (National Commission on Excellence in Education, 1983, pp. 25–26).

Although it emphasized the need for students to learn more academic content, the Commission stressed that the educational objectives recommended in *A Nation at Risk* should apply equally to the college-bound and to those not planning to continue their formal education after high school (1983, p. 25).

In 1983, the NSB Commission on Pre-College Education in Mathematics, Science and Technology also made similar, though more detailed, recommendations about the desired outcomes of mathematics and science education. It too stressed instructional objectives that apply not only to college-bound, preprofessional students, but to all students. At the most general level, these outcomes included "the ability to write for a purpose, apply higher-level problem-solving skills, and analyze and draw conclusions, rather than minimal basic skills such as the rote memorization of facts" (NSB, 1983, p. 12).

In the same report, the NSB Commission recommended that the federal government finance and maintain "a national mechanism to measure student achievement and participation in a manner that allows national, state, and local evaluation and comparison of educational progress." The Commission further recommended that this mechanism build upon the current National Assessment of Educational Progress (NAEP). It argued that achievement and participation should be measured against the Commission's primary objective—"the highest quality education and highest participation level in the world by the year 1995." The Commission then made clear that "quality education" should be defined according to the outcome criteria it had specified.

At first glance, this recommendation seems quite straightforward and appears to provide sufficient guidance to those charged with designing such an assessment mechanism. However, upon closer examination, two problems emerge. First, it does not specify the extent to which the expected outcomes articulated by federal agencies such as ED and NSF are the same as those that states and local districts expect their students to achieve, and toward which they are directing policy and practice. If the outcomes expected by states and local districts differ from those of the federal agencies, then not only would the information produced by a national indicator system lack external validity, it would be of little use to either policymakers or practitioners. Unfortunately, there is currently no systematic information about what states and local districts expect mathematics and science education to accomplish, or about how those expectations vary across the country.

A second problem is the extent to which the expected outcomes are likely to change over time, either absolutely or in their relative importance, and how such change might be accommodated by an indicator system. Even if the expected outcomes defined by NSF and ED were consistent with state and local outcomes, they are clearly not immutable. New technological developments and the changing needs of the national economy necessitate the redefinition of mathematics and science objectives. Shifting political priorities also lead to redefinition. NSF's own history of precollegiate mathematics and science education, which moved from an emphasis on more effective training for future scientists to a combined focus on this objective and greater scientific literacy for all students, demonstrates the importance of an adjustable indicator.

State and Local Definitions of Expected Outcomes. Somewhat ironically, state and local definitions of expected outcomes are often not as precise as those articulated at the national level, and much less is known about them. Yet state and local action exerts the strongest influence on the shape of mathematics and science education.

States vary considerably in the extent and specificity with which they have defined mathematics and science objectives—for example, Georgia recently mandated a statewide basic curriculum, and in preparation for its development by the state board of education, the Governor's Education Review Commission outlined student outcomes in several areas, including mathematics, science, and computer education (see Appendix 10.1).

Although a growing number of states are moving in the same direction as Georgia, the majority do not have a statewide curriculum. But several of those that do have articulated, at least implicitly, expected outcomes through such mechanisms as statewide assessment testing, the type of courses required for graduation, and curriculum guidelines developed at the state level. These mechanisms relate to the input and process variables discussed below, but their specific focus and the skills emphasized also suggest which science and mathematics outcomes are considered important by state officials. While the number of states for which such objectives are at least implicit is growing, some states still do not specify expected outcomes in any form at all, or do so only in the area of minimal competencies.

Although anecdotal evidence indicates significant variation among the states, we lack systematic information about state goals in mathematics and science education. For example, most states publish curriculum guides that can serve either as capacity-building instruments suggesting how particular subjects might be taught or as part of a state mandate to ensure that students acquire certain academic competencies. Yet there is little current research about what is included in each of those guides, the extent to which they actually affect local practice, or how they vary across states.

Even when state policymakers take specific actions such as increasing the number of courses required for graduation, their expectations about what a policy should achieve are not always clear. Conversations with legislators and state board members suggest that they support these changes because of a sense that students should obtain more scientific and technical knowledge. They also recognize that the nature of the workforce is changing due to technological developments, and they believe that their states' economies will benefit from a more scientifically literate population. Beyond expressing these general beliefs, however, many members of the state policy community (particularly those outside the educational establishment, such as legislators) have not defined precise outcomes for the initiatives they have enacted.

In addition to curriculum guides, statewide assessments provide insights into what state governments view as the expected outcomes of mathematics and science education. As of June 1987, 40 states were testing students in mathematics, and 29 were testing in science, with the number in both categories growing (CSSO, 1988). Although we lack information about the comparability of science tests across states, recent research has compared the content of statewide assessments in mathematics. Burstein et al. found that of the 22 states that test in grades 1–3, 14 test in 4 out of 5 major skill areas; in grades 4–6, 9 of the 36 states with assessments test in all 5 skill areas and 19 more test in 4 areas; in grades 7–9, 34 states test in at least 4 skill areas. In grades 10–12, however, 18 states do not administer any type of mathematics test (1985: 4.13). In addition, 11 states include higher-order subskills as part of their mathematics assessment for at least one grade-level category. Burstein et al. acknowledge that their analysis of statewide assessments is only an initial exploration, but continuation of such research may be an effective way of determining which instructional outcomes are the most widely accepted across the country and therefore the most likely candidates for inclusion in a national indicator system.

If our knowledge about how state governments view mathematics and science objectives is limited, our information about the local level is virtually non-existent. As at the state level, most information about what local schools and districts view as desirable outcomes comes, by inference, from an examination of local tests and curriculum. Even this inferential exercise, however, is limited by a lack of sufficient data. Relevant studies are typically based on school-level evidence or on a detailed content analysis of curriculum and testing materials. For example, Goodlad reports great curricular similarity among 38 schools in the teaching of mathematics. He concludes that in the schools of his sample, mathematics is a "body of fixed facts and skills to be acquired, not . . . a tool for developing a particular kind of intellectual power in the student" (1984, p. 209). Goodlad also noted a lack of certainty about the importance of science as a topic of precollegiate study; an amorphous science curriculum at the elementary level; and a disjuncture between the actual topics studied and the expressed intention of teachers to instill scientific and critical thinking skills in their students (1984, pp. 215–216).

Somewhat at odds with this picture of uniformity across the curriculum are studies comparing the content of textbooks and standardized tests. In studies of 4th grade mathematics, Freeman and his colleagues found significant diversity of content and little overlap between the most frequently used texts and standardized tests, suggesting a lack of consensus about what should be taught (and, by implication, what should be learned) at that level (1983). Similarly, Burstein et al. confirmed the contention of some states that NAEP does not adequately reflect their own curricula (1985).

Once again, we are left with three basic questions: (1) What do states and local districts believe should be the outcome of science and mathematics education? (2) How much do these expectations vary across the country? (3) How consistent are they with federal goals? It is also unclear whether the curriculum and tests from which outcome goals have been inferred reflect the actual expectations of policymakers and their constituents, or whether those audiences either have not articulated precise objectives or have failed to link policy goals with practice.

In sum, the political system's choice of policy objectives is critical in defining the expected outcomes that a national indicator system will need to measure. Unfortunately, the precision with which the federal level has articulated such outcomes is often not reflected at the state and local levels. In addition, more systematic data are needed about the range of state and local goals and how those goals have been translated into policy and practice. Relying only on the federal outcomes would result in a system that has little relationship to the governmental levels that actually determine the contours of mathematics and science education, and one that poses serious external validity problems.

Taking into account the expected outcomes of mathematics and science education from the perspective of the policy community involves not just the empirical task of identifying how those outcomes are defined, but also the normative one of deciding how much weight should be given to them. For the most part, policymakers do not want to specify, in any but the most general way, educational outcomes. However, when state and local officials articulate more detailed policy objectives, as they are doing now, it usually means that they believe professional educators are not performing adequately. Whether this is a fair or accurate assessment is an issue that cannot be resolved by designers of a national indicator system. They must accept the fact that professional judgments have to be accommodated within the norms of democratic accountability as they apply to schools. Probably the most effective way for system designers to balance these sometimes competing values is to establish a process for defining expected outcomes that is viewed as legitimate by both practitioners and policymakers.

Indicator System Uses

The tradeoffs involved in addressing different policymaker audiences become clear when we examine the various uses an indicator system can serve. These could conceivably include any or all of the following purposes:

- To provide a broad overview of the status of mathematics and science education in the United States.
- To serve as an accountability mechanism by reporting data about how well schools and students are performing.
- To improve policy and practice by providing information about which approaches seem to be working.

Clearly, neither NSF nor the designers of any other indicator system can control the uses to which the information generated is put. However, they can design the system in ways that minimize the likelihood that data will be used for purposes they deem inappropriate (e.g., by the selection of indicators, the level at which they are disaggregated, and how they are reported).

We interviewed about twenty policymakers representing potential users within the Congress, Executive Office agencies, NSF, ED, and state government. In addition to questions about their individual information needs, we asked what they consider to be the most important purpose an indicator system might serve. Their responses are summarized as part of the discussion of each potential use.

Providing a Broad Overview. The provision of an overview of mathematics and science education is probably the function of greatest interest to national policymakers. Such information could be used by NSF and ED officials in their "bully pulpit" role (Jung and Kirst, 1986). They could discuss in greater detail how American students are performing in comparison with students in other countries and how mathematics and science instruction and achievement have changed over time; they could use indicator results to exhort states and local districts to do better. Such information would also provide federal officials with guidance about where to target their own limited program efforts. For this purpose, the mathematics and science indicator system would function much like NAEP currently does. It would collect data representative of different regions, types of school districts (e.g., urban/rural/suburban), and students (by race, sex, grade level, etc.), but would not provide information specific to any individual state.

State and local policymakers would find such a system of only limited value. Like NAEP results or the national commission reports that have been issued over the past several years, this type of indicator system might serve as a prod to state and local action, and it could be used by supporters of educational reform as one rationale for new initiatives to improve mathematics and science education. However, once such measures were enacted, national data that could not be disaggregated at least to the state level would be of little or no use to the policy community. To inform local practice, indicator system data must also be disaggregated in such a way as to allow comparisons across different types of schools and districts.

An alternative that still serves primarily the overview function is an indicator system analogous to individual states participating in NAEP, with the data then reported on a state-by-state basis (Alexander and James, 1987). Such a system would focus primarily on outcome indicators and the resource and process measures associated with particular outcomes. Because it would not be designed for accountability or policy modification purposes, this system would not measure in any detail policy-specific variables such as the use of state curriculum guides or whether textbooks and student assessments are consistent. Rather, this system would allow states to compare the performance of their students with that of students elsewhere and would give a general sense of modal inputs and classroom practices (e.g., amount of instructional time on particular subjects, teacher qualifications, etc.) in the state. At this time, such a general picture would be useful in many states. For local districts, however, the indicator system would provide only general information about the relationship between practice and effects in districts of similar size and characteristics.

Despite these limitations, an indicator system designed to provide a broad overview of mathematics and science education could play a major role in policymakers' efforts to define more precisely the policy problems that confront them. One dimension of problem definition consists of a basic set of facts that most people can agree upon (e.g., that student test scores have declined, that fewer college students are choosing mathematical and scientific majors). The marshaling of such facts is facilitated by the existence of relevant indicators that describe the state of the policy system and provide benchmarks for comparing current conditions with those of earlier times or different places (Kingdon, 1984). Good indicator data can, for example, inform policymakers about the scope of a problem, e.g., whether it is widespread or confined to a particular ethnic group, age level, or geographic area.

However, the information that fewer students are becoming science majors tells policymakers only that a problem exists. If they are to address a given problem effectively, they need to know what factors affect the outcomes of interest. Consequently, an indicator system must provide information not only about particular outcomes (e.g., student participation in mathematics and science courses), but also about factors believed to be linked to those outcomes. It must be based on an underlying model of the educational system that identifies variables of interest to policymakers and specifies, as well as possible, the relationships among them. Policymakers can use such information to define a problem and to identify the factors most likely to be related to an observed change. In this sense, an indicator system can aid the problem definition process, since better indicators would presumably lead to more precise definitions of policy problems and a more informed choice of solutions.

In sum, a system that provides an overview can be an important resource for policymakers. By providing a mechanism for comparing trends over time, such a system can signal whether or not there are sufficient numbers of students in the scientific manpower pipeline. By generating information about relationships among key factors in the educational system, the indicator system can also identify the grade levels at which a problem is beginning to surface, the types of students who are most affected, and whether changes in such factors as teacher qualifications or curriculum content are likely to remedy the problem.

Indicator system information is just one factor, however, and usually not the most important one, in shaping policy decisions. What policymakers actually do about a problem such as the scientific manpower pipeline will depend on how critical they consider this problem to be in relation to other policy problems; their own beliefs about how people become scientists; and the political resources they have and the constraints they face. This caveat is not meant to discourage the development or to lessen the assumed importance of an indicator system. Rather, it is to suggest that system designers are likely to produce a much more effective system if they understand the role of information in a policy context.

Without exception, the policymakers we interviewed said that describing the condition of mathematics and science education is the most important function an indicator system can serve. They believe a broad range of information should be included in this descriptive or overview function. Respondents talked about wanting to know what the "health" of mathematics and science education is, and needing a system that identifies trends that may help in anticipating future problems. In addition to an interest in general trend data, respondents were particularly interested in information about those factors over which they can exert some leverage. Within this general framework, they want data that will help inform the choices they need to make, given limited resources. For example, they want information about the tradeoffs involved in using money for teacher salaries as compared with buying laboratory equipment or reducing class size.

Serving as an Accountability Mechanism. An indicator system that permits comparisons across states could ostensibly function as a kind of accountability mechanism. It could provide policymakers and the public with information about how well students in a particular state are performing on standardized achievement measures and how their participation levels in mathematics and science education compare with those in other states. This information could then be used in assessing how well various policymakers and practitioners are doing in providing high-quality mathematics and science education and imposing rewards or sanctions for that performance. In other words, the accountability function moves an indicator system beyond serving as simply a source of information to actually using that information to demand or stimulate improvements in schooling.

However, the use of a national indicator system for such a purpose presents several problems. First, there is the question of whether a federal agency like NSF ought to be involved in the process of holding states and local school districts accountable for what is essentially a state and local function. The policymakers we interviewed uniformly argued that accountability for mathematics and science education should not be a function of a national indicator system. In their view, accountability, beyond that needed to make certain its own programs are operating appropriately, is not a federal responsibility. At the same time, respondents believe that the federal government can provide information that states might use as part of their own accountability systems.

In addition to the question of appropriateness, there is the issue of feasibility. Since mathematics and science education is ultimately delivered in individual schools and classrooms, an effective accountability mechanism requires that data be collected at that level. Although some states collect primarily district-level data, most recognize the need to collect school-level and even student-specific data if they are to influence and monitor the educational change process.

Political accountability also assumes that government officials are held responsible not only for the general performance of the system, but also for the policies they enact and implement. Consequently, an indicator system that monitors for accountability purposes would need to collect data related to specific policies (e.g., on teacher training, textbook selection, course requirements). Given the cost and administrative capacity required to collect such data in even one state, it is unreasonable to expect that a national indicator system could accommodate the level of detail needed to hold individual states and districts accountable. In addition, a national indicator system may assume considerably less variability across jurisdictions than actually exists. States and local school districts have different political traditions that define acceptable policy actions; they also vary in the nature and extent of their educational problems, and in the policy instruments they use to address those problems. Even if a national indicator system were sensitive to such variation, it would minimize differences because of the way educational indicators are measured.

The federal government thus can design and operate a national indicator system to provide a broad overview of the status of mathematics and science education, but the system is unlikely to be an effective accountability mechanism. Although it can prod states or local districts to encourage higher-quality mathematics and science education, the federal government lacks the authority to punish or reward performance. A national-level indicator system also cannot provide the level of detail about individual schools or specific policies needed for true accountability. Consequently, such a system could not replace state and local efforts, and accountability will almost certainly continue as a state and local responsibility.

Improving Policy and Practice. Because it also measures the factors associated with particular outcomes, a monitoring system might be useful for identifying approaches that seem to work in improving mathematics and science education. The policy community could use this information to modify or fine-tune its activities. Policymakers we interviewed felt that since improving practice is clearly within the mission of NSF and other relevant federal agencies, this would be an appropriate function for a national indicator system. Respondents argued that NSF should provide information about practices that are consistently related to valued outcomes for students, and that this would be an appropriate function of a national monitoring system.

However, improving policy and practice, like providing accountability, raises major feasibility questions. To target resources effectively or to modify policies, policymakers need information about unintended consequences and potential problems at the individual district level, or even the school or classroom level. Past research has shown that understanding the relationship between top-down policy and local practice often requires micro-level data. Consequently, the aggregate indicators of a national monitoring system may not measure state policy and local practice variables in sufficient detail to enable the identification of effective approaches to mathematics and science education.

Nevertheless, an indicator system can provide a general framework within which to examine effective practices. For example, a series of small-scale studies could be designed to focus on the school resource and process variables that, at the aggregate level, show a positive relationship with desired outcomes. In other words, the indicator system data could be used to determine what domains of schooling were the most fruitful to examine, and the in-depth studies could conceptualize the variables of interest in the same way as the indicator system does. In this way, data from the two sources could be integrated. The indicator system data could suggest which relationships to explore, and the in-depth studies could probe those factors that are difficult to measure validly with aggregate indicators. The more intensive studies could also examine feasibility issues, such as the relative costs of different approaches, the professional capacity required to implement them, and any unintended consequences that might result.

In sum, providing a broad overview of mathematics and science education is the most important purpose a national indicator system can serve for the policy community. General trend data and information about key components of the educational system would be a critical resource for policymakers as they attempt to identify and define policy problems. Although the information a national system would generate would be only one factor shaping policy decisions, the system could play a significant role in influencing what mathematics and science education issues are considered and what policy solutions are proposed.

The role that a national indicator system is likely to play, however, as either an accountability mechanism or an impetus for policy adjustment will be a diffuse one. The general consensus is that the accountability function is not an appropriate role for the federal government. In addition, a national indicator system will not be able to assess whether particular state or local policies are producing their intended effects or whether resources are being used effectively. But if a national indicator system includes more intensive analyses of specific schooling components, it could inform the policy community about which generic approaches are associated with improved mathematics and science education. Policymakers are currently searching for alternatives to mandates, but they lack sufficient information about the extent to which other approaches such as incentives or local capacity-building strategies are likely to be effective. An indicator system, in conjunction with several well-focused, in-depth studies, might be a very useful source of such information. It cannot, however, assist policymakers in modifying the design of specific state or local policies.

Some Consequences of Producing Useful Information

As the discussion thus far indicates, any system that generates policy-relevant information will be used in a political environment fueled by competing values and interests, and system designers need to be aware of how such a system might affect the policy context. For example, educational indicators can assist in identifying problems that, once recognized, become candidates for government action. Those wishing to expand the role of government will use these data to advance their position, while those espousing a more limited role may seek to discredit the data. Indicator system designers and managers must recognize that their data may become politicized, but they also need to guard their own independence and neutrality. Others, not system managers, give the data political meaning.[2] Similarly, if indicator data clarify the current status of mathematics and science education, that information might affect public support for schools. However, the direction in which support levels might be affected is not immediately obvious. One could hypothesize that positive trends might increase support levels. But it is equally plausible that indicators of relatively high achievement in mathematics and science might result in public complacency. Regardless of the direction in which public opinion moves, indicator system data may affect support levels and thereby constrain the range of available choices. Policymakers may be forced to act when they did not plan to, or they may be pressured to consider a particular set of alternatives.

Indicator data can also lead policymakers to focus on one aspect of a policy problem at the expense of others (MacRae, 1985). For example, indicator information might direct attention to those components of schooling that are easiest to measure, at the expense of more complex aspects. Moreover, the use of indicator data is likely to generate (or at least highlight) a set of opportunity costs. As Wildavsky argues, movement on any indicator can be maximized, as long as society is willing to ignore all other indicators (1979).

---

[2]I am grateful to Paul Hill for stressing the importance of this point.

The impact that an indicator system can have on how policymakers and the public view education should not be an argument against making such a system policy-relevant. However, it does emphasize the need to be attentive to the nature of the policy context. System designers can influence the way their information is used by the way they disseminate it. For example, focusing on one indicator to the exclusion of others can be mitigated by stressing the relationships among key components of schooling. As Bardach (1983) notes, all policy information is context-dependent. Whether and how it is used depends on the environment into which it is disseminated. Consequently, system designers can influence how information is used by understanding the needs of different audiences and the broader policy context in which indicator system information is disseminated (e.g., what other issues are on the policy agenda, how authority is distributed, what resources are available).

Not only does the policy community provide a major rationale for developing an indicator system, its actions can affect the major domains of schooling, and in turn, how indicator system data are interpreted. These effects are discussed below.

THE POLICY CONTEXT AS A MONITORING SYSTEM COMPONENT

The policy context becomes an indicator system component when policymakers enact and implement policies designed to change key aspects of schooling. These actions may then become factors that help explain changes in input, process, and output variables. In choosing to increase the number of science courses required for high school graduation, mandating that teachers obtain an undergraduate degree in an academic discipline rather than in education, or providing additional funds for updated texts, the political system chooses to pursue its policy objectives in a particular way.

This approach or combination of approaches must be taken into consideration in the design of an indicator system: It may be significant in explaining variations in system outcomes across geographic areas and types of students and change over time. Policy actions can affect the type and level of inputs, and, if successfully implemented, they may also influence school processes. One task in designing an indicator system, then, is to identify those policies that are likely to affect relevant input and process variables and determine whether they have been implemented and are thus capable of actually affecting mathematics and science education.

Policies Exerting a Potential Influence
on the Central Features of Schooling

At the federal level, both ED and NSF fund programs in mathematics and science education. NSF is currently spending about $90 million annually on precollegiate programs to develop instructional materials, prepare teachers, and provide informal science education in out-of-school settings such as museums. ED spends about $119 million, primarily to help local districts improve inservice teacher training and retraining in mathematics and science. Because these programs are so small relative to state and local efforts, their effects are not likely to be observed in a national indicator system or to influence the substance or level of major input and process variables.

Rather, the policy that will have an effect on these variables will be state and local policy. We have already discussed state assessments as an area of growing interest. These assessments can potentially affect what is taught and how it is taught. Preliminary evidence suggests that current state assessments exert the greatest effect on the elementary school curriculum (e.g., the sequencing of mathematical skills across grade levels); at the high school level, the greatest effect is on the lowest-achieving students. However, as more states and local districts move beyond the testing of competencies in basic skills to standardized subject-matter assessments, the effects of state assessments on the curriculum are likely to grow.[3]

Thirty-seven states have increased the number of mathematics courses required for high school graduation, and 28 have increased the number of science courses. Of the states that have graduation requirements in mathematics, 2 require one course, 32 require two courses, and 10 require three courses for high school graduation. The majority of states with science requirements (30) mandate two courses for high school graduation; 8 states require one course; and 4 require three courses. These state policies compare with the NSB Commission's recommendation that high school students be required to take at least three years of mathematics and three years of science and technology.

The implementation of new course requirements is by no means straightforward: Course content can be diluted, and classes can be taught by unqualified teachers. Nevertheless, research indicates that students learn more if they are exposed to more content (Wolf, 1977; Good et al., 1978; Brophy and Good, 1986; Raizen and Jones, 1985).

---

[3]As part of a project for the Center for Policy Research in Education (CPRE), researchers at Rutgers, RAND, and the University of Wisconsin-Madison examined the effect of state policies on local schools in six states and ten schools in each of those states. The findings cited here are included in OERI State Accountability Study Group (1988).

Thus, we should expect these new standards policies to shape the indicators in a national system.

However, the effect of the new requirements is unlikely to be uniform across all students. For example, most increases in state course requirements do not affect college-bound students because those students were already meeting (and often exceeding) the new state minimums. These students are more affected by increased university admissions requirements, the most common change being an increase in the number of required laboratory science courses. State course requirements for high school graduation, on the other hand, are significantly affecting lower-achieving students. Preliminary evidence suggests that these students are taking more academic courses, although they are often lower-level courses, such as general or consumer mathematics and general science. At the same time, however, urban schools report higher course failure rates (20 to 35 percent of the students in some schools fail at least one course a semester), and a greater need for remediation. Given these rather significant and widespread differences across types of students, a national indicator system would be expected to reveal changes in such factors as course enrollments and, eventually, in achievement, and that shifts in state policy would account for much of the change. At the same time, we would expect that the effects of standards policies on indicator system outcomes are likely to diminish over time as more states require the same number and type of courses, thus reducing the current natural variation.

A number of states are moving to implement a more uniform curriculum across all districts, at least for the teaching of basic skills. This effort could very well mean that state-developed curriculum guides, which traditionally have exerted little impact on local practice, may become more important in shaping classroom processes. One potentially powerful way for states to shape local curriculum is through efforts to make curriculum guidelines, textbooks, and statewide assessments consistent with each other. As noted, several states conduct statewide assessments, and 21 have state-level textbook adoption policies (Anderson, 1984). Even in states without a mandated basic curriculum, efforts are being made to exert greater influence over what has traditionally been a local process. California, for example, has developed model curricular standards for high school mathematics and science instruction, including examples of the type of literature and problems to present to students. The state is also moving toward making its assessment tests consistent with this curriculum and stressing higher-order thinking skills. In addition, the California State Board of Education has required textbook publishers to upgrade science and mathematics texts as a condition for state adoption. Whether states will be successful in changing classroom practice remains to be seen, but this new emphasis on shaping instructional processes and content should be taken into account in designing an indicator system.

Two other variables that are ostensibly open to policy manipulation are instructional time and teacher characteristics. *A Nation at Risk* and *Action for Excellence* both recommended that the length of the instructional day and year be extended as a means of improving educational quality. Those recommendations have been criticized because research indicates that the quantity of instructional time is a relatively minor factor in explaining student achievement, as compared with how that time is spent (Karweit, 1983; Levin, 1983). States and local districts have made modest changes in the length of the school year, usually increasing it to between 180 and 190 days—significantly less than the 200 to 220 days recommended in *A Nation at Risk*. Similarly, states have either required or provided incentives for increasing the school day to six or seven periods. However, the seven-hour school day recommended in *A Nation at Risk* is by no means the norm. State and local reluctance to extend the school day and year stems not so much from agreement with the cautions of researchers as from the cost implications of such changes. Estimates indicate that extending the school day by 20 percent (from 6.5 to 8 hours) would cost more than $20 billion annually; lengthening the school year from 180 to 220 days would also cost more than $20 billion (Odden, 1984). Consequently, states have made only minor changes in the quantity of instructional time and have tried to influence its quality through staff development efforts that sensitize teachers to how classroom time might be used more effectively. These efforts are neither widespread nor systematic enough to be measured reliably in an indicator system. Clearly, instructional time and its use constitute a significant factor in an indicator system, but one that is unlikely to be affected by the larger policy context.

Over the past few years, every state has enacted policies altering the ways teachers are to be trained, evaluated, or compensated, and many have made significant changes in all three areas. There has been a particular focus on mathematics and science teachers because of reported shortages in these areas. How these policy initiatives might be represented in an indicator model is still quite problematic, however.

Policymakers assume that the aggregate effect of all the new policy measures will be to improve the quality of the teaching force and, in turn, student academic performance. But these initiatives vary significantly from state to state; they assume a long time horizon to achieve their intended effects (i.e., 10 years or more); they are several stages removed from the factors that exert a direct effect on student achievement; and in some cases, they represent unexamined assumptions about the link between policy and effects (e.g., the relationship between performance-based compensation and student achievement).

Therefore, while gross measures such as the proportion of teachers teaching outside their field of certification or teacher salary levels might be included in an indicator model, a more complex representation of the teacher policy context is probably not only unnecessary at this point, but also difficult to conceptualize and measure. This is not to argue that teacher-related variables should not be included in an indicator model, or even that policy-specific variables related to teachers should not be considered at some future time. Rather, it is to suggest that at this point, teacher policy is too variable and volatile to affect in any systematic way either the teacher variables or the system outcomes likely to be included in an indicator model. This situation will probably change as we learn more about the relationships among teacher policies, instructional processes, and student effects, and as teacher policies are modified to reflect more accurately teachers' professional orientations and incentive structures. Right now, however, it appears that the distribution of teacher characteristics, like instructional time, is not a domain that is significantly shaped by the policy context.

Measuring the Effects of the Policy Context

Incorporating the policy context into a national indicator system is not an easy task. By purpose and design, an indicator system attempts to measure key features of schooling in a uniform way across states, local districts, schools, and students. Yet educational policies, even those addressing ostensibly the same problem, can differ significantly across jurisdictions in their intended effects, the instruments used, their targets, and their time frames. Consequently, teacher policy and student standards cannot be measured in a completely generic way. Moreover, an indicator system is designed to measure the core features of schooling. Even though the actual numerical value of these indicators may vary over time and place, the way the indicator is defined remains essentially the same. The focus of public policy, on the other hand, can vary significantly over time and place, depending on policymaker and constituent priorities. For example, in the 1970s, state policy focused almost solely on school finance; in the 1980s, it shifted to student standards and teacher policies. In the coming decade, policy may focus on how schools are organized and governed or on the curricula they teach. The challenge for an indicator system, then, will be to capture the effects of these major policy shifts, while still concentrating on the core (and essentially stable) features of schooling.

Finally, both the current state of research and the nature of public policy place significant limitations on the incorporation of the policy context into an indicator system. The body of research on policy formation and implementation accumulated over the past 15 years has established the conditions under which policy is translated into school- and classroom-level practice, but it does not address the links between changes in practice and changes in outcomes (e.g., Elmore, 1978; Berman and McLaughlin, 1978; McDonnell and McLaughlin, 1980). On the other hand, microlevel research on teaching and learning and on the organizational climate of schools typically specifies the relationship between practice and effects, but says little about the impact of policy on those domains (see the other chapters in this volume for the relevant discussion). It is only within the past few years that these two strands of research have begun to be integrated, so the links from policy to school practice and on to student effects are not yet well understood.

The nature of policy itself places significant limitations on the integration of policy into an indicator system. Policy analysts typically think of a particular policy as embodying a set of causal assumptions which assume that if policymakers take "x" action (e.g., enact regulations, appropriate funds), then outcome "y" will occur. However, policy implementation research has indicated quite clearly that such causal assumptions are rarely borne out in practice. To begin with, policies may be enacted but not implemented; or they may be implemented in different ways across targets; or they may produce varying effects on different subpopulations. All of these scenarios confound a linear conception of policies and their effects. In addition, because many education policies are designed to improve outcomes, such as student learning, which are influenced by a complex set of factors, the independent effect of any single policy intervention is often difficult to determine (Berryman and Glennan, 1980).

These problems suggest that there is no straightforward way to ensure that the policy context is included as an indicator system component. However, there are four strategies that can be used in the short term, while research on the links among policy, practice, and effects continues.

First, as an adjunct to the national indicator system, there should be a mechanism that periodically tracks state and local policy developments. Such a system would need to identify (1) significant changes in state policy and emerging trends in local policy; (2) what the policy community views as the intended effects of those policies; and (3) the extent of their implementation. These data could then be linked to indicator system data on those core features of schooling that the policies are expected to influence. Although policies may vary considerably from place to place, we would expect that some policies are sufficiently widespread and similar to exert a discernible effect on major schooling domains (e.g., policies regulating course requirements and student assessments). The policy tracking mechanism would sensitize indicator system users to possible explanations for changes in key indicators.

Second, capturing the effects of the policy context reinforces the need to include a variety of school process measures in a national indicator system. Many policies cannot be expected to produce their ultimate effects (e.g., changes in teaching behavior or in student attainment) for at least five to ten years. However, it is reasonable for policymakers to ask whether or not components of schooling such as the qualifications of incoming teachers or course offerings and content have changed in ways that are consistent with the intent of their policies. An indicator system of the type described in this volume could provide such useful policy information. Data about changes in input and school process factors cannot inform policymakers about whether their policies "worked" in some ultimate sense, but they can indicate whether those changes are moving schools in desired directions.

A third way to deal with limitations stemming from the nature of public policy is to make certain that an indicator system contains multiple effects measures. By using a number of measures, each of which contributes a different facet of information about the status of mathematics and science education, we can limit the effect of irrelevant factors and develop a more comprehensive and valid picture of policy effects (Campbell and Stanley, 1963). Including such measures as student course participation, in addition to achievement, will not completely solve the difficulties inherent in identifying the effects of specific policies, but it will make the estimates more precise.

Finally, an indicator system that takes into consideration the policy context should include a set of adjunct studies that explore the policy implications of the data the system generates. Such studies would provide a very important feedback loop into the policymaking process. Through them, policymakers could learn about the effects of the policies they have already enacted: Are they producing their desired effects on the core features of schooling? Are they producing different effects on different kinds of students? Are they generating unintended consequences? At the same time, policy studies could signal emerging trends and problems that policymakers will have to deal with in the future. Such studies would combine indicator system data, information obtained from the policy-tracking mechanism, and perhaps, in-depth case studies of either particular schooling domains and the policies currently affecting them or categories of policies and their effects.

CONCLUSIONS

This analysis of the policy context suggests that the legitimacy of a national indicator system will ultimately depend on how its usefulness is judged by the policy community. That community will support such a system politically and be willing to participate in it if its members believe the system takes into consideration their concerns; its outcome indicators reflect federal, state, and local goals; and aggregate policy effects, to the extent that they influence the core features of schooling, can be measured.

Particularly important is ensuring that NSF's notion of desirable mathematics and science outcomes is compatible with the more diffuse, though no less important, objectives embodied in state and local policy and practice. In their national leadership role, agencies like NSF and ED can significantly influence states and local districts in defining what they expect mathematics and science education to achieve. Yet support for a federal effort, at a time when the federal level is definitely the junior partner in education, depends on NSF making certain that its suggested approaches take into consideration the preferences and capacity of the governmental levels that have actual responsibility for educating students. By acknowledging that the policy context represents both the major rationale for the system and a critical component of that system, indicator efforts in mathematics and science education can avoid the mistakes of past endeavors and can provide an analytical bridge between the worlds of policy and practice.

Appendix 10.1

ILLUSTRATIVE STATE-LEVEL DEFINITION OF REQUIRED BASIC-SKILL OUTCOMES

The following definitions of basic-skill outcomes for students in mathematics, science, and computer education are excerpted from the report of the Governor's Review Commission in Georgia. The letter I stands for Introduce (initial instructional activities); D stands for Develop (activities that elaborate and expand the skill); R stands for Reinforce (activities that strengthen an already acquired skill).

Grades			
K–4	5–8	9–12	
			In the area of Mathematics, the student is able to:
I	D	R	perform, with reasonable accuracy, the computation of addition, subtraction, multiplication, and division, using natural numbers, fractions, decimals, and integers.
I	D	R	make and use measurements in both traditional and metric units.
			use the mathematics of
I	D	R	— integers, fractions, and decimals
	I	D,R	— ratios, fractions, and percentages
	I	D,R	— roots and powers
	I	D,R	— use basic algebraic concepts (such as missing addends and unknown variables) and geometric concepts (basic shapes and geometric relations).
I	D	R	make estimates and approximations and judge the reasonableness of a result.
I	D	R	formulate and solve a problem in mathematical terms
I	D	R	select and use appropriate approaches and tools in solving problems (mental computation, trial and error, paper-and-pencil techniques, calculator and computer).

Grades			
K–4	5–8	9–12	
I	D	R	use basic concepts or probability and statistics (for example, understand the likelihood of events occurring, know how to compute the average).

In reasoning and solving problems, the student is able to:

I	D	R	identify and formulate problems.
I	D	R	propose and evaluate ways to solve problems.
I	D	R	locate and evaluate information needed to solve problems.
I	D	R	distinguish between fact and opinion.
I	D	R	reach a valid and supportable conclusion.

The **computer** has emerged as a basic tool for acquiring and organizing knowledge, communicating, and solving problems. To compete successfully in postsecondary academics and in the increasingly technological workplace,

the student leaving high school is able to:

	I	D,R	demonstrate a basic awareness of when and how computers may be used in daily life.
	I	D,R	demonstrate a basic knowledge of how computers work and of common computer technology.
(a)	I	D,R	demonstrate some ability to use the computer and appropriate software for self-instruction, problem solving, work processing, and collection and retrieval of information.

Science instruction should enable the student to:

I	D,R		understand that matter has structure and is found in various conditions.
I	D,R		demonstrate a basic understanding of energy, its nature, its limits, and its uses.
I	D,R		understand that machines extend the physical capacities of human beings.
I	D	D,R	demonstrate a basic understanding of the interrelationships between people and the earth and its natural resources.
I	D,R	D,R	exhibit a basic scientific understanding of the varieties of living organisms and the relationships among them.
I,D	D,R	R	use the basic principles of decisionmaking as outlined in the scientific method of problem solving.

^aInstruction made available to all students, but participation not required.

REFERENCES

Abhyankar, S.B. (1977). A comparative laboratory study of the effects of two teaching strategies on sixth grade students' attitudes and self-confidence in science (Ph.D. dissertation, Florida State University, Tallahassee, 1977). *Dissertation Abstracts International, 38,* 2023A.

Achievement Council. (1985). *Excellence for whom?* Oakland, CA: The Achievement Council.

Adelman, C. (1983). *Devaluation, diffusion, and the college connection: A study of high school transcripts, 1964–1981.* (ERIC Document Reproduction Service No. ED 228 244). Washington, DC: National Commission on Excellence in Education.

Adler, Mortimer, J. (1982). *The Paidiea proposal: An educational manifesto.* New York: MacMillan Co.

Advisory Commission on Intergovernmental Relations. (1986). *Measuring state fiscal capacity: Alternative methods and their uses.* Washington, DC. ACIR Report M-150.

Ahlgren, A., & Walberg, L.J. (1973). Changing attitudes toward science among adolescents. *Nature, 245,* 187–190.

Aiken, L.R. (1982). Writing multiple-choice items to measure higher-order educational objectives. *Educational and Psychological Measurement, 42,* 803–806.

Akers, J. (1984, January). Not all math texts are created equal. *Learning, 12,* 34–35.

Aldrich, H. (1983, July 27). Teacher shortage: Likely to get worse before it gets better. *Education Week.*

Alexander, K.L., Cook, M., & McDill, E.L. (1978). Curriculum tracking and educational stratification: Some further evidence. *American Sociological Review, 43*(1), 47–66.

Alexander, K.L., & McDill, E.L. (1976). Selection and allocation within schools: Some causes and consequences of curriculum placement. *American Sociological Review, 41,* 963–980.

Alexander, K.L., Natriello, G., & Pallas, A.M. (1985, June). For whom the bell tolls: The impact of dropping out on cognitive performance. *American Sociological Review, 50,* 409–420.

Alexander, L., and James, H.T. (1987). *The nation's report card: Improving the assessment of student achievement.* Washington, D.C.: National Academy of Education.

American Association for the Advancement of Science. (1984). *Equity and excellence: Compatible goals.* Washington, DC: American Association for the Advancement of Science.

American Association for the Advancement of Science. (1985). *Project 2061: Phase I.* American Association for the Advancement of Science, Washington, DC.

American Association of Physics Teachers. (1982). *AAPT guidelines for high school physics programs.* Stony Brook, NY: American Association of Physics Teachers.

American Chemical Society. (1984, October). *Tomorrow: The report of the task force for the study of chemistry education in the United States.* Washington, DC: American Chemical Society.

American Council on Education. (1983, June 8). Demographic imperatives: Implications for educational policy. Report on the forum *The demographics of changing ethnic populations and their implications for elementary-secondary and postsecondary educational policy.* Washington, DC: American Council on Education.

Anderson, B. (1984). State policy on textbooks: Three key questions. *ECS Issuegram.* Denver, CO: Education Commission of the States.

Anderson, C.S. (1982). The search for school climate: A review of the research, *Review of Educational Research, 52*(3), 368–420.

Anderson, C.W., & Smith, E.L. (1983). *Children's conceptions of light and color: Developing the concept of unseen rays.* Paper presented at the Annual Meeting of the American Educational Research Association. Montreal, Canada.

Anderson, C.W., & Smith, E.L. (1986). Teaching science. In V. Koehler (Ed.), *The educator's handbook: A research perspective.* New York: Longman.

Anderson, J. (1981). Achievement and participation of women in mathematics, *Journal for Research in Mathematics Education, 12,* 356–372.

Andrews, J.W., Blackmon, C.R., & Mackey, J.A. (1980). Preservice performance and the National Teacher Examinations. *Phi Delta Kappan, 61*(5), 358–359.

Antonnen, R.G. (1969). A longitudinal study in mathematics attitude. *Journal of Educational Research, 62,* 467–471.

Anyon, J. (1981). Social class and school knowledge. (1981). *Curriculum Inquiry, 11,* 3–40.

Armbruster, B.B., & Anderson, T.H. (1981). Analysis of science textbooks: Implications for authors. In J.T. Robinson, (Ed.), *Research in science education: New questions, new directions.* Washington, DC: National Institute of Education.

Armor, D.J., Conry-Oseguera, P., Cox, M., King, N., Pascal, A., Pauly, E., Zellman, G., McDonnell, L. (1976). *Analysis of the school preferred reading program in selected Los Angeles minority schools.* Santa Monica, CA: The RAND Corporation.

Armstrong, J. (1981). Achievement and particiation of women in mathematics. *Journal for Research in Mathematics Education, 12,* 356–372.

Armstrong, J.M. (1980). *Achievement and participation in mathematics: An overview.* Washington, DC: National Institute of Education.

ASCUS (Association for School, College, and University Staffing) (1984). *Teacher supply/demand.* Madison, WI: ASCUS.

Association of California Urban School Districts. (1985). *Dropouts from California's urban school systems: Who are they? How do we count them? How can we hold them (or at least educate them)?* Final Report by the Urban School Districts Task Force on Dropouts.

Association for Supervision and Curriculum Development (ASCD) (1985). *With consequences for all.* Alexandria VA: ASCD.

Averch, H.A., Carroll, S.J., Donaldson, T., Kiesling, H., & Pincus, J. (1972). *How effective is schooling? A critical review and synthesis of research findings.* Santa Monica, CA: The RAND Corporation.

Ayers, J.B., & Qualls, G.S. (1979). Concurrent and predictive validity of the National Teacher Examinations. *Journal of Educational Research, 73*(2), 86–92.

Azumi, J.E., & Madhere, S. (1983, April). *Professionals, power and performance: The relationships between administrative control, teacher conformity, and student achievement.* Paper presented at the annual meeting of the American Educational Research Association, Montreal, Canada.

Bachman, J.G., Green, S., & Wirtanen, D. (1971). Dropping out — Problem or symptom? *Youth in transition (Volume III).* Ann Arbor: Institute for Social Research, The University of Michigan.

Baker, E.L. (1984). Evaluating educational quality: A rational design. In *The use of testing and evaluation for assessing educational quality and improving school practice.* University of California, Los Angeles, Center for the Study of Evaluation.

Bandura, A. (1977). Self-efficacy: Toward a unifying theory of behavioral change. *Psychological Review, 84,* 191–215.

Bardach, E. (1983). *The dissemination of policy research to policymakers.* Unpublished manusucript.

Barr, R. & Dreeben, R. (1983). *How schools work.* Chicago: University of Chicago Press.

Barth, R. (1979). Home-based reinforcement of school behavior: A review and analysis. *Review of Educational Research, 49,* 436–458.

Bassham, H., Murphy, M., & Murphy, K. (1964). Attitude and achievement in arithmetic. *Arithmetic Teacher, 11,* 66–72.

Bauer, R. (1966a). *Social indicators.* Cambridge, MA: M.I.T. Press.

Bauer, R.A. (1966b). Social indicators and sample surveys. *Public Opinion Quarterly, 30,* 339–352.

Becker, H.J. (1982–1984). *School uses of microcomputers: Reports from a national survey,* Nos. 1–4. Center for the Social Organization of Schools. Baltimore, MD: The Johns Hopkins University.

Becker, H.J. (1986). *Computer survey newsletter.* Baltimore, MD: Johns Hopkins University Center for the Social Organization of Schools.

Becker, H.S., Geer, B., & Hughes, E. (1968). *Making the grade: The academic side of college life.* New York: Wiley.

Begle, E.G. (1979). *Critical variables in mathematics education.* Washington, DC: Mathematical Association of America and National Council of Teachers of Mathematics.

Bell, D. (1972). On meritocracy and equality. *The Public Interest, 29,* 29–68.

Benbow, C.P., & Stanley, J.C. (1980). Sex differences in mathematical ability: Fact or artifact. *Science, 210*(4475), 1262–1264.

Benbow, C.P., & Stanley, J.C. (1982). Consequences in high school and college of differences in mathematical reasoning ability: A longitudinal perspective. *American Educational Research Journal, 19,* 598–622.

Bentzen, M.M. (1975). *Changing schools: The magic feather principle.* New York: McGraw-Hill.

Berliner, D. (1976). Impediments to the study of teacher effectiveness. *Journal of Teacher Education, 27*(1), 5–13.

Berliner, D.C. (1979). Tempus educare. In P.L. Peterson and H.L. Walberg (Eds.), *Research on teaching: Concepts, findings, and implications.* Berkeley, CA: McCutcheon Publishing.

Berliner, D. (1984). The half-full glass: A review of research on teaching. In P.L. Hosford (ed.), *Using what we know about teaching (pp. 51–77). Alexandria, VA: Association for Supervision and Curriculum Development.*

Berman, P., & McLaughlin, M.W. (1975–79). *Federal programs supporting educational change,* Volumes I-IX. Santa Monica, CA: The RAND Corporation.

Berry, B. (1986). Why bright college students won't teach. *Urban Review 18*(4), 269–280.

Berryman, S., & Glennan, T.K. (1980). An improved strategy for evaluating federal programs in education. In J. Pincus (Ed.), *Educational evaluation in the public policy setting.* Santa Monica, CA: The RAND Corporation.

Berryman, S. (1983). *Who will do science?: Minority and female attainment of science and mathematics degrees: Trends and causes.* New York: The Rockefeller Foundation.

Bidwell, C.E., & Kasarda, J.D. (1975). School district organization and student achievement. *American Sociological Review, 40,* 55–70.

Bishop, J.M. (1977). Organizational influences on the work orientations of elementary teachers. *Sociology of Work and Occupation, 4*(2), 171–208.

Blank, R.K., & Raizen, S.A. (1985). *Approaches to measuring the implemented curriculum.* Paper prepared for a meeting of the Colloquium on Indicators of Precollege Science and Mathematics Education. Washington, DC: National Research Council.

Blank, R., & Raizen, S.A. (1985). *Teacher quality in science and mathematics education: Planning for a National Research Council study.* Unpublished manuscript. Washington, DC: National Research Council.

Blase, J.J. (1982). A social-psychological grounded theory of teacher stress and burnout. *Education Administration Quarterly, 18*(4), 93–113.

Blaug, M. (1985). Where are we now in the economics of education? *Economics of Education Review 4(1),* 17–28.

Bloch, E. (1986). Basic research and the economic health: The coming challenge. *Science, 232,*(4750), 595–599.

Blosser, P.E. (1984). Attitude research in science education. *ERIC clearinghouse for science, mathematics, and environmental education, 1,* 1–8.

Bock, R.D., & Moore, E.G.J. (1986). *Advantage and disadvantage: A profile of American youth.* Hillsdale, NJ: Lawrence Erlbaum Associates.

Borg, W.R. (1980). Time and school learning. In C. Denham & A. Lieberman (Eds.), *Time to learn.* Washington, DC: National Institute of Education.

Boyd, W.L. (1979). The changing politics of curriculum policy making for American schools. In J. Schaffarzick & G. Sykes (Eds.), *Value conflicts and curriculum issues: Lessons from research and experience.* Berkeley, CA: McCutchan Publishing.

Bowles, S. (1969). *Education production function: Final report,* U.S. Department of Health, Education, and Welfare, Office of Education. Washington, DC.

Bowles, S., & Levin, H.M. (1968). The determinants of scholastic achievement—An appraisal of some recent evidence. *Journal of Human Resources, 3,* 3–24.

Bransford, J., Sherwood, R., Vye, N., & Rieser, J. (1986). Teaching thinking and problem solving. *American Psychologist, 41*(10), 1078–1089.

Braswell, J. (1978, March). College board scholastic aptitude test. *Mathematics Teacher, 71,* 168–180.

Bredeson, P.V., Fruth, M.J., & Kasten, K.L. (1983). Organizational incentives and secondary school teaching. *Journal of Research and Development in Education, 16,* 52–56.

Bridge, R.G., Judd, C.M., & Moock, R.R. (1979). *The determinants of educational outcomes.* Cambridge: Ballinger.

Bridges, E.M., & Hallinan, M.T. (1978). Subunit size, work system interdependence, and employee absenteeism. *Educational Administration Quarterly, 14*(2), 24–42.

Brody, L., & Fox, L.H. (1980). An accelerative intervention program for mathematically gifted girls. In L.H. Fox & D. Tobin (Eds.), *Women and the mathematical mystique.* Baltimore: Johns Hopkins University Press.

Brookover, W., Beady, C., Flood, P., Schweitzer, J., & Wisenbaker, J. (1979). *School systems and student achievement: Schools can make a difference.* New York: Praeger.

Brophy, J. (1986). Teacher influences on student achievement. *American Psychologist, 41*(10), 1069–1077.

Brophy, J.E., & Evertson, C. (1974). *Process-product correlations in the Texas teacher effectiveness study: Final report.* Austin, TX: Research and Development Center for Teacher Education.

Brophy, J.E., & Evertson, C. (1977). Teacher behavior and student learning in second and third grades. In G.D. Borich (Ed.), *The appraisal of teaching: Concepts and process.* Reading, MA: Addison-Wesley.

Brophy, J.E., & Good, T.L. (1986). Teacher behavior and student achievement. In M.C. Wittrock (Ed.), *Handbook of research on teaching* (pp. 328–375). New York: Macmillan.

Brown, B.W., & Saks, D.H. (1980). Production technologies and resource allocations within classrooms and schools: Theory and measurement. In R. Dreeben and J. A. Thomas (Eds.), *The analysis of educational productivity. Volume 1: Issues in microanalysis.* (pp. 53–118). Cambridge, MA: Ballinger, Cambridge.

Brown, J.S., & Burton, R. (1978). Diagnostic models for procedural bugs in basic mathematical skills. *Cognitive Science, 2,* 155–192.

Brown, J.S., & Van Lehn, K. (1980). Repair theory: A generative theory of bugs in procedural skills. *Cognitive Science, 4,* 379–426.

Brumby, M. (1981). Learning, understanding, and 'thinking about' the concept of life. *Australian Science Teachers Journal, 27*(3), 21–25.

Bruner, J. (1960). *The process of education.* Cambridge, MA: Harvard University Press.

Bruner, J. (1971). *The relevance of education.* New York: W. W. Norton.

Bruno, J.E. (1981). Designs of incentive systems for staffing racially isolated schools in large urban districts: Analysis of pecuniary and nonpecuniary benefits. *Journal of Educational Finance, 7*(2), 149–167.

Bureau of Labor Statistics (1982). *Employment and training report of the president, 1982: Employment and earnings.* Washington, DC: U.S. Bureau of Labor Statistics.

Bureau of the Census (1973). *Statistical abstract of the United States: 1973,* 94th ed. Washington, DC: U.S. Department of Commerce.

Bureau of the Census (1980). 1980 Census of Population, Vol. 1, chapter C (PC 80-1-C).

Bureau of the Census (1983). *Statistical abstract of the United States: 1984,* 104th ed. Washington, DC: U.S. Department of Commerce.

Burnett, R.W. (1944). The science teacher and his objectives. *Teachers College Record, 45,* 241–251.

Buros, O.K. (1961). *Tests in print.* Highland Park, NJ: The Gryphon Press.

Burstein, L. (1980). The role of levels of analysis in the specification of educational effects. In R. Dreeben & J. A. Thomas (Eds.), *The analysis of educational productivity, volume 1: Issues in microanalysis* (pp. 119–190). Cambridge, MA: Ballinger.

Burstein, L., Baker, E.L., Aschbacher, P., & Keesling, J.W. (1985). *Using state test data for national indicators of education quality: A feasibility study.* Final report of the state tests as quality indicators project. Los Angeles: University of California, National Center for Education Statistics, Center for the Study of Evaluation.

Byrne, C.J. (1983). *Teacher knowledge and teacher effectiveness: A literature review, theoretical analysis and discussion of research strategy.* Paper presented at the meeting of the Northeastern Educational Research Association. Ellenville, NY.

Calfee, R.C., & Brown, R. (1979) Grouping students for instruction. In *Classroom management, seventy-eighth yearbook of the National Society for the Study of Education.* Chicago: University of Chicago Press.

California Assembly Office of Research. (1985). *Dropping out, losing out: The high cost for California.* Sacramento, CA: Joint State Publications Office.

California Commission on the Teaching Profession. (1985). *Who will teach our children?* Sacramento, CA: California Commission on the Teaching Profession.

California State Department of Education. (1984a). *California high school curriculum study: Paths through high school.* Sacramento, CA: California State Department of Education.

California State Department of Education. (1984b). *Performance report for California schools: Indicators of quality.* Sacramento, CA: California State Department of Education.

Campbell, D.T., & Stanley, J.C. (1963). *Experimental and quasi-experimental design for research.* Chicago: Rand-McNally.

Capper, J. (1985). *Proposal to develop and disseminate core content goals in mathematics and science.* A proposal submitted to the National Science Foundation, Council of Chief State School Officers, Washington, DC.

Carnoy, M., & Levin, H. (1985). *Schooling and work in the democratic state.* Stanford, CA.: Stanford University Press.

Carpenter, T.P., Corbitt, M.K., Kepner, H.S., Lindquist, M.M., & Reys, R.E. (1980, September). NAEP note: Problem solving. *Mathematics Teacher, 73*(6), 427–433.

Carpenter, T.P., Matthews, W., Lindquist, M.M., & Silver, E.A. (1984). Achievement in mathematics: Results from the national assessment. *Elementary School Journal, 84*(5), 85–95.

Carroll, C.D. (1985). *High school and beyond tabulation: Background characteristics of high school teachers.* Washington, DC: NCES.

Carroll, S.J., and Park, R.E. (1983). *The search for equity in school finance.* Cambridge, MA: Ballinger Publishing Co.

Casserly, P. (1979). *Factors related to young women's persistence and achievement in mathematics.* Washington, DC: National Institute of Education.

Catterall, J.S. (1986). *On the social costs of dropping out of school.* Stanford, CA: Stanford Educational Policy Institute. Program Report No. 86-SEPI-3.

Center for Statistics (1986, March 18). *Plan for the redesign of the elementary and secondary data collection program.* (Working paper). Washington, DC: U.S. Department of Education, Office of Educational Research and Improvement.

Centra, J.A., & Potter, D.A. (1980). School and teacher effects: An interrelational model. *Review of Educational Research, 50,* 273–291.

Chambers, J. (1978). Educational cost differentials and the allocation of state aid for elementary/secondary education. *The Journal of Human Resources, 13*(4), 459–481.

Chambers, J. (1980). The development of a cost of education index: some empirical estimates and policy issues. *Journal of Education Finance 5*(3), 262–281.

Champagne, A.B., Klopfer, L.E., & Gunstone, R.F. (1980). *A model of adolescents' understanding of physical phenomena and its application to instruction.* Paper presented at the Annual Meeting of the American Educational Research Association, 14 April, 1981, Los Angeles, CA.

Champagne, A.B., Klopfer, L.E., & Gunstone, R.F. (1982). Cognitive research and the design of science instruction. *Educational Psychologist, 17*(10), 31–53.

Chapman, D.W. (1984). Teacher retention: The test of a model. *American Education Research Journal, 21*(3), 645–659.

Chapman, D.W., & Hutcheson, S.M. (1982). Attrition from teaching careers: A discriminant analysis. *American Educational Research Journal, 19*, 93–106.

Chipman, S.F., & Thomas, V.G. (1984, September). *The participation of women and minorities in mathematical, scientific, and technical fields.* Paper commissioned by the Committee on Research in Mathematics, Science, and Technology Education of the National Research Council Commission on Behavioral and Social Sciences and Education, Washington, DC.

Cicourel, A.V., & Kitsuse, J.I. (1963). *The educational decision makers* Indianapolis: Bobbs-Merrill.

Clark, D., Lotto, L., & McCarthy, M. (1980, March). Factors associated with success in urban elementary schools. *Phi Delta Kappa,* 467–70.

Clark, D.L., Lotto, L.S., & Astuto, T.A. (1984). Effective schools and school improvement: A comparative analysis of two lines of inquiry. *Educational Administration Quarterly, 20,*(3), 41–68.

Clement, J. (1979a). *Limitations to formula-centered approaches to problem solving in physics and engineering.* Amherst, MA: University of Massachusetts at Amherst. (ED 214 755).

Clement, J. (1979b). *Common preconceptions and misconceptions as an important source of difficulty in physics courses.* Amherst, MA: University of Massachusetts at Amherst. (ED 214 755).

Clement, J. (1982). Students' preconceptions in introductory physics. *American Journal of Physics, 50*(1), 66–71.

Cohen, M. (1983). Instructional, management, and social conditions in effective schools. In A. Odden & L.D. Webb (Eds.), *School finance and school improvement: Linkages for the 1980s,* Fourth Annual Yearbook of the American Education Finance Association. Cambridge, MA: Bollinger.

Cohn, E. (1979). *The economics of education*. Cambridge, MA: Ballinger Publishing Co.

Cohn, E., & Millman, S.D. (1975). *Input-output analysis in public education*, Cambridge, MA: Ballinger.

Coleman, J. (1961). *The adolescent society*. New York: The Free Press.

Coleman, J. (1968). The concept of equality of educational opportunity. *Harvard Educational Review, 38*, 7–22.

Coleman, J., Campbell, E.Q., Hobson, C.J., McPartland, J., Mood, A.M., Weinfeld, F.D., & York, R.L. (1966). *Equality of educational opportunity*. U.S. Department of Health, Education, and Welfare, Office of Education (OE-38001), Washington, DC: U.S. Government Printing Office.

Coleman, J.S., Hoffer, T., & Kilgore, S. (1982). *High school achievement: Public and private schools compared*. New York: Basic Books.

College Entrance Examination Board. (1983). *Profiles, college bound seniors*. New York: Author.

College Entrance Examination Board. (1986). *Keeping the options open*. New York: College Entrance Examination Board.

Comber, L.C., & Keeves, J.P. (1973). *Science education in nineteen countries: An empirical study*. New York: John Wiley and Sons.

Combs, J., & Cooley, W.W. (1968). Dropping out: In high school and after high school. *American Educational Research Journal, 5*, 343–363.

Commission on Professionals in Science and Technology. (1986). *Professional women and minorities*. Washington, DC: Commission on Professionals in Science and Technology.

Committee on Coordinating Educational Information and Research. (1985, October). *CCSSO center on assessment and evaluation (draft report)*. Washington, DC: Council of Chief State School Officers.

Conference Board of the Mathematical Sciences. (1983) The mathematical sciences curriculum, K-12: What is still fundamental and what is not. Report to the National Science Board Commission. In *Educating Americans for the 21st century: Source materials*. Washington, DC: National Science Board, National Science Foundation.

Conference Board of the Mathematical Sciences. (1983). *New goals for mathematical sciences education*. Washington, DC.

Conference on Goals for Science and Technology Education, Grades K-12 (1983). A revised and intensified science and technology curriculum grades K-12 urgently need for our future. In *Educating Americans for the 21st Century: Source materials*, Washington, DC: National Science Board, National Science Foundation.

Cooley, W.W., & Klopfer, K. (1961). *Manual for the test on understanding science.* Princeton, NJ: Educational Testing Service.

Cooley, W.W., & Leinhardt, G. (1980). The instructional dimensions study. *Educational Evaluation and Policy Analysis, 2,* 7–25.

Cooley, W.W., & Reed, H.B. (1961). The measurement of science interests: An operational and multidimensional approach. *Science Education*, 45, 320–326.

Cooney, T.J., & Dossey, J.A. (1981). *Classroom processes: The linkage between intentions and outcomes.* Unpublished manuscript. University of Georgia.

Council of Chief State School Officers. (1988, February). State data available on indicators of science/math education. draft. Washington, D.C.: author.

Council of Chief State School Officers. (1985). *Profile of current national activities describing education in the United States.* Unpublished manuscript. Washington, DC: Council of Chief State School Officers.

Cox, H., & Wood, J.R. (1980). Organizational structure and professional alienation: The case of public school teachers. *Peabody Journal of Education, 58*(1), 1–6.

Crandall, D.P., & Loucks, S.F. (1982–3). *People, policies, and practices: Examining the chain of school improvement*, Vols. I-X. Andover, MA: The Network.

Creswell, J.L. (1980). A study of sex related differences in mathematics: Achievement of black, chicano, and anglo adolescents. As cited in S.M. Malcom, Y.S. George, & M.L. Matyas (1985). *Summary of research studies on women and minorities in science, mathematics and technology.* Washington, DC: American Association for the Advancement of Science.

Crocker, R.K., Bartlett, K.R., & Eliott, H.G. (1976). A comparison of structured and unstructured modes of teaching science process activities. *Journal of Research in Science Teaching, 13,* 267–274.

Cronbach, L.J., & Snow, R.E. (1977). *Aptitudes and instructional methods: A handbook for research on interactions.* New York: Irvington.

Crosswhite, F.J., Dossey, J.A., Swafford, J.O., McKnight, C.C., & Cooney, T.J. (1985). *Second international mathematics study: Summary report for the United States.* Washington, DC.: National Center for Education Statistics.

Cruikshank, D.R. (1985). Uses and benefits of reflective teaching. *Phi Delta Kappan, 66,* 315–336.

Cuban, L. (1979). Determinants of curriculum change and stability, 1870–1979. In J. Schaffarzick & G. Sykes (Eds.), *Value conflicts and curriculum issues: Lessons from research and experience.* Berkeley, CA: McCutchan Publishing.

Cuban, L. (1984). Transforming the frog into a prince: Effective schools research, policy, and practice at the district level. *Harvard Educational Review, 54,*(2), 129–151.

Daly, R.E. (1981). *A causal analysis of satisfaction, performance, work environment and leadership in selected secondary schools.* A Study of Schooling (Technical Report No. 31). Los Angeles: University of California, Graduate School of Education.

Dar, Y., & Resh, N. (1986). Classroom intellectual composition and academic achievement. *American Educational Research Journal, 23,*(3), 357–374.

Darling-Hammond, L. (1984). *Beyond the commission reports: The coming crisis in teaching.* Santa Monica, CA: The RAND Corporation.

Darling-Hammond, L. (1985). *Equality and excellence: The educational status of black Americans.* New York: College Entrance Examination Board.

Darling-Hammond, L., & Hudson, L. (1986). *Indicators of teacher and teaching quality.* Santa Monica, CA: The RAND Corporation.

Darling-Hammond, L., Wise, A.E., & Pease, S.R. (1983). Teacher evaluation in the organizational context: A review of the literature. *Review of Educational Research, 53*(3), 285–328.

Darling-Hammond, L., & Wise, A.E. (1985). Beyond standardization: State standards and school improvement. *Elementary School Journal, 85*(3), 315–336.

Davis, D.G. (1986). *A pilot study to assess equity in selected curricular offerings across three diverse schools in a large urban school district: A search for methodology.* Paper presented at the Annual Meeting of the American Educational Research Association, San Francisco, CA.

Deese, J. (1981). Text structure, strategies, and comprehension in learning from scientific textbooks. In J.. Robinson, (Ed.), *Research in science education: New questions, new directions.* Washington, DC: National Institute of Education.

de Neufville, J.I. (1975). *Social indicators and public policy: Interactive processes of design and application.* New York: Elsevier Scientific Publishing Company.

de Neufville, J.I. (1978–79). Validating policy indicators, *Policy Sciences, 10,* 171–188.

DeWolf, V.A. (1981). High school mathematics preparation and sex differences in quantitative abilities. *Psychology of Women Quarterly, 5*, 555–567.

Doyle, W. (1977). Paradigms for research on teacher effectiveness. In L.S. Shulman (Ed.), *Review of research in education*, Vol. 5. Itasca, IL: Peacock Publishers.

Doyle, W. (1983). Academic work. *Review of Educational Research, 53*(2), 159–199.

Doyle, W. (1985). Classroom organization and management. In M.C. Wittrock (Ed.), *Handbook of research on teaching* (3rd ed.), 392–431. New York: Macmillan.

Driver, R., & Easley, J. (1978). Pupils and paradigms: A review of literature related to concept development in adolescent science students. *Studies in Science Education, 5*, 61–84.

Driver, R., & Erickson, G. (1983). Theories-in-action: Some theoretical and empirical issues in the study of students' conceptual frameworks in science. *Studies in Science Education, 10*, 37–60.

Druva, C.A., & Anderson, R.D. (1983). Science teacher characteristics by teacher behavior and by student outcome: A meta-analysis of research. *Journal of Research in Science Teaching, 20*(5), 467–479.

Duncan, O.D. (1967). *Toward social reporting: Next steps.* New York: Russell Sage Foundation.

Dunteman, G.H., Weisenbecker, J., & Taylor, M.E. (1979). *Race and sex differences in college science program participation.* Triangle Park, N.C.: Research Triangle Institute.

Dwyer, C.A. (1974). Influence of children's sex role standards on reading and arithmetic achievement. *Journal of Educational Psychology, 66*(6), 811–816.

Eckland, B.K. (1980). The efficient use of educational data: A proposal for the national longitudinal study of the high school class of 2002. In C.E. Bidwell & D.M. Windham (Eds.), *The analysis of educational productivity, volume II: Issues in macroanalysis* (pp. 93–152). Cambridge, MA: Ballinger.

Edmonds, R.R. (1979). Effective schools for the urban poor. *Educational Leadership, 37*, 15–27.

Education Commission of States. (1983). *A 50-state survey of initiatives in science, mathematics, and computer education.* Denver, CO: Education Commission of States.

Education Commission of States. (1984). *Current status of state assessment programs. (Clearinghouse notes.)* Denver, CO: Education Commission of States.

Educational Policies Commission. (1966). *Education and the spirit of science.* Washington, DC: National Education Association. (ED 011 507).

Educational Research Service. (1986). *Class size research: A related cluster analysis for decision making.* Arlington, VA: ERS.

Educational Testing Service. (1987, May). *Learning by doing.* Princeton, NJ: Educational Testing Service. (Report No. 17-HOS-80)

Eisner, E.W. (1982). *Cognition and curriculum: A basis for deciding what to teach.* Longman, NY.

Eisner, E.W., & Vallance, E. (1974). Five conceptions of curriculum: Their roots and implications for curriculum planning. In Eisner, E.W., & Vallance, E. (Eds.), *Conflicting conceptions of curriculum.* Berkeley, CA: McCutchan Publishing.

Ellett, C.D., & Walberg, H.J. (1979). Principals' competency, environment, and outcomes. In H.J. Walberg (Ed.), *Educational environments and effects: Evaluation, policy, and productivity.* Berkeley, CA: McCutchan Publishing.

Elmore, R.F. (1978). Organizational models of social program implementation. *Public Policy, 26,* 185–228.

Elstein, A.S., Shulman, L.S., & Sprafka, S.A. (1978). *Medical problem solving: An analysis of clinical reasoning.* Cambridge: Harvard University Press.

Ennis, R.H. (1985). A logical basis for measuring critical thinking skills. *Educational Leadership, 43*(2), 44–48.

Epstein, J.L., & Becker, H.J. (1982). Teacher practices of parent involvement: Problem and possibilities. *Teachers College Record, 83,* 103–113.

Erickson, F. (1975). Gatekeeping the melting pot. *Harvard Educational Review, 45,* 44–70.

Erlwanger, S. (1975). Case studies of children's conceptions of mathematics. *Journal of Children's Mathematical Behavior, 1*(3), 157–283.

Esposito, D. (1973). Homogeneous and heterogeneous ability grouping: Principal findings and implications for evaluating and designing more effective educational environments. *Review of Educational Research, 43,* 163–179.

Etzioni, A. (1979). Indicators of the capacity for social guidance. *The Annals of the American Academy of Political Science, 388,* 25–34.

Etzioni, A., & Lehman, E.W. (1967). Some degree in 'valid' social measurement. *The Annals of the American Academy of Political Science, 373,* 1–15.

Evaluation Technologies, Inc. (1982). *A classification of secondary school courses.* Washington, DC: National Center for Education Statistics. (ED 217 579)

Fantini, M. (1980). *Community participation: Alternative patterns and their consequences on educational achievment.* Paper presented at the American Educational Research Association Annual Meeting.

Feibel, W. (1978). *Effects of training on the transition from concrete to formal reasoning in college students.* Unpublished doctoral dissertation. Santa Cruz, CA: University of California at Santa Cruz.

Fennema, E. (1984). Girls, women, and mathematics. In E. Fennema & M.J. Ayer (Eds.), *Women in Education.* Berkeley: McCutchan.

Fennema, E., & Carpenter, T.P. (1981). Sex-related differences in mathematics: Results from national assessment," *Mathematics Teacher, 74,* 554–559.

Fennema, E. (1980). *Multiplying options and subtracting bias.* Reston, VA: National Council of Teachers of Mathematics.

Fennema, E., & Sherman, J.A. (1977). Sex-related differences in mathematics achievement, spatial visualization, and affective factors. *American Educational Research Journal, 14,* 51–72.

Fennema, E., & Sherman, J.A. (1978). Sex-related differences in mathematics achievement and other factors: A further study. *Journal for Research in Mathematics Education, 9,* 189–203.

Ferris, A. (1981). Developing social indicators of inequity in education: Working paper. In D. Guilford, *Indicators of equity in education.* Washington, DC: National Research Council of the National Academy of Sciences.

Festinger, L. (1957). *A theory of cognitive dissonance.* Stanford, CA: Stanford University Press.

Fey, J.T. (1982). Mathematics Education. *Encyclopedia of Educational Research.* Fifth edition, Vol. 3, 1166–1182.

Filby, N., Barnett, B., & Bossert, S. (1982) *Grouping practices and their consequences.* San Francisco: Far West Laboratory for Educational Research.

Findlay, W.G., & Bryan, M.M. (1971). *Ability grouping: 1970 status, impact, and alternatives.* Athens, GA: University of Georgia, Center for Educational Improvement.

Fisher, C., Berliner, D., Filby, N., Marliave, R., Cahen, L., & Dishaw, M. (1980). Teaching behaviors, academic learning time, and student achievement: An overview. In C. Denham & A. Lieberman (Eds.), *Time to learn.* Washington, DC: National Institute of Education

Flowers, A. (1984). Preparation of teachers: Myths and realities. In J.L. Taylor (Ed.)., *Teacher shortage in science and mathematics: Myths, realities and research.* Washington, DC: National Institute of Education.

Fraser, B.J. (1978). Development of a test of science-related attitudes. *Science Education*, 62(4), 509–515.

Frataccia, E.V., & Hennington, I. (1982). *Satisfaction of hygiene and motivation needs of teachers who resign from teaching.* Paper presented at the annual meeting of the Southwest Educational Research Association, Austin, Texas.

Frederiksen, N. (1984). The real test bias: Influences of testing on teaching and learning. *American Psychologist, 39*(3), 193–202.

Frederiksen, N., & Ward, W.C. (1978). Measures for the study of creativity in scientific problem solving. *Applied Psychological Measurement, 2*(1), 1–24.

Freeman, D., Belli, G., Porter, A.C., Floden, R., Schmidt, W., & Schwille, J. (1981). The consequences of different styles of textbook use in preparing students for standardized tests. (Research Series No. 107). East Lansing, MI: Institute for Research on Teaching, Michigan State University.

Freeman, D.J., Belli, G.M., Porter, A.C., Floden, R.E., Schmidt, W.H., & Schwille, J.R. (1983a). The influence of different styles of textbook use on instructional validity of standardized tests. *Journal of Educational Measurement, 20*(3), 259–270.

Freeman, D.J., Kuhs, T.M., Porter, A.C., Floden R.E., Schmidt, W.H., & Schwille, J.R. (1983b). Do textbooks and tests define a national curriculum in elementary school mathematics? *Elementary School Journal, 83*(5), 501–513.

Fullan, M. (1982). *The meaning of educational change.* Teachers College Press, Columbia University.

Furr, J.D., & Davis, T.M., (1984). Equity issues and microcomputers: Are educators meeting the challenge. *Journal of Educational Equity and Leadership, 4*, 93–97.

Gage, N.L. (1978). *The scientific basis of the art of teaching.* New York: Teachers College Press.

Gagne, R.M. (1968). Educational technology as technique. *Educational Technology, 8*, 5–13.

Galambos, E.C. (1985). *Teacher preparation: The anatomy of a college degree.* Atlanta: Southern Regional Education Board.

Gamoran, A. (1986). *The stratification of high school learning opportunities.* Paper presented at the annual meeting of the American Educational Research Association, San Francisco.

Gardner, P.L. (1975). Attitudes to science: A review. *Studies in Science Education, 2*, 1–41.

Gauld, C. (1982). The scientific attitude and science education: A critical reappraisal. *Science Education, 66*(1), 109–121.

Gauld, C., & Hukins, A.A. (1980). Scientific attitudes: A review. *Studies in Science Education, 7*, 129–161.

Gay, G. (1980). Conceptual models of the curriculum planning process. In *Considered action for curriculum improvement.* Yearbook for the Association for Supervision and Curriculum Development (ASCD). Alexandria, VA: ASCD

Gilbert, J.K., & Watts, D.M. (1983). Concepts, misconceptions, and alternative conceptions: Changing perspectives in science education. *Studies in Science Education, 10*, 61–98.

Gilmartin, K.J. (1981). The concept of equality of educational opportunity. In D. Guilford, *Indicators of equity in education.* Washington, DC: National Research Council of the National Academy of Sciences.

Giroux, H.A. (1980). Beyond the limits of radical educational reform: Toward a critical theory of education. *The Journal of Curriculum Theorizing, 2*(1), 20–46.

Glaser, R. (1983). *Education and thinking: The role of knowledge.* (Tech. Rep. No. PD5–6). Pittsburgh: University of Pittsburgh.

Glasman, N.S., & Bimianinov, I. (1981). Input-output analyses of schools. *Review of Educational Research, 51*(4), 509–539.

Glass, G.V., & Smith, M.L. (1978). *Meta-analysis of research on the relationship of class size and achievement.* Boulder, CO: University of Colorado, Laboratory of Educational Research.

Glenn, B.C., & McLean, T. (1981). *What works? An examination of effective schools for poor black children.* Cambridge, MA: Harvard University, Center for Law and Education.

Glidewell, J.C. (1983). Professional support systems: The teaching profession. In A. Madler, J.D. Fisher, & B.M. DePaulo (Eds.), *Applied research in help-seeking and reactions to aid.* New York: Academic Press.

Good, T., & Grouws, D. (1977). Teaching effects: A process-product study in fourth grade mathematics classrooms. *Journal of Teacher Education, 28*, 49–54.

Good, T., & Grouws, D. (1979). The Missouri mathematics effectiveness project: An experimental study in fourth grade classrooms. *Journal of Educational Psychology, 71*, 355–362.

Good, T., Grouws, D.A., & Beckerman, T.M. (1978). Curriculum pacing: Some empirical data in mathematics. *Journal of Curriculum Studies, 10*, 75–81.

Good, T., & Marshall, S. (1984). Do students learn more in heterogeneous or homogeneous groups? In P.P. Peterson, L.C. Wilkinson, & M.T. Hallinan (Eds.), *The social context of instruction* (pp. 15–38). New York: Academic Press.

Goodlad, J.I. (1975). *The dynamics of educational change.* New York: McGraw-Hill.

Goodlad, J.I. (1984). *A place called school: Prospects for the future.* New York: McGraw Hill.

Goodlad, J.I., & Klein, M.F. (1970). *Behind the classroom door.* Worthington, OH: Charles A. Jones Co.

Goodlad, J.I., Klein, M.F., Tye, K.A. (1979). The domains of curriculum and their study. In J. I. Goodlad and Associates, *Curriculum inquiry: The study of practice.* New York: McGraw-Hill.

Gordon, W. (1957). *The social system of the high school.* Glencoe, IL: The Free Press.

Governor's Education Review Commission. (1984). *Priority for a quality basic education.* A second report to Governor Joe Frank Harris and the Georgia general assembly. Georgia: Author.

Grant, C.A., & Sleeter, C. (1986). Race, class, and gender in education research: An argument for integrative analysis. *Review of Educational Research, 56*(2), 195–211.

Green, B.F. (1981). A primer of testing. *American Psychologist, 36*(10), 1001–1011.

Greene, M. (1984). The impacts of irrelevance: Women in the history of American education. In E. Fennema & M.J. Ayer (Eds.), *Women in education.* Berkeley: McCutchan.

Griffin, G.A. (1979). Levels of curricular decision-making. In J. I. Goodlad and Associates, *Curriculum Inquiry.* New York: McGraw-Hill.

Guilford, D., & Hartman, H. (1981). *Indicators of equity in education.* Washington, DC: National Research Council of the National Academy of Sciences.

Gump, P.V. (1967). *The classroom behavior setting: Its nature and relation to student behavior* (Final Report). Washington, DC: U.S. Office of Education, Bureau of Research. (ERIC Document Reproduction Service No. ED 015 515).

Gurin, P., Gurin, G., Lao, R.C., & Beattie, M. (1969). Internal-external control in the motivational dynamics of Negro youth. *Journal of Social Issues, 25*, 29–53.

Guthrie, J.W., & Reed, R.J. (1985). *Educational administration and policy.* Englewood Cliffs, NJ: Prentice Hall, Inc.

Guthrie, L.F., & Leventhal, C. (1985, April). *Opportunities for scientific literacy for high school students.* Paper presented at the Annual Meeting of the American Educational Research Association, Chicago.

Haladyna, T., Olsen, R., & Shaughnessy, J. (1983). Correlates of class attitude toward science. *Journal of Research in Science Teaching, 20*(4), 311–324.

Haladyna, T., & Shaughnessy, H. (1982). Attitudes toward science: A quantitative synthesis. *Science Education, 66*(4), 547–563.

Haladyna, T., & Thomas, G. (1979). The attitudes of elementary school children toward school and subject matters. *Journal of Experimental Education, 48*(1), 18–23.

Hall, G., Jaeger, R.M., Kearney, C.P., & Wiley, D.E. (1985, December 20). *Alternative for a national data system on elementary and secondary education.* A report prepared for the Office of Educational Research and Improvement. Washington, DC: U.S. Department of Education.

Hallinan, M.T., & Sorenson A. (1983). The formation and stability of ability groups. *American Sociological Review, 48*(6), 838–851.

Hallinan, M.T., & Sorensen, A. (1985). *Effects of ability grouping on growth in academic achievement.* Unpublished manuscript.

Halpern, G. (1965). *Scale properties of the interest index.* Princeton, NJ: Educational Testing Service.

Hamblin, R.L., Hathaway, C., & Wodarski, J.S. (1971). Group contingencies, peer tutoring, and accelerating academic achievement. In E. Ramp and W. Hopkins (Eds.), *A new direction for education: Behavior analysis,* 41–53. Lawrence, KS: The University of Kansas, Department of Human Development.

Hamilton, S.F. (1981). The social side of schooling: Ecological studies of classrooms and schools. *The Elementary School Journal, 83*(4), 313–334.

Haney, W. (1984). Testing reasoning and reasoning about testing. *Review of Educational Research, 54*(4), 597–654.

Haney, W. (1985). Making testing more educational. *Educational Leadership, 43*(2), Oct., 4–15.

Hanson, S. (1986). *The college preparatory curriculum across schools: Access to similar types of knowledge?* Paper presented at the annual meeting of the American Educational Research Association, San Francisco.

Hanushek, E. (1970, February). *The production of education, teacher quality and efficacy.* Paper presented at the Bureau of Educational Personnel Conference, Washington, DC.

Hanushek, E. (1981). Throwing money at schools. *Journal of Policy Analysis and Management, 1*(1), 19–41.

Harms, N.C. (1982). Project synthesis: Summary and implications for teachers. In N.C. Harms & R. Yager (Eds.), *What research says to the science teacher,* Vol. III. Washington DC: National Science Teachers Association.

Harnischfeger, A., & Wiley, D.E. (1976). The teaching-learning process in elementary schools: A synoptic view. *Curriculum Inquiry, 6,* 5–43.

Harnischfeger, A., & Wiley, D.E. (1980). Determinants of pupil opportunity. In R. Dreeben & J.A. Thomas (Eds.), *Issues in microanalysis: Analysis of educational productivity*, Vol. 1. Cambridge, MA: Ballinger.

Hauser, P.M. (1975). *Social statistics in use.* New York: Russell Sage Foundation.

Hawley, W.D., Rosenholtz, S., Goodstein, H.J., & Hasselbring, T. (1985). Good schools: What research says about improving student achievement. *Peabody Journal of Education, 61*(4), 1–178.

Heckman, P.E., Oakes, J., & Sirotnik, K.A. (1983). Expanding the concepts of renewal and change. *Educational Leadership, 40*(7), 26–32.

Heller, J., & Reif, F. (1982). *Prescribing effective human problem-solving processes: Problem description in physics.* Berkeley, CA: University of California at Berkeley. (ERIC Document Reproduction Service No. ED 229 276).

Henry, N.B. (Ed.). (1947). *The forty-sixth yearbook of the National Society for the Study of Education. Part I: Science education in American schools.* Chicago: National Society for the Study of Education.

Henry, N.B. (Ed.). (1960). *The fifty-ninth yearbook of the National Society for the Study of Education. Part I: Rethinking science education.* Chicago: National Society for the Study of Education, 1960.

Hess, F. (1985). The socialization of the assistant principal: From the perspective of the local school district. *Education and Urban Society, 18*(1), 93–106.

Heyns, B. (1974). Selection and stratification in schools. *American Journal of Sociology, 79*(6), 1434–1451.

Heyns, B. (1978). *Summer learning and the effects of schooling.* New York: Academic Press.

Heyns, B., & Hilton, T.L. (1982). The cognitive tests for high school and beyond: An assessment. *Sociology of Education, 55*, 89–102.

Hilton, T.L., & Berglund, G.W. (1974). Sex differences in mathematics achievement: A longitudinal study. *Journal of Educational Research, 67*, 231–237.

Horn, E.A., & Walberg, H.J. (1984). Achievement and interest as functions of quantity and level of instruction. *Journal of Educational Research, 77*, 227–232.

Hort, S., Stiegelbauer, S.M., & Hall, G.E. (1984). How principals work with other change facilitators. *Education and Urban Society.*

Horwitz, R.A. (1979). Effects of the 'open classroom.' In H.J. Walberg (Ed.), *Educational environments and effects: Evaluation policy and productivity.* Berkeley, CA: McCutchan.

House of Representatives, Congressional Record—House. (1975, April 9). H.2585, as quoted in Schaffarzick, J., "Federal Curriculum Reform: A Crucible for Value Conflict," in J. Schaffarzick & G. Sykes (Eds.), (1979). *Value conflicts and curriculum issues: Lessons from research and experience.* Berkeley, CA: McCutchan Publishing.

Howe, T.G., & Gerlovich, J.A. (1982). *National study of the estimated supply and demand of secondary science and mathematics teachers.* Ames, IA: Iowa State University.

Howell, F.M., & Freese, W. (1982). Early transition into adult roles: Some anticedents and outcomes. *American Educational Research Journal, 19,* 51–73.

Hoy, W.K., Tarter, C.J., & Forsyth, P. (1978). Administrative behavior and subordinate loyalty: An empirical assessment. *Journal of Educational Administration, 16*(1), 29–38.

Huberman, A.M., & Miles, M. (1984). Rethinking the quest for school improvement: Some findings from the DESSI study. *Teachers College Record, 86,* 34–54.

Hudson, L. (1986). *Item-level analysis of sex differences in mathematics achievement test performance.* Unpublished doctoral dissertation. Ithaca, NY: Cornell University.

Hueftle, S.J., Rakow, S.J., & Welch. W.W. (1983, June). *Images of science: A summary of results from the 1981–82 National Assessment in Science.* Science Assessment and Research Project, University of Minnesota.

Hunter, M. (1983). *Mastery teaching.* El Segundo, CA: TIP Publications.

Hurd, P.D. (1986). Perspectives for the reform of science education. *Kappan, 67,* 353–358.

Husen, T. (Ed.) (1967). *International study of achievement in mathematics: A comparison of twelve countries.* (Vols. 1 & 2.) New York: John Wiley.

Inhelder, B., & Piaget, J. (1958). *The growth of logical thinking from childhood to adolescence.* New York: Basic Books.

International Association for the Evaluation of Educational Achievement (IEA) (1980). *Second international mathematics study: Classroom processes questionnaire.* University of Illinois, Champagne-Urbana, IEA, U.S. National Coordinating Center.

Jackson, P. (1968). *Life in classrooms.* New York: Holt, Rinehart, & Winston.

Jaeger, R.M. (1978). About educational indicators: Statistics on the conditions and trends in education. In L.S. Shulman (Ed.), *Review of research in education, 6,* 276–315.

Jencks, C., Smith, M., Acland, H., Bane, M.J., Cohen, D., Gintis, H., Heyns, B., & Michelson, S. (1972). *Inequality: A reassessment of the effects of family and schooling in America.* New York: Basic Books.

Johnson, M.L. (1984). Blacks in mathematics: A status report. *Journal for Research in Mathematics Education, 15,* 145–153.

Johnston, K.L., & Aldridge, B.G. (1984). The crisis in science education: What is it? How can we respond? *Journal of College Science Teaching, 14*(1), 20–28.

Jones, C., Clarke, M., McWilliams, H., Crawford, I., Stephenson, C.B., & Tourangeau, R. (1983) *High school and beyond 1980 sophomore cohort first follow-up (1982) data file users manual.* Report to the National Center for Education Statistics (contract OE-300-78-0208). Washington, DC: National Center for Education Statistics.

Jones, C., Rowen, M.R., & Taylor, H.E. (1977). An overview of the mathematics achievement tests offered in the admissions testing program of the college entrance examination board. *Mathematics Teacher, 70,* 197–208.

Jones, J.D., Vanfossen, B., & Spade, J. (1985). *Curriculum placement: Individual and school effects using the high school and beyond data.* Paper presented to the annual meeting of the American Sociological Association.

Jones, L.V. (1984). White-black achievement differences: The narrowing gap. *American Psychologist, 39*(11), 1207–1213.

Jones, L.V., Burton, N.W., & Davenport, E.C. (1984). Monitoring the achievement of black students. *Journal for Research in Mathematics Education, 15,* 154–164.

Jones, L.V., Davenport, E.C., Bryson, A., Bekhuis, T., & Zwick, R. (1986). Mathematics and science test scores as related to courses taken in high school and other factors. *Journal of Educational Measurement, 23*(3), 197–208.

Jung, R., & Kirst, M. (1986). Beyond mutual adaptation, into the bully pulpit: Recent research on the federal role in education. *Educational Administration Quarterly.*

Kaagan, S. (1980). Cooperation-competition, culture, and structural bias in classrooms. In S. Sharan et al. (Eds.), *Cooperation in education.* Provo, UT: Brigham Young University Press.

Kaagan, S., & Smith, M.S. (1985) Indicators of educational quality. *Educational Leadership, 43*(2), 21–24.

Kahle, J.B. (1982). *Can positive minority attitudes lead to achievement gains in science?* Analysis of the 1977 national assessment of educational progress, attitudes toward science. *Science Education, 66*(4), 539–546.

Kahle, J.B. (1983, April). *The disadvantaged minority: Science education for women and minorities.* Presentation at the National Science Teachers Association Convention, Dallas.

Karweit, N. (1976). Quantity of schooling: A major educational factor? *Educational Researcher, 5,* 1976, 15–17.

Karweit, N. (1983). *Time-on-task: A research review.* Baltimore, MD: Johns Hopkins University. Center for Social Organization of Schools. Report No. 332.

Kasarda, J. (1986, October 29). Testimony before a subcommittee of the Joint Congressional Economic Committee, as cited in *Education Week.*

Kingdon, J.W. (1984). *Agendas, alternatives, and public policies.* Boston: Little, Brown.

Kirkland, M.C. (1971). The effects of tests on students and schools. *Review of Educational Research, 41*(4), 303–350.

Kirst, M.W. (1984). *Who controls our schools?* New York: W. H. Freeman and Co.

Klein, M.F. (1980) *Teacher perceived sources of influence on what is taught in subject areas, a study of schooling* (Tech. Rep. No. 15). Los Angeles: University of California.

Klitgaard, R.E., & Hall, G.R. (1973). *A Statistical search for unusually effective schools.* Santa Monica, CA: The RAND Corporation.

Klitgaard, R.E., & Hall, G.R. (1974). Are there unusually effective schools? *Journal of Human Resources, 10*(3), 90–106.

Kolata, G.B. (1980). Math and sex: Are girls born with less ability? *Science, 210,* 1234–1235.

Kooker, E. (1976). Changes in grade distributions associated with changes in class attendance policies. *Psychology, 13,* 56–57.

Kounin, J.S. (1970). *Discipline and group management in classrooms.* New York: Holt, Rinehart & Winston.

Kuhs, T.M., Schmidt, W.H., Porter, A.C., Floden, R.E., Freeman, D.J., & Schwille, J.R. (1979). *A taxonomy for classifying elementary school mathematics content* (Research Series No. 4). East Lansing, MI: Michigan State University, Institute for Research on Teaching.

Kulik, C.L., & Kulik, J.A. (1982). The effects of ability of grouping on secondary school students: A meta-analysis of evaluation findings. *American Educational Research Journal, 19*(3), 415–428.

Ladd, H.F. (1975). Local education expenditures, fiscal capacity, and the composition of the property tax base. *National Tax Journal, 28*(2), 145–158.

Lamke, T.A., Nelson, M.J., & Kelso, P.C. (1960). *Henmon-Nelson tests of mental abilities: Revised edition.* New York: Houghton Mifflin.

Land, K.C. (1975a). Social indicator models: An overview. In K.C. Land & S. Spilerman (Eds.), *Social indicator models.* New York: Russell Sage Foundation.

Land, K.C. (1975b). Theories, models and indicators in social change. *International Social Science Journal, 27,* 7–37.

Land, K.C., & Felson, M. (1976). A general framework for building dynamic macro social indicator models: Including an analysis of changes in crime rates and police expenditures. *American Journal of Sociology, 82,* 565–604.

Langan, J. (1981). Notes on equity and equality. In Guilford, D. et al., *Indicators of equity in education.* Washington, DC: National Research Council of the National Academy of Sciences.

Lantz, A.E., & Smith, G.P. (1981). Factors influencing the choice of nonrequired mathematics courses. *Journal of Educational Psychology, 73*(6), 825–837.

Larabee, D.F. (1984). Setting the standard: Alternative policies for student promotion. *Harvard Educational Review, 54,* 67–87.

Larkin, J.H. (1981). Cognition of learning physics. *American Journal of Physics, 49*(6), 534–541.

Larkin, J.H., McDermott, J., Simon, D.P., & Simon, H.A. (1980a). Models of competence in solving physics problems. *Cognitive Science, 4,* 317–345.

Larkin, J., McDermott, J., Simon, D.P., & Simon, H.A. (1980b). Expert and novice performance involving physics problems. *Science, 80*(20), 1335–1342.

Lee, V.E. (1986). *The effect of curriculum tracking on the social distribution of achievement in Catholic and public secondary schools.* Paper presented at the annual meeting of the American Educational Research Association, San Francisco.

Leinhardt, G., & Greeno, J. (1986). The cognitive skill of teaching. *Journal of Educational Psychology, 78*(2), 75–95.

Leinhardt, G., & Seewald, A.M. (1981). Overlap: what's tested, what's taught? *Journal of Educational Measurement, 18,* 85–96.

Lenny, E. (1977). Women's self confidence in achievement settings. *Psychological Bulletin, 84,* 1–13.

Lester, F.K. (1980). Research on mathematical problem solving. In R.J. Shumway (Ed.), *Research in mathematics education,* (pp. 286–323). Reston, VA: National Council of Teachers of Mathematics.

Levin, H.M. (1972). *The cost to the nation of inadequate education.* Report to the Select Committee on Equal Educational Opportunity of the United States Senate. Washington, DC: U.S. Government Printing Office.

Levin, H.M. (1980). Educational production theory and teacher inputs. In C.E. Bidwell & D.M. Windham (Eds.), *The analysis of educational productivity. Volume II: Issues in macroanalysis.* Cambridge, MA: Ballinger.

Levin, H.M. (1983). *About time for educational reform.* Stanford, CA: Institute for Research on Educational Finance and Governance.

Levin, H.M. (1986). *Educational reform for disadvantaged students: An emerging crisis.* Washington, DC: National Education Association.

Levine, A.G., McGuire, C.H., & Nattress, L.W. (1970). The validity of multiple-choice tests as measures of competence in medicine. *American Educational Research Journal, 7,* 69–82.

Levine, D.M. (1975). 'Inequality' and the analysis of educational policy. In D.M. Levine & M.J. Rane (Eds.), *The 'inequality' controversy: Schooling and distributive justice.* New York: Basic Books.

Levy, G.E. (1970). *Ghetto school.* New York: Pegasus Press.

Lieberman, A., & Miller, L. (1984). *Teachers, their world, and their work: Implications for school improvement.* Alexandria, VA: Association for Supervision and Curriculum Development.

Lightfoot, S.L. (1983). *The good high school: Portraits of character and culture.* New York: Basic Books.

Lindblom, C.E., & Cohen, D.K. (1979). *Usable knowledge.* New Haven, CT: Yale University Press.

Litt, M.S., & Turk, D.C. (1983, April). *Stress, dissatisfaction, and intention to leave teaching in experienced public high school teachers.* Paper presented at the annual meeting of the American Educational Research Association, Montreal.

Little, J.W. (1982). Norms of collegiality and experimentation: Workplace conditions of school success. *American Educational Research Journal, 19*(3), 325–340.

Locke, E.A. (1976). The nature and causes of job satisfaction. In M. Dunnett (Ed.) *Handbook of industrial and organizational psychology.* NY: Rand-McNally.

Lockheed, M.E. (1984). Sex segregation and male preeminence in elementary classrooms. In E. Fennema & M.J. Ayer (Eds.), *Women in education.* Berkeley, CA: McCutchan, 1984.

Lockheed, M.E. (1985). *Understanding sex/ethnic related differences in mathematics, science, and computer science for students in grades four to eight.* Princeton, NJ: Educational Testing Service.

Lortie, D.C. (1975). *Schoolteacher: A sociological study.* Chicago: University of Chicago Press.

Los Angeles Unified School District. (1985). *A study of student dropout in the Los Angeles unified school district.* Report to the Superintendent and Board of Education.

Lynn, L.E., Jr. (Ed.). (1978). *Knowledge and policy: The uncertain connection.* Washington, DC: National Academy of Sciences.

Maccoby, E.E., & Jacklin, C.N. (1974). *The psychology of sex differences.* Stanford, CA: Stanford University Press.

Macdonald, J.B., & Zaret, E. (Eds.), (1975). *Schools in search of meaning.* Yearbook of the Association for Supervision and Curriculum Development (ASCD). Alexandria, VA.

Mackenzie, D.E. (1983). Research for school improvement: An appraisal and some trends. *Educational Researcher, 12*(3), 5–17.

MacRae, D., Jr. (1985). *Policy indicators.* Chapel Hill, NC: University of North Carolina Press.

MacRae, Duncan, Jr., & Lanier, Mark W. (1985). The use of student improvement scores in state and district incentive systems. In D. MacRae & R. Haskins (Eds.), *Policies for America's public schools: Teachers, equity & indicators* (pp. 213–239). Norwood, NJ: Ablex.

Madaus, G.F., Kellaghan, T., Rakow, E.A., & King, D.J. (1979). The sensitivity of measures of school effectiveness. *Harvard Educational Review, 49*(2), 207–230.

Madden, N.A., & Slavin, R.E. (1983). Mainstreaming students with mild academic handicaps: Academic and social outcomes. *Review of Educational Research, 53*(4), 519–570.

Madden, N.A., & Slavin, R.E. (1987). Effective classroom programs for students at risk, *Center for research on elementary and middle schools*, The John Hopkins University.

Mahoney, M.J. (1979). Psychology of the scientist: An evaluative review. *Social Studies of Science, 9*, 349–357.

Malcom, S. (1986, October). *Equality and excellence in mathematics education: The continuing challenge.* Paper prepared for the National Forum of the College Board.

Malcom, S.M., George, Y.S., & Matyas, M.L. (1985). *Summary of research studies on women and minorities in science, mathematics and technology.* Washington, DC: American Association for the Advancement of Science.

Mann, D., & Fenwick, S. (1985). *The impact of impact II: 1982–1983.* Report to the Exxon Education Foundation. New York: Columbia University, Teachers College.

Maslow, A.H. (1968). Some educational implications of the humanistic psychologies. *Harvard Educational Review, 38*, 685–696.

Matthews, W. (1984). Influences on the learning and participation of minorities in mathematics. *Journal of Research in Mathematics Education, 15*, 84–95.

Mayeske, G., Wisler, C.E., Beaton, Jr., A.E., Weinfeld, F.C., Cohen, W. M., Okada, T., Proshek, J.M., & Tabler, K.A. (1972). *A study of our nation's schools*, Washington, D.C: U.S. Office of Education.

McDill, E., Natriello, G., & Pallas, A. (1985, April). *Raising standards and retaining students: The impact of the reform recommendations on potential dropouts* (Report No. 358). Baltimore: Johns Hopkins University, Center on Social Organization of Schools.

McArthur, D. (1985). Developing computer tools to support performing and learning complex cognitive skills. In K. Pedzek, D. Berger, & B. Banks (Eds.), *Applications of cognitive psychology: Computing and Education*. Hillsdale, NJ: Lawrence Erlbaum.

McBay, S.M. (1986). *Review of issues and options related to increasing the number and quality of minority science and mathematics teachers*. Paper prepared for the Carnegie Forum on Education and the Economy.

McBride, J.R. (1985). Computerized adaptive testing. *Educational Leadership, 43*(2), 25–28.

McCorquodale, P. (1983). *Social influences on the participation of Mexican-American women in science*. Tucson, AZ: University of Arizona Department of Sociology.

McDill, E.A., & Rigsby, L.C. (1973). *The structure and process in secondary schools: The academic impact of educational climates*. Baltimore: Johns Hopkins University Press.

McDill, E.L., Natriello, G., & Pallas, A.M. (1986). A population at risk: Potential consequences of tougher schools standards for student dropouts. *American Journal of Education, 94*(2), 135–181.

McDonald, F.J., & Elias, P. (1976). *Beginning teacher evaluation study, Phase II*. Executive summary report. Princeton, NJ: Educational Testing Service.

McDonnell, L.M., & McLaughlin, M.W. (1980). *Program consolidation and the state role in ESEA Title IV*. Santa Monica, CA: The RAND Corporation.

McGuire, C.H., & Babbott, D. (1967). Simulation technique in the measurement of problem-solving skills. *Journal of Educational Measurement, 4*(1), 1–10.

McKeachie, W.J., & Kulik, J.A. (1975). Effective college teaching. In F.N. Kerlinger (Ed.). *Review of research in education* (Vol. 3). Itasca, IL: F. E. Peacock.

McKnight, C.C., Crosswhite, F.J., Dossey, J.A., Kifer, E., Swafford, S.O., Travers, K.J., & Cooney, T.J. (1987). *The underachieving curriculum: Assessing U.S. school mathematics from an international perspective*. Champaign, IL: Stipes Publishing.

McLaughlin, M.W., & Marsh, D.D. (1978). Staff development and school change. *Teachers College Record, 80*(1), 69–94.

McLean, L. (1985). *Drawing implications for instruction from item, topic, and classroom-scores in large-scale science assessment.* Paper prepared for the Annual Meeting of the American Educational Research Association, Chicago.

McPartland J.M., & Becker, H.J. (1985, September). *A model for NCES research on school organization and classroom practices.* Johns Hopkins University, Center for Social Organization of Schools.

Meara, H., Fallis, M., & Hallett, A.C. (1983). *Class coverage in the Chicago public schools: A study of teacher absences and substitute coverage.* Chicago: Chicago Panel on Public School Finances.

Medley, D.M. (1979). The effectiveness of teachers. In P.L. Peterson & H.J. Walberg (Eds.), *Research on teaching.* Berkeley, CA: McCutchan Publishing Corp.

Messick, S., Beaton, A., & Lord, F. (1983). *National assessment of educational progress reconsidered: A new design for a new era.* (NAEP Report 83-1). Princeton, NJ: National Assessment of Educational Progress.

Michelson, S. (1970). The association of teacher resources with children's characteristics. In A. Mood (Ed.), *Do teachers make a difference?* Washington, DC: U.S. Department of Health, Education, and Welfare, Office of Education.

Miller, J. (1983). Scientific literacy: A conceptual and empirical review. *Daedalus, 112,*(2), 29–48.

Mitroff, I.I., & Mason, R.O. (1974). On evaluating the scientific contribution of the appollo moon missions via information theory: A study of the scientist-scientist relationship. *Management Science: Applications, 20,* 1501–1513.

Moore, B.E., & Moore A.J. (1975, March). *Possible influences on student attitudes toward involvement with science: Curricular, demographic, and personal factors.* Paper presented at the Annual Meeting of the National Association for Research in Science Teaching, Los Angeles. (ERIC No. Ed. 104 665).

Moos, R.H. (1979). *Evaluating educational environments.* San Francisco: Josey-Bass.

Moos, R.H., & Moos, B.S. (1978). Classroom social climate and student absences and grades. *Journal of Educational Psychology, 70,* 263–269.

Morgan, R. (1975). An exploratory study of three procedures to encourage school attendance. *Psychology in the Schools, 12,* 209–215.

Munby, H. (1983a). *An investigation into the measurement of attitudes in science education.* Columbus, OH: Ohio State University, SMEAC Information Reference Center. (ED 237 347)

Munby, H. (1983b). A common curriculum for the natural sciences. In G.D. Fenstermacher & J.I. Goodlad (Eds.), *Individual differences and the common curriculum.* Eighty-second yearbook of the National Society for the Study of Education. Chicago: University of Chicago Press.

Munday, L.A., & Davis, J.C. (1974). *Varieties of accomplishment after college: Perspectives on the meaning of academic talent.* (ACT Research Report No. 62.) Iowa City, IA: American College Testing Service.

Murnane, R.J. (1982). Interpreting the evidence on school effectiveness. *Teachers College Record, 83*(1), 19–35.

Murnane, R.J. (1985, June). *Do effective teachers have common characteristics: Interpreting the quantitative research evidence.* Paper presented at the National Research Council Conference on Teacher Quality in Science and Mathematics, Washington, DC.

Murnane, R.J. (1987). Improving education indicators and economic indicators: The same problems? *Educational Evaluation and Policy Analysis, 9*(2), 101–116.

Murnane, R.J., & Phillips, B.R. (1981). Learning by doing, vintage, and selection: Three pieces of the puzzle relating teaching experience and teaching performance. *Economics of Education Review, 1*(4), 453–465.

Murnane, R.J., & Raizen, S.A. (1988). *Improving indicators of the quality of science and mathematics education in grades K–12.* Washington, DC: National Academy Press.

National Advisory Committee on Mathematics Education (1975). *Overview and analysis of school mathematics: grades K–12.* Washington, DC: Conference Board on the Mathematical Sciences.

National Alliance of Black School Educators. (1984). *Saving the African-American child.* Washington, DC: National Alliance of Black School Educators.

National Assessment of Educational Progress (1981–82). *Demonstration package. Exercises illustrative of 1981–82 assessment of mathematics.* (13-DP-22) Princeton, NJ: NAEP.

National Assessment of Educational Progress User's Bulletin. (undated). *Plans for the 1985–86 assessment.*

National Assessment of Educational Progress. (1975). *Selected results for the National Assessment of Science: Scientific procedures and principles* (Science Report No. 04-S-02). Denver, CO: Education Commission of the States.

National Assessment of Educational Progress. (1976–77). *Demonstration package illustrating the kinds of exercises which were used in the 1976–77 assessment of science and in a pilot assessment of basic skills.* (08-DP-22). Princeton, NJ: NAEP.

National Assessment of Educational Progress. (1977–1978). *Mathematics objectives, second assessment.* Denver, CO: Education Commission of the States.

National Assessment of Educational Progress. (1980). *Mathematics technical report: Summary volume.* Denver, CO: Education Commission of the States.

National Assessment of Educational Progress. (1983). *Third national mathematics assessment: Results, trends, and issues.* Denver, CO: Education Commission of the States.

National Assessment of Educational Progress. (undated). NAEP field-test teacher questionnaire. Princeton, NJ: National Assessment of Educational Progress.

National Association of Biology Teachers. (1983). *New directions in biology teaching: Perspectives for the 1980s.* In F.M. Hickman & J.B. Kahle (Eds.). Reston, VA: National Association of Biology Teachers.

National Center for Education Statistics. (1982). *The condition of education, 1982 edition.* Washington, DC: U.S. Department of Education.

National Center for Education Statistics. (1983). *The condition of education, 1983 edition.* Washington, DC: U.S. Department of Education.

National Center for Education Statistics. (1984). *The condition of education.* Washington D.C.: United States Department of Education

National Center for Education Statistics. (1985a). *Academic requirements and achievement in high school* (FRSS Report No. 15). Washington, DC: U.S. Department of Education.

National Center for Education Statistics (1985b). *An analysis of course offerings and enrollments as related to school characteristics.* Washington, DC: U.S. Department of Education.

National Center for Education Statistics. (1985c). *High school and beyond: An analysis of course-taking patterns in secondary schools as related to student characteristics.* Washington, DC: U.S. Department of Education.

National Center for Education Statistics. (1985d). *The condition of education, 1985 edition.* Washington, DC: U.S. Department of Education.

National Commission on Excellence in Education. (1983). *A nation at risk: The imperative for educational reform.* Washington, DC: U.S. Government Printing Office.

National Council of Teachers of Mathematics. (1980). *An agenda for action: Recommendations for school mathematics of the 1980s.* Reston, VA: Author.

National Council of Teachers of Mathematics. (1981). *An agenda for action and priorities in school mathematics.* National Council of Teachers of Mathematics. Reston, VA: Author.

National Education Association (1981). *Status of the American public school teacher.* Washington, DC: Author.

National Research Council. (1985). *Mathematics, science, and technology education: A research agenda.* Washington, DC: National Academy Press.

National Science Board Commission on Precollege Education in Mathematics, Science and Technology. (1983). *Educating Americans for the 21st century: Source materials.* Washington, DC: National Science Foundation.

National Science Board. (1985). *Science indicators: The 1985 report.* Washington, DC: The National Science Foundation.

National Science Foundation (1975). *Pre-college science curriculum activities of the National Science Foundation.* Washington, DC: Author.

National Science Foundation (1976, January). *The National Science Foundation and pre-college science education; 1950–1975.* Report prepared for the Subcommittee on Science, Research, and Technology of the Committee on Science and Technology, U.S. House of Representatives, 94th Congress, 2nd Session.

National Science Foundation (1980). *What are the needs in precollege science, mathematics, and social science education? Views from the field.* Washington, DC: Author.

National Science Foundation (1986). *Women and minorities in science and engineering* (NSF 86-301). Washington, DC: National Science Foundation.

National Science Teachers Association. (1971). School science for the 70's. *The Science Teacher, 38*(8), 46–51.

National Science Teachers Association. (1982). *Science-technology-society: Science education for the 1980s.* Position statement. Washington, DC: Author.

Nay, M.A., & Crocker, R.K. (1970). Science teaching and the affective attributes of scientists. *Science Education, 54*(1), 59–67.

Neale, D.C., Gill, N., & Tismer, W. (1970). Relationship between attitudes toward school subjects and school achievement. *Journal of Educational Research, 63*(5), 232–237.

Newfield, J.W., & Wisenbaker, J.M. (1985). *Student selection of a challenging high school program of studies.* Paper presented at the Annual Meeting of the American Educational Research Association, Chicago.

Noddings, N. (1979). NIE's national curriculum development conference. In J. Schaffarzick & G. Sykes (Eds.), *Value conflicts and curriculum issues: Lessons from research and experience.* Berkeley, CA: McCutchan Publishing.

Noland, T.K. (1986). *The effects of ability grouping: A meta-analysis of research findings.* Unpublished doctoral dissertation. University of Colorado, Boulder.

Noll, V.H. (1933). The habit of scientific thinking. *Teachers College Record, 35,* 1–9.

Oakes, J. (1981). *Tracking policies and practices: School-by-school summaries, a study of schooling* (Tech. Rep. No. 25). Los Angeles: University of California, Graduate School of Education.

Oakes, J. (1985). *Keeping track: How schools structure inequality.* New Haven, CT: Yale University Press.

Odden, A. (1984). Financing educational excellence. *Phi Delta Kappan, 65,* 311–318.

OERI State Accountability Study Group, (1988). *Creating responsible and responsive accountability systems,* Washington, DC: U.S. Government Printing Office.

Office of Management and Budget. (1974). *Social indicators.* Washington, DC: Government Printing Office.

Osborne, R.J. (1981). Children's ideas about electric current. *Science Teacher, 29,* 12–19.

Osborne, R.J., & Wittrock, M.C. (1983). Learning science: A generative process. *Science Education, 67*(4), 489–508.

Page, F.M., Jr., & Page, J.A. (1982). Perceptions of teaching that may be influencing current shortage of teachers. *College Student Journal, 16,* 308–311.

Page, R. (1987). Lower-track classes at a college-preparatory high school: Caricatures of educational encounters. In G. Spindler (Ed.), *Interpretive ethnography of education at home and abroad.* Hillsdale, NJ: Lawrence Erlbaum Associates.

Pallas, A.M. (1984). The determinants of high school dropout. Unpublished Ph.D. dissertation. Baltimore, MD: The Johns Hopkins University.

Pallas, A.M., & Alexander, K.L. (1983) Sex differences in quantitative SAT performance: New evidence on the differential coursework hypothesis. *American Educational Research Journal, 20,* 165–182.

Parsons, J.E., Kaczala, C.M., & Meece, J.L. (1982). Socialization of achievement attitudes and beliefs: Classroom influences. *Child Development, 53,* 322–339.

Partlett, M., & Hamilton, D. (1976). Evaluation as illumination. In G.V. Glass (Ed.), *Evaluation studies review annual.* Beverly Hills, CA: Sage.

Patton, M.Q. (1978). *Utilization-focused evaluation.* Beverly Hills, CA: Sage.

Pederson, K.G. (1970). Teacher migration and attrition. *Administrator's Notebook, 18*(8), 1–13.

Peng, S.S., Owings, J.A., & Fetters, W.B. (1982). *Effective high schools: What are their attributes?* Paper presented at the Annual Meeting of the American Statistical Association, Cincinnati, OH.

Peng, S.S., Takai, R.T., & Fetters, W.B. (1983). High school dropouts: Preliminary results from the high school and beyond survey. Paper presented at the 1983 annual meeting of the American Educational Research Association.

Penrick, J.E., & Yager, R.E. (1983). The search for excellence in science education. *Phi Delta Kappan, 64*(8), 621–623.

Persell, C.H. (1977). *Education and inequality: The roots and results of stratification in America's schools.* New York: The Free Press.

Peterson, P.L. (1976). *Interactive effects of student anxiety, achievement orientation, and teacher behavior on student achievement and attitude.* Unpublished doctoral dissertation. Stanford, CA: Stanford University.

Peterson, P.L. (1979). Direct instruction reconsidered. In P.L. Peterson & H.J. Walberg (Eds.), *Research on teaching.* Berkeley, CA: McCutchan.

Peterson, P.L., & Fennema, E. (1985). Effective teaching, student engagement in classroom activities, and sex-related differences in learning mathematics. *American Educational Research Journal, 22,* 309–335.

Peterson, P.L., & Walberg, H.L. (Eds.). (1979). *Research on teaching.* Berkeley, CA: McCutchan.

Peterson, P.L., Swing, S.R., Braverman, M.T., & Buss, R. (1982). Students' aptitudes and their reports of cognitive processes durng direct instruction. *Journal of Educational Psychology, 74,* 535–547.

Peterson, P.L., Swing, S.R., Stark, K.D., & Waas, G.A. (1984). Students' cognitions and time on task during mathematics instruction. *American Educational Research Journal, 21*(3), 487–515.

Peterson, R.W., & Carlson, G.R. (1979). A summary of research in science education—1977. *Science Education, 63,* 497–500.

Piaget, J., & Inhelder, B. (1969). *The psychology of the child.* New York: Basic Books.

Polya, G. (1957). *How to solve it.* (2nd ed.) New York: Doubleday.

Polya, G. (1962). *Mathematical discovery: On understanding, learning and teaching problem solving.* (Vol. 1.) New York: Wiley.

Polya, G. (1965). *Mathematical discovery: On understanding, learning and teaching problem solving.* (Vol. 2.) New York: Wiley.

Porter, A.C., Schmidt, W.J., Floden, R.E., & Freeman, D.J. (1978). Practical significance in program evaluation. *American Educational Research Journal, 15,* 529–539.

Powell, A.G., Farrar, E., & Cohen, D.C. (1985). *The shopping mall high school.* Boston: Houghton Mifflin.

Powell, J., & Steelman, L.C. (1984). SAT Performance of the states. *Harvard Education Review, 54*(4), 389–412.

Prakash, M.S., & Waks, L.J. (1985). Four conceptions of excellence. *Teachers College Record, 87,* 79–101.

Purkey, S.C., & Smith, M.S. (1983). Effective schools: A review. *Elementary School Journal, 83*(4), 427–452.

Quellmalz, E.S. (1985, October). Needed: Better methods for testing higher-order thinking skills. *Educational Leadership, 43*(2), 29–36.

Quirk, T.J., Witten, B.J., & Weinberg, S.F. (1973). Review of studies of the concurrent and predictive validity of the National Teacher Examinations. *Review of Educational Research, 43,* 89–114.

Raizen, S.A., & Jones, L.V. (Eds.). (1985). *Indicators of precollege education in science and mathematics: A preliminary review.* Washington, DC: National Academy Press.

Ramirez, M., & Casteneda, A. (1974). *Cultural democracy, biocognitive development, and education.* New York: Academic Press.

Ranbom, S. (1985, May 22). E.T.S. readying computer-based 'test of the future'. *Education Week,* p. 9.

Raschke, D.B., Dedrick, C.V., Strathe, M.I., & Hawkes, R.R. (1985). Teacher stress: The elementary teacher's perspective. *Elementary School Journal, 85,* 559–564.

Rehberg, R.A., & Rosenthal, E.R. (1978). *Class and merit in the American high school.* New York: Longman.

Resnick, D.P., & Resnick, L.B. (1985, April). Standards, curriculum and performance: A historical and comparative perspective. *Educational Researcher, 14,* 5–20.

Resnick, L.B. (1976). Task analysis in instructional design: Some cases from mathematics. In D. Klahr (Ed.), *Cognition and instruction.* New York: Lawrence Erlbaum.

Rivlin, A.M. (1973). Measuring performance in education. In M. Moss (Ed.), *Studies in income and wealth* (pp. 411–437). New York: Columbia University Press.

Roberson, S.D., Keith, T.Z., & Page, E.B. (1983). Now who aspires to teach? *Educational Researcher, 12*(6), 13–21.

Rock, D., Braun, H.I., & Rosenbaum, P.R. (1984). *Excellence in high school education: Cross-sectional study, 1972–1980. Final report.* Princeton, NJ: Educational Testing Service.

Rock, D., Braun, H.I., & Rosenbaum, P.R. (1985). *Excellence in high school education: Longitudinal study, 1980–1982. Final report.* Princeton, NJ: Educational Testing Service.

Rock, D., Hilton, T.L., Pollack, J., Ekstrom, R.B., & Goertz, M.E., (1985, January). *A study of excellence in high school education: Educational policies, school quality, and student outcomes: Psychometric analysis.* Report submitted to the U.S. Department of Education, National Center for Education Statistics. Princeton, NJ: Educational Testing Service.

Roe, A. (1961). The psychology of scientists. *Science, 134,* 456–459.

Rogers, C.R. (1962). Toward becoming a fully functioning person. In *Perceiving, behaving, becoming: A new focus for education,* Yearbook of the Association for Supervision and Curriculum Development (ASCD), Alexandria, VA.

Romberg, T.A., & Stewart, D.M. (1987). *The monitoring of school mathematics: Background papers. Volume I: The monitoring project and mathematics curriculum.* University of Wisconsin-Madison, School of Education, Wisconsin Center for Education. Program Report 87–1.

Romberg, T.A. (1983). A common curriculum for mathematics. In G.D. Fenstermacher & J.I. Goodlad (Eds.), *Individual differences and the common curriculum, eighty-second yearbook of the National Society for the Study of Education.* Chicago: University of Chicago Press.

Romberg, T.A. (1984). *School mathematics—options for the 1990s. Volume 1: Chairman's report of a conference.* U.S. Government Printing Office, Washington, DC.

Rosenbaum, J.E. (1976). *Making inequality: The hidden curriculum of high school tracking.* New York: Wiley.

Rosenbaum, J.E. (1980). Social implications of educational grouping. In D.C. Berliner (Ed.), *Review of Research in Education, 8,* 361–401.

Rosenholtz, S.J. (n.d.). *The organizational context of teaching.*

Rosenholtz, S.J. (1985). Effective schools: Interpreting the evidence. *American Journal of Education, 93,* 352–388.

Rosenholtz, S.J., & Simpson, C. (1984). The formation of ability conceptions: Developmental trend or social construction. *Review of Educational Research, 54,* 31–63.

Rosenholtz, S.J., & Smylie, M.A. (1983, December). *Teacher compensation and career ladders: Policy implications from research.* Paper commissioned by the Tennessee General Assembly's Select Committee on Education.

Rosenholtz, S.J., Bassler, D., & Hoover-Dempsey, K. (1985). *Organizational inducements for teaching.* Interim report submitted to the University of Illinois, National Institute of Education.

Rosenthal, R., & Jacobson, L. (1968). *Pygmalion in the classroom.* New York: Holt, Rinehart, and Winston.

Roth, K.J., Smith, E.L., & Anderson, C.W. (1983). *Students' conceptions of photosynthesis and food for plants.* Paper presented at the annual meeting of the American Educational Research Association, Montreal.

Rotter, J.B. (1975). Some problems and misconceptions related to the construct of internal versus external control of reinforcement. *Journal of Consulting and Clinical Psychology, 43,* 56–67.

Rowan, B., Bossert, S.T., & Dwyer, D.C. (1984). Research on effective schools: A cautionary note. *Educational Researcher, 12*(4), 24–31.

Rowe, M.B. (1983, Spring). Science education: A framework for decision-makers. *Daedalus, 112*(2), 123–142.

Rumberger, R. (1983). Dropping out of high school: The influence of race, sex, and family background. *American Educational Research Journal, 20,* 199–220.

Rumberger, R. (1985). The shortage of mathematics and science teachers: A review of the evidence. *Educational Evaluation and Policy Analysis, 7*(4), 355–369.

Rumberger, R.W. (1986). *School dropouts: A problem for research, policy and practice.* Report No. 86-SEPI-16. Stanford, CA: Stanford Education Policy Institute.

Rutter, M. (1983). Effective schools. In L. Shulman & G. Skyes (Eds.), *Handbook of teaching and policy.* NY: Longman.

Rutter, M., Maughan, P.M., & Ouston, J. (1979). *Fifteen thousand hours: Secondary schools and their effects on children.* Cambridge, MA: Harvard University Press.

Ryan, W. (1972). *Blaming the victim.* New York: Vintage Books.

Sarason, S. (1971) *The culture of the school and the problem of change.* Revised 1982. Boston: Allyn and Bacon.

Schaffarzick, J., & Sykes, G. (1979). Preface. In J. Schaffarzick & G. Sykes (Eds.), *Value conflicts and curriculum issues: Lessons from research and experience.* Berkeley, CA: McCutchan Publishing.

Schalock, D. (1979). Research on teacher selection. In D.C. Berliner (Ed.), *Review of research in education* (Vol. 7). Washington, DC: American Educational Research Association.

Scheyer, P., & Stake, R.E. (1977). A program's self-evaluation portfolio. As cited in D. Hamilton, *Making sense of curriculum evaluation: Continuities and discontinuities in an educational idea.* In L.S. Shulman (Ed.), *Review of research in education* (Vol. 5). American Educational Research Association.

Schlechty, P.C., & Vance, V.S. (1983). Institutional responses to the quality/quantity issues in teacher training. *Phi Delta Kappan, 65,* 94–101.

Schmidt, W.H. (1983) High-school course taking: A study in variation. *Journal of Curriculum Studies, 15*(2), 167–182.

Schoenfeld, A.H. (1979). Explicit heuristic training as a variable in problem-solving performance. *Journal for Research in Mathematics Education, 10,* 174–187.

Schoenfeld, A.H. (1982). Measures of problem-solving performance and of problem-solving instruction. *Journal for Research in Mathematics Education, 13*(1), 31–49.

Schoenfeld, A.H. (1983). The wild, wild, wild, wild, wild world of problem solving. *For the Learning of Mathematics, 13*(3), 40–47.

Schofield, H.L. (1982). Sex, grade level, and the relationship between mathematics attitude and achievement in children. *Journal of Educational Research, 75,* 280–284.

Schunk, D.H. (1981). Modeling and attributional effects on children's achievement: A self-efficacy analysis. *Journal of Educational Psychology, 73*(1), 93–105.

Schunk, D.H. (1982). Effects of effort attribution feedback on children's perceived self-efficacy and achievement. *Journal of Educational Psychology, 74*(4), 548–556.

Schunk, D.H. (1983). Ability versus effort attributional feedback: Differential effects on self-efficacy and achievement. *Journal of Educational Psychology, 75*(6), 848–856.

Schwab, J.J. (1974). The concept of the structure of a discipline. In E. W. Eisner & E. Vallance (Eds.), *Conflicting conceptualizations of curriculum.* Berkeley, CA: McCutchan Publishing,

Schwille, J., Porter, A., Belli, A., Floden, R., Freeman, D., Knappen, L., Kuhs, T., & Schmidt, W.J. (1981). *Teachers as policy brokers in the content of elementary school mathematics.* East Lansing, MI: Michigan State University, Institute for Research on Teaching.

Scientific Manpower Commission (1983). *Professional women and minorities.* Washington DC: Professional Manpower Commission.

Scriven, M. (1967). The methodology of evaluation. In *AERA monograph series on curriculum evaluation.* Chicago: Rand-McNally.

Scriven, M. (1974). Evaluation perspectives and procedures. In W.J. Popham (Ed.), *Evaluation in education.* Berkeley, CA: McCutchan.

Sells, L. (1982). Leverage for equal opportunity through mastery of mathematics in S.M. Humphreys (Ed.), *Women and minorities in science: Strategies for increasing participation.* Washington, DC: American Association for the Advancement of Science.

Sewell, W.H., Hauser, R.M., & Featherman, D.L. (1976). *Schooling and achievement in American society.* New York: Academic Press.

Shane, H.G., & Tabler, M.B. (1981). *Educating for a new millenium.* Bloomington, IN: Phi Delta Kappa Educational Foundation.

Shavelson, R.J. (1981). Teaching mathematics: Contributions of cognitive research. *Educational Psychologist, 16*(1), 23–44.

Shavelson, R. (1983). Review of research on teachers' pedagogical judgments, plans, and decisions. *Elementary School Journal, 83,* 392–414.

Shavelson, R.J. (1985). *The Dodds class of 1982: Characteristics of students remaining in the same high school, 1980–1982.* Santa Monica, CA: The RAND Corporation.

Shavelson, R., & Dempsey-Atwood, N. (1976). Generalizability of measures of teaching behavior. *Review of Educational Research, 46,* 553–611.

Shavelson, R., McDonnell, L., Oakes, J., & Carey, N. (1987). *Indicator systems for monitoring mathematics and science education.* Santa Monica, CA: The RAND Corporation.

Shavelson, R.J., Oakes, J., & Carey, N. (1987). A conceptual indicator model of changes in school mathematics. In T.A. Romberg & D.M. Stewart (Eds.), *The monitoring of school mathematics: Background papers.* Madison, WI: Wisconsin Center for Education Research.

Shavelson, R.J., & Salomon, G. (1986). A reply. *Educational Researcher, 15*(2), 24–25.

Shavelson, R., Webb, N., & Burstein, L. (1986). Measurement of teaching. In M. Wittrock (Ed.), *Handbook of research on teaching* (3rd ed.). New York: Macmillan.

Shea, B. (1976). Schooling and its antecedents: Substantive and methodological issues in the status attainment process. *Review of Educational Research, 46*(4), 463–526.

Sheldon, E.B. (1975). The social indicators movement. In D.R. Krathwohl (Ed.), *Educational indicators: Monitoring the state of education.* Princeton: Educational Testing Service.

Sheldon, E.B., & Freeman, H.E. (1971). Notes on social indicators: Promises and potentials. *Policy Sciences, 1,* 97–111.

Sheldon, E.B., & Moore, W.E. (1968). *Indicators of social change.* New York: Russell Sage Foundation.

Sheldon, E.B., & Parke, R. (1975). Social indicators. *Science, 188,* 693–699.

Sherman, J.A. (1980). Mathematics, spatial visualization, and related factors: Changes in girls and boys, grades 8–11. *Journal of Educational Psychology, 72,* 476–482.

Sherman, J.A., & Fennema, E. (1977). The study of mathematics by high school girls and boys: Related variables. *American Educational Research Journal, 14*, 159–168.

Sherman, L.W., & Thomas, M. (1986). Mathematics achievement in cooperative versus individualistic goal-structured high school classrooms. *Journal of Educational Research, 79*(3), 169–172.

Shonfield, A., & Shaw, S. (Eds.). (1972). *Social indicators and social policy.* London: Heinemann Educational Books.

Shug, M.C. (1983). Teacher burnout and professionalism. *Issues in Education, 1*(2, 3), 133–153.

Shulman, L.J. (1985). Paradigms and research programs in the study of teaching: A contemporary perspective. In M.C. Wittrock (Ed.), *Handbook of research on teaching* (3rd ed., pp. 3–36). New York: Macmillan.

Shulman, L.S., & Elstein, A.S. (1975). Studies of problem solving, judgment, and decision making: Implications for educational research. In F.N. Kerlinge (Ed.), *Review of Research in Education, 3*, 3–42. Itasca, IL: Peacock.

Shymansky, J.A., Kyle, W.C., Jr., & Alport, J.M. (1983). The effects of new science curricula on student performance. *Journal of Research in Science Teaching, 20*(5), 387–404.

Sieber, R.T. (1979). Classmates as workmates: Informal peer activity in the elementary school. *Anthropology and Educational Quarterly, 10*, 207–235.

Siebert, A.F., & Likert, R. (1973). *The Likert school profile measurements of the human organization.* Paper prepared for the annual meeting of the American Educational Research Association.

Simon, H.A. (1979). How big is a chunk? In H.A. Simon (Ed.), *Models of thought.* New Haven, CT: Yale.

Simpson, R.D. (1977). Relating student feelings to achievement in science. In *What research says to the science teacher*, Vol. I. Washington, DC: National Science Teacher's Association.

Sirkin, J.R. (1985, November 27). How state chiefs established indicators for cross-state comparisons. *Education Week, 5*(13), 15.

Sirotnik, K.A. (1979). *Development and psychometric analyses of major scales utilized in a study of schooling. A study of schooling in the United States.* (Tech. Rep. No. 4.) Los Angeles, CA: University of California, Graduate School of Education.

Sirotnik, K.A. (1986). *Critical perspectives on the organization and improvement of schooling.* Norwell, MA: Kluwer Academic Publishers.

Sirotnik, K.A., & Oakes, J. (1981). Contextual appraisal for schools: Medicine or madness? *Educational Leadership, 39*, 164–179.

Sizemore, B., Brossard, C.A., & Harrigan, B. (1983). *An abashing anomaly: The high achieving predominantly black elementary school.* Final report. Pittsburgh: University of Pittsburgh.

Sizer, T. (1984). *Horace's Compromise.* Boston, MA: Houghton Mifflin.

Slavin, R.E. (1978). Separating incentives, feedback, and evaluation: Effects on academic performance and student attitudes. *Journal of Educational Psychology, 70,* 532–538.

Slavin, R.E. (1987). *Cooperative learning.* New York: Longman.

Slavin, R. (1986). *Ability grouping and student achievement in elementary schools: A best evidence synthesis.* Unpublished manuscript. Johns Hopkins University.

Slavin, R. (1987). *A review of research on elementary ability grouping.* Baltimore: Johns Hopkins University Center for Effective Elementary Schools.

Sleeman, D.H. (1982). Assessing aspects of competence in algebra. In D.H. Sleeman & J.S. Brown (Eds.), *Intelligent tutoring systems* (pp. 185–200). London: Academic Press.

Sleeman, D.H., & Smith, M.J. (1981). Modeling student's problem solving. *Artificial Intelligence, 16,* 171–187.

Smith, J.P., & Welch, F.R. (1986). *Closing the gap: Forty years of economic progress for blacks.* Santa Monica, CA: The RAND Corporation.

Smith, L., & Sanders, K. (1981). The effects on student achievement and student perception of varying structure in social studies content. *Journal of Educational Research, 74,* 333–336.

Smith, W.S. (1982). *Career oriented modules to explore topics in science.* Lawrence, KS: University of Kansas, School of Education.

Soar, R.S. (1977). An integration of findings from four studies of teacher effectiveness. In G.D. Borich (Ed.), *The appraisal of teaching: Concepts and process.* Reading, MA: Addison-Wesley.

Soar, R.S., & Soar, R.M. (1976). An attempt to identify measures of teacher effectiveness from four studies. *Journal of Teacher Education, 27,* 261–267.

Sorensen, A.B. (1970). Organizational differentiation of students and educational opportunity. *Sociology of Education, 50,* 355–376.

Spady, W.G. (1976). The impact of school resources on students. In W. G. Sewell, R.M. Hauser, & D.L. Featherman (Eds.), *Schooling and attainment in American society.* New York: Academic Press.

Stage, E., Kreinberg, N., Eccles, J., & Rossi Becker, J. (1985). Increasing the participation and achievement of girls and women in mathematics, science, and engineering. In S.S. Klein (Ed.), *Handbook for achieving sex equity through education.* Baltimore: The Johns Hopkins University Press.

Stake, R.E. (1967). The countenance of educational evaluation. *Teachers College Record, 68*, 523–540.

Stake, R.E., & Easley, J. (Eds.). (1978). *Case studies in science education.* Urbana, IL: University of Illinois.

Stallings, J. (1976). How instructional processes relate to child outcomes in a national study of Follow Through. *Journal of Teacher Education, 27*, 43–47.

Stallings, J. (1980). Allocated academic learning time revisited, or beyond time on task. *Educational Researcher, 19*(11), 11–16.

Stallings, J., & Kaskowitz, D. (1974). *Follow through classroom observation evaluation 1972-1973.* Menlo Park, CA: Stanford Research Institute.

Statistical Abstract of the United States. (1985). Washington DC: United States Bureau of the Census.

Steinberg, L., Blinde, P.L., & Chan, K.S. (1982). Dropping out among language minority youth: A review of the literature. *Review of Educational Research, 54*(1), 113–132.

Steinkamp, M.W., & Maehr, M.L. (1984). Gender differences in motivational orientations toward achievement in school science: A quantitative synthesis. *American Educational Research Journal, 21*(1), 39–59.

Stern, D., Paik, I., Catterall, J.S., & Nakata, Y. (in press). With and without high school diplomas. *Economics of Education Review*

Sternberg, R.J., & Baron, J.B. (1985, October). A statewide approach to measuring critical thinking skills. *Educational Leadership, 43*(2), 40–43.

Stipek, D.J., & Weisz, J.R. (1981). Perceived control and academic achievement. *Review of Educational Research, 51*(1), 101–137.

Stroup, A.L., & Robbins, L.N. (1972). Research notes: Elementary school dropout among black males. *Sociology of Education, 45*, 212–222.

Summers, A.A., & Wolfe, B.L. (1975). *Equality of educational opportunity quantified: A production function approach.* Department of Research, Federal Reserve Bank of Philadelphia.

Summers, A.A., & Wolfe, B.L. (1977). Do schools make a difference? *American Economic Review, 67*(4), 639–652.

Suydam, M. (1980). Untangling clues from research on problem solving. In S. Krulik (Ed.), *Problem solving in school mathematics, 1980 Yearbook of the National Council of Teachers of Mathematics.* Reston, VA: National Council of Teachers of Mathematics.

Swenson, L.S. (1970). The Michelson-Morley-Miller experiments before and after 1905. *Journal of Historical Astronomy 1*(1), 56–78.

Task Force on Education for Economic Growth. (1983). *Action for excellence: A comprehensive plan to improve our nation's schools.* Washington, DC: Education Commission of the States.

Taylor, C.W., & Ellison, R.L. (1967). Biographical predictors of scientific performances. *Science, 155,* 1075–1080.

Thomas, J., & Tyack, D. (1983). Learning from past efforts to reform the high school. *Phi Delta Kappan, 64*(6), 400–406.

Tobin, D., & Fox, L.H. (1980). Career interests and career education: A key to change. In L.H. Fox & D. Tobin (Eds.), *Women and the mathematical mystique.* Baltimore: Johns Hopkins University Press.

Traub, R., Weiss, J., & Fisher, C., with Musella, D., Kahn, S. (1973). *Openness in schools: An evaluation of the Wentworth county Roman Catholic school board schools.* Toronto: Educational Evaluation Center, Ontario Institute for Studies in Education.

Travers, R.M.W. (1983). *How research has changed American schools: A history from 1840 to the present.* Kalamazoo, MI: Mythos Press.

Trickett, E.S., & Moos, R.H. (1973). Social environment of junior high and high school classrooms. *Journal of Educational Psychology, 65*(1), 93–102.

Trickett, E.S., & Moos, R.H. (1974). Personal correlates of contrasting environments: Student satisfaction in high school classrooms. *American Journal of Community Psychology, 12,* 1–12.

Trimble, K. & Sinclair, R.L. (1986). *Ability grouping and differing conditions for learning: An analysis of content and instruction in ability-grouped classes.* Paper presented at the annual meeting of the American Educational Research Association, San Francisco.

Tye, B. (1985). *Multiple realitites: A study of 13 American high schools.* Lanham, MD: University Press of America.

Tye, K. (1985). *The junior high: School in search of a mission.* Lanham, MD: University Press of America.

Tyler, R. (1949). *Basic principles of curriculum and instruction.* Chicago: University of Chicago Press.

United States Commission on Civil Rights. (1978). *Social indicators of equality for minorities and women.* Washington, DC: United States Commission on Civil Rights.

United States Department of Commerce (1982). *Current population report.* Series P-20.

United States Department of Education. (1984a, 1985, 1986, 1987). *State education statistics.* Office of Planning, Budget, and Evaluation, Planning and Evaluation Service.

United States Department of Education. (1984b). *The nation responds: Efforts to improve education.* Washington DC: U.S. Government Printing Office.

United States Department of Health, Education and Welfare (1969). *Toward a social report*. Washington, DC: U.S. Government Printing Office.

Usikin, Z. (1980, Summer). What should *not* be in the algebra and geometry curricula of average college-bound students? *Mathematics Teacher, 73,* 413–424.

Valverde, L.A. (1984). Underachievement and underrepresentation of hispanics in mathematics and mathematics-related careers. *Journal for Research in Mathematics Education, 15,* 123–133.

Vance, V.S., & Schlechty, P.C. (1982). The distribution of academic ability in the teaching force: Policy implications. *Phi Delta Kappan, 64,* 22–27.

Vanfossen, B.E., Jones, J.D., & Spade, J.Z. (1985). *Curriculum tracking: Causes and consequences.* Paper presented at the annual meeting of the American Educational Research Association, Chicago.

Venezky, R.L., & Winfield, L.F. (1979). Schools that succeed beyond expectations in reading. *Studies in Education.* Newark, DE: University of Delaware.

Vockell, E.L., & Lebone, S. (1981). Sex-role stereotyping by high school females in science. *Journal of Research in Science Teaching, 39,* 563–574.

Vygotsky, L.S. (1978). *Mind in society: The development of higher psychological processes.* Cambridge, MA: Harvard University Press.

Wagenaar, T. (1984). *Occupational aspirations and intended field of study in college.* Washington, DC: National Center for Education Statistics.

Waite, L., & Berryman, S. (1984). *Women in nontraditional occupations: Choice and turnover.* Santa Monica, CA: The RAND Corporation.

Walberg, H.J. (1969a). Predicting class learning: An approach to the class as a social system. *American Educational Research Journal, 14,* 529–542.

Walberg, H.J. (1969b). Social environment as a mediator of classroom learning. *Journal of Educational Psychology, 60,* 443–448.

Walberg, H.J., Haertel, G.D., Pascarella, E., Junker, L.K., & Boulanger, F.D. (1981). Probing a model of educational productivity in science with national assessment samples of early adolescents. *American Educational Research Journal, 18,* 233–249.

Walberg, H.J., & Tomlinson, T.M. (1986). *Academic work and educational excellence: Raising student productivity.* Berkeley, CA: McCutchan Publishing Co.

Walberg, H.J., & Waxman, H.C. (1983). Teaching, learning, and the management of instruction In D.C. Smith (Vol. Ed.), *Essential knowledge for beginning educators.* Washington, DC: American Association of Colleges for Teacher Education and ERIC Clearinghouse on Teacher Education.

Walberg, H.J. (1984). Families as partners in educational productivity. *Phi Delta Kappan,* 65(6), 397–400.

Walberg, H.J., Fraser, B.J., & Welch, W.W. (1986). A test of a model of educational productivity among senior high school students. *Journal of Educational Research, 79,* 133–139.

Walker, D.F. (1981). Learning science from textbooks: Toward a balanced assessment of textbooks in science education. In J.T. Robinson (Ed.), *Research in science education: New questions, new directions.* Washington, DC: National Institute of Education.

Walker, D.F. (1985). Curriculum and Technology. In A. Molnar (Ed.), *Current thought on curriculum.* Association for Supervision and Curriculum Development, ASCD. Arlington, VA.

Wang, M.C., & Walberg, H.J. (Eds.) (1986). *Adapting instruction to individual differences.* Berkeley: McCutchan Publishing Co.

Ward, B. (1979). *Attitudes toward science: A summary of results from the 1976–77 national assessment of science.* Denver, CO: Education Commission of the States.

Ward, W.C., Frederiksen, N., & Carlson, S.B. (1980). Construct validity of free-response and machine-scorable forms of a test. *Journal of Educational Measurement, 17*(1), 11–29.

Ware, N.C., & Lee, V. (1985). *Predictors of science major choice in a national sample of male and female college students.* Cambridge: Radcliffe College.

Warren, D.R. (1974). *To enforce education: A history of the founding years of the United States Office of Education.* Detroit: Wayne State University Press.

Warren, J.W. (1979). *Understanding force.* London: John Murray Publishers.

Watts, D.M. (1982, May). Gravity: Don't take it for granted. *Physics Education, 17*(5).

Webb, N.M. (1980). A process-outcome analysis of learning in group and individual settings. *Educational Psychologist, 15,* 69–83.

Webb, N.M. (1982). Group composition, group interaction, and achievement in cooperative small groups. *Journal of Educational Psychology, 74*(4), 475–484.

Webb, N.M. (1984a). Sex differences in interaction and achievement in cooperative small groups. *Journal of Educational Psychology, 76*(1), 33–44.

Webb, N.M. (1984b). Stability of small group interaction and achievement over time. *Journal of Educational Psychology, 76*(2), 211–224.

Webb, N.M. (1984c). Microcomputer learning in small groups: Cognitive requirements and group processes. *Journal of Educational Psychology, 76*(6), 1076–1088.

Webb, N.M., & Cullian, L.K. (1983). Group interaction and achievement in small groups: Stability over time. *American Educational Research Journal, 20*(3), 411–423.

Wehlage, G.G., & Rutter, R.A. (1985). Dropping out: How much do schools contribute to the problem? Madison, WI: Wisconsin Center for Education Research.

Weiner, B. (1972). *Theories of motivation: From mechanism to cognition.* Chicago: Rand-McNally.

Weiner, B. (1977). An attributional approach for educational psychology. In L. Shulman (Ed.), *Review of research in education* (Vol. 4, pp. 179–209). New York: Plenum.

Weiner, B. (1979). A theory of motivation for some classroom experiences. *Journal of Educational Psychology, 71,* 3–25.

Weiss, C.H. (1979). The many meanings of research utilization. *Public Administration Review, 39,* 426–431.

Weiss, I. (1978). *Report of the 1977 national survey of science, mathematics, and social studies education.* Research Triangle Park, NC: Center for Educational Research and Evaluation.

Weiss, Iris S. (1982). Report of the 1977 survey of science, mathematics, and social studies education. *American Educational Research Journal, 19,* 145–153.

Weiss, L., Pace, C., & Conaway, L.E. (1978). *The visiting woman scientists pilot program. Highlights report.* Research Triangle Park, NC: Research Triangle Institute.

Welch, W.W. (1983, February 8–10). *Research in science education: Review and recommendations.* Paper presented at the Conference on Teacher Shortage in Science and Mathematics: Myths, Realities, and Research. Washington, DC: National Institute of Education.

Welch, W.W. (1985). Attitudes towards science. In T. Husen & T.N. Postlewaite (Eds.), *International encyclopedia of education: Research and studies.* New York: Pergamon Press.

Welch, W.W., Anderson, R.E., & Harris, L.J. (1982). The effects of schooling on mathematics achievement. *American Educational Research Journal, 19,* 145–153.

Wescott, D.N. (1982, June). Blacks in the 1970s: Did they scale the job ladder? *Monthly Labor Review,* 29–38.

Whimbey, A. (1985, October). You don't need a special 'reasoning' test to implement and evaluate reasoning training. *Educational Leadership, 42*(2), 37–39.

Whipple, G.M. (Ed.) (1932). *The thirty-first yearbook of the National Society for the Study of Education. Part I: A program for teaching science.* Chicago: National Society for the Study of Education.

Wildavsky, A. (1979). *Speaking truth to power: The art and craft of policy analysis.* Boston, MA: Little Brown.

Wiley, D.E. (1976). Another hour, another day: Quantity of schooling, a potent path for policy. In W.H. Sewell, D.L. Featherman, & R.M. Hauser (Eds.), *Schooling and achievement in American society,* New York: Academic Press.

Wiley, D.E., & Harnischfeger, A. (1974). Explosion of a myth: Quantity of schooling and exposure to instruction, major educational vehicles. *Educational Researcher, 3,* 7–12.

Willower, D.J., & Jones, R.G. (1963). When pupil control becomes an institutional theme. *Phi Delta Kappan, 45,* 107–109.

Willson, V.L. (1983). A meta-analysis of the relationship between science achievement and science attitude: Kindergarten through college. *Journal of Research in Science Teaching, 20*(9), 839–850.

Winkler, J., Shavelson, R.J., Robyn, A., & Feibel, W. (1984). *How effective teachers use microcomputers for instruction.* Santa Monica: The RAND Corporation.

Wisconsin Center for Education Research. (1984). *Special analyses of high school and beyond 1980 and 1982 seniors.* Unpublished paper. University of Wisconsin.

Wisconsin Center for Education Research. (1984). *Effect of taking mathematics courses on mathematics achievement.* Unpublished data analysis.

Wittrock, M.C. (1974). Learning as a generative process. As cited in Jones. (1984). *Educational Psychologist, 11,* 87–95.

Wolf, R.M. (1977). *Achievement in America.* New York: Teachers College Press.

Wolf, R.M. (1979). Achievement in America. In H.J. Walberg (Ed.), *Educational environments and effects* (pp. 313–330). Berkeley, CA: McCutchan.

Wolfe, L.M., & Ethington, C.A. (1986). *Race and gender differences in a causal model of mathematics achievement.* Paper presented at the annual meeting of the American Educational Research Association, San Francisco.

Yager, R.E. (1981a). The importance of terminology in teaching K-12 sciences. *Journal of Research in Science Teaching, 20*(6), 577–588.

Yager, R.E. (1981b). Science education. *ASCD curriculum update.* Association for Supervision and Curriculum Development, Alexandria, VA.

Yudin, L., Ring, S., Nowakiwska, M., & Heinemann, S. (1973). School dropout or college-bound: Study in contrast. *Journal of Educational Research, 67,* 87–93.

INDEX

Ability grouping, 50–51, 134–135 (*see also* Tracking)

Absenteeism, 54

class environment and, 141, 142

Academic performance indicators, 231–233

Academic press (*see* Press for achievement)

Access to knowledge, 42–43

curriculum and, 49–50

operationalizing, 61–63

resources and, 47–48

student outcomes and, 46–52

time and, 48–49

Achievement (*see also* Press for achievement)

access to instruction and, 200–211

class time and, 48–49

course-taking as predictor of, 204–209

Achievement indicators, 147–166, 167–168

criteria for measuring, 154–157

importance of, 180–181

Achievement scores, school resources and, 43–44

Action for Excellence, 263

Administrative leadership, 59–60

Administrative priorities, press for achievement and, 56

Advisory Commission on Intergovernmental Relations (ACIR), 35

Aid to Families with Dependent Children (AFDC), 34, 36

American College Testing (ACT) program, 28, 150*t*–151*t*, 152–153

Aptitude relevance, in achievement tests, 154, 155*f*, 156–157

Arithmetic concepts, model of, 107–108, 108*f*

Assignments, 49, 127–128, 129–130

"At risk" students, definition of, 193*n*

Attention in class, 168–169

Attitude indicators, 171–180, 189–191

Attitude measures and achievement, 171–172

Attitudes

and approach to thinking, 177–179

and extracurricular participation, 169–170

gender- and race-linked differences, 212–215

importance as indicators, 179–180

teacher, 76–77

toward science, 172–173

ways to improve, 172

Attitude scales, reliability of, 173

Attitude survey, 171–172

Attrition patterns, teacher, 83–84

Average daily attendance (ADA), 33–34

Average daily membership (ADM), 34

Black students (*see also* Minorities; Race, class, and gender; Social indicators)

attitudes toward science, 174, 175

science activities and, 129

Blue ribbon panels, 166

Books in the home, dropouts and, 231

Budgets, 29, 30*f*, 31, 33 (*see also* Costs; Funding; Resource indicators)

importance as indicators, 17–18

California, 35

definition of dropout, 234

model curricular standards, 262

Proposition 13, 198

California Achievement Tests, 148*n*

California Assessment Program, 34

California Commission on the Teaching Profession, 199

Careers, student attitudes toward, 174–175

Census Bureau, dropout research by, 229, 235, 236–237

Center for Education Statistics (CES), 239, 239*n*

course-taking data, 170

longitudinal studies, 148

on misassignment, 82

Certification, 68, 74, 78*f*

319

326 INDICATORS FOR MONITORING MATHEMATICS AND SCIENCE EDUCATION